INTERPRETING POLITICS

An Introduction to Political Science

CHANDLER & SHARP PUBLICATIONS IN
POLITICAL SCIENCE

General Editor: Victor Jones

INTERPRETING POLITICS

An Introduction to Political Science

PETER C. SEDERBERG

University of South Carolina

 Chandler & Sharp Publishers, Inc.
San Francisco

This book includes the following copyright materials, which are reprinted with the permission of the copyright owners and publishers:

The Soldier and the State: The Theory and Politics of Civil-Military Relations. Samuel P. Huntington. Harvard University Press, 1957.

The Limits to Growth: A Report for THE CLUB OF ROME'S *Project on the Predicament of Mankind*, by Donella H. Meadows, Dennis L. Meadows, Jórgen Randers, William W. Behrens III. A Potomac Associates book published by Universe Books, New York, 1972. Graphics by Potomac Associates.

Social and Cultural Dynamics. Pitirim Sorokin. Porter Sargent Publishers, Inc. 1957.

Library of Congress Cataloging in Publication Data

Sederberg, Peter C   1943-
   Interpreting politics: An introduction to political science.

   (Chandler & Sharp publications in political
science)
   Bibliography: p.
   Includes index.
   1. Political science.   I. Title.
JA66.S43   320   77-1657
ISBN 0-88316-529-5

To my son Per

Contents

Preface

This book surveys the concerns of that loose collectivity of those who call themselves political scientists. Thus it is explicitly an introduction to the entire discipline as distinguished from a simplified exposition of some particular area deemed representative, elementary, basic, or prerequisite. Hence it is necessarily wide in range and rather eclectic. A primary goal is to insure that no matter what subsequent courses in political science a student may take, the subject matter, the concepts, and the analytical frameworks will not be completely alien. This same goal applies to the introductory course in political science.

To progress toward this goal, the introductory book should be fundamentally analytical in approach. Its immediate goal should go beyond providing a mere survey of contemporary problems or catering to an assumed student interest by attempting inevitably dated "relevance." The goal should be to furnish a more durable relevance by explaining concepts that political and other social scientists have devised as they organize their investigations of ever-shifting political reality. The strengths and limitations of those concepts should also be explored.

Readings for the introductory course should fit this goal. They should be relatively inclusive in substance so the student gains some knowledge of both empirical and normative problems in political life; of all levels in the political process—local, national, international, foreign, domestic. They should provide a sample of events and decisions that exhibit the major concepts and analytical frameworks used by political scientists. Both readings and textbook should give the student some opportunity for insight into the underlying links and the disparate interests in the discipline of political science.

The textbook should be clear in its presentation of these ideas, avoiding as much as possible the sometimes obscure and convoluted vocabulary of the social sciences while still remaining true to the content.

The tensions among these multiple goals probably suggest why I feel the need for, and the need to write, "another introductory text." They also isolate the obstacles in the path of writing it. I have sought to introduce the interests of the discipline in a meaningful way by providing a diverse selection of topics. I have drawn upon the insights of political analysts ranging from classical political philosophers to contemporary "political behavioralists." I have employed, for a unifying theme, the multifaceted problems of power. They have served me satisfyingly as an organizing principle for the many concerns of this book. Despite the obvious shortcomings of the power concept, I see power problems as central to the students' intuitive ideas about political life; moreover, they pervade the study and application of politics.

Many people have assisted me in the development of this book. Special thanks must go to Professors Victor Jones and William Kreml, who read all or part of the manuscript and made numerous substantive suggestions. The clarity of the final product owes much to the keen editorial assistance of Jon Sharp and especially Willis L. Parker. My wife, Nancy B. Sederberg, read the manuscript in its many permutations and improved greatly both its style and its substance. Finally, the thousands of students whom I have taught over the past decade deserve special mention, for they furnished me a "teaching-learning laboratory" for the ideas and approaches developed in *Interpreting Politics*.

Peter C. Sederberg

December, 1976

INTERPRETING POLITICS

An Introduction to Political Science

Part One

THE STUDY OF POLITICAL LIFE

"The proper study of mankind is man," observes the poet Alexander Pope. One area of human activity has always attracted study—*politics*, or the manner by which communities organize themselves. In part, this fascination arises from morbid impulses, for communities, by acting or failing to act, have been responsible for some of the great calamities of history. And now the human race confronts problems ranging from the threat of war to the spread of pollution, problems that can be managed only through politics: creative and responsible politics.

The substantive areas of political life that could be studied include questions that range from how the broader social environment impinges upon specifically political action to detailed examinations of the structure and functions of political organizations. Often, though, political scientists, like their colleagues in the other social sciences, appear more concerned with *how to study* their subject than with the subject itself. The basic issue concerns the extent to which the social sciences can be considered "scientific." So, before turning to more substantive matters, Chapter I surveys some of the problems involved in the scientific study of society and polity.

Political scientists, once they have gone beyond the basic methodological debate, pursue a variety of interests. Some concept or theme must be found to unify this diversity. Chapter II suggests that the idea of "power" can be used to organize the interpretation of politics.

Chapter I The Scientific Study of Society

The scientific mind has dominated intellectual activity over the past century. Even its critics define their world views by reference to science, if only through reacting against it. This dominance is rooted both in science's proven ability to reveal the proverbial "secrets of nature" and in its utility for developing technologies of control. For good or ill, the "natural" or physical sciences have reinforced humanity's power to reshape its environment. Not surprisingly, those scholars concerned with the study of society—the social scientists—attempt to use the powerful intellectual tools of the natural scientists in hopes of achieving equivalent success.

An unsympathetic survey of the works produced by social scientists might conclude that the relation between their fields and "real" science is akin to that between astrology and astronomy. The struggle of social scientists to be scientific often seems to result only in their becoming incomprehensible. Many works of social science appear obscured by a screen of turgid prose and unfathomable techniques. Despite the inevitable occurrence of jargon, however, the product of social scientific research is probably more easily understood by the average lay person than are the investigations of natural scientists. This relative ease does not mean that the knowledge produced is any less significant. Obviously, the activities in which people participate and the forms of interaction they devise should be more comprehensible to them than are those processes they did not create (for example, the actions of poker players as compared with the behavior of subatomic particles).

Some social philosophers, though, decry the tendency to emulate the methods of the natural scientists, because they believe that the subject matter of the social world is qualitatively different from that of the natural world. Human beings, they argue, are thinking and purposive creatures whose doings cannot be understood through a slavish parody of modes of analysis developed to study the inanimate or, at best, unselfconscious world.[1] In order to understand human behavior some account must be taken of the motives of those who are doing the behaving and of the meaning they assign to their acts. Motives and meaning, however, are subjective in nature and are not directly knowable to the observer. One does not suppose that rocks have motives. It seems, then, that a social investigator who attempts to deal with these factors would be placed in the position of having to guess at internal states of mind. Such efforts clearly differ from what appears to be the normal observational field of the natural scientist.

This conclusion, though, is too hasty. Social scientists do not simply try to feel what the people they are studying feel. Nor do they abandon all attempts to deal with motivation and meaning; rather, they assess these indirectly from what the actors say and do. Clearly, such efforts are imperfect, for people do not always say what they really feel (a particular problem in public-opinion surveys); neither are observed actions necessarily the actions that were intended. Nevertheless, social scientists explicitly or implicitly assign typical motives to account for the behavior they observe. These typifications must be continually checked through constant observation and corrected if they are not in accord with the observed behavior. The debate over the use of scientific method in the social sciences arises out of a confusion between what is done (the typification of subjective states of mind) and the way it is done (empirical observation and logical systemization). The former distinguishes the social from the natural sciences, while the latter provides the basis for possible linkages between them.[2]

The nature of the social world does raise certain problems for scientific study. In order to discuss these problems, it is necessary first to identify those areas in which the social and natural sciences can share a common perspective. These can be classified under three topics: fundamental assumptions about the nature of scientific knowledge; methodological goals and procedures for the formulation and testing of propositions; and the relevant conclusions of the other sciences.[3]

FUNDAMENTAL ASSUMPTIONS OF SCIENTIFIC INQUIRY

Science, in simple terms, is a perspective on the world, a way of looking at things.[4] Like other perspectives, it reveals some aspects of existence, obscures others, and is not even concerned with still others. A basic truth, but one often ignored, is that science is a limited tool of knowledge. The recognition of these limitations does not imply the downgrading of scientific accomplishments, but only the necessity for being aware of other areas of knowledge and experience which are beyond the purview of science. Therefore, adoption of the fundamental assumptions of science in the study of society constitutes a *restriction*, but one that may produce more significant results than unsystematic and impressionistic forms of investigation.

Usually, the basic limiting condition of scientific inquiry is formulated in terms of the dichotomy between "fact" and "value." Science, presumably, can establish only the validity of statements of fact; whether a fact is "good" or "evil" is a question beyond science's capabilities—literally *meta*physical. While such a formulation has some validity, it crudely oversimplifies the actual limits on scientific investigation. First, "facts" are not as real and objective as they often appear. Second, some value questions can be discussed scientifically. Third, the forms of knowledge beyond science are more extensive than simple questions of value.

The overemphasis on the factual base of science generates a kind of vulgar empiricism which obscures the selectivity of the scientific perception of the world. Facts, or empirical data, cannot be viewed as indifferent bits of reality; rather, they are selected by the operations of the mind of the scientist out of a possibly infinite universe of "facts." Indeed, one of the purposes of scientific method is to provide the observer scientist with criteria to judge the relevance that the various data have to the understanding of the phenomenon under examination. Questions of relevance imply a kind of value judgment, the basis for which is explanatory utility. Scientific investigation, moreover, seldom restricts itself to the accumulation of data. It generally involves analysis at levels of abstraction far removed from the empirical observations upon which it rests.

These qualifications aside, scientists assume that scientific analysis can determine the validity of only those statements ultimately founded on empirical or observable data. Even this validity can be established only in the negative sense that a proposition has not yet been *in*validated by contradictory evidence. Since *all* the facts will never be known, only some of them, scientific propositions remain provisional, for the possibility always exists that a new discovery will disprove previously accepted knowledge. The necessity for empirical validation in turn relates to the assumption that data on the physical world are essentially objective, that two independent observers will be able to reach an agreement about what they see. Clearly, other types of knowledge are not so easily shared. To use a rather extreme example, the nuclear physicists working on the weapons development of two competing ideological systems would be able to concur on statements about the physical processes involved in producing a nuclear reaction, while violently disagreeing on statements about the values of the systems which they are severally defending. One question is scientific in nature while the other is beyond science. One political scientist distinguishes between the two kinds of knowledge illustrated above by arguing that scientific knowledge is "intersubjectively transmissible" from one consciousness to another, while the moral evaluation of the respective political systems is "intersubjectively nontransmissible" or personal in nature.[5] One could argue that all knowledge, including that based on empirical data, is filtered through each person's individual consciousness and is, therefore, personal.[6] Indeed, one can never be sure that what one person sees as a chair or the color red is identical to what another sees. Despite these difficulties, the distinction is a useful one; in fact, it would be difficult to carry out scientific investigations without it.

By establishing that science limits itself to the examination of propositions that are in essence intersubjectively transmissible one does not, however, prevent some valid scientific inquiries into problems of value. As was noted earlier, the criteria of scientific method are themselves ways of determining value in some sense—that of significance or relevance to the problem under study. Questions of value, especially in the social world, usually involve broader issues of good and evil, of the desirable and undesirable. Even with this more broadly construed meaning, science can make a contribution. Essentially, the question whether something is "valuable" can be answered *scientifically* only in relation to:

a.   some goal or purpose for the pursuit of which it is or is not useful (valuable), or to

b.   the ideas held by some person or group regarding what is or is not valuable.[7]

Therefore, values can be discussed scientifically in the following ways:[8]

1.   What are the *immediate purposes* people are pursuing at a particular place or time?

2.   What are their *ulterior purposes*?

3.   Are *conflicting purposes* being pursued?

4.   In the case where the goals are abstract ideals (freedom, justice, or the like), what *meanings* are associated with these abstractions?

5.   What *biological or biographical background* is associated with a person's espousal of a particular end?

6.   What is the *probability of achieving* the end with any means?

7.   What are the *foreseeable consequences or risks* involved in the pursuit of the purpose at hand, irrespective of the choice of means?

8.   How are people *influenced* to pursue or drop the pursuit of any purpose?

9.   What is the *function* of the purposes and the manipulation of them in the various spheres of social life?

10.   Are the means *suitable* to achieve the end?

11.   Are there *other means* which might achieve the end more efficiently?

12. What are the *foreseeable consequences and risks* involved in applying the chosen means?
13. How can the choice of means be *influenced*?
14. What is the *function* of the selection and manipulation of means in social life?
15. If a quality is cherished, does the person or thing *actually* possess that quality and to what degree?

In short, the "truth" of so-called ultimate values cannot be scientifically established, but once these values have been asserted, a wide range of value questions can be subjected to scientific analysis, at least in principle.

In any case, the issue of ultimate values is not the only one beyond the scope of science. Numerous intuitive insights, personal and unique experiences and subjective feelings, in addition to simple value beliefs, also are not intersubjectively transmissible. Such intuitions and feelings are an important component of an individual's comprehension of the world, especially the social world. That this type of insight cannot be directly translated into scientific knowledge underscores the point that the criterion of empirical validation and transmissibility is a limitation.

Genius, whether scientific or artistic, appears rooted in this area of deeply personal and subjective knowledge; the task of scientific genius is to restate this subjective insight into a transmissible form. In this process of restatement, some of the content of the original insight will invariably be lost. For this and other reasons, scholars who wish to examine foreign political or social systems are commonly urged to live in the foreign environment for a substantial length of time, during which they can experience intimately the interpersonal responses and the sensations that accompany their subject matter—seeing, hearing, smelling, tasting, touching. These experiences may not be readily apparent in the final write-up of the research, but they will certainly deepen the understanding of the problem studied.

BASIC METHODOLOGICAL GOALS AND PROCEDURES OF SCIENTIFIC INQUIRY

Assuming that social scientists confine themselves to forms of knowledge that are in principle transmissible, the question remains: "What are they to do with this knowledge?" What they attempt to do constitutes the second major area of sharing with the natural sciences, namely the methodological goals and procedures of scientific investigation.

The goals of science are commonly summed up by the trinity of *explanation*, *prediction*, and *control*. Explanation is the prime mover; the other two follow from it. Indeed, the essence of science is the explanation of empirically defined phenomena by relating them into ordered patterns.[9] Once satisfactory explanations have been made, the conditions under which a given event will occur can be isolated and, consequently, its reoccurrence can be predicted. Knowledge of the necessary and sufficient conditions of occurrence, in turn, increases the likelihood that the event can be controlled. Insofar as the natural sciences have achieved these goals, human power over the environment has increased. This last characteristic deserves special emphasis, for social scientists in applying their knowledge attempt to control people, not things. At a time when the problems created by ill-considered interference in the physical universe are increasingly apparent, the effort to expand control over the social world should provoke ever more searching inquiries.

A scientist, in any case, does not spend time simply gathering "raw" data; rather, he or she strives to provide some order to this data through the process of *generalization*. Once a generalization has been made, certain implications can be deduced which help achieve the goal of prediction and suggest ways of further testing the original proposition. In very basic terms, scientific investigation consists of the alternation of induction (or reasoning from the specific data to the general statement) with deduction (reasoning from the general statement to expectations about the data). The "strength" of a science's explanatory power resides in the nature of the generalizations made in that science.

The power of a generalization can be evaluated according to its *scope* (the range and variety of the phenomena it relates to one another) and its *probability* (the nearness to certainty in their relationship). One problem afflicting political and other social sciences is that when the degree of probability of a proposition is high, the scope is often narrow; but as the generalization becomes less narrow and more inclusive, its probability declines.[10] A simple example will help make this clear.

All generalizations are probability statements. In the natural sciences, however, some general statements are so probable that the likelihood of their nonoccurrence approaches zero. Thus, they become universal generalizations and can be stated in the following form: "All blue-collar workers in the United States vote Democratic." This proposition is obviously false. Unfortunately, political science can produce few general statements that approach 100-percent certainty. Those that do demonstrate a high degree of probability tend to be rather narrow; that is, they are not very "general" generalizations.

As the generalization's degree of probability declines, it may be possible to assign odds to it; for example: "Three out of four blue-collar workers vote Democratic," or "The probability that blue-collar workers vote Democratic is .75." While clearly not so strong as the universal statement ("all . . ."), such a generalization can prove quite useful. Numerical probabilities can be assigned to some statements in political science, but again the scope tends to be quite limited. Three out of four blue-collar workers may have voted Democratic in a particular election, but this proposition will not hold true over a number of elections. Therefore, its predictive capacity remains low. The problem of change over time also affects the physical sciences, but usually to a lesser degree. Consequently, even universal relationships in physics may not be universal if the time frame is expanded to several billion years. Conversely, that which has been previously invalidated may at some time in the future be accurate. In the sciences, nothing is ever proven or disproven in any final or ultimate sense.

As the generalization's scope expands, more of its probability may be lost. In order to take the time factor into account, the above example could be weakened to a mere tendency statement: "Blue collar workers *tend* to vote Democratic." This is a generalization that can be supported reasonably well with data drawn over time from election statistics in the United States, but even though the scope is broader, the decline in probability weakens the statement's explanatory and predictive power. In the social sciences, most of the generalizations that purport to be true over time are of this sort.

Generalizations in the sciences are directed at answering a number of different questions.[11] The most common of these questions concerns the "cause" of the phenomenon under examination. For example, with all other relevant variables held constant, event A will cause event B (invariably, or n percent of the time, or some of the time). The image of causality commonly is one of a simple linear relationship between pairs of variables where the causal flow is a sequence of events that can be clearly isolated. Unfortunately, such mechanistic causality has little relevance to the social world, where multiple variables interact with one another in complex relationships that make it difficult to identify the "dependent" and "independent" factors in any clear-cut fashion.

Another approach to causality inquires into the interactions of one element in a system of related parts.[12] Such an analysis might seek to identify the contribution of this element to the system's continued existence or collapse. One could investigate, for example, the ways schools teach political values supportive of the established order. This method of analysis is commonly called "functional." On a more ambitious scale, a scientist might study the operation of the system as a whole, with respect both to the relationships among its parts and the interactions between the system and its environment. Whole-systems analysis adopts the position that complex systems can be understood only if multiple variables are taken into account. It leaves itself open to the criticism that, at least with regard to the social world, such an approach requires vast amounts of information. Systems analysis consequently often tends to be overabstract and relatively detached from the empirical reality of the social world. Nevertheless, the image of the "political system" functioning in a broader social context, processing "demands" and "supports" into "outputs" whose impact is then fed back into the system, constitutes an important idea in contemporary political science (see Figure I-1).

Figure I-1   A Simple Model of the Political System

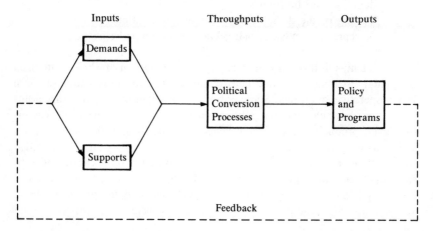

Generalization is more tenuous in a multivariable than in simple two-variable analysis. One reason is that if each element in a system can be linked to any other element only in terms of a probability statement that is less than 100-percent in degree, then the likelihood of the entire system functioning in the hypothesized manner is the product of all the component probabilities. That is, if the "odds" are .75 (or 3 to 1, or 3 in 4) that event A causes event B, and .70 that event B causes event C, then the product .75 × .70 = .525 is the odds that event A has a causal relationship to event C. This example provides another reason why increasing the scope of a generalization often leads to a decline in its probability, for a systems analysis can be viewed as a complex generalization linking a number of subsidiary statements.

From an empirical base, through the process of generalization or explanation, the scientist proceeds in a systematic fashion to produce knowledge that is intersubjectively transmissible; in other words, that can be tested and confirmed or invalidated by another, independent observer. The steps of scientific procedure have been itemized in numerous ways, none of which necessarily conforms with the process followed by any particular scientist. An ideal series of these steps can be the following:[13]

   1.   Identification of a problem; formulation of some preliminary ideas on
        the relationships that might be found.

2. Observation of what appears to be the data set relevant to the problem.
3. Description of the data, including classification and measurement of that which can be measured.
4. Inductive generalization, producing testable hypotheses.
5. Deduction from the generalization as to what further supportive evidence should be found.
6. Testing of the deductions by further observations.
7. Acceptance, revision, or rejection of the hypotheses.

No scientist follows all of these steps in a rigorous fashion. Often an individual researcher will contribute to only one or two, for scientific research is a cooperative enterprise. Some critics of the output of contemporary political science have charged that political scientists too often stop at the descriptive level, producing few testable generalizations, if any (this situation has been changing to some extent in recent years). But, in any case, generalizations if they are to be of any use must be constructed on accurate and substantial observation—good description. In certain areas of investigation, especially in the study of foreign political systems, good descriptive materials are often lacking, leading to the production of generalizations that are little more than speculation.

RELEVANT CONCLUSIONS OF THE OTHER SCIENCES

Finally, the social sciences can draw upon the relevant conclusions of the physical and biological sciences. The key word here is *relevant*. Since people are physical beings, some of the discoveries of the physical sciences are useful to the understanding of their behavior. Many of these findings, like the principles of gravitation, are taken as givens; to study the effects of these givens on political behavior would appear trivial (curiously, there may be some relation between the gravitational pull of the moon and aggressive actions, so perhaps studies as bizarre as this may be useful). As social scientists move into the field of biology, however, many research findings become of critical importance—for example, works investigating the biochemical basis of mental illness. Research into genetics produces controversies of as much interest to the social as the natural scientist, for instance the debates over the natural "superiority" or "inferiority" of women or blacks. Some ethologists and others argue that genes influence not only physical characteristics of people but social ones as well.[14]

Whatever the merits of the various sides of these controversies, they illustrate the growing attention paid to the impact of people's biological nature on their social and political life. Further research of biologists and geneticists will undoubtedly be of continued concern for social scientists.

The Significant Agreements

The discussion of the propositions of natural science that are shared by the social scientist can be summarized as follows:

1. *Science is based on observable facts.* It assumes that two observers can come to an agreement on what these facts are and agree or disagree about what their significance is. Certain types of personally appropriated knowledge, such as feelings and intuition, are beyond the scope of scientific investigation.

2. *Science is a generalizing activity.* The point is not simply to count and measure, but also to link discrete but related items together into ordered patterns. In this way a "fact" is explained. One could argue that these generalizations should in turn be subsumed by an even more general statement, and so on, until a broad, encompassing theory is constructed. The factual base, however, must never be lost, and even the most abstract conceptualizations should have some empirical reference by which they can be tested.

3. *Science is logical.* It utilizes both inductive and deductive logic. The generalizations must be internally consistent, and contradictions among hypotheses must be resolved. The implications of related general statements must be logically consistent.

4. *Science is open-ended.* Revision constantly occurs. Statements can never be proven (or, for that matter, disproven) in any final sense. At times, this revision may be incremental, that is, based on the careful elaboration of basically accepted propositions. At other times, the revision may be quite fundamental, causing the whole perspective of a science to shift, as in the abandonment of a geocentric for a heliocentric view of the solar system or, more recently, in the subsuming of the Newtonian by the Einsteinian view of the physical universe. Scientific "truth" is always provisional and never dogmatic.

5. *Science has some "nonlogical" characteristics.* Many of the real advances in scientific thought come through the intuitive insights of thinkers of great genius. They are then able to transform these insights into scientifically acceptable terms that can be understood by their less gifted fellows and ultimately supported by empirical evidence.

PROBLEMS AFFECTING THE SCIENTIFIC STUDY OF THE SOCIAL WORLD

The social sciences are often considered "weak" in comparison with the natural sciences; however, this weakness casts no necessary reflection on the intelligence of social scientists. The complexity of their subject matter—human beings—is the primary cause of this apparent weakness. Many of the obstacles created by the nature of the subject matter are not unique to the social arena; natural scientists must also cope with them, though generally to a lesser degree. Some of these obstacles may profitably be identified and discussed.

The Impact of Values on the Observers and Their Research

Scientists are commonly conceived as objective, "value-free" investigators disinterestedly searching out answers to the puzzles that intrigue them. In fact, making the choice of what puzzle to examine is making a kind of value statement. Though this point is commonly conceded, the image of free scientific minds—responding only to what interests them and to the requirements of their science—is retained. This image is unsatisfactory, for it leaves unexamined the sources of scientific interest and the ways by which the requirements of science are determined. The former are, in part, tied to the investigator's personal values, and the latter are a function of perceived social needs.[15] And though social values affect the development of personal ones, the two can be analyzed separately.

Scientists are human beings, and they do not become automatons when engaged in research. Rather, they bring to that research all the psychological baggage that makes up their personalities, including conscious and unconscious biases. These, naturally, are going to have some impact on what the scientists see as important. This consequence, sometimes called "selective perception," may lead observers to see only that which fits into certain preconceived notions. As an ideal, scientists are supposed to be open-minded enough to recognize contradictory evidence and revise their conclusions accordingly. Moreover, a scientist's research should provide sufficient means for other scientists to evaluate and validate these conclusions. Both of these expectations can act as checks on personal bias. While the effects may thereby be lessened, one would be foolish to discount completely the possibility of bias and the distortions it can cause.

Related to the problem of biases affecting research is the myth of the dispassionate scientist. Again, human frailty must be recalled. Someone who has invested considerable time and effort in a project commits a portion of his or her personality to its outcome. The committed scientist will be unlikely to take criticism in a completely uninvolved fashion. Scientific disputes can be quite emotional, as contending scientists resist views contrary to their own.

Such problems occur in all areas of scientific investigation, but plausible reasons exist for expecting them to be more serious in the social sciences. The research of natural scientists can be more easily isolated from their personal lives than can the research of social scientists. The possibility that the observer's biases will exert some influence appear much higher in the study of the social world, where the problems more directly involve the scientist's own emotions. One response of some social scientists has been to deal at a level of abstraction high enough to make the human element *appear* relatively remote. Economists have been particularly successful in this regard. The process of abstraction reaches its extreme apex in the jargon of military pseudoscience, in which murder is referred to as "termination with extreme prejudice" and civilians are killed in "friendly bombing strikes." Critics of such dehumanization of the social sciences argue that it is just as prejudicial, and far more undesirable, than passionate involvement. And not the social sciences only—even those who study the physical and biological world can no longer ignore the impact of their research on the life of man. More natural scientists are becoming directly involved in social and political problems, as is seen in studies of the impact of environmental pollution or technological change on society.

Societal goals also affect scientific inquiry. Again, the idealized portrait of the scientist—as a person insulated from "irrelevant" pressures arising out of social and, specifically, political sources—is misleading. In part, the effect of social goals relates back to the personal biases of the scientist—neither the goals nor the biases are learned in a vacuum; rather, their development is influenced by the values of associates and the prevailing social mores of the time. Dominant views about the needs of society direct, to some extent, the course of scientific research. This statement may appear fairly innocuous, except for the fact that these opinions on social needs have no necessary relationship to the requirements for the advance of scientific knowledge. More often than not, the perceived needs reflect the interests of the powerful. One need not be a Marxist to see some validity in the argument that all aspects of the established culture, including science, reflect the interests of the dominant economic groups. Scientific research is seldom any longer carried out by the gifted loner working in a basement laboratory; rather, it involves team effort and a considerable amount of money. These funds come increasingly from government and from the research and development budgets of large private corporations. Certainly, one can question whether research thus directed approximates the ideal of free inquiry, whatever the contributions made to national defense or product desirability.

Natural scientists, however, gain some latitude in consequence of the apparent abstractness of their concerns; research in problems that interest them is often tolerated and funded because of the faith that "pure" (that is, not immediately relevant) research will have some future payoff for the funding organization. Social scientists, because their investigations are of more direct interest to the general public and require its cooperation, find it more difficult to insulate themselves from social pressures. One difficulty is that their research often involves possible infringements on citizens' prerogatives to a far greater extent than does research in the natural sciences. For example, reasonably clear limits exist as to how far a social scientist can pry into people's lives in his quest for information. Another difficulty is that research, especially that funded by the government, quite usually reflects the interests of the regime. Uncomfortable conclusions may still be reached, such as the Walker Commission's findings of a "police riot" in Chicago at the 1968 Democratic convention or the Kerner Commission's warnings of increasing racial division in America, but the motivating premise of each study is the preservation of the system. Not surprisingly, though Soviet and United States natural scientists increase their contacts with one another, the social scientists continue to view each other as apologists for their respective regimes.

Despite the qualifications of the scientific ideal which must be recognized because of the influence of values on research, scientific knowledge in the social sciences can still be developed. Even a relatively biased approach may reveal characteristics of the social world that are obscured by other lines of investigation. Few would deny, for example, the real contribution of Karl Marx to the understanding of the relationships between the economic and the sociopolitical systems, even though they dissent from his passionate commitment to revolution. Moreover, if the social scientist adheres to the goal of verifiability, others will be able to evaluate his conclusions and compensate for the impact of his biases. Scientific "objectivity" is not the monopoly of any one scientist; rather, it emerges from the free interplay of information and scholarly criticism.

The Complexity and Diversity of Human Beings

A generalization commonly rests on points of similarity existing among the items covered by the general statement. Increasing the complexity and distinctiveness of the items makes it more difficult to construct generalizations of either high probability or inclusiveness. Social scientists seem to confront this problem to an extreme extent, for not only are human beings complex psychobiological organisms, but also each person is distinguishable from all others by the characteristics produced through his or her own genetic heritage and life experiences. Moreover, a person can choose from among alternative courses and pursue consciously selected goals. Some social philosophers argue that these individuating traits and self-awareness make it impossible to study human behavior in the same way that one would study that of molecules, or even that of other animals. Even though this position may be exaggerated, the social sciences undoubtedly confront a difficult and complex object.

In some sense, everyone is unique, in that no one individual is identical to any other. The uniqueness of each person, however, should not be taken as implying that everyone is completely unlike all others. Areas of likeness do exist, and these provide the grounds for scientific generalizations. At the very least, humans have in common certain physical traits. Additionally, all humans possess certain needs that must be fulfilled in some fashion. Psychologist Abraham Maslow provides a suggestive list of these needs: (1) physical needs, as for food, water, and shelter; (2) safety needs—insurance of survival and continued fulfillment of physical needs; and (3) psychological needs, such as the need for love, esteem, and self-actualization.[16]

Other patterns of commonality may also be present, at least among people of the same culture. Shared language, for example, provides both a means of communication and a common structure for thought processes. Cultural value expectations contribute similar experiences to different people. Regularized patterns of behavior are taught to all members of a society. Indeed, when one pauses to think of the inherent complexity of an accepted and habitualized social process like road travel, one cannot fail to be impressed with the amount of likeness that does exist. Complex norms of social interaction have been so deeply impressed on most people, leading to their expectations of others' behavior, that periodic and relatively trivial breakdowns of these patterns may lead to an exaggerated emphasis on the uniqueness and unpredictability of human individuals.[17] Of course, social scientists are often interested in explaining the unexpected, the breakdowns in the social order; nevertheless, the importance of these shared patterns for the comprehension of social action and the creation of valid generalizations should not be underestimated.

Cultural Diversity

Beyond the existence of certain common physical and psychological needs, the preceding argument for other grounds of similarity assumes a certain degree of cultural homogeneity. Only by growing up in the same cultural setting do people learn the same norms and expectations. A different culture, with its own language, values, symbols, and myths makes a different learning experience. This is a question of degree, for any two cultures may be more or less distinct and less or more similar. The greater the degree of similarity, for example, among an assortment of nations, the more likely that individual life experiences will be similar. The greater the differences among cultures, the more difficult it will become to make strong, cross-cultural general statements. Indeed, a social scientist encounters significant barriers to simply understanding a foreign culture; to devise explanations that are valid in different cultural contexts is still more difficult.

Though cultural heterogeneity poses certain problems for social scientists, some mitigating factors must also be taken into account. First, since human beings possess essentially the same organism with essentially like needs, even apparently strange values and institutions are not inherently unknowable, even though not immediately comprehensible to an outside observer. In order to understand another culture, it may be necessary to learn its language and traditions and live among its people for an extended length of time. In short, a person gains an understanding of another culture in precisely the same way he learns about his or her own. And, it should be remembered, even one's own is never completely learned.

Second, though various cultures can be analytically distinguished from one another, any distinction should not obscure the fact that communication and subsequent blurring of boundaries occur among them. Cultural exchanges have existed for as long as the cultures themselves, but not until this century has it been possible to speak accurately of an emerging world culture, although its contours are not clear, and much discussion about it remains speculative. Few deny the importance of the communications revolution and the growing interdependence among all states. No one can successfully isolate himself from the impact of what others do to spaceship Earth. The implication of this increased communication and dependence is that the distinctiveness of the various cultures will diminish as common concerns and organizations to deal with these concerns become more important. Though this process has been often tagged "Westernization" or "Americanization," the world culture will be more likely an amalgam of that which is found valuable in each culture's efforts to cope with its environment. Social scientists may find it both easier and more fruitful, therefore, to focus on the similarities rather than on the differences that exist among them.

Third, though handicapped by their own cultural preconceptions, observers outside a culture also possess an advantage: They do not have the preconceptions of the inside social scientists. There are different kinds of intellectual blinders, and sometimes being socialized within a particular culture may prevent analysts from seeing characteristics of their own society which are apparent to outside observers. This problem, in part, relates back to the impact of values on research. Foreign social scientists, though they may lack the rich cultural background of the member, may be able to reveal what has been ignored by the latter. One of the most perceptive interpretations of American democracy, for example, was made by the nineteenth-century French aristocrat Alexis de Tocqueville.[18] Since no one can ever claim more than partial knowledge, it is always useful to combine differing perspectives in order to achieve a more complete picture.

The Ability to Learn and Change Behavior

Individual and cultural diversity inhibit the scope of generalizations in the social sciences. The ability of humans to learn and change their behavior decreases the probability that any particular statement will hold true over time. The problem of behavior modification also exists, to some degree, in the natural sciences—viruses become resistant to antibiotics, insects thwart the effects of pesticides, and even the "basic laws" of the physical universe may alter over time. People in their social interactions are far more susceptible to change. Each individual's worldly existence can be viewed as a process of becoming; no one is ever finalized into an unalterable state until death. Larger social units (institutions, societies) also constantly change, though at differing rates. This change, and the consequent decline in any proposition's certitude over time, weakens the predictive power of the social sciences.

The predictive capability of the social sciences is not, however, by any means eliminated. Despite the apparent mutability of some aspects of human behavior, other aspects remain fairly stable. Basic personality traits are learned relatively early and continue fairly unaltered throughout a person's life. Many institutions retain fundamental characteristics for decades, and each new generation that grows up within these structures learns supportive values and behavior. Admittedly, human life is not long in comparison with the eons over which some physical relations remain relatively unchanged. Enough continuity exists, though, to provide accurate expectations of impressive consistency in the social world, at least over the short run. Finally, it is also possible to investigate and generalize about the processes through which new behavior is learned (see Chapter XI).

The Limitations on Experiment

The classic technique of coping with a complex problem in the natural sciences is to experiment under controlled conditions. The relationship under examination is separated from other potential influences, or at least these are held constant to the greatest extent possible. Usually, this relationship is conceived in terms of "independent" and "dependent" variables, and the effect of changes in the former on the behavior of the latter is carefully measured. In most cases, the relationship studied is abstracted from a more complex "reality," for example, the assumption of zero resistance in Newtonian physics. Such simplifications are justified because through them more fundamental interactions are understood.

Social scientists often find it difficult to conduct the natural scientist's kind of controlled experiments; a greater multitude of variables may affect any problem of interest, making it difficult to identify all of them, much less to control for their impact. Some psychologists and sociologists have been able to construct relatively controlled conditions in experiments involving isolated small groups or individuals. Political scientists, however, tend to be concerned with *public* action, which by definition cannot be isolated in a laboratory. They must analyze complex systems of elements with no clear idea of how the multiple factors affect one another. Moreover, social scientists, and even medical researchers and other biological scientists, become deeply involved in controversy if they appear to be experimenting or collecting data on human beings in an unethical fashion.

Social scientists have been ingenious in finding partial substitutes for the capacity to conduct experiments. These methods can be loosely termed arguments by analogy. The means most commonly used, perhaps the fundamental means, is comparison. In its simplest form, comparison involves the systematic investigation of a similar problem in different contexts. In political science, comparative politics suggests cross-national comparisons (for instance, the functions of political parties in presidential as compared with parliamentary systems). Comparisons also can be made on any level of analysis (for example, the provision of welfare services in high- and low-income states of the United States). In any such analogy, the points of similarity must outweigh the points of difference—there must be adequate grounds for comparison. Though the specification of direct causal relations is less likely than in laboratory experiments, an idea of the effects of different conditions can be acquired.

Some social scientists are unsatisfied with the lack of rigor that characterizes comparisons among systems in the world and so have attempted to construct simulations of the complex interactions of the elements of a society. These simulations may be created by individuals adopting certain roles (such as foreign-policy decision makers in "war games") or by programming a computer with what is assumed to be an approximation of the real system. Various elements in the simulation can then be altered and the reaction of the other elements to this change studied. The utility of simulations rests precisely on the observer's ability to change selected variables at will—an opportunity usually denied to social scientists in their studies of the "real" world. The basic requirement involves the strength of the analogy; that is, the accuracy of the simulation's representation of reality. If the underlying assumptions are incorrect, the results will be false no matter how complex the game or program may be. The use of simulations will be further examined in Chapter XV.

Though perhaps not as esthetically pleasing as controlled experiments, the comparative method and the simulation method have their usefulness. Even the natural sciences use them where ordinary experiment would be prohibitively costly, as in the testing of the effect of stress on a bridge or airplane design. These techniques are not necessarily second-best substitutes for experimentation. They may reflect more accurately than experiments the interactions among the parts of complicated systems that characterize the social, as well as parts of the natural, world.

The Limited Quantifiability and Measurability of Social and Political Data

An essential aspect of scientific investigation is the accurate measurement of the phenomena under examination. The attempt to measure assumes that the essential aspects of the data are quantifiable in some sense. The crudest form of measurement is the classification of the data according to a scheme of categorization (thus one might try to classify political systems as being either "authoritarian" or "democratic"). A more useful scale would rank the items being measured (for example, rank the systems as being more or less democratic). The most powerful scale quantifies the exact size of the interval between two comparable phenomena and, if the scale can be anchored at a zero point, permits mathematical manipulation of the data. These four scales are called respectively nominal, ordinal, interval, and ratio.

The social sciences encounter certain difficulties in measuring their concerns, especially along interval and ratio scales.[19] First, some important political and social events are wholly unique occurrences and cannot be readily compared with anything else. One could argue that all social events are of this sort, an assumption which would allow only narrative histories of the flow of unique happenings. Many descriptive histories reflect, implicitly or explicitly, such an orientation. Most social scientists, however, try to deal with aggregates, despite the nonreplicability of historical events. In their attempts to aggregate social data, they begin to confront other problems.

Some important social and political phenomena, though they can be aggregated conceptually, are impossible to measure in a quantifiable fashion that would make them comparable. The emphasis on quantification can lead to an excessive concern for only those aspects of social life which are easily quantifiable. For example, election returns are easily counted and compared. The intensity of feelings behind a particular vote, however, is not so susceptible of measurement (though some indirect measures have been devised); to ignore the problem for this reason is absurd. The problem is not simply an intellectual one, for both moral and practical issues are involved. In a democracy, should a relatively indifferent majority prevail over an intensely committed minority? What would be the impact on stability if members of this minority were denied redress of their grievances by the majority?

Another problem in social measurement arises when a multidimensional phenomenon is measured by only one or a few indicators. Again, this is more than an intellectual issue, for overconcentration on one or two measures can lead to faulty decisions. This problem has become important with respect to the use of economic measures of social well being or of profit and loss. Economic indicators are certainly relevant, but their obvious quantifiability tends to obscure the importance of other factors; a country's social health cannot be measured simply by the money-unit growth in the gross national product. The deteriorating quality of the environment also demonstrates the need to develop other indicators. The cost of cleaning up the environment, owing to its easy measurement in terms of taxpayers' dollars, hides other costs of failing to undertake this cleanup—costs in terms of the citizens' mental and physical health, and possibly even survival.

Since the social sciences' problems often involve data that are not directly measurable, indirect measures are sometimes used; that is, more accessible data are drawn upon under the assumption that they provide some indication of the less measurable phenomenon. If, for example again, the intensity of voter preferences cannot be measured directly, some indirect measures can be hypothesized. A committed person, it may be argued, is more likely to become involved in political activity. On this reasoning those who vote are more intensely involved than those who don't; those who are active in various political groups are, in turn, more committed than those who simply vote. One also could, undoubtedly, count the number of hours invested in political activities to distinguish among the activists.

This example is rather crude, but it illustrates both the potential and the problems of indirect measures. The validity of an indicator rests on the logic of the link between the immeasurable and the measured. The weaker the link, the more misleading the indirect measure will be. Though intensity of feelings probably has some impact on the amount of political activity, other factors contribute to both participation and noninvolvement. Participation as an indirect measure of intensity will decline in validity as the importance of these other factors rises. Moreover, another distortion can arise out of the tendency to define the original problem as being equivalent to the measurable phenomenon: intensity of feeling becomes defined as participation, or native intelligence as performance on an intelligence test.

The difficulties in implementing any systematic measurement in the social sciences, as well as the absence of "hard" data on many areas of social life, sometimes lead to a kind of "ritualistic scientism" on the part of social scientists who too slavishly follow criteria of quantifiability.[20] The tendency to concentrate on narrowly defined, essentially trivial problems because they are easily quantified and the pseudo-scientific manipulation of basically unsound data constitute examples of scientism. Social scientists should not allow quantifiability to dictate their concerns; nor should they claim, either directly or by laying down a smokescreen of sophisticated techniques, more than the data base will support.

Figure I-2   Obstacles to the Scientific Study of Society

Obstacles	Mitigating Circumstances
1. Impact of personal and social values on research.	Free and open scholarly discussion and criticism.
2. Complexity of individual human beings.	Common basic needs, similar biological organism; sometimes common cultural experience.
3. Cultural diversity.	Common basic needs, growing communication; emergence of world culture.
4. Ability of humans to learn and change behavior.	Relative stability of basic predispositions; ability to learn about the learning process.
5. Limited capacity for controlled experiment.	Substitutes for experiment (simulations, etc.); comparative method.
6. Difficulties encountered in the quantification and measurement of social phenomena.	Development of indirect measures; multiple indicators; computerized data manipulation.

THE STRENGTH OF THE SOCIAL SCIENCES[21]

The awe in which many people hold the physical and biological sciences appears primarily founded in the impact these sciences have on the world. If the natural sciences were confined to the arcane formulations of "pure" theory with no technological implications for everyday life, they might still be respected, as everything mysterious generally is; but they also would be considered largely irrelevant. In fact, most technological advances up to the nineteenth century were not systematically connected with any abstract empirical theory, and the position of the scientist was considerably less prestigious.

This state continues to characterize the condition of the social sciences: the "technological" advances in the social and political spheres are as great as those of the natural sciences, if not greater. They are, however, largely unaccompanied by any supporting structure of abstract theory, except to a partial degree and after the fact. The lack of "anticipatory" theory to point to new technologies is a major difference between the social and the natural sciences. This situation is changing as suggestions for new ways of organizing social life are being presented by social scientists, especially in the areas of economics and psychology.

If, however, the strength of an area of knowledge is demonstrated by its impact, then social scientific knowledge can easily be assessed and compared with natural scientific knowledge. In contrast to material technology, which is external to human beings and acts upon them, people act *within* their social inventions and often fail to recognize these inventions for the achievements they are. Yet the multitude of ways people have organized themselves to carry out complex tasks, ranging from political control and economic production to scientific research itself, is at least as significant as the applications of the natural sciences. Most of the latter would have little impact if they were not applied through social and political organizations.

Thus, the impact of social knowledge and the multiplicity of social and political organizations are at least as crucial to everyday life as the technological output of the natural sciences. Where the natural sciences appear superior is in the construction of abstract, interrelated systems of generalizations supported by concrete evidence in the real world. The social sciences, as distinct from the accomplishments of commonly held social knowledge, are not as well articulated and have not produced systems of generalizations comparable to those of the natural sciences. This difference in theory-building reflects two fundamental characteristics of examinations of the social world. First, as has been stated in the previous section, the subject matter of the social sciences is considerably more complex than that of the physical or even the biological sciences, and this complexity has an obvious impact on the scientist's ability to make valid generalizations. Second, perhaps more is known of the social world, and this knowledge makes it difficult to simplify or, more accurately, to oversimplify.

The consequent proposition generates some objections: The accomplishments of the social sciences must be evaluated in light of both the complexity of the subject matter and the recognition of this complexity by social scientists. It appears that as natural scientists delve more deeply into the physical universe, their formulations become increasingly complex. For example, neither simple Newtonian physics nor the original conception of the structure of the atom go far in illuminating the work in contemporary physics. Natural scientists have often rested on established views only to have them undermined by the admission of new and complicating evidence. Social scientists, however, have been less able to deceive themselves with their oversimplifications. The complexity of the social world can be directly and immediately experienced. In part, then, the inability of social scientists to produce esthetically pleasing general theory may be explicable not through their ignorance but through their knowledge—knowledge of the diversity of the phenomena to be explained.

One final caveat: In most of this discussion the pursuits of the natural and social sciences have been considered as basically distinct. This view neglects the ways in which they impinge on one another. As was previously argued, the organization of scientific research and the application of its technological findings are largely social and political problems. On the other hand, advances in the natural sciences and particularly in the biological sciences may conceivably contribute to the solution of one problem of the social sciences: the diversity and mutability of the social world. It soon may be possible to utilize recent discoveries to control behavior and even to homogenize the human race through genetic manipulation. This "possible future," along with some others, will be taken up in the final chapter.

SOME DEMANDING QUESTIONS

The effort to make the study of society and polity scientific raises at least four questions to which every social scientist should give some thought:

1.   To what extent does the subject matter of the social sciences—purposive human behavior—affect the relevance of the methods of the natural sciences for the study of the social world? What problems do the social sciences encounter, and how might those who conduct social investigations compensate for them?

2.   If scientific method is only one limited way to knowledge, how can other ways (such as those of the philosopher or artist) be drawn upon to complement scientific knowledge?

3.   Should scientific inquiry be limited in any way? The logic of science dictates working to expand knowledge and to enhance the ability to predict and control. Some natural scientists doubt whether certain areas should be further researched, such as those concerning the development of new strains of infectious micro-organisms or the genetic manipulation of human beings. Should similar considerations limit social-scientific research? If so, how are such limits to be established and enforced?

4.   Related to the problem of limiting the substance of research is that of the proper limits on its conduct. To what extent is it justifiable for social scientists to manipulate, deceive, or spy upon their subjects in order to carry out their research objectives?

The answers to these questions are beyond the competence of science, yet that does not mean they should be ignored. Social scientists must not forget the meaning behind the mythic images of the scientist as Faust or Frankenstein. The unexamined, unbounded pursuit of knowledge, like the quest for other forms of power, can corrupt the pursuer and devastate the society.

Chapter II   The Search for a Focus:
The Problem of Power

Political science, if a coherent discipline, might justifiably be expected to have a reasonably well-defined subject area. Such an expectation, however, is not met. Most people intuitively "know" what the study of politics entails, yet no neat formula exists defining the boundaries of inquiry to everyone's satisfaction.[1] To complicate the situation further, political scientists, whatever they may be studying, show little hesitation about borrowing anything that appears useful from any of the other social sciences—a habit which, in turn, makes their output rather eclectic.[2] The interests of political scientists range from the micro- to the macrocosmic: from the ways a child learns about political life to the methods by which a nation-state makes war and peace. Any interpretation of the basic concerns of political science needs to establish some organizing focus, if not a clear definition of its subject matter.

Traditionally, and commonsensically, the study of politics concentrates on those institutions in a society that can reasonably be described as "governing" that social system. The nature of these institutions varies from system to system. Sometimes, the specifically political institutions appear easily identifiable, because they are set forth in formal constitutions; whereas, in others, the organs of political action may not be clearly differentiated from more broadly construed social and cultural institutions.

While the institutional approach has considerable merit and cannot be ignored, it begs the question as to how to distinguish between political and nonpolitical action. The political analyst confronts this problem even with respect to contemporary constitutional systems, for many political or quasi-political activities are not mentioned in these formal documents of governance. For example, the venerable Constitution of the United States shows

24

little concern with the political role of the mass media and none at all about the operations of political interest groups and parties. Consequently, most scholars go beyond these formal documents and attempt to delineate the boundaries between political concerns and broader social concerns by identifying what are thought to be the distinctive characteristics of what political systems do and/or how they do it.

What Political Systems Do

One of the more durable general statements on what political systems do is that of David Easton: The political system engages in the *authoritative allocation of values* (what people desire) for the social system as a whole.[3] Other social organizations may allocate some values among their members (as does the family or a church), but only the allocations of the political system are authoritative for the entire society. If a family or a church makes such society-wide allocations, as in a monarchy or a theocratic state, then it becomes a fundamental part of the political system. When an individual or social group attempts to influence the allocation, for example through voting or political lobbying, these acts become political. The values allocated by the political system can be quite limited as in a feudal system, or can affect almost every aspect of a citizen's life as in the contemporary welfare state.

Since the basic condition of human existence is scarcity, the allocation of values necessarily involves conflict over their distribution. Thus, a related perspective on what the political system does involves the *resolution, or at least the regulation, of conflict* over the value distribution for the whole society. Again, conflict occurs and is regulated on levels below the societal one through activities which become quasi-political (one can speak, therefore, of politics in a corporation or even a family). The conflict approach concentrates on the process by which values are allocated. Usually, this concern leads to another, that of power, for a common assumption is that the relative power position of the participants in a conflict will determine its outcome.[4]

Identifying the distinctive traits of the political system as being authoritative value allocation and conflict resolution/regulation leads to some further questions: Does "authoritative" mean *really* authoritative or simply claiming such authority? In either case, what makes an allocation authoritative for a whole society? Indeed, what is meant by a "whole" society? In an increasingly interdependent world, one could argue that the only "whole" system is the emerging world society, and the supposedly sovereign nation-states no more represent independent systems than do the various subsystems within their increasingly permeable boundaries. Some of these difficulties may be resolved by turning from what political systems do to how they do it.

How Political Systems Carry Out Their Functions

Some political scientists argue that the distinctive characteristic of the political system is the exercise or threat of "physical coercion" which underlies all its activities. This observation echoes the familiar dictum that political power grows out of the barrel of a gun. The political system, from this point of view, attempts to claim a *monopoly over the control of coercion.*[5] If other groups or individuals exercise coercion, they do so with either the tacit or explicit toleration of the system or in violation of the system's prerogatives. A political system's authoritative allocation of values rests ultimately on this claim to monopoly.

Though this argument isolates an interesting characteristic, it still retains some ambiguities. First, what constitutes coercion? Sanctions can be of a very subtle sort, and the definition is hardly sharpened by extending the concept to cover everything from psychological deprivation to physical imprisonment and death. If coercion is defined this broadly, then the political system can never make a realistic claim to monopoly. Second, some theorists attach importance to the idea of "legitimate" coercion—legitimate in that its exercise is viewed as right. Such legitimacy, however, can only be asserted; the extent to which the assertion is true is a matter for research. In fact, two or more competing claims to legitimacy may co-exist in the same system.

The presumed monopoly, nevertheless, serves to distinguish analytically among relatively independent systems, their dependent subsystems, and the interactions among whole systems. A political subsystem (for example, a local government) exercises coercion only as a part of a larger unit; it cannot claim a monopoly in its own right. Additionally, no international system exists that can plausibly claim such a monopoly and thereby make the nation-state systems into subsystems. This situation could change. Established national systems could break up, as Pakistan did in 1971, or an effective world system could emerge. Currently, realistic claims to a coercive monopoly are generally made only by nation states.

Together, these three aspects (value allocation, conflict management, and claims to coercive monopoly) provide some loci for political analysis. The definitional discussion remains at a fairly abstract level, however, and consequently provides little glue with which to bind an inquiry into the multiple interests of political scientists. Another concept, that of power, may provide better cohesion. Yet the use of "power" as an organizing idea in political science provokes disagreement, and its utility and shortcomings must be examined.

POWER AS *THE* FUNDAMENTAL POLITICAL CONCEPT

Politics always implies power relationships. Even the classical political philosophers discuss the impact of alternative power distributions on the quality of political life. Some, like Thomas Hobbes (1588-1679), make the quest for power into the central dynamic of their entire political theory. Hobbes argues that all men, motivated by a desire for security, strive for dominion over one another, leading to a ceaseless war of each against all until the state was created to bring order into human existence.[6] The identification of power as a basic organizing principle or motivating force in political life continues to the present day. Hans Morgenthau asserts that all nation states, like the men in a Hobbesian state of nature, struggle to insure their security by increasing their power. Therefore, the quest for power is also an essential trait of "politics among nations."[7] Other political scientists also view political relationships as power interactions:

> Politics as power consists fundamentally of relations of superordination and subordination, of dominance and submission, of governors and the governed. The study of politics is the study of these relationships.[8]

Political scientists who adopt this position investigate such aspects of the power question as the sources of power (what gives a person or group power and under what circumstances), the distribution of these power resources, the consequences of this distribution for the political system, and the impact of the exercise of power or the ends for which it is used.

Those who argue for the centrality of power to the understanding of politics can also point to the importance of power questions in everyday political discourse: Political issues are commonly defined in terms of power relations. Debate swirls around such topics as whether the United States is becoming a second-rate power or whether the presidency is becoming too powerful vis-à-vis Congress. The relative power of groups is seen as determining their impact on the political process (power is ascribed to the "military-industrial complex"; newly mobilized minorities rally around programs for black, red, Chicano, or woman power). Even the roles of individuals in government are defined in terms of the power they appear to exercise—for example, the relative influence attributed to Henry Kissinger and Secretary of State William Rogers during Nixon's first term, or the analyses of former House Ways and Means Committee Chairman Wilbur Mills's rise and and decline as a congressional power broker (1939-1974). The fact that political-power discussions are popular among ordinary citizens need not be taken as irrefutable proof that power must necessarily be the central concept of political science. Power conditions, however, cannot be facilely dismissed if the discussions of political behavior are going to be intelligible to those who are doing the behaving.

Those who make power the organizing concept of the study of politics have not gone unchallenged. Perhaps the most important criticism is that "power" has little value as a *scientific* concept. Vagueness often detracts from its utility as it is stretched to cover phenomena ranging from brute force to the "power of an idea whose time has come." The absence of precision leads to problems in operationalizing the concept; that is, in defining ways power can be measured and compared. Consequently, many political scientists choose to focus on more easily defined and measured phenomena, abandoning direct concern with questions of power.

A second major objection to the primacy of power in the study of politics rises from the question whether power is, in any sense, the basic motivating force of political action. People seek power for a variety of purposes, some few admittedly for its own sake, others for selfish ends, and still others for altruistic purposes. One could assert that both Adolf Hitler and Martin Luther King sought power, but the comparison would be invidious if it ended there. The critical problem from this perspective involves the uses made of the power sought. Moreover, it is unlikely that all people at all times pursue power; other problems concern them during much of their time. The concept of power, like the equally vague idea of "self-interest," by attempting to explain everything, explains nothing.

POWER: SOME DEFINITIONS

Some of the problems noted above can be illustrated through a survey of several attempts to define "power." Among the more notable efforts are the following:

> Power is the probability that one actor within a social relationship will be in a position to carry out his will despite resistance, regardless of the basis on which this probability rests.—*Max Weber*
> Power relationships are those subsets of relations among social units such that the behavior of one or more units depends in some circumstances on the behavior of others.—*Robert Dahl*
> Power is the ability to affect social activities.—*Marvin Olsen*
> Power is a capacity to overcome part or all of the resistance, to introduce changes in the face of opposition (this includes sustaining a course of action or preserving a status quo that would otherwise have been discontinued or altered). —*Amitai Etzioni*
> A has power over B to the extent that he can get B to do something B would not otherwise do.—*Robert Dahl*
> The amount of power A has over B with respect to order w (by A) and response

x (by B) is (a) the probability that when A does w, B does x, minus (b) the probability that when A does not do w, B does x.—*William Riker*

These definitions, though varied, share some elements and difficulties. Most of them suggest that power is not an abstract "thing" or pure possession, but something that must be seen in a relationship. Its existence is recognized in an interaction, not a static state. Several of the statements imply that power can be measured in terms of the resistance overcome; under this implication, commanding an action that would have been done without the order fails to provide a test of the commander's power. Some of the definitions appear to be quite "scientific," with the relationship stated in exact logical terms.

Despite the apparent precision and agreement, closer investigation reveals certain problems. All the definitions appear to include a wide and unspecified range of possible manifestations of power, as well as unelaborated sources of power. The qualification of overcoming resistance adds little to one's understanding since resistance can be overcome through motivations as varied as fear and love. Even the specificity of Riker's formulation (the last definition) is of dubious value unless elements of the relation (orders, responses, and probabilities) are empirically defined.

Additionally, some critics note that the emphasis on power as a relation, exhibited in all the definitions except possibly Olsen's general statement, fails to cover adequately the nature of the power phenomenon.[9] Seeing power only in explicit order/response interactions obscures the structural characteristics of power, as when a particular institutional framework or established "rules of the game" reflect and support an established power distribution, or when habitualized behavior maintains the existing stratification system. A political scientist must not only try to examine overt political issues where power relations will be openly manifested, but also must discover those issue areas which have been excluded from the sphere of normal politics. The "mobilization of bias," which factors certain questions into the political process while excluding others, reflects the distribution of power in a more profound sense than the results of overt political action.[10] The power analyst, therefore, must concern himself both with the actions of A and B and with the more difficult question of who is favored by the existing demarcation of the boundaries of legitimate political discourse.

POWER AS AN ORGANIZING THEME
OF POLITICAL INQUIRY

The concept of power, though intuitively an important element in political life, lacks the specificity and empirical content necessary for it to serve as the "first principle" of political inquiry, the kind of universal explanation that subsumes all particular political behavior. Political life is too complex to be easily comprehended by so diffuse a concept. Scientific research into politics, to be fruitful, must concentrate on more narrowly defined problems that are amenable to systematic investigation. Nevertheless, though the generalized idea of power possesses little explanatory credibility, it can still be used in a thematic fashion to draw together the disparate inquiries of political scientists. In this way, power questions can be woven into the multifaceted areas of interest in the study of politics, not in an attempt to pass power off as a general theory but simply to illuminate some common associations among the diverse directions of political science.

In the following chapters, some of the major concerns of political scientists and philosophers are discussed, in terms both of empirical investigations and normative evaluations. The problem of power will be used to provide a certain amount of continuity to what otherwise might appear to be an unconnected narrative of the discrete investigations of a pseudo science.

Part Two

FUNDAMENTAL POLITICAL RELATIONS

Why do some people and groups have a greater impact on the development of social relations than others? The simple answer, seemingly obvious, is that they have more power. This reply, though, merely raises other questions: Why do they have more power? Where does it come from? The answers, discussed in Chapter III, involve identifying the sources of power in social relations and how these are converted into specifically political outcomes.

If one person has power, then another must obey. What are the motives for obedience and how are they related to the sources of power in society? Obedience is often associated with the threat or experience of coercion, but not necessarily or exclusively. Citizens may obey political authorities because they feel morally obligated to do so. In fact, the basis for moral obligation to the state has excited philosophical debate for 2500 years. On the other hand, the problem of obligation also raises the question whether disobedience is ever justified. These issues are taken up in Chapter IV.

The general interest in who has power in society leads to the specific issue of "who governs?" This question establishes a fundamental area of political inquiry; the answer helps one understand the operations of a political system and provides a basis for comparison with other systems in the world. Unfortunately, a simple solution is often difficult to discover, as an examination of the contending "theories" of who governs in the United States amply illustrates. Some general conclusions, however, can be reached, and comparisons with other political systems can bring these conclusions into sharper focus. In Chapter V, therefore, the situation in the United States is contrasted briefly with that in the Soviet Union.

Competition for scarce social-power resources and disagreements over the uses to which they should be put means that social and political relations often entail conflict. These conflicts need not be destructive—actually they can serve a creative and vitalizing role in a system as long as their consequences are contained. Chapter VI

31

examines the sources of conflict, the different dimensions along which conflicts can be compared and contrasted, and the processes by which conflict might be resolved or regulated.

Conflict, of course, can become violent. In Chapter VII the nature and causes of political violence are explored, as are some major regime strategies for containing social discontent. The problems of revolutionary war and terror are given special attention, and the chapter concludes with an examination of some of the ethical problems raised by the use of violence in political relations.

Chapter III   The Source of Power

Social interaction can be viewed as a quasi-economic process in which the participants pursue diverse ends through the manipulation and exchange of social-power resources.[1] The unequal *distribution* of such resources enables some individuals or groups to have a greater impact on social outcomes than others; in this sense, they possess more power. Even in highly centralized systems, however, the weakest person has at least one potential resource: his or her life. Political power refers to the ability to shape those outcomes that can be plausibly labeled public policy.

The mere possession of a power resource does not guarantee a voice in the political process. As it does in the more narrowly defined economic system, the relation between supply and demand determines the value of a particular resource, renders it *relative*. Under conditions of increasing scarcity, a resource increases in value and its controller can become more effective. Likewise, a resource may be in demand in one area of social life and be considered irrelevant in another.

Still another factor, in addition to distribution and relative value, determines effectiveness: the *skill* with which a particular resource is managed. A "power-rich" person may squander this "wealth," while one with significantly fewer resources may skillfully manipulate them for maximum advantage, invest them wisely, and grow in power over time. The judicious *combination* of two or more separate resources often multiplies their value to a level greater than the sum of their independent values.

Political scientists find all these aspects important for the study of the determinants of public policy within a system, as well as a major basis of comparison among systems. Only the basic contours of these issues can be examined in this chapter, though subsequent chapters will further elaborate some areas. The next two sections identify a number of the primary resources drawn upon in contemporary political systems and suggest some possible interactions among them. The concluding part investigates several related questions about power relations in society.

POWER RESOURCES

The impact of social power, whether in a relational or a structural sense, is not confined to the political arena; rather, it permeates all social action. Consequently, most power resources are not specifically political in nature, but can be used for broader social purposes. At times, a person who appears resource-rich in an area of private social activity may find it difficult to translate this private power into public outcomes. For example, wealthy Chinese businessmen in Southeast Asia, though dominating economic activity, are often excluded from direct political participation and must invest considerable funds (for instance, in bribery) to gain some indirect access to the government. Though most of the resources analyzed below are not specifically political and cannot be automatically equated with political power, they can usually be used for such ends and will be discussed from this perspective.

Economic Resources

When asked what gives a person power, most Americans will probably reply "money." Simple monetary wealth plays an important role in most systems, but in the United States the pursuit of this resource assumes, at times, obsessive proportions. Actually, the ability to exchange money for political power is somewhat restricted, even in the United States. The extremely wealthy no longer "buy" public officials quite so flagrantly as they did in the nineteenth century, though evidence of such purchases occurs more frequently as one moves from the national to the state and local levels of government.[2] The purchase of specific public decisions through bribery (see Chapter IX) still occurs, though probably not on a scale of some other countries or of previous times. The political uses of money in the United States have become more indirect and subtle. For an example, effective campaigns for office demand considerable funds. The large donor to a political campaign may not expect to "own" a legislator, but he most certainly expects in the future to gain privileged access and at least a hearing for his views. Some of the abuses during the 1972 presidential campaign led to further constraints being placed on even these indirect exchanges of monetary resources for political decisions. Nevertheless, money can still be exchanged for other resources that may in turn command significant political power potential.

The power associated with monetary wealth raises the question of its origin and suggests a more fundamental economic power resource: the control of the means of production, basically land, labor, and capital. According to Marxist theory, the control of the means of production is the primary power resource; all else is secondary:[3] economic relationships underlie all other forms of social, cultural, and political interaction. Those who control productive activities, therefore, direct the political system and shape social and cultural values as well. In his historical analysis, Marx argues that power shifted in the past from the class that controlled the land (feudal lords) to those who controlled capital (the bourgeoisie) and that it would finally be seized by those who controlled labor (the proletariat).

Though Marxism can be criticized both for its overemphasis on purely economic power resources and for the inaccuracy of some of its predictions, it remains a significant and important analysis of the nature of power relations. Those who control the means of production can often translate this economic power into political outcomes, as studies of big business and organized labor demonstrate.[4] Marx, however, did not foresee that two such concentrations of economic power could coexist and to some extent counterbalance one another in the same system.[5] Further, in some countries private groups do not control the means of production. In the Soviet Union, for example, large-scale private ownership has been abolished and labor does not really exist as an independent force. The political leadership exercises more direct control over economic resources than does this leadership in the United States.

Marx also failed to anticipate the growing importance of a new means of production and thus the growth of a new power resource: the control of needed knowledge and skills. Considerable debate continues over the precise impact of the technocratic and managerial elites. John Kenneth Galbraith and others argue that the managerial class, not the legal owners, exercises primary control over the industrial system, because the managers have the skills necessary to operate complex economic enterprises.[6] This power shift occurs whether the owners are the stockholders of a capitalist system or the political leadership in a socialist one (the growing influence of public bureaucracies parallels that of private ones).

Whether or not a technocratic elite rises to pre-eminence in postindustrial societies, possession of a desired skill or specialized knowledge gives people a resource they may be able to exchange or use to shape public policy. Even those who perform relatively low-level functions can exert considerable power within a system if they are able to act in concert. A strike by unskilled factory workers clearly demonstrates this power resource made possible through organization (see Organizational Resources, below). When a sizeable proportion of all workers go on a general strike, they can even threaten the continued existence of a regime, as they did in France in May 1968.

Economic power resources, then, include more than simple monetary wealth. Anyone who performs a necessary task in the productive process controls some potential power. Clearly, some individuals are favored by the unequal distribution of economic resources, but even the relatively powerless can shape sociopolitical outcomes if they are able to act cohesively.

Status Resources

In every social order some individuals are esteemed and others defer to them and follow their wishes. Those esteemed individuals control status resources. People acquire status in diverse ways. In some societies, accidents of birth can determine a person's rank in a stratified status hierarchy. Instead or in addition, a person may be able to exchange other power resources for status, as when someone is respected because of economic success or because of a skill he or she possesses. Even intangible qualities like personal magnetism or beauty may confer status. Generally, cultural values determine the nature of status resources in a society; what is considered a source of high status in some societies may be held in contempt in others. Status resources also change over time. For example, professional soldiers occupied the lowest social rank in traditional Chinese culture, but in postrevolutionary China they have moved to a higher level, possibly the highest.

Status constitutes a source of power because others follow an esteemed person out of the belief that he can better see the correct course of action. This element of faith helps to distinguish status from the more materialistic power resources.[7] If the followers question the recommendations, however, then status has failed to gain compliance and other resources must be brought to bear.

A person may possess status in one area of social life and not in another. When a doctor recommends a course of treatment, for example, his patient usually accepts his advice on faith. He seldom questions the doctor's background, training, and motives; rather, he defers to the doctor's status as a presumed expert. Perhaps the doctor also will be able to sway his patient similarly on issues of national health-care policy, because the patient may believe that the physician's expertise carries over to this related area. If, however, the doctor begins to make recommendations on national-defense policy, his opinions will most likely be challenged because he has clearly gone beyond the usual area within which deference is granted him. Since the effectiveness of status resources originates in faith, the doctor can be described as a victim of a credibility gap. Even those who occupy positions of generally high status, like the presidency of the United States, may find this resource a diminishing asset if the people no longer have faith. Failure of a recommended course of action can produce this result.

One of the most powerful manifestations of status resources is charismatic political leadership. *Charisma* means much more than simple personal popularity. Max Weber developed the concept to describe the nature of the relationship existing between the great religious leaders of history—Christ, Moses, Mohammed, Buddha—and their followers.[8] In these extraordinary cases, the followers confer ultimate status on their leaders, believing them to be set apart from ordinary men by a gift of grace which implies divinity or, at least, privileged access to the Godhead. Consequently, the leader is "uniquely capable of cognitively structuring or restructuring the world."[9] In the contemporary world, this special status has been most closely approximated by some Asian and African leaders who led their peoples to independence (Sukarno, Nkrumah, Gandhi, Mujibur Rahman). This impressive faith, however, has been often shattered by the failure of the leaders to fulfill all the expectations they raised. While it lasts, though, charismatic status can be converted into impressive political power.[10]

Status as a power resource (rather than a mere formal ranking) depends on the psychological quality of faith and, as such, can be quite volatile. These psychological dynamics, moreover, can be manipulated. A leader may be able to generate faith in himself through the utilization of powerful symbolic appeals and of the mass media. Adolf Hitler's image as an all-powerful leader was enhanced by the settings of his mass rallies.[11] In this case, he was able to convert other power resources into a form of status. Other politicians, on a less grandiose scale, have been able to convert status in one area into a political position. However, the very fluidity which encourages manipulation can lead to deference being withdrawn with equal rapidity.

Information Resources

As a social order grows more complex, accurate and readily accessible information becomes essential to successful performance. Control over information, then, is another power resource. The ability to gather and, conversely, the ability to withhold information can be a primary determinant of relative power positions. Many civil libertarians, for example, believe that the centralization of information resources in the national government poses a threat to individual freedom and political choice. The government continually expands its intelligence-gathering apparatus and moves toward more efficient systems of data retrieval and assessment. Soon, all the information on citizens gathered by every agency of government on all levels may be centrally stored and instantaneously accessible. On the other hand, the individual citizen and even his elected representatives encounter significant obstacles in acquiring information on how public organizations function and make decisions.[12] The distribution of information resources of this sort appears skewed in the government's favor.

The serious implications of this distribution can be graphically demonstrated by the consequences of such resource concentration in more authoritarian systems. "Totalitarianism" implies a form of rule wherein the government has complete access to the lives of its subjects but they have none to the government. Commonly, totalitarianism is equated with all-pervasive coercion, but the more essential trait may be the elimination of the citizens' privacy through a complete centralization of control over information resources.[13]

The ability to gather or withhold information suggests another information resource: the means by which information is transmitted, primarily the mass media. Again, government control of transmission characterizes authoritarian systems. In the United States, critics on both the political right and left attack what they see as the excessive power of a private media establishment. Though often castigated for taking controversial editorial positions or revealing sensitive information, mass media seem to have their crucial role less in the area of specific opinion formation than in the general definition of the range of acceptable political discussion. Some issues are never adequately discussed because they are not factored into the arena of legitimate political discourse. Naturally, in a system where the political regime controls the content of the media, the boundaries of political discourse remain rather constricted. Even in systems of privately controlled media, all the conceivable policy alternatives seldom receive equal attention, equal space, or equal time.[14]

Information exchange involves both a transmitter and a receiver. Control of information transmission furnishes one source of power and the ability to shape the receiver constitutes another. Consequently, control over the process by which people assimilate information can be a source of power. The enterprise of education is not neutral. All social systems devote some effort toward insuring that supportive attitudes are learned by each generation. People learn values and orientations that affect the way they view the world. As with other forms of information resources, an authoritarian system often attempts to exercise control over as many phases of this learning process as possible, whereas greater decentralization exists in a more open society. Revolutionaries also see their role as an educational one, at least in part, for they recognize that until a "revolutionary consciousness" exists, support for a revolutionary redistribution of resources is unlikely. Any person can contribute to the shaping of another's consciousness, but other education resources are also unequally distributed (see Chapter XI).

Physical Coercion Resources

Physical coercion, or its threat, is often considered the resource of last resort; when all else fails, coercion can be used to shape behavior in the desired direction. Basically, coercion includes any act intended to damage a person or to damage what he values. So defined, the range of coercive acts extends from the slight and the subtle to the extensive and the overt. *Physical* coercion refers to a narrower range of actions where the destructiveness has a recognizable, direct, physical dimension (thus forms of "psychological coercion" are excluded from consideration).

The political regime generally attempts to delineate the boundaries of what is deemed legitimate physical coercion, though so doing does not give it a monopoly on coercive resources. Everyone possesses some coercive potential which could be exchanged for other resources if one were willing to accept the risk. The crime rates attest to this potential. Moreover, the use of this resource need not be confined to the private arena, but can be directed against the state. Naturally, under normal circumstances, a private individual probably will not receive the best of this exchange, given the preponderant resource position of the regime. Nevertheless, coercive resources may be spent attacking the regime, if the attacker is willing to accept the cost. The state's superior position depends, in part, on its organizations of physical coercion—the police and the armed forces. If antiregime forces are able to improve their relative position, either through organizing their own coercive resources or undermining the coherence of the regime's, their chances of converting this particular resource into political outcomes increase (see Chapter VII).

Political Resources

Authority and legitimacy are the specifically political power resources, though both terms often have wider implications than the restricted meanings given here. Individuals possess *political* authority when they are able to speak for the regime in a certain area, that is, are authorized to state policy. As with other power resources, the value of various authority roles varies. In a political democracy, the individual voter has a modest position of authority. When voting, the citizen in effect speaks for the regime in the selection of certain public officials. Though a single voter may not appear particularly potent, when thousands or millions concert their votes they can become very important. In the past, this political resource could be exchanged directly for other resources—for example, money. This kind of exchange is frowned upon in most contemporary democracies, and so the transaction occurs on a more esoteric level, where the citizens give a candidate their support in exchange for general policy or ideological promises.[15] The value of the vote fluctuates. In close elections, the bids for it may be quite high. In uncontested elections, its value as an authority resource may be close to zero (though it may have some value as a source of legitimacy).

Other authority roles command considerably more value in exchange. Most are continuous rather than intermittent, and people who hold such positions speak for the regime on a wider range of activities. In systems of constitutional government, however, even the chief executive's authority is institutionally limited, while contemporary autocratic rulers are restricted by the necessity to have a *de facto* division of authority. The value of political authority also depends on the position of the government in terms of other resources. If the regime controls considerable economic resources, for example, the political authorities able to allocate those resources will probably command a high price in exchange for access to them or influence over them. Alternatively, a bankrupt regime would find the value of its authority roles quite diminished. In the past, the value of a political office could be directly measured, for it was often sold to the highest bidder. Indeed, the sale of public offices provided a major source of revenue for the British monarchy up until the nineteenth century. Currently, the exchanges, as with the vote, usually occur at the more abstract level of support (taxes, obedience, and the like) given in the expectation of acceptable government performance.

Another factor which can affect a regime's overall resource position is its legitimacy. As used here, *political* legitimacy refers to the beliefs of the people as to the *moral rightness* of the regime, that is, as to whether they have a *moral* obligation to follow the wishes of the political authorities. The legitimacy resources of a regime vary with respect to what sectors of the population view regime commands as legitimate and within what boundaries.

Even a well established regime may encounter some dissidents who refuse to grant it any legitimacy. In the United States, for example, some radicals reject the government completely and are willing to use violence against it. If such sentiments were to spread, the position of the government would be severely undermined. Even those who do consider the regime legitimate often place some limitation on their allegiance. In a constitutional system, in fact, some limits on legitimate regime action are formally defined. Thus, the United States government cannot legitimately attempt to establish an official state religion. In other systems, customary rights and obligations may effectively constrain the sphere of legitimate regime activities.

Legitimacy is an important regime resource because feelings of moral obligation prompt people to give up resources they control without receiving fair value in exchange (except in some generalized psychological sense of satisfaction).[16] Consequently, a relatively legitimate regime acquires needed resources at a lower unit cost than an illegitimate one. As legitimacy declines, a regime must extract needed resources through more concrete inducements or threats of coercion.

Political authority, legitimacy, and status affect one another. When a people view their regime as legitimate, they will probably endow the office-holders of that regime with relatively high status and will often defer to their wishes. Those who hold positions in an illegitimate regime will receive little deference. Naturally, the value of being able to speak for a regime (of having authority) will be greater under conditions of legitimacy. Alternatively, a leader who possesses exceptionally high personal status (charisma) may be able to confer legitimacy on the political institutions and policies with which he associates.[17]

Organizational Resources

Organization can be viewed as an amplifier of other power resources.[18] Almost everyone controls some small resource reserve, but solitary action has little impact on sociopolitical outcomes. Organization brings disparate resource holders together and directs them toward a common end. Generally, the ability to act in concert creates for the whole a greater potential power than that of the sum of the parts acting separately.

The value of organizational resources depends primarily on two factors: the value of the resource being organized and the quality of the organization. Obviously, not all organizations are equally relevant to the social process—an organization of butterfly collectors would most likely possess little power because of the nonessential character of butterfly collecting. The value of a resource, however, may not be readily apparent. Individual garbagemen do not appear to carry out a highly valued function, but if they are able to act together, they quickly demonstrate their collective importance.

The quality of an organization depends on four interrelated criteria:[19]

1. *Adaptability*: A strong organization must be able to adapt to changing circumstances and confront new challenges. Citizens may organize in an ad hoc fashion to redress a particular grievance and may even be quite effective in dealing with that specific task. They often fail to exercise continuing power after the initial purposes have been achieved because of the inability to adapt the organization to new ends. Even apparently powerful organizations can face difficulties to which they cannot adjust, as in the case of the collapse of an army after a defeat. Paradoxically, victory too may encourage organiza-

tional breakdown. Adaptability seems best fostered by continual, middle-range challenges that test organizational flexibility without seriously threatening extinction.

2. *Complexity*: Complexity essentially refers to the degree of differentiation or division of labor in an organization. A complex organization is usually large, but not all large organizations are complex. Differentiation can apply both to the hierarchical structure of authority and to the multiplicity of distinct functions performed within an organization. Contemporary bureaucracies (both public and private) are the most common complex organizations. A local citizens' group consisting of a chairman, a secretary, and a body of undifferentiated members exemplifies a simple organization.

3. *Coherence*: The extent to which the organizational parts function as a coherent whole also affects organizational quality. Coherence and complexity, in fact, may be somewhat contradictory, for as complexity increases, so do problems of maintaining coherence. A situation where the various subdivisions begin to pursue incompatible ends hardly improves organizational quality. Simple organizations do not automatically avoid coherence problems, though, for they generally lack internal discipline, and individual members often balk at subordinating themselves to group purposes.

4. *Autonomy*: Quality also is contingent on the degree of independence from external control. No organization can be completely autonomous; at the very least, it must engage in resource exchanges with other power holders. The central issue is whether the organization engages in these exchanges to maximize internally selected or externally imposed goals. A "company union," for example, serves not the ends of the workers who make up its membership but rather those of the management of the firm. Organizational autonomy also provides a measure of the degree of centralization in a political system. In a pluralist system, private groups can be freely formed and possess a reasonable amount of autonomy. But even in the United States, the most familiar example of political pluralism, most organizations must conform to certain government regulations governing their behavior. In more authoritarian systems, social organizations are commonly subordinated to the regime.

All four criteria, taken together, indicate organizational quality. They need not vary in the same direction, for an organization could be high in one area and low in another. Indeed, as is suggested above, increasing complexity may threaten coherence.

THE EXCHANGE OF POWER RESOURCES

Most social interaction consists of the manipulation and exchange of resources in the pursuit of individual or group goals. In politics, the participants attempt to maximize their control over specifically political resources (authority and legitimacy), as well as over other resources controlled by the regime. The nature of this process can be most clearly illustrated when money serves as a medium of exchange, for then a quantitative measure exists for what is given and received. But often the exchange process is considerably more subtle. The holder of one resource may appear to receive others though seeming to spend nothing of his own. This appearance may be caused by the very high exchange value of his resource. Another cause may be "payment" deferred to some future time. In still another, the exchange may be psychological and qualitative, rather than material, hence more difficult to perceive or recognize.

Some of the complexities of the process of social exchange are illustrated in Chart III-1. The holder of political resources, for example, can exchange them for other resources in various ways. An officeholder may give a decision in exchange for a bribe. A relatively strong authority and legitimacy position for the regime as a whole increases its ability to collect taxes, though the people may expect certain policies and programs in return for their material support. Failure to produce these may reduce the regime's capacity to authoritatively extract taxes in the future. An analogous position probably exists with respect to status. Most people, under normal circumstances, will give some deference to high public officials; but, if these officials perform poorly, their status may decline. Officials can also use their position to gain access to the media, as well as to acquire the information necessary for decision making. However, the value of authority in this area again appears in part dependent on the performance expectations of the people. Poor performance may make it necessary for the regime to invest other resources at its disposal (money, coercion) to control the media or to gather information. Those in certain positions of authority direct the police and the armed forces, but these groups, too, expect something in return, and if these expectations are unfulfilled the disappointed may become insubordinate (see Chapter X). Finally, officials can use their authority and legitimacy to direct and control the activities of their subordinates. In some cases, then, the exchange is quite overt. In others, the return is deferred, in the sense that people follow authoritative directives, under the assumption that the policies declared by the authorities will approximate their expectations. Finally, citizens may give up some of their resources to the regime because they feel morally obligated to do so.

The remainder of the chart provides further examples of how the various resources may be traded off for one another. Economic resources can be used to buy numerous other economic resources: political decisions or access to top political figures; respect, through philanthropy; information and access to the media; armaments, to increase coercive power; and, in general, they can be

Chart III-1 Examples of Resource Exchange

	RESOURCES RECEIVED					
RESOURCES INVESTED	*Political*	*Economic*	*Status*	*Information*	*Coercion*	*Organization*
Political	Use the authority of one political office to influence another.	Exchange government decisions for bribes.	Use government position to gain respect.	Use government position to gain access to media.	Use government position to direct armed forces.	Use government position for the authoritative coordination of activities.
Economic	Pay bribes for government decisions.	Exchange one economic resource for another.	Use economic resources to buy respect.	Use money to buy access to media.	Use money to buy arms.	Use economic resources as an incentive for cooperation.
Status	Use social respect to gain government position.	Use social position to acquire economic resources.	Use status in one area of social activity to gain it in another.	Use social status to gain access to media.	Use social status to protect oneself from coercion.	Use status to unite faithful for a common purpose.
Information	Use control of media to influence government.	Exchange access to media for money.	Use control of media to acquire social status.	Exchange one piece of information for another.	Give information in exchange for protection from coercion.	Use information to coordinate organization.
Coercion	Use armed forces to seize control of government.	Use arms to seize money.	Use force to extract deference from others.	Use threat of coercion to gain information.	Exchange one coercion resource for another.	Coerce coordination.
Organization	Use organization to unite supporters into a political party.	Use organization to unite producers into a monopoly.	Use organization to unite faithful into a church.	Use organization to unite local transmitters into a network.	Use organization to unite armed men into an army.	Use one organization to organize in another area.

used as an incentive for cooperative activity. Status resources may be drawn upon by prestigious persons seeking public office and used for extracting material support from the "faithful" or for gaining access to the media. High status may also protect a person from official coercion (in this case, he gains in that he does not lose—he avoids a negative consequence). When the status resource is deference to the same leader, it may be invested or spent to unite the followers in a common endeavor. Control of relevant information resources enables a person to shape political opinions, sell desired information, use media to build status, give information in exchange for protection, or coordinate the activities of an organization. Coercive resources, obviously, can be drawn upon to eliminate political opponents, extort material resources, extract information, or force cooperation. Coercion, when directed at the perceived enemies of political order, may even increase the status of the coercer in the eyes of other regime supporters.

Organization multiplies the effectiveness of individual power holders. The organization of political support creates a political party; the organization of an area of production, a monopoly; the organization of the faithful, a church; the organization of information transmitters, a communications network; the organization of armed men, an army. Organization improves one's power position over time.

This discussion of power resources does not capture the full complexity and dynamism that characterize sociopolitical exchanges. Further elaborations could discuss the problem of opportunity costs (using resources in one way usually implies that alternatives cannot be explored) and the effects of constantly fluctuating rates of exchange. Strategies for maximizing the potential of resources at one's disposal also deserve examination. The more important power resources, however, have been identified and some of their interrelationships suggested.

THE DISTRIBUTION AND MEASUREMENT
OF POWER RESOURCES

In addition to identifying the sources of power and examining their uses, power analysts explore other related problems, such as the distribution of power resources and the measurement of power.

The study of the effects of various power distributions is thousands of years old. Aristotle developed one of the earliest comparative typologies based on three basic types of power distribution (whether one, few, or many ruled) and whether the dominant group ruled for the common good or in their own selfish interest (Figure III-2).[20] Aristotle argues that each form of rule draws primarily upon a particular power resource. Monarchy and aristocracy are based on merit (status) and skill in rulership; tyranny, on physical coer-

Figure III-2   Aristotle's Typology of Forms of Rule

		PURPOSES SERVED	
		Common Good	*Selfish Interest*
TYPE OF POWER DISTRIBUTION	*Rule of One*	Monarchy	Tyranny
	Rule of the Few	Aristocracy	Oligarchy
	Rule of the Many	Polity	"Democracy"

cion; oligarchy, on control of wealth; and democracy (Aristotle used the term to describe the distorted form of rule by the many), on the sheer numbers of the poorer classes. Subsequent analyses over the next 2500 years produced more complex typologies of the source and distribution of power in innumerable political systems, but the basic questions remain direct descendants of Aristotle's pioneering effort. Among the enduring problems are:[21]

1.   What are the characteristics of the Rulers and the Ruled?
2.   How do the Rulers and the Ruled compare in numbers?
3.   Do the Rulers and the Ruled typically come from different classes, strata, regions, or other groupings?
4.   What historical changes have occurred in the characteristics of the Rulers and the Ruled?

These questions and the complex sociological, economic, and political inquiry they imply continue to form a fundamental part of contemporary political investigation (see Chapter V). Understanding of conflict and stability within political systems also depends on knowledge of the distribution of power (see Chapters VI and VII).

Power analysts also concern themselves with problems of measurement. The concept of power, as argued in Chapter II, can be criticized as too vague and too inclusive to be susceptible to precise measurement. At best, one can make only crude ordinal comparisons among power holders; that is, one individual or group can be recognized as more powerful than another, but the precise difference cannot be stated.

Focusing on power resources, however, may facilitate measurement. Monetary power resources obviously submit most readily to measurement and comparison. Other power resources may be measurable indirectly. Formalized hierarchies, for example, give some idea of relative authority. Polling and interview techniques may be used to identify those who have high status in a community. Systematic studies of organizational quality can be implemented. None of these alternatives may be completely satisfying, but in order to learn about the distribution of power the attempt must be made to compare power resources. And in addition, some idea of relative power positions can be gained through the analysis of resource exchanges over time.

A related approach might be to develop indicators of a controller's (C) power over a responder (R) in a specific order/response situation. Among the possibly relevant factors are:[22]

1. The probability that R will comply with the order.
2. The number of persons in R.
3. The amount of change in R's position, attitudes, or psychological state.
4. The speed with which R changes.
5. The reduction in the number of alternatives open to R.
6. The degree of R's threatened or expected deprivation.

Such questions direct attention to some more specific areas of power research.

Viewing power as an order/response relationship, however, tends to obscure its structural characteristics, which largely determine what issues become subjects for debate in the first place. Structural power must be measured indirectly, because its impact lies in what does *not* occur. As conflict increases, so does the value of seeing power primarily in direct order/response relations. Under conditions of consensus, though, structural perspectives of power become important.

This chapter investigated some of the primary sources of power in society and how they might be exchanged for one another. Some brief remarks were also made on the problems of distribution and measurement. The problem of power can also be approached from the opposite direction: Why do men obey? This question is the concern of the next chapter.

Chapter IV Obedience and Power

MOTIVES FOR OBEDIENCE

People obey for a variety of reasons: habit, desire, fear, and obligation.

Habit

The vast preponderance of a person's rule-conforming behavior is nearly automatic, or habitual. Human beings would be unable to function if they consciously considered each step they took into the complex social world. Consequently, from the day of birth, an infant learns how to act in social situations, and though the initial lessons are consciously absorbed, they eventually become ingrained as habits.

The complexity of these habits of conformance is staggering, though usually unrecognized.[1] One has only to consider the amount of social learning of norms and procedures that facilitates the flow of traffic in a city to realize the importance of such learning for the preservation of order. When a beginning driver first masters the rules of the road, he is aware of every move and is probably a little awkward in his operations. As he gains experience, though, his driving becomes both accomplished and more automatic. So dependent are people on these learned responses that even minor breakdowns are cause for considerable alarm.

Even seemingly trivial habits of obedience are not politically neutral. Such responses help to maintain order and preserve the status quo, including the existing distribution of power resources. Some groups are clearly favored by a particular status quo, while others are disadvantaged. Habit generally supports the structure within which power relations and exchanges occur. A person, of course, may not learn these supportive patterns of behavior and thus acquire "bad" (that is, disruptive) habits and be considered "antisocial." The process and problems of learning, or socialization, will be further considered in Chapter XI.

People's actions, however, are not completely habitualized. At least their initial learning is conscious and motivated by some external goal. Moreover, they periodically rise out of their habitualized state and consider their actions and alternatives, at which time other motivations become important determinants of obedience or disobedience. In fact, choice appears to become conscious most often when disobedience, or nonconformance, is considered.

Desire

Once habit fails, a person can be motivated to obey another's will by appealing to the desire for a reward. When two individuals each control a resource the other desires, they can serve one another through a mutually beneficial exchange. A resource-rich person or group can dispense rewards to build a following. The success of appeals to this motive depends on the individual's assessment of a number of factors:

1.   The *"value"* of the reward.
2.   The *probability* that the promised reward will indeed be given.
3.   The *time lag* between rendering the service and receiving the reward.
4.   The value and certainty of the rewards for *alternative actions* (thus, what are the expected fruits of disobedience?).

As the value of the promised reward increases, along with the certainty of its being awarded within a reasonable time, the probability of obedience increases, assuming the evaluations of alternative courses of action remain constant. If the probability of receiving the reward declines or if it is postponed to some vague future date, the effectiveness of promises of even large rewards will diminish.

Governments can offer many rewards for rule-conforming behavior. These rewards, however, are often "collective goods"; that is, citizens may benefit from them whether or not they obey the laws. For example, both the taxpayer and the tax evader benefit from the efforts of the government to provide for the national defense or a clean environment. Naturally, little positive incentive exists to pay for a service which one would receive anyway, especially when the value of disobedience is judged high. Also, if the people doubt the government's ability to fulfill its promises, their desire to provide the requested support will most likely be low.

Some rule conformance may be motivated by a clearly recognized, positive self-interest. Thus, drivers may follow traffic laws because of a conscious recognition that their own safety and ease of travel are enhanced. Others may be prompted by rewards of considerable abstraction. For example, Supreme Court Justice Oliver Wendell Holmes is reputed to have remarked that "taxes are the price I pay for civilization." Governments, unfortunately, cannot depend on such enlightened self-interest or abstract values to produce rule compliance. When habit and desire fail, obedience can be motivated by fear.

Fear

The fear of being punished for a failure to obey certainly motivates much consciously conforming action. Basically, the strength of motivation through fear depends on factors similar to those of desire for reward:

1. The *severity* of the threatened punishment.
2. The *probability* that the threats will be imposed.
3. The *time lag* between the act of disobedience and the punishment.
4. The *attractiveness* of the anticipated rewards (see above) for disobedience.

The severity of punishment affects the probability of obedience only when not undermined by the other factors. If potential criminals believe that the probability of their being captured is quite low, even the threat of severe punishment may be a weak deterrent. They may, of course, be mistaken in their evaluation of the probabilities. The effectiveness of a punishment promised at some distant time (like the after-life) also may have little impact on immediate action. Finally, the anticipated fruits of disobedience must be considered. Some people will take considerable risks if they believe the stakes high.

Punishment and the threat of punishment possess one advantage from the regime's point of view. Though many government services (rewards) are collective in nature and thus indivisible, punishment can often be inflicted on specific offenders. This specificity provides a more precise tool for motivating obedience.

One final note: The factors that determine the relative effectiveness of threats of punishment and promises of reward appear more objective than they in fact are. Severity of punishment, for example, depends upon the values of the person threatened. Commonly, deprivation of life is considered to be the most severe threat; however, people do sacrifice their lives to protect other values like the boundaries of their country or the lives of their loved ones. Similarly, the value of a promised reward may be assessed differently by different persons. Calculations of value and severity, therefore, are fundamentally subjective in nature.

Obligation

One other motive may encourage conformance to another's wishes or to laws: feelings of moral obligation. One thus motivated chooses to obey not because of the expectation of a specific reward or the fear of punishment; rather, one obeys because such actions are believed to be right and are mandated by moral principles. Perhaps the person can be said to receive a psychic reward or gratification in return for obedience, but any such expectation is quite different from the calculations of relatively materialistic *quid pro quo* exchanges.

Every established sociopolitical order attempts to devise some grounds on which its citizens will feel obliged to obey the laws. Fear and desire require substantial resource expenditure by the regime, as does the process of instilling supportive habits. If people feel morally bound to obey, however, they not only resist sizeable temptations but also require little in the way of concrete rewards or threats, at least over the short run. One potential drawback exists, though, for a regime that establishes the moral basis of obedience thereby usually defines the conditions when disobedience is permissible or even required.

Clearly, some of the power resources discussed in the preceding chapter are more relevant to the manipulation of one motivation for obedience than another. Control of the instruments of physical coercion, for example, can be used to play on the motivation of fear, while certain economic resources can be used to reward obedience. Feelings of moral obligation, especially to the political regime, depend on legitimacy resources, whereas in essentially private interactions certain status resources might produce such feelings of obligation.

At the formative stage, habits of obedience require resource expenditure. Certain actions must be rewarded or punished and feelings of moral obligation reinforced. After the desired responses have been deeply implanted, resource expenditure will decline as the desired response comes to be automatic. Even strong habits, however, require some kind of periodic reinforcement or they may eventually be extinguished. As techniques of behavior control and modification increase in sophistication, the role of habit in maintaining the social order may further expand in the future. A perfectly habitualized society would have to be completely static and surprise-free, as changing environments require active decision making.

THE GROUNDS OF MORAL OBLIGATION TO THE STATE

The question of *why* people obey is essentially an empirical one. The problem of when citizens *should* obey is normative in nature and for more than two millennia has received the attention both of political philosophers and of regimes. As with most issues of political values, a number of positions have been advocated, which illustrate the development of political philosophy.

Perhaps the most ancient principle of obligation is *tradition*; that is, certain rules or rulers are followed because they have been sanctified by customs that stretch back into the immemorial past.[2] Traditional legitimacy remains important in many contemporary cultures and even plays a role in modern societies. When a father orders his son to act in a certain way because that is the way he behaved at his son's age, he invokes tradition. Tradition also limits the grounds of obligation. A person who grows up in one tradition will not feel bound by another and may even view it as evil. Many cultures recognize this limitation, hence treat people from other areas as "strangers" or "aliens" and may even confine them to special areas. Witness American ghettos, where immigrants, blacks, and other minorities have been isolated, in part because the dominant groups fear the population elements that have not absorbed the prevailing system of cultural norms. Within a particular culture, a ruler who fails to live up to the traditional requirements of his office may find his support waning.

Tradition, then, provides somewhat ambiguous support for a ruler. The *theocratic* principle, however, appears more inclusive. Theocracies lay claim to the people's obedience because the ruler either is a god or represents one. The rulers of some of the great bureaucratic empires of the past (Egypt, Rome, Inca) all asserted their own divinity. Medieval kings, though, were often limited by the traditional rights and privileges of the nobility, wherefore centralizing monarchs like Louis XIV of France found the doctrine of the divine right of kings useful in the struggle to consolidate their power. The efficacy of such claims rests on the people's acceptance of the ruler's assertion of divinity (the ultimate status resource). Once the principle is established, all commands, no matter how subversive of tradition, become morally binding.

Divinity, though, can be contested. The early Christians refused to accept the Roman emperor as god, precipitating a three-hundred-year legitimacy crisis. Ultimately, in Western Europe, this confrontation was resolved in one of the more historic political compromises: divine authority was consolidated in the hands of the Roman church which, in turn, validated the authority of the secular rulers. Though this division solved one problem, it set the stage for a thousand years of struggle between church and state over the limits of their respective spheres of authority.

The Greek philosophers Socrates (470?-399 B.C.) and Plato (427-347 B.C.) also examined the question of moral obligation to the state. The *Socratic* principle essentially holds that if a person lives in and accepts the benefits of a system, he also must accept its laws, even if they do not always work to his advantage.[3] Socrates was sentenced to death by an Athenian jury on what appear to have been trumped-up charges, yet he turned down an opportunity to escape and dutifully followed the court's sentence. He might have developed a different position had he not been over seventy years old. Nevertheless, the Socratic principle of obligation perhaps influences the behavior of tourists in a foreign country. Certainly, they have no patriotic loyalty to that country, nor did they participate in the formation of its laws. As guests, however, they may well feel obligated to respect the laws of the host country while enjoying its benefits.

The *Platonic* theory of obligation asserts that justice requires that those few enlightened ones who understand the nature of the "good" should rule and that all others should follow. Consequently, either philosophers must rule or rulers must become philosophers.[4] Presumably, no lesser mortal could claim such morally grounded obedience, and the philosophers who are not kings because of some perversion of power constitute a law unto themselves. Though Plato's argument might appear rather abstract, communist parties assert a similar principle in legitimizing their rule. The party, especially the leadership, claims to understand the basic "laws of history," and this knowledge uniquely qualifies it for rulership. Naturally, if the party is not in power, the existing regime must be historically ignorant and should be removed, by revolution if necessary. Those who advocate a rule of experts or technocrats also echo the Platonic theory of obligation.

Somewhat related to the Platonic rationale is the argument that the ruler must be obeyed when his commands are in accordance with *natural law*, which reflects universal principles of justice. A ruler's failure to follow natural law dissolves obligation.[5] Unlike the Platonic idea of the good (or the communist understanding of the forces of history), which is accessible only to the chosen few, the principles of natural law are presumably available to all those capable of exercising "right reason." Unfortunately, "reasonable men" have continually disagreed over the exact content and meaning of such law. Natural-law theory continues to be of importance, for it contributed to the development of the doctrine of natural rights, which libertarians argue must be respected by all forms of good government. This doctrine found its most recent reincarnation in the United Nations Universal Declaration of Human Rights.

Other important principles of obligation are found in various *contract theories*, especially those associated with the English political philosophers Thomas Hobbes (1588-1679) and John Locke (1632-1704). Essentially, this theory develops the myth that social and political systems originate in a contractual agreement among human beings in the "state of nature" who subordinate themselves to political authority in order to secure the advantages denied them in their natural condition. Hobbes, being something of a pessimist, views this natural state as one of continual war of each against all, where life is "solitary, poor, nasty, brutish, and short."[6] In order to preserve their lives, people make a compact giving a sovereign complete authority to rule. In exchange for their obedience, the citizens expect the sovereign to protect their lives. If the sovereign fails to do this the contract is dissolved. Hobbes went so far as to argue that a man sentenced to death for a high crime would no longer be bound by the contract and could justifiably attempt to escape (in contrast to Socrates' position).[7]

Locke, however, holds a more optimistic opinion of life in the state of nature.[8] Though not a ceaseless war, the competition for scarce resources does necessitate some system of conflict regulation. For Locke, the mythical contract is a two-part affair, one creating a basic political society and the other defining a specific form of rule (such as representative democracy, monarchy, or the like). Unlike Hobbes, Locke believes that it is possible to eliminate the political regime without destroying the underlying social order. Locke argues that the regime is created to protect liberty and property, as well as life, and that a regime's failure to fulfill the broader conditions of this contract dissolves the obligation to it. Hobbes's doctrine implies that a sovereign can be replaced only after he ceases to protect life (at that point people would be back to the state of nature anyway). Locke's theory justifies rebellion against a tyrant who, though protecting life, fails to protect liberty or property. Dissolution of the government, however, does not reduce citizens to their natural state. Interestingly, both Hobbes's pessimism and Locke's optimism found support in English political history of the seventeenth century. Hobbes witnessed the execution of a king (Charles I, d. 1649) and the ravages of a civil war. Locke lived through the "Glorious Revolution" of 1688, when James II was removed from power by Parliament and a new king (William III), more to Parliament's liking, was installed with little bloodshed.

Contract theory, especially that of John Locke, influenced the leaders of the American Revolution and constitutes the basic rationale of the Declaration of Independence. Jefferson asserts in his document that governments are instituted by men to protect the "unalienable Rights" of "Life, Liberty, and the Pursuit of Happiness." When a government fails to secure these rights, "it is the Right of the People to alter or to abolish it, and to institute a new Government . . ."[9] Ironically, the precise words of the Declaration occur in the Statement of Principles of the Black Panther Party to justify their dissent from the established order.[10]

The concept of *democratic legitimacy* largely evolved out of contract theory. Basically, individuals are believed to be morally bound by the decisions of the people *(vox populi, vox Dei*—the voice of the people is the voice of God). A problem arises, though, in determining exactly what constitutes the "people's voice." If a decision is unanimous, the problem is minimal, though the French philosopher Jean Jacques Rousseau (1712-1778) argues that a decision to be binding must be in the people's "true" interest—what he calls the general will—and the "will of all" might be mistaken about this interest.[11] Rousseau, though, leaves somewhat unclear how the general will is to be discovered. In any case, unanimity is seldom achieved, especially in large political systems. Consequently, contemporary theories of democratic legitimacy combine principles of majority rule and respresentative democracy with certain guarantees of minority rights (for instance, free speech).[12] If a law passes in accordance with these various conditions, the people are obligated to obey it.

Democratic theories, then, share with contractual ones the concern that particular conditions be met. Contract theory, however, primarily emphasizes substantive issues (life, liberty, property), while democratic theory concentrates on procedural areas (the process by which a law is passed or a regime comes to power). Strictly speaking, a bad law correctly passed would be binding, though discontented citizens could make use of the avenues provided by the democratic order to alter this law. If a law or a regime should come into being in violation of democratic procedures (as through a *coup d'état*), the people would not be morally bound to obey it.

The doctrine of *philosophical anarchism* denies that any external power can claim morally imperative obedience from an individual.[13] It asserts, rather, that adults must be completely morally autonomous, that is, obliged only to follow the dictates of their consciences. Insofar as any individual morally binds himself to any government, no matter how it is constituted, he loses his autonomy. Philosophical anarchists might indeed obey a command for other reasons—fear of punishment or desire for reward—but never because they felt morally obliged to conform. Acquiescence, therefore, is subject to immediate withdrawal if the conditions rewarding or coercing it are removed.

Directly opposed to the claims of moral autonomy made by the philosophical anarchists is the argument for complete submission in the *organic theory* of obligation.[14] Organicism holds, essentially, that the people gain their life and meaning from the social order of which they are a part. Just as a hand cannot be considered autonomous from the rest of the body, neither can the individual be considered independent from the state. Organicism implies that the whole political order is something greater than the sum of the parts, that each citizen serves some function in the whole, and that some members are worth more to the continuation of the "body politic" than others (as in a physical body, where one can survive the loss of a hand or a foot, but not of a heart or a brain). Organic theory draws on many elements of Western political thought from Plato through Rousseau and Hegel (1770-1831), and came to a perverted culmination in the crude ideology of the Nazis.

The question of moral obligation to a political regime is irrelevant in the theories of both anarchism and organicism, though for opposite reasons. In anarchism, morally autonomous adults cannot abdicate their responsibility by binding themselves to an external power. In organicism, the idea of autonomous individuals is meaningless, and if a subordinate part were to rebel against the whole, it would be taken as a sign of disease in the body politic.

This survey of various theories of obligation illustrates the answers given to the question of why and when citizens should obey, ranging from complete submissiveness to complete autonomy. The variety suggests that no universally acceptable answer will ever be formulated, though philosophers and rulers will continue to assert one or another. Perhaps the complexity of the ethical problem limits the possibility of a simple answer, and one must be satisfied with a more ambiguous and tentative analysis. In this regard, the doctrine of civil disobedience not only asserts the periodic necessity to disobey, but also the practical necessity for obedience most of the time.

BETWEEN SUBMISSION AND AUTONOMY: THE DOCTRINE OF CIVIL DISOBEDIENCE[15]

The definition of the grounds of moral obligation to the state, as was noted above, often implies the circumstances justifying disobedience. Conversely, the doctrine of civil disobedience, in arguing the case for certain types of disobedience, justifies rule conformance under most conditions. Generally, the principles of obligation discussed above assert that obedience is required when the laws conform with some ideal (tradition, the conditions of a "contract," democratic process, and so on). Submission to laws, however, can also be viewed as a lesser evil, accepted in order to avoid two greater ones. People without law rapidly degenerate into a condition of strife and violence. Unless law also binds the ruler, however, turmoil will simply be replaced by tyranny. The middle way of law which is binding on both rulers and ruled is preferable to either extreme.

Human law, though, is fallible and may not conform with basic principles of justice; that is, particular laws may not be compatible with the underlying purposes of the system of law. Therefore, one's sense of justice may require that a law be disobeyed, after other avenues of redress have been exhausted. Martin Luther King, Jr. (1929-1968) and Mohandas Gandhi (1869-1948) advocated this idea, though elements of the doctrine can be traced back at least to the early Christians.

In a rule of law in conformity with justice, just selective disobedience to an unjust law must fulfill certain conditions: First, though the unjust law is violated, the essential rightness of the system of law is affirmed. Consequently, the effects of disobedience on the whole system of law must be carefully weighed. If the risks to the system are greater than the presumed benefits of disobedience, then the lesser injustice must be endured. Second, since the system of law is accepted, the *civil* violator must be willing to accept the consequences of his actions and go unresistingly to jail. Third, the selective resistance must be nonviolent so as to minimize the damage done to the rest of the system.

Martin Luther King, especially in his early civil-rights protests, fulfilled all three conditions in his acts of civil disobedience. First, he believed in the underlying principles of governance in the United States and thought that legalized discrimination on the basis of race violated these basic principles. Drawing attention to these unjust legal practices through his disobedience, he hoped that their true nature would be recognized and that they would be expunged from the legal system. To dramatize his fundamentally supportive position, he willingly accepted the penalties attached to the violation of these laws, in the expectation that this behavior would further publicize his position and that the higher courts, in any case, would declare the laws unconstitutional. His nonviolence at once further emphasized his support of the basic system and won him considerable sympathy, as pictures of police violence were broadcast throughout the nation.

Gandhi, in his struggle to convince the British to quit India, rejected more than a mere few unjust laws; rather, he denounced the entire system of British colonial rule and demanded complete independence. Though he attempted to keep his battle nonviolent and willingly accepted imprisonment (as did hundreds of other Indian nationalists) to dramatize his cause, the *swaraj* (self-rule) movement was not a true civil-disobedience campaign because of the comprehensiveness of the aim and the totality of the rejection of the system of rule. To the extent that the conflict was kept nonviolent, it might be considered a "civil" revolution.

The effectiveness of Martin Luther King's strategy depended on the accuracy of his evaluation of the basic justness of the system. If the unjust racist laws that he and his followers disobeyed were, indeed, deviant cases in an otherwise acceptable order, then the oppressed minorities could reasonably expect redress as soon as the incompatibility was demonstrated. If, however, the entire system of laws was corrupt, then selective symbolic disobedience would have little effect. Similarly, though Gandhi rejected an entire system of rule, he still relied upon the basic ethical qualities he assumed to exist in most of the British. Eventually, he believed, the basic rightness of his struggle (he called this *satyagraha*, or "truth-force") would become apparent to even the most stubborn imperialist.

Some dissidents, obviously, share neither King's acceptance of the fundamental legal order nor even Gandhi's faith in the humanity of his opponents. During the 1960's, radical movements in the United States concluded that the problems of America were interconnected. Domestic racism, the war in Vietnam, the power of large corporations, the maldistribution of wealth, and so on were no longer viewed as unfortunate occurrences in an otherwise healthy society. Rather, they all were deemed symptomatic of the sickness of the system itself. (Interestingly, in the last years of his life, King appeared to move away from his original position by seeing a relationship between Vietnam and domestic racism.) Consequently, the radicals' resistance to that order became increasingly violent, and they certainly no longer accepted the legal consequences of their acts.

The doctrine of civil disobedience, then, is a limited one, which establishes the conditions for obedience, as well as justifying disobedience under certain circumstances. As the rejection of the system of law becomes more inclusive and as the weapons chosen become more destructive, resistance moves away from simple disobedience toward revolution (see Figure IV-1). The doctrine of civil disobedience does not justify revolutionary violence— the right to revolution, if it is believed to exist, must be established on other grounds.

Figure IV-1   Forms of Resistance to Law

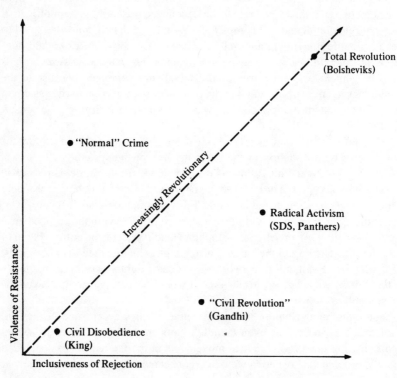

SOME AREAS FOR INQUIRY

The problem of obedience and power raises some interesting areas for political inquiry:

1.   How does a particular regime elicit obedience from its citizens? What is the mix of rewards, punishments, and moral inducements, and how does this mix change over time? What is the role of habit in maintaining the established order? How do the regimes of different political systems compare along these lines?

2.   On what grounds does a regime claim legitimacy; that is, how does it try to engender in the citizens feelings of moral obligation to political authority? How effective are these claims? How do the grounds of moral obligation change over time? How do these grounds differ from system to system?

3.   The two preceding groups are essentially empirical in nature. Also of importance is the philosophical issue of disobedience. Does an individual ever have the right to disobey political authorities? If so, under what conditions?

4.   Finally, in any political system one might inquire: Who is obeying whom, or more precisely, who governs?

Chapter V Who Governs? [1]

Those holding positions of political authority govern a political system. Who, however, "governs" these officeholders? Some truth lies in the Marxist assertion that the political authorities merely serve the ruling class, whose power depends on the control of the instruments of production. Other analysts, though rejecting the Marxist emphasis on economic resources, agree that the real governors are those who control the preponderance of general social power resources (wealth, skill, organization, and the like), and who convert this general power position into specific political outcomes. Political authority, from this viewpoint, remains a highly dependent variable. Critics of this position argue that public officials possess power in their own right, as well as the ability to initiate action and control other resource holders. If Marxism defines one extreme of this debate, the other would be represented by those who advocate a "great man" theory of politics and history.

The exchange model developed in Chapter III encourages a more complex conclusion. [2] Political authority is one resource among many that exist in society and are exchanged for one another. A strong demand for authority drives up its price in terms of other resources; those who control authority positions are thereby put in an advantageous situation enabling them to initiate and direct the course of public policy. If political authority suffers a deflation, the holders of other and more valued resources are thereby able to increase their control over the development of public policy. Only if the value of political-authority resources should fall to zero would public officials be completely dependent on other power holders; only if the value of all other resources should fall to zero would officials be completely independent. Neither extreme seems particularly probable; however, the rate of exchange and, consequently, the balance of independence and dependence can vary greatly over time and among different systems.

The following discussion approaches this complex and shifting problem from two directions. First, some major interpretations of the "real" governors of the United States political system are surveyed. Second, to place the United States in comparative perspective, several general observations on who governs in the Soviet Union are contrasted with the United States experience.

CONTENDING VIEWS ON WHO GOVERNS IN THE UNITED STATES

The problem of "who governs" appears to be essentially an empirical one, but supposedly objective descriptions often include an implicit or explicit defense or critique of the existing order. The complexity of the process of political decision making in the United States provides evidence for several not completely compatible answers. At the risk of some oversimplification, the four primary positions may be stated; they are that the country is governed by (1) the people (through their elected representatives); (2) organized special-interest groups; (3) a single power elite or (4) competing elites. Each position takes some account of the others. These four answers are critically examined in turn, and a provisional synthesis is attempted in the concluding part of this section.

The People Govern

The United States was founded on the idea of popular sovereignty: that all power resides in the people and that the public officials gain their authority from the people. Whatever the contribution of the myth of popular sovereignty to government legitimacy (and a wide variety of regimes in the world today invoke it), it fails to guarantee that the people truly govern themselves. For to do so, the people should be able to participate effectively in the making of all political decisions that affect their lives. Though the governing processes of some small groups approximate this ideal, it obviously does not characterize the way public policy usually develops. The United States is not a pure *participatory* democracy.

The people might nevertheless be said to govern if the system meets four conditions of *representative* democracy.

1. *The elected representative must be responsible to the people.* Representation alone does not mean people's rule. All it means is that one person stands in place of another person or group.[3] A demagogic leader might claim

to represent the "people's" will. The key question invokes responsibility: to whom are the representatives responsible—to themselves, to a special-interest group, or to their whole constituency? One continuing debate in politics concerns the extent to which elected representatives should obey the will of their constituents, assuming it can be discovered, or follow their own judgment. No easy answer can be given, but to the degree that representatives deviate from the will of their constituents, however justifiably, the people are that much less their own governors. The representatives, moreover, might respond more readily to the needs of powerful special interests rather than to those of the general public.

In order to maximize the responsibility of the representatives to their entire constituency, at least three conditions need to be met: First, terms in office should be kept short, forcing elected officials to report back to the people and renew their mandates frequently. Second, effective routes of access to the representatives should be available between elections, so that the people can continue to communicate their views. Third, the people should retain the power to intervene directly in the governing process. One way of meeting this condition is through use of *initiative*, *referendum*, and *recall* provisions that exist in some state constitutions. Initiative provisions enable voters to legislate by placing a proposal on the ballot through petition. Referendum provisions require that before certain measures become law, they must be submitted to the voters for approval. Recall provisions give the voters the power to remove an official before his term expires. The effectiveness of these measures depends on the ease with which they can be implemented.

The institutionalized methods of government in the United States lack many of the structural devices that help to insure popularly responsive representatives. Indeed, the original Constitution deliberately excluded some of them. The House of Representatives, with relatively short two-year terms, was intended to be fairly responsive to the people. Both the Senate (six-year term) and the president (four-year term), however, were originally indirectly elected. The longer terms of office were designed to isolate these officials from the swings of public opinion. The Supreme Court, in effect, remains a lifetime appointment, and the vast federal bureaucracy is neither directly controlled by the people nor easily managed by the elected officials (see Chapter IX). Additionally, no provisions equivalent to initiative, referendum, and recall exist at the national level. Even constitutional amendments are referred not to the people but to the state legislatures.

Some democratization has occurred over the years, especially with respect to extension of the right to vote, provision for the direct election of senators (Amendment XVII), and reduction of the independent role of the Electoral College. The country, however, still does not possess formal structures of government completely supportive of people's rule. Moreover, the informal processes by which influence is exercised between elections tend to make officials more responsive to those groups who possess significant power resources. The importance of informal processes suggests a second condition if the people as a whole are to be accurately described as governing through their elected representatives.

2. *All citizens must possess sufficient power resources to participate effectively in the political process.*

Sufficiency and effectiveness need not mean complete equality in the distribution of resources; rather, each citizen must possess enough of some politically relevant resource to make his or her voice heard. To some extent the vote serves this function, for at least at election time candidates must justify themselves to gain or retain office. Elected officials, though, are not equally responsive to every member of their districts. Some members are more important, perhaps because they make large donations or organize a block of voters. And between elections, power inequalities increase in importance, for it is then that the general promises of the campaign are translated into specific policies. The ability to influence both day-to-day legislative action and the administrative system that enforces the laws becomes far more important than shaping the platitudes of the campaign. In order to have this influence, one must control sufficient resources to apply continuous pressure on the representatives and the administrative system. The average citizen does not possess the power to participate in this level to any significant degree.

3. *The range of alternatives open to the citizens also affects the significance of their participation.* Political activity means little if it simply involves the affirmation of policies decided upon by the regime. Rather, there must be some competition among parties and ideas.

Competition, like responsiveness and equality, is a matter of degree. Presumably, representative dmocracy requires competition between two or more parties for the voters' support. The problem, though, is not quite so simple. First, even in a country ruled by a single party, there may be some internal competition. In Tanzania, for example, the ruling party, the Tanzanian African National Union (TANU) has nominated two candidates for each office and allowed the voters to choose between them. Second, even where two or more parties compete in elections, the amount of "real" choice available to voters may still be limited. The Democratic and Republican parties are sometimes castigated as "tweedledee and tweedledum" because they both develop essentially moderate political positions. Consequently, though voters in the United States have some choice, the available alternatives do not represent the full range of the ideological spectrum.

Beyond the simple competition of parties, the sociopolitical environment ought to encourage the development and expression of diverse opinions. The basic liberties of free speech, press, and assembly guaranteed in the Bill of Rights, insofar as they are respected, begin to provide such an environment. Competition among ideas seems to require also that the contending positions be adequately presented to the people. Adequate presentation depends on sufficient resources; access to the means of mass communication must be purchased in some way. The formal right of free speech means little unless one can gain a hearing. Consequently, groups who lack conventional resources (money, position) will try to gain a hearing by staging a disruption of some kind. Despite this alternative route, the "marketplace of ideas" in the United States is about as free as the economic marketplace. Just as giant corporations dominate the economy through their concentrated economic power, certain political positions dominate the media because of the power resources supporting them. The problem is less one of majority oppression of minority rights than one of a minority of significant power holders shaping majority opinion in the first place.

Even assuming that the elected officials respond to the people's wishes, that all citizens possess sufficient power resources to make themselves heard, and that meaningful choices are open to them, self-government is still not guaranteed. It depends further on the quality of the participation.

4. *The quality of the participation in a true democracy must be quite high in terms of the levels of activity, knowledge, and "rationality."* The fact that people control sufficient resources to participate effectively means little if they choose not to participate. Apathetic citizens do not govern themselves; rather, they abdicate their position to those more interested. The United States system, however flawed, offers a number of avenues of participation, from periodic voting through continuous political activity. Many citizens do not take advantage even of the least of these, failing to vote except in presidential elections. The participation in local contests often falls below 25 per cent. Even fewer citizens are active on a more steady basis. One reason for this noninvolvement is that those with resources choose to invest them elsewhere. Whatever the cause, this behavior does not lead to self-government.

Political activity, in order to result in self-government, must further be informed and "rational." The citizens' choice must be intelligent. This requirement entails, first, that they know their own preferences. Though such self-knowledge may seem automatic, most people probably fail to identify their core interests and/or to recognize that many of their goals may be incompatible with one another. Preferences need not be completely consistent, but contradictions should at least be recognized. Second, citizens must be sufficiently knowledgeable about the nature and consequences of the available alternatives to make a choice compatible with their values. Voters in the United States generally lack the necessary information about both policy issues and contending candidates for office. Even when they make choices, they are often ill informed. Ignorance, then, lessens the significance of the voters' participation. As political issues grow more complex, those who control information and knowledge can increase their impact on political outcomes, and the less informed relinquish what power they once possessed. Rational participation, in sum, implies that people's choices reflect their preferences, that ends and means are consistent.

The conditions for representative democracy are imperfectly met in the United States. This imperfection does not deny that the people retain some capacity to affect the course of public policy. Indeed, a substantial argument could be made that a gradual process of democratization, extending back two hundred years, continues to expand the people's power. Nevertheless, the ideal still fails to adequately describe the real, and the question "who governs" must be answered in a different fashion.

Interest Groups Govern

If the ideal of representative democracy is not fully realized in the United States, how, then, is the system governed? A second perspective focuses on the interest groups which appear to mediate relations between the rulers and the ruled.[4] This interpretation is commonly referred to as the group or pluralist thesis. Interest groups may be defined as collections of individuals "who are linked by particular bonds of concern or advantage, and who have some awareness of these bonds."[5] Interest groups can be classified into four basic types:[6]

1.   *Anomic*: Anomic groups develop with relatively spontaneous expressions of a common interest, such as a riot or a demonstration. Actually, very few outbursts of mass discontent are completely spontaneous—even riots can be deliberately provoked and directed. As the activity becomes less spontaneous, it approximates more organized forms of interest expression.

2.   *Nonassociational*: The nonassociational category includes various kinship, religious, status, regional, or class groups who express their interests only intermittently. These groups lack an ongoing organization and procedures for defining the nature and means of interest expression. Rather, they operate only when the outside world impinges greatly on their concerns. If this external pressure is continuous, these groups will begin to develop an ongoing organization, thereby becoming another type.

3.   *Institutional*: Social systems include a variety of organizations whose primary function is something other than interest expression. Thus, government bureaucracy administers policy, the military defends the state from internal and external enemies, and churches save souls. Yet these organiza-

tions may also represent what they see as their interests. The military and civil bureaucracies lobby for increased appropriations, and churches support or oppose legislation they believe affects morals or their rights. This secondary function of interest expression is probably inevitable, but it can begin to subvert the primary purpose of the organization (see Chapter IX).

4. *Associational*: Associational groups are organizations that exist primarily to represent interests and are most commonly identified with the term "interest group." Examples include labor unions, business and professional associations, civic, consumer, and other groups. When nonassociational groups set up a continuing structure—like the N.A.A.C.P.'s representation of the interests of the black community—they become associational in character. These are the groups that generally engage in political lobbying.

The pluralist position sees power as dispersed, but not among individuals so much as among these interest groups, especially the latter two types. Competition among these groups determines the shape of public policy. The output of the political system is viewed as largely dependent on the interactions among the various groups involved in a particular policy area. Simply put, policy outcomes can be determined by carrying out a kind of "vector analysis" of the relative power positions of the competing groups.

The political system, then, includes a kind of "dual representation": the formal structures of political representation (Congress, the state legislatures, and similar bodies) and the interest groups that provide a form of functional representation. The day-to-day process of governance is largely left to the interactions between these two sets of representative bodies. The elected officials, moreover, recognizing the relative passivity of the average voter, and continually confronting the demands of organized interests, respond more to the latter than the former.

Politics, then, consists of bargaining and compromise among these various groups, refereed by the political authorities. Policy change develops gradually as the relative power balance among the contending groups shifts. No one group dominates the political system; indeed, if one group appears to be growing too powerful, it generally stimulates the growth of an opposing group.[7] Big business and big labor, for example, in a sense feed off each other. Though no single group can completely fulfill its positive objectives, it can usually veto those proposals that seriously threaten its core interests.[8] Average citizens, though not politically active, retain some residual power through periodic voting and by supporting those groups which advance their interests. In fact, the pluralist thesis assumes that most people have their various interests represented by a variety of groups which cross-cut rather than reinforce one another. Total identification with a single group can lead to compartmentalization of society and a breakdown in orderly social interaction.

The proponents of the pluralist thesis do not view their conclusions as an unfortunate, if more accurate, description of the governing process in the United States. Rather, they believe more direct forms of democracy can degenerate into mass politics and even totalitarianism.[9] Perhaps if people were angels, direct democracy or completely responsive representative democracy would work. Given the emotional and ill-informed participation of the average citizen, the intervening interest groups, who function as the primary political actors, serve to moderate the political process.

Pluralist theorists see in direct democracy several dangers that a pluralist system presumably avoids. First, direct democracy almost inevitably produces majority tyranny, for the various minority interests have no way of protecting themselves. In a pluralist system, they can organize into groups and participate in policy making or at least can veto policies that seriously damage their position. Second, assuming that mass participation is necessarily ill-informed, the decisions of a mass democracy could lead to disaster, given the complex nature of contemporary social problems. Organized interest groups, however, possess the resources to gather and evaluate relevant information in forming their positions, hence the decisions in which they participate should be of considerably higher quality. Third, mass opinions are subject to wide swings that create political instability. Interest groups, because they identify with a specific area of concern, hold more stable positions through time. The dispersal of power among these groups, and their presumed inclination toward bargaining and compromise, produce an equilibrium.

Advocates of pluralism see a fourth danger. They often view mass democracy as only one step away from tyranny. This somewhat paradoxical connection between mass democracy and tyranny can be clarified by recalling the mediating role of interest groups. Direct democratic involvement in politics produces instability, which in turn increases the likelihood that some strong man will try to impose order in the name of the people (as did Napoleon after the French Revolution). In a pluralist society, the power of the interest groups protects the people from overinterference by the regime and, at the same time, insulates the regime from the potential instability of mass involvement. In a mass democracy, moreover, the citizen stands alone facing the government. Interest groups, in short, constitute middle-level power holders that the government cannot bully as easily as it could bully an atomized citizenry. Consequently, in a totalitarian system, the regime discourages the creation of independent groups and even horizontal communication among the citizens. Such relations can create potential competitors to the regime's claim to total power.

The pluralist interpretation of the United States power structure not only purports to be an adequate empirical answer to "who governs," but appears to be a preferable alternative as well. Again, as with the democratic answer, some supporting evidence can be found. Political observers since the nineteenth century have noted the American inclination to form groups to achieve social and political objectives.[10] Moreover, close analysis of certain policy areas, especially of those involving questions of domestic social and economic policy, reveals patterns of group interaction that resemble the pluralist model. The argument, though, collides with the complexity of politics in the United States and, consequently, has been criticized for both its descriptive and normative deficiencies.

A Power Elite Governs

Another school of thought on the nature of the governmental process competes with the pluralist model. Though not necessarily rejecting the desirability of certain aspects of democracy, these analysts argue that every large-scale society is ruled by a power elite and that the United States is not different. With respect to the system in the United States, this perspective is most commonly identified with C. Wright Mills and his disciples.[11] Mills and others level a number of substantive criticisms at the pluralist model:

1.   *The pluralist model fails to account for the widespread feelings of political powerlessness among Americans.* A sense of power or efficacy can arise from two sources:[12] First, an individual might believe himself or herself to be personally powerful, that is, able to affect political outcomes. This confidence would be characteristic of citizens in a perfect participatory democracy. Second, a person, though not feeling personally powerful, may think that other groups or individuals adequately represent his interests. This kind of efficacy characterizes the pluralist model. No doubt some Americans feel efficacious in one or both ways, yet many others do not. Therefore, both of these descriptions of the United States political system are, at best, partial.

2.   *These feelings of powerlessness result in part from the fact that many people do not belong to significant intermediary groups.* Hence they have no organizational representative to compensate for feelings of personal powerlessness. Among the underrepresented interests are those groups that possess few power resources (such as the poor) or groups that are difficult to organize (such as consumers). Other interests are overrepresented and are able to shape public policy to suit their own special needs. They may still compete and compromise among themselves, but the outcomes do not reflect a balancing of all the potential interests affected. The pluralist thesis could become more accurate as new interests, previously unorganized, enter into the political system. During the 1960's, for example, minorities became more vocal in articulating their interests; consumer and environmental groups began to participate more extensively in policy making. Big economic interests no

longer went unchallenged. Other problems, however, continue to plague the pluralist position, despite the proliferation of new groups.

3. *Even if people belong to a significant group, they are often alienated from its internal processes.* In any organization, especially as it grows larger and more complex, some leaders must exist to plan and implement activities. These leaders use their power to maintain their position within the group. Thus, sociologist Robert Michels formulates his famous "iron law of oligarchy": "Who says organization, say oligarchy."[13] Consequently, even if interest groups could effectively participate in decision making (a concession most elite theorists refuse to make), the interests of the rank-and-file membership would still not be represented. Rather, those in the oligarchy dominating the organization tend to use it primarily to further their own interests. The average organization member has little voice in or control over organizational affairs. Though somewhat overdrawn, this portrait of membership alienation and powerlessness can be supported by some examples, such as the United Mine Workers before the defeat of Tony Boyle.

4. *Finally, and most importantly, the elite theorists argue that the pluralist thesis fails to account for the relative power positions of the various groups that do participate.* Unless they are approximately equal in power, it may still be possible to identify a power elite by isolating those few who exercise the greatest impact on policy.

In order to make their point, elite theorists must do more than simply criticize the pluralist thesis; they must in addition identify plausible candidates for recognition as the ruling elite. Those who advocate an elite interpretation of the American system must demonstrate the existence of a general-purpose elite; that is, one which is able to determine government policy over a wide range of key issues.[14]

A number of possible general-purpose elites have been suggested, including finance capitalists (that is, investment bankers who control both industry and government); the top families (who control wealth, status, and government); and "peak" associations, like the National Association of Manufacturers (these presumably coordinate the activities of various elements of the elite).[15] None of these hypothesized elites, however, demonstrate sufficient cohesion or wide enough influence to qualify as a ruling elite.

C. Wright Mills develops a more complex argument.[16] First, he declares that the power elite in the United States consists of three interrelated groupings: the top political, military, and corporate leadership. Second, he argues that the top-level financiers and corporation lawyers can be included because they serve as go-betweens and unifiers of the three primary elements. Third, he does not deny that other power holders exist, like Congress and special-interest groups; rather, he relegates them to the middle levels of political influence. The "big" issues of war or peace, prosperity or recession, are decided by this tripartite power elite. Congress and other power holders may have an impact on lesser issues, though primarily through reaction rather than initiation.

Mills defines his dominant group broadly enough to be a general-purpose elite, *if* these elements actually operate in a cohesive manner. He argues that they interlock in a number of ways: First, their objective interests commonly coincide, especially since the end of World War II. They may periodically conflict over specifics, but they agree on overall policy trends. The phrase "military/industrial complex" sums up this continuity of interest, because the big corporations and the military presumably benefit from large defense appropriations and hence support attitudes and political leaders who advocate such expenditures. Second, Mills argues that the career patterns of the three elements frequently mesh. Generals become corporate directors or assume civilian government positions, and corporate executives are recruited for top government positions. Third, the social and educational backgrounds of the members of the power elite coincide. They generally come from high-status families (with the partial exception of the military) and they go to the same prestige schools. In this latter case, the military academies could be considered prestige schools, and their graduates are disproportionately represented at the highest ranks. Fourth and finally, through their control of the avenues of upward mobility, the elite is able to select for promotion those who demonstrate reliable support of elite views.

Mills's rather bleak description of the United States power structure, then, consists of three levels: (1) a relatively unified power triad who make all the important decisions; (2) a relatively ineffectual collection of middle-level power holders who counterbalance one another, as in the pluralist argument, but succeed primarily in canceling themselves out of effective political participation; and (3) a mass public, alienated from the middle-level power holders and unable to affect the power elite who run the system. Unlike those who hold to the pluralist description of United States political process, Mills makes it abundantly clear that what he describes is not his preference. Nevertheless, though elite theorists identify some of the weaknesses of the pluralist argument, their analysis, even in the fairly complex Millsian form, has been criticized as an oversimplification.

The elite thesis seems applicable to a society in which three conditions obtain. The first of these is a significantly unequal distribution of power resources. An elite, if it is to have elite quality at all, must be a relatively small minority controlling the majority of the power resources in a society. Were the resources to be more equally distributed, the size of the group controlling a preponderance of them would increase. At complete equality, no less than a majority of the citizens could control a majority of the society's power resources. A majority elite is a contradiction in terms. The distribution of power in the United States, though not so much skewed as it is in some other countries, seems sufficiently unequal to meet this first condition; a relatively small minority does possess preponderant power.

The second condition is a substantially united outlook in the members of the power-rich minority. The fact of unequal resource distribution does not by itself create a power elite, and the critics of the elite thesis believe that its proponents exaggerate the unity of the relatively powerful. Power relations in the United States are far too complex and amorphous to support much unity. The very structure of government, which divides political authority not only among three branches at the national level but also among fifty states and thousands of units of local government, encourages a politics of negotiation, not domination.[17] Elite theory ignores the importance of veto groups, competitive elections, "loyal" opposition, and the routes of access to the system which provide nonelites with opportunities for both influence and obstruction.

The third condition has to do with objectives. If the members of a minority elite do not, at least broadly, share common objectives, it would seem doubtful that they could apply power effectively enough to govern. Moreover, the elite argument often implies that the objectives of the elite and the mass are necessarily incompatible, though the masses may be too befuddled to realize it. Insofar as the elite favors the status quo and the nonelites possess at least a potential interest in change, the assertion of incompatibility is valid. Social and political relations, however, seldom polarize to such an extent. Elite and mass interests may coincide on numerous areas of policy, especially after the power distribution has been legitimized. Moreover, the basic source of legitimacy that justifies the distribution of power often limits its exercise as well. In fact, some observers argue that elite groups in the United States give stronger support to democratic norms than does the public at large.[18]

Countervailing Elites Govern

When the conditions for a single power elite do not exist, nevertheless minority groups having some characteristics of elites may concentrate power resources and apply them for more or less compatible objectives, perhaps interchanging governing power with one another, perhaps compromising in coalitions. Neither is necessarily explicit. This countervailing-elite thesis does not completely abandon the insights of the elite argument; rather, it develops something of a synthesis of the pluralist and elite models.[19] First, it accepts the position that the unequal distribution of power in a society creates elites, but argues that in the United States no single group possesses enough power to be considered a general-purpose or ruling elite. On the contrary, the dispersed nature of power resources generates numerous, competing special-purpose elites.[20] These special-purpose elites are not equally involved in every issue. They become concerned only when the political process affects their core interests. In this respect, they resemble pluralist interest groups. Unlike the political actors in the pluralist model, those in the countervailing-elite model need not have any specific group affiliation. Nor is policy simply a dependent variable, the product of the interaction of competing private groups. Rather, competition among the elites provides "space" for skillful politicians to manipulate groups and actively shape political outcomes. Finally, competition enables members of the nonelite to affect policy, if they choose to make the effort. Perhaps Ralph Nader, who affected political outcomes before he organized his numerous ancillary organizations, represents what a truly dedicated citizen can still accomplish in the relatively open system of the United States. He won legislative victories over some of the corporate elements that Mills assumed to be the power elite.

The countervailing-elite thesis, like the power-elite theory, views most citizens as relatively passive. This apathy, however, supposedly results not from helplessness and hopelessness, but from feelings of *relative* satisfaction. Most citizens control a few resources (at the least, some time that they could devote to political activities), but they choose to allocate them in the pursuit of essentially private goals and happiness. Private "investment" appears more attractive than public activity, until the costs of political inactivity rise sufficiently to encourage a reallocation of resources. This passivity does not mean that nonparticipating citizens are completely satisfied, only that they are not discontented enough to engage in political action. As political decisions impinge more intensely on their lives, people are provoked out of their inactivity and, because of the system of competing elites, can have an impact on public policy.

The apathy of average citizens, from the countervailing-elite perspective, may even be required for the successful operation of the political system. If the competing elites are better informed and more strongly attached to the norms of the political system than the masses, increased participation could lead to a decline in political civility and intelligent policy choices. In a sense, the countervailing-elite system functions best when most citizens believe they could have an effect, but do not act on this belief because they would rather allocate their resources toward the pursuit of private goals.

Not surprisingly, the attempted synthesis of the countervailing-elite interpretation of who governs America fails to satisfy everyone.[21] Power-elite theorists, especially, criticize the countervailing-elite model on both empirical and normative grounds: that it fails to adequately describe political decision making in the United States and, in any case, that it certainly is not desirable.

First, the countervailing-elite thesis largely ignores the structural characteristics of power, focusing exclusively on the relational aspects. Some competition among elite factions most certainly occurs, but only over those issues which are included on the agenda for discussion. This "agenda" is largely determined by those who have power. Therefore, not all potential policy alternatives, especially not those that threaten established power positions, are even discussed, much less implemented. This limitation of the agenda can be seen in the debate over health care. The accepted alternatives concern whether a national health insurance program should be implemented by the government or through private insurance companies; no national political figure is seriously advocating a socialized health service such as exists in Great Britain. Thus, elites compete over secondary issues; on fundamental power concerns they are united.

Second, political inactivity need not be a sign of relative satisfaction. Some account must also be taken of the weapons of repression that block access to the political system. For example, anyone who attributes the non-participation of blacks in the South before the mid-1960's to relative satisfaction would have to be completely blind to the "legal" obstacles and illegal coercion that prevented blacks from voting. Also, noninvolvement may be the result of cynical apathy; that is, the belief that the system will fail to respond no matter how much effort one invests in political activity. Cynical apathy is a sign not of relative satisfaction but of despair.

Third, in emphasizing the importance of competing elites and skillful politicians, the countervailing-elite approach tends to ignore the impact of class identities and social movements on the political process. Those who make this criticism often adopt a quasi-Marxist position and stress the importance of class and status factors in structuring political positions and attitudes, as well as in providing a basis for mass movements to transform society. Neither the rise of unionized labor as a political force in the late nineteenth century nor the equal-rights movements of the 1960's and 1970's can be adequately classified as the politics of competing elites.

Who, Then, Governs?

Each of the positions developed above appears to draw on some supporting evidence, but does not draw enough to claim to be the exclusive interpretation of the United States political process. Each analysis reveals a part of a complex and multifaceted situation but by focusing on one aspect tends to obscure others. To a large extent, the answer to the question "who governs" is determined by what areas are chosen for analysis. Historical studies of the extension of the franchise, the development of egalitarian welfare legislation, and the expanding role of public opinion could conclude that the United States, for good or ill, has become increasingly democratic over the last 200 years. Examination of the legislative process, particularly the activities of the lobbies, produces evidence for the pluralist model. The role of the president and his top military and civilian advisors in shaping national-security policy, as with the increasing United States entanglement in Vietnam, suggests that certain critical areas of public life are controlled by an approximation of a power elite. Each interpretation reveals and conceals, but together they suggest some general characteristics of who governs in the United States:

1.   Power is unequally distributed; some potential groups are underrepresented. The inequalities, however, are probably not as great as in many other contemporary political systems (see below).

2.   The distribution of power is shifted continually as new elements enter into the political equation and old ones diminish at least in relative influence.

3.   Power in the system must be viewed in both relational and structural terms. The former is seen in the regular competition among established personalities, programs, and groups. The latter is indirectly suggested by the policies that go unconsidered and the people that go unheard because they have been excluded from the agenda of legitimate political discourse or lack the power resources to make their voices heeded.

4.   The "elite" is divided into many competing subgroups; and though these may share an interest in the preservation of their advantages, they nevertheless differ over questions of policy and the relative power distribution among themselves.

5.   The competition among elite groups, changes in the distribution of power, and the democratic provisions in the formal institutional framework provide nonelites some access into the political system. Like power, however, access is also unequally distributed.

6.   Political noninvolvement has a number of causes. Some citizens are politically inactive because they would rather pursue private happiness; others have either given up hope or else fear becoming involved in political action.

The United States is not a pure democracy. Indeed, whether a pure democracy could exist in the complicated large-scale organizational environments characterizing contemporary societies is very doubtful. In such an environment, complete consensus becomes highly improbable, and policy directions will be determined by those individuals and groups that are strategically placed.[22] To say that "the few" rather than "the many" make political decisions does not mean that the United States is dominated by a coherent power elite. Strategic power positions may be more or less widely distributed, more or less accountable to the many, and more or less susceptible to changes over time. The extent to which the governing process in the United States can be described as relatively open might be revealed by a brief discussion of "who governs" in another political system.

WHO GOVERNS IN THE U.S.S.R.—THE PARTY ELITE[23]

The idea of democracy informs most inquiries into who governs in the United States. Analysts attempt to demonstrate either that the governing process, if not perfect, is relatively democratic (for instance, the pluralist and countervailing-elite interpretations), or that it should be criticized for being insufficiently democratic (the elite thesis). Similarly, the image of totalitarianism lurks behind most Western interpretations of the Soviet political system. Some observers try to substantiate that the U.S.S.R. exemplifies a "mature" totalitarian system, while others argue that it is evolving, liberalizing, and can no longer be accurately labeled "totalitarian."

Perhaps the major reason for the difference in general orientation toward the two polities lies in their contrasting histories. Karl Deutsch notes that the American and Soviet revolutionary experiences differed radically.[24] The United States began in a situation of relative plenty and equality, whereas the Russian tradition was one of scarcity, inequality, and exploitation. Second, the American people prior to the Revolution had decades of practice in self government. In contrast, Russian political history was one of uninterrupted autocratic rule. Third, the act of revolution and the creation of a new constitutional order in the United States, though not excessively optimistic, were based on a fundamental faith in men's ability to forge a workable community of interest. The Bolshevik revolution, however, was rooted in the Marxist theory of antagonistic class interests, and the new rulers, after seizing power, had to fight a bloody civil war to crush all the internal enemies of their rule. Fourth, the right to pursue happiness stated in the Declaration of Independence expressed a faith that people could choose what was best for themselves. Lenin, to the contrary, distrusted the spontaneous desires of the masses and believed that a highly disciplined revolutionary vanguard must lead the people to their "true" happiness. Finally, the American political tradition has been primarily one of moderation and compromise, the Soviet tradition one of ruthlessness with those who deviated from the correct path. Given this past, therefore, it is not surprising that the Soviet system is autocratic and that the point of debate revolves around whether this autocracy can be described as "total."

Totalitarianism implies two basic, interrelated conditions: First, the political system is extremely hierarchical and centralized. Second, the political leadership maintains nearly total control over all other aspects of social and economic life. This latter condition distinguishes totalitarianism from simple autocracy or tyranny. The absolute monarch, though centralizing nearly all political authority resources into his own hands, does not attempt to control the entire lives, indeed the thoughts, of his subjects. On the other hand, contemporary welfare states, especially those existing in Scandinavia, affect and regulate almost every aspect of life from "the womb to the tomb." They are not totalitarian because power resources remain relatively dispersed, and the people retain some control over the state.

Two analysts of totalitarianism further enumerate its characteristics as including:[25]

1.   An elaborate, comprehensive ideology legitimizing the rule of the political elite.

2.   A single mass party dominating the government and penetrating into all sectors of society. The party is highly centralized and supplies the "priesthood" to promote and interpret the ideology.

3.   The use of terror not only to subdue real and imagined enemies, but also to fragment the population and prevent the appearance of any competitive power centers.

4.   Complete domination of the means of mass communication, as well as attempts to control the educational process.

5.   A nearly complete monopoly of physical coercion resources.

6.   A centrally controlled economy, including the domination of all economic organizations such as unions, trade associations, and professional groups.

The Soviet Union most closely approximated these characteristics during the rule of Josef Stalin (1928-1953). During this twenty-five-year period, the system was governed by a small power elite consisting of the top-level leadership of the Communist Party apparatus, the government administration (including economic managers), the secret police, and the military. Stalin, by skillfully playing on the fears and rivalries of these leaders, was able to consolidate considerable power in his own hands. Opponents of the regime were terrorized into oblivion, and the arena of legitimate political discourse was completely defined by the governing elite.

Stalin's death intensified the conflict among his subordinates. By 1958 Khrushchev and his supporters in the Communist Party emerged victorious over other rivals within the party, the secret police (Beria), the government bureaucracy (Malenkov), and the military (Zhukov). Khrushchev, though, never attained the level of personal power possessed by Stalin. His ouster in 1964 did little to alter the central political position of the Communist Party bureaucracy. The issue of who governs the Soviet Union, then, depends on the nature of the party organization and whether other power centers can significantly shape its actions.

Four areas of activity reveal the role of the party in the Soviet system: penetration, centralization, recruitment, and ideological legitimacy.

Penetration: The Communist Party is a mass organization of more than 13 million members and candidate members. These come from all occupations, and they commonly form the core of almost every other social grouping. Primary party units exist in organizations ranging from collective farms and factories to military formations and universities. Party members occupy leadership positions in any significant nonparty structure. Additionally, ancillary organizations like the Komsomol (Young Communists) further extend the party's reach. The party parallels the government structure from the local level to the highest organ of the central government, with overlapping membership at every level. Therefore, the party penetrates into almost every area of social and political activity.

Centralization: Penetration, by itself, may simply provide a mechanism for democratic control and participation. The party organization, however, is hierarchically structured, with each unit strictly subordinated to the one above it. The Politburo and Secretariat stand at the peak of the organizational pyramid. The full time bureaucrats or *aparaty* are the heart of the party organization. They control its day-to-day activities. The Secretariat regulates this apparatus by exercising ultimate authority over recruitment and promotion. The party apparatus, in effect, constitutes an elite within an elite. In 1974, only around 2 percent of the membership of 12.7 million were *aparaty*, but party bureaucrats made up 60 percent of the Politburo's membership. Beyond the bureaucratization of authority, each individual member is subject to strict party discipline. The principle of democratic centralism allows for debate before a decision has been reached, but after the party line has been defined, all members must adhere to it.

Recruitment: The Communist Party is not an open organization; not everyone can join. Recruitment and promotion take place largely through a process of co-optation. The selection process includes a careful initial screening and a period of trial membership at each level of the hierarchy. Thus, there are even "candidate" members of the Politburo. Additionally, the leadership periodically institutes purges of the membership to eliminate those who fail, for one reason or another, to fulfill their responsibilities. Purges commonly occur after a shift in the relative power positions of those at the highest levels. These methods of recruitment and periodic purification help insure that those who join and rise in the party are loyal and disciplined. Since the Secretariat holds ultimate authority over this co-optative process, its members can insure that their supporters occupy middle-level leadership positions. Moreover, as people distinguish themselves in other forms of social activity, they can be tapped for membership, both as a reward and as a means of control.

Ideological legitimacy: Marxist-Leninist ideology legitimates the political authority of the party, while party ideologues, in turn, interpret the ideology. A faction attempting to use another organization (such as the army) to usurp the position of the party bureaucrats would be opposing the primary tradition of legitimacy in the political system. Party primacy has been promulgated for so many decades that its position undoubtedly has been institutionalized to some extent. Thus, Khrushchev's fall was engineered not by a group outside the party but by a coalition within the Politburo. These men owed their position in some cases to Khrushchev but had grown powerful and discontented enough to act independently of him.

Essentially, then, the Soviet Union is governed by a small elite of professional party functionaries who dominate a highly centralized mass organization extending throughout the social, economic, and political systems. Though the party elite is clearly preeminent, some evidence suggests that its control is not total. Among these indicators are:

1. *The Growing Complexity of the Soviet Economy and Society:* Total central control probably becomes increasingly difficult to sustain in a complex society. The control systems, whether police, party, or centralized economic planning, grow more and more costly and less able to provide the necessary coordination. Therefore, some decentralization of decision-making authority may be necessary for efficiency of operations. Technological experts must be given greater latitude to make judgments according to the imperatives of their expertise without being constantly second-guessed by party bureaucrats. Some decentralization has occurred, especially in the areas of scientific investigation and economic production, but progress has not been steady. Party officials recognize the dilemma they face: either threaten performance or relinquish some of their authority.

2. *The Apparent End to One-Man Rule:* Neither Khrushchev nor Brezhnev appears to have dominated the system as totally as did Stalin. Other members of the power elite exercise more independence than did Stalin's lieutenants, as is indicated by the fact that Stalin was removed only by death, but Khrushchev by his colleagues.

3. *The Apparent End to Widespread Terror:* Total control requires that all other potential centers of power be neutralized, and terror provides a powerful mechanism of neutralization. Because of its essentially capricious nature, terror becomes a costly and disruptive force in a complex society which requires considerable order to function effectively. Even Stalin appeared to realize that the system could not indefinitely endure terrorization at the levels of the late 1930's. Additionally, the top party officials seem to fear a replication of the bloody purge which decimated their own ranks during that decade. The police still pervade the Soviet system, but they are more restrained than in earlier years.

4. *The Emergence of Other Semi-Independent Centers of Power:* Some observers argue that something akin to interest groups exists in the U.S.S.R. Perhaps these are not as independent as those in the United States, but they are active enough to have some impact on policy formation and implementa-

tion. One analyst identifies eight primary pressure groups:[26] (a) The scientists, technicians, and managers of the nuclear and space programs. (b) The chief planners and managers of heavy industry. (c) The trade unions. (d) Municipal administrators. (e) Agricultural interests, particularly the managers of the state farms. (f) The military, who often act in concert with the interests favoring weapons research and heavy industry. (g) Academicians, especially those in various research institutes. (h) Journalistic and literary groups.

Despite the apparent loosening of the Soviet system, it can still be more accurately described as ruled by a power elite than can the United States. Participation by the great mass of the Soviet people is largely confined to the affirmation and dedicated implementation of official policy. Other groups must direct their attention to influencing party officials, for all political authority remains consolidated in their hands. Additionally, each of the groups mentioned above is penetrated by the party. Finally, no real opposition exists, with the possible exception of a few dissenting intellectuals who have little internal impact because they lack the necessary power resources.

CONCLUDING OBSERVATIONS

In all contemporary political systems, a minority rules the majority. To conclude, however, that this is all one needs to know about the governing process of over 100 independent nation-states would be mistaken. The previous analysis of the United States and the Soviet Union suggests some critical questions about these and other systems for examination:

1.   What are the origins of the elite(s)? Do they have homogeneous or heterogeneous backgrounds? Do they come from a particular class, region, ethnic, or racial group? Have they traditionally exercised power? How did they come to power? How is the composition changing over time?

2.   How are the power resources distributed in the system? Upon what resources do the elites primarily rely? How are social-power resources transformed into specifically political authority resources? How has the distribution changed over time?

3.   How do the elites maintain themselves in power? What is the mix of coercion and consensus in their rule?

4.   How unified are the various elements of the elite? Unity is a matter of degree, but three basic levels can be distinguished: (a) Total consensus: Under conditions of total consensus, no member of the elite dissents from the established position. Party discipline in the Soviet Union approximates this extreme. (b) Competitive consensus: The various elements of the elite com-

pete with one another, but within a "tradition of political contest" and a framework of formal and informal rules and norms.[27] The United States political system approximates this position. (c) Total competition: Elite competition, at this extreme, occurs without any limitations and, consequently, produces considerable political instability. At its worst, this conflict leads to civil war or revolution, as recently happened in Pakistan, Nigeria, and Vietnam.

5.   What purposes are being served by the government? Who benefits and who pays? The range of activities of the contemporary welfare state suggests a form of rule less exploitative than earlier political systems.

How these questions are answered will give considerable insight into the openness of a political system to initiatives from the masses and its responsiveness to their needs. In addition, the questions provide some information on the sources of political stability and instability. A casual review of the political experience of the twentieth century reveals considerable political conflict and violence, as people rebelled against rulers whom they believed to be oppressive. Therefore, the sources and consequences of conflict and violence deserve further attention.

Chapter VI

Conflict and Conflict
Regulation

TWO VIEWS OF SOCIETY

Justice "means nothing but what is to the interest of the stronger party."[1]
These words, attributed by Plato to the Greek sophist Thrasymachus (c. 400
B.C.), introduce one of the earliest statements of what might be called the
coercion view of society.[2] Thrasymachus argues that in any political order,
the ruling groups use their power to enforce a conception of justice which
essentially supports their position and interests. Their subjects either accept
this version of justice or suffer the consequences of dissent. Might, in short,
defines right. Marx echoes this description of the social order in his analysis
of capitalist society, in which the ruling class uses the instruments of the state
to enforce its interests (witness the laws protecting private property). Naturally, the oppressed classes do not necessarily accept their position and may well
prefer to bring about a change. The sociopolitical system, under these circumstances, will be characterized by the coercion of some of its members by
others, a situation that provokes continuous conflict and creates a constant
pressure for change.

In contrast with the conflict view of society, the *integrationist* position
stresses consensus and stability over time.[3] Conflict signifies a breakdown or
disease in the body politic, in contrast to the normal state of affairs in which
each member plays a role in maintaining the system, and all the members
carry out their functions in a well-integrated fashion. Instead of coercion of
the ruled by the rulers, agreement exists on the basic values which support the
status quo. Plato, in rebutting Thrasymachus, develops a theory of the "good
society" in which philosophers direct the policy of the state, a class of
guardians protects it from internal and external enemies, and a subject class
supports the rest with productive activities. Each of the three contributes to

the maintenance of the whole by playing its assigned role. Acceptance of one's proper position in society is Plato's definition of justice.[4]

Neither the simple coercion nor the integrationist view provides an adequate perspective on society. Rather, they complement one another, and, depending on the problem being discussed, one or the other will generally prove useful. Consequently, the analysis of a system's political culture or the investigation of the process by which this culture is transmitted from generation to generation reflects essentially integrationist concerns. These subjects are discussed later, in Chapter XI. In this chapter and Chapter VII, the emphasis is closer to that of the conflict position.

THE SOURCES OF CONFLICT

Conflict suffuses all social life, from the relations within a family to the interaction among nation states. Conflict, therefore, characterizes that social behavior identified as "political"—from the ritualized adversary relationship between defense and prosecution attorneys at a trial through the free-wheeling but nonetheless restricted conflict of the election campaigns to the unrestricted conflict of a total war. In each of these cases, however, the origins remain essentially the same—conflict develops over the distribution and use of power resources.

Conflict over the distribution of power resources develops because they are scarce and are usually unequally distributed. Most political systems can be roughly divided into rulers—those who control the preponderance of the power resources—and ruled. The former share a fundamental interest in maintaining the status quo, while the latter presumably have an interest in altering it more in their favor.[5] Since the rulers generally constitute a minority of the population, this type of conflict can be called "elite/mass vertical conflict" (*a* in Figure VI-1). Advocates, as well as analysts, of revolution see such extreme polarization existing in a society just prior to upheaval. Thus, Marx believed that the middle classes and smaller capitalists would be thrust down into the proletariat during the final years of the capitalist stage, thereby eliminating all middle-range power holders and increasing the pressure for change. In this case, the masses possess the *potential* power, but until they acquire the consciousness and organization to actualize it, they continue to be dominated by the ruling class.

But the continuation and expansion of the middle classes has softened the starkness of Marx's simple model and helped make him a poor prophet. Middle-range power holders do exist and, when numerous enough, they tend to moderate the seriousness of vertical power conflicts (*b* in Figure VI-1). The middle classes, because they possess some store of power resources, frown upon proposed redistributions that appear to threaten their position and aspir-

Figure VI-1.   Conflict over the Distribution of Power

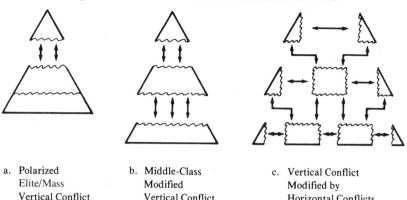

| a. Polarized
   Elite/Mass
   Vertical Conflict | b. Middle-Class
   Modified
   Vertical Conflict | c. Vertical Conflict
   Modified by
   Horizontal Conflicts |

ations. Since they do not occupy elite positions, however, they retain some interest in moderate reform. This interest can be seen, for example, in middle-class irritation concerning the tax loopholes available to the very rich in the United States. The middle classes could become radicalized if their power position were significantly challenged—revolutionary if the threat appears to come from the elite, reactionary if the threat originates in rising lower-class groups. The middle class can also serve as a buffer between the truly disadvantaged and the upper strata of the power pyramid.

Power conflicts, moreover, are often complicated by horizontal competition among elements in the same stratum of power (c, Figure VI-1). These horizontal conflicts cross-cut vertical ones, and thereby can moderate them still further. Even the elite may not be unified, a fact the consequences of which are explored later in this chapter. Such multiple power conflicts provide an inadequate base for revolution, but the consequences of extreme factionalization can be equally devastating to social tranquility by hindering cooperative activity and even causing the complete disintegration of the system.

One final factor affects power conflicts. The preceding discussion implies that a person or group rich in one power resource will be rich in others; if poor, they will be consistently poor. But this consistency need not be the case. A person could conceivably be powerful in one area of social life and not in another. A man, for example, may possess considerable status among his family and friends but still be relatively powerless in affecting the course of public policy. The sense of self worth given by these relatively limited status resources may be sufficient to lessen the tensions produced by political powerlessness, especially if political effectiveness is not highly valued. Even a powerful group may find it has greater impact on some policy areas than on others or is rich in one resource but not in others. The distribution of power resources can cross-cut rather than reinforce a single power hierarchy, again moderating the seriousness of conflict over any one power resource.

In addition to conflicts over the basic distribution of power resources are those over the use or purpose served, that is, over policy. It must be emphasized, however, that power and policy conflicts are inextricably intertwined: Policy is the other side of the coin of power.[6] The conflicts encountered in stable societies and "normal" politics often involve simply policy issues. This will be the case only if an underlying consensus exists on the appropriate distribution of power. If this consensus breaks down, policy conflict will begin to reflect alternative positions on the proper distribution of power.

Generally, when the goals of policy are agreed upon, conflict tends to occur over the most effective means to pursue those ends/goals and does not seriously threaten the existing distribution of power resources. As agreement on the fundamental purposes of policy erodes, policy conflict increasingly involves basic power issues. Of course, neat analytical distinctions between "ends" and "means" are often difficult to maintain in practice, because one merges into the other. Conflicts over tax policy, for example, might be interpreted as a simple disagreement over the best means of supporting accepted governmental operations. The definition of tax policy, however, can also profoundly shape the distribution of economic power resources. The graduated income tax in the United States was intended to promote a modest redistribution of wealth from the richest sectors to the lower and the lower middle classes. Over the years, numerous qualifications that favor the very wealthy have been written into the tax laws, and the middle classes appear to be bearing the preponderance of the tax burden. Advocates of tax reform, therefore, become involved in conflicts of both means and ends, of policy and power.

Revolutionary regimes strikingly illustrate the interconnections between policy and power. Revolutionaries wish to instigate a radical redistribution of power, and their preferred policies reflect this desire: expropriation of the holdings of large landowners, takeover of privately owned industries, steeply graduated income taxes, hundred-percent inheritance taxes, wide-scale welfare programs for the poor, and so on. The late President Salvador Allende of Chile attempted to implement such policies during his brief tenure in office, thereby provoking conflict—not mild conflict over means, but violent resistance from the middle and upper classes, as well as from some foreign investors and the CIA, who believed their power positions to be threatened. Their resistance ultimately culminated in the violent overthrow of the Allende regime by the military in 1973. Similarly, the conflicts between Stalin and Trotsky in post-revolutionary Russia reflected an intense struggle for power. Stalin's ultimate victory enabled him both to implement his policy preferences and to eliminate his opponents.

Policy conflicts, under some circumstances, can cross-cut rather than reinforce power conflicts. This cross-cutting can occur in two primary ways. First, elements of the same power stratum may disagree over policy. Middle-class Americans belong to both the Republican and Democratic parties and are divided among themselves over the appropriate course of policy, while agreeing with fellow party members of different class backgrounds. The Democratic party, in particular, has been frequently successful in forging a heterogeneous coalition of supporters.

Second, two different levels of a power hierarchy may advocate policies opposed by a third. Some analysts have argued that civil-rights legislation in the United States was supported by a coalition of lower- and upper-level power holders, sometimes at the expense of the lower middle class.[7] Such a policy alliance would ameliorate the potential power conflict between the extremes while reinforcing that between the lowest and the next to lowest levels. Some of George Wallace's political success can be explained by his ability to galvanize the frustration felt by lower middle-class groups against both the upwardly mobile elements of minority groups and the "establishment" that supports their rise.

THE DIMENSIONS OF CONFLICT

Though conflict may be all-pervasive, social and political life need not be plagued by the constant threat of collapse. Some conflicts are so trivial that they receive little attention. Others, though possibly quite significant, are strictly regulated so that they occur in a quite orderly fashion. Clearly, some method of distinguishing among the nature and consequences of different conflict situations needs to be developed.

Actualization and Latency

Perhaps the most fundamental question concerns whether the presumed conflict actually exists; whether it is *manifest* or is merely *latent* in the social situation.[8] Obviously, from the presumed participants' standpoint, a conflict they fail to recognize does not exist. Thus, though the powerless appear to have an interest in changing the distribution of resources, and the powerful an interest in maintaining it, this conflict can remain latent. The ruled, in this case, may accept the legitimacy of the rulers' position and passively bear their own deprived condition. In the United States, many lower-class citizens accept the established order as legitimate, even though this support results in their continued subordination. One mark of a skillful ruler is the ability to minimize the actualization of this potential conflict.

Objections may be raised against the very concept of latency. Either a conflict is recognized as such by the contending parties, or it cannot be meaningfully discussed. Often the idea of latent conflict simply disguises the outside observer's belief that such a conflict *should* exist. Indeed, the fact that it has not become manifest simply indicates the low level of consciousness on the part of one or more of the presumed adversaries. Ultimately, the identification of so-called latent conflicts may become an exercise in self-deception for an observer who wishes that a particular conflict existed. Revolutionary intellectuals in an essentially nonrevolutionary society sometimes exhibit this tendency: They see latent conflicts everywhere, but also see limited perception on the part of the masses that prevents them from seeing their "true" interests. Consequently, the revolutionary must lead the befuddled masses to enlightenment and revolutionary conflict. Thus, Lenin was dismayed at the propensity of the workers to be satisfied with what he viewed as minor material gains rather than complete control of the instruments of production. For this reason he advocated the creation of a disciplined, elite cadre party of dedicated revolutionaries who would serve as the vanguard of the proletarian revolution.[9]

Despite the potential for self-deception, the concept of latent conflict retains its utility, if for no other reason than that it directs attention to the problem of anticipating why and where new conflicts might erupt. Beyond this, it suggests that people can be manipulated to act in ways which appear harmful to their own well-being. Basically, the worth of the concept of latency is grounded in the undeniable fact of scarcity and exclusivity: What one person possesses or controls is often denied to another. To ignore the meaning of potential or latent conflict under these circumstances would seem excessively shortsighted.

Intensity

At the most general level, the intensity of a conflict refers to the degree to which an individual or group is involved. A low-intensity conflict receives only divided attention, while a high-intensity one can become so obsessive that all aspects of life are interpreted in terms of it. The degree of intensity varies directly with the perceived importance of the issues involved in the conflict. The determinants of perceived importance are the *salience* and *number* of values affected by the conflict.[10]

Salience refers simply to the fact that each person sees some things as being more central to his existence than others. Everyone possess a crude hierarchy of values, and conflicts over high-ranking values are more intense than those over lower-ranked ones, other things being equal. Most people, for example, place a high value on continued life; therefore, conflicts threatening the lives of the contestants are quite intense, as where the outcome of competition for basic necessities determines which of the contending parties survives. When necessities are secure, then further conflicts over material goods might decline in significance, and other issues could become more salient.[11]

Marxists believe that the working classes will discover the paramount importance of the control of the means of production in determining the quality of all aspects of their lives and that economic conflicts with the capitalist class will then involve the workers' most salient values. Similarly, nationalist leaders in Asia and Africa hoped that the value of national independence would assume so great an importance in the minds of the native peoples that the intensity of the conflict between them and the colonial rulers would cause any internal conflicts to pale into insignificance. After independence, however, domestic value concerns such as the allocation of government resources increase in salience, and internally divisive conflicts often occur.

The salience of a particular value often depends on certain psychological dynamics, for example, the amount of effort that a person expends to reach or maintain a given value position. A reinforcing exchange may take place: a person sacrifices to attain a desired goal which, in turn, becomes all the more valued because of the sacrifice—and thus justifies even further sacrifices. The greater the sacrifice made for a particular goal, the more salient it becomes and more intense the conflicts triggered by challenges to it. This dynamic helps explain the fervor of a recent convert to a faith (religious or secular) who has had to struggle to rid himself of previous conflicting beliefs. It also provides the psychological basis for the conventional wisdom that one born to freedom appreciates it less than does one who fought for it.

The salience of a particular value also tends to be increased if competition over it is seen as zero-sum rather than positive-sum in nature. In a zero-sum conflict, winnings equal losses; the victor's gains must therefore be at somebody else's expense; a poker game is an example of a zero-sum conflict. In a positive-sum conflict, however, winnings exceed losses, so it is possible for the winners to redistribute some of their gains to compensate the losers. In effect, this benefit has occurred in many Western economies during periods of economic growth. Governments have adopted certain policies like the graduated income tax and welfare programs to reallocate some of the gains of the winners in economic competition to the losers, with the result that nearly everybody's standard of living improved. Competition for economic resources has been, that is, positive-sum in nature, hence has diminished in intensity. If the economic pie ceases to grow, however, conflicts over its division will most likely increase in intensity.

The number of values involved also affects the intensity of a conflict.[12] As the number of values involved increases, so also does the intensity. Conflicts may be compartmentalized from one another; that is, stresses in one area of life may be seen as unconnected with any other. Thus, workers' wage disputes with their employers might appear unrelated to their criticisms of the national political leadership. A revolutionary attempts to persuade people that all their frustrations are interconnected and should be seen as facets of the same conflict. Marxists, for example, not only emphasize the salience of economic values (especially control over the means of production), but also argue that all other aspects of the workers' deprived condition (such as their political powerlessness, their low social status, their cultural deprivation) are caused by their subordinated economic position.

Many conflicts, then, involve not one single value but a number of issues that reinforce rather than cross-cut each other. Racial conflict in the United States, for example, is more than a problem of skin color; it involves questions over the distribution of economic, status, and political-power resources as well. Even basic living patterns (blacks concentrated in decaying central cities and whites "fleeing" to the suburbs) reinforce the conflict. In South Africa, the racial basis of the power distribution is far more marked than it is in the United States, creating a potentially volatile situation. Perhaps after blacks gain political and economic power more in line with their numbers, the apparent salience of racial identity will decline. The conflict between Catholics and Protestants in Northern Ireland is another case where multiple values are involved.

Definition

Conflicts also differ according to the degree of specificity with which they are defined. For example, most industrial strikes in the United States are fairly *specific* in nature, focusing on one issue (wages) or on a closely related set of issues. A general strike designed to bring about the fall of a political regime possesses more *diffuse* definition. Normal election campaigns, in which the candidates and political parties they represent clash over a wide range of policy issues, also exemplify rather diffuse conflicts.

A second element of definition concerns the degree to which the contenders adopt an *instrumental* approach to the conflict. Do they possess a reasonably detailed set of goals and methods of achieving them or are they simply expressing their emotions? Every conflict is going to be a mix of instrumental and emotional attitudes, but the proportions differ. The participants in a spontaneous riot, for example, are more likely giving vent to their pent-up rage and frustration than following well-planned methods designed to achieve concrete objectives. The opposing sides in a war, however, develop overall strategic goals and attempt to formulate tactics to achieve these ends.

Both relatively specific and diffuse conflicts can be approached instrumentally. A campaign or a general strike, though diffuse, could be carefully planned to achieve a clearly conceived set of objectives (electoral victory, the collapse of a regime). The instigators of a riot could be very instrumental in their orientation, provoking people's diffuse fury to promote their own objectives. Many specific conflicts are quite instrumental in nature. The participants in an industrial strike are not particularly interested in going on a diffuse rampage through their factory; rather, they follow a controlled set of tactics designed to pressure the management to meet certain precise demands. Other specific conflicts, however, may be highly emotional in character, especially when the psyches involved are deeply intertwined: the oedipal conflict, for example, in which the son competes with his father for his mother's affections. Though specific in focus, this conflict is nevertheless deeply emotional in character. An essentially noninstrumental response is for the son to repress and deny his feelings, supposedly producing adult neuroses or even psychoses.[13]

Destructiveness

The destructiveness of a conflict relates to the weapons chosen by the participants to express their hostility. Destructiveness can be measured simply by the amount of physical damage done to the combatants and their possessions. Bodies can be counted and property or money losses added up to arrive at an approximation of the degree of destruction. Some conflicts cause little or no damage, such as a normal election campaign in which the only immediate losses are the time and money invested by the candidates. The destructiveness of a strike, though not immediately obvious, may be quite extensive if measured in terms of the impact on the entire economy, as well as the direct costs in terms of workers' wages and company profits.

On a more subtle level, the damage done to all of the participants' values must be considered in order to accurately estimate the destructiveness of a conflict. Individuals also possess nonmaterial values, and conflicts which damage them may be seen as more destructive than ones which harm only material wellbeing. "Objective" indicators such as deaths and property damage provide some estimate; however, people may also be damaged in subjective, psychological ways. A war, for example, may both hurt a country's material base and kill many of its citizens, but the most grievous loss may be that of national independence and self-respect. A conflict analysis that focused only on the physical dimension would miss the point. The cost of the Vietnam war for the United States, from this perspective, includes not only the loss in money and lives but also the damage to domestic political institutions and the international prestige of the country. The direct physical consequences of a conflict, therefore, might be only an indirect measure of the impact on other values.

Cohesiveness

The dimension of cohesiveness refers to the amount of organization and unity characterizing the conflicting groups. Clearly, one side may be more cohesive than the others involved, and if the difference grows too great, the conflict would most likely be resolved in favor of the more organized. Cohesiveness depends on the ability of the members of a group to agree on a common set of purposes and to work cooperatively and effectively for their realization. The more cohesive group will also usually make more efficient use of the resources at its disposal. In a sense, even a single individual could be characterized as more or less cohesive. Thus, one man might "know his own mind" and work in a disciplined and efficient fashion to accomplish his goals, while another might be torn by doubt and indecision and be unable to work effectively at any task. The latter would clearly be at a disadvantage in a situation that places him in competition with the former.

Extent

The extent of a conflict can be measured along two lines: its *scope* and its *duration*.[14] Basically, as used here, the scope of the conflict refers to the number of people involved: the more people, the wider the scope. On a more qualitative scale, the kinds of people participating in a conflict should be investigated. A conflict that involves representatives of a wider range of social or political groups might be considered wider in scope than one involving fewer identifiable groups. Thus, scope could be thought of in terms of the number of functional groups engaged, not simply individuals. On a still more qualitative level, the importance of the conflicting groups to the functioning of the sociopolitical system could be considered. A conflict that embroils certain core elite groups would be considered of greater scope than one involving only groups at the periphery of the system. Scope, in this sense, involves not numbers but rather the extent of the implications and the impact of the conflict on the system.

In this context, it must be noted that conflicts often consist of more than two sides. In fact, several parties may take distinct and incompatible positions. The conflict in Northern Ireland, usually defined as being between Protestants and Catholics, actually is more complex. First, both the Protestants and the Catholics are divided into extremists and moderates. Second, both the British and the Irish Republican governments take part. Finally, the British government itself is divided on what policy to follow. The scope of a conflict, therefore, consists not only of the number of individuals or groups engaged, but also the number of distinctive and conflicting positions developed.

The second aspect of the extent of a conflict concerns its duration; that is, how long it lasts, measured in days, weeks, or years. Underlying this apparently straightforward definition, however, is a more difficult conceptual problem: Does the conflict have a reasonably well-defined beginning and end, or is its duration essentially open-ended? The designation of duration may often be an arbitrary decision of the analyst. In studying the Arab-Israeli conflict, an observer might simply focus on the 1967 Six Day War, but the origins stretch back into the nineteenth century (or, perhaps, to the time when Moses led the people to the Promised Land) and the quarrel may continue indefinitely into the future. In fact, the realistic pursuit of stability, whether domestic or international, should be concerned less with the resolution of conflicts than with their containment and regulation (see the section on conflict resolution and regulation). Nevertheless, it may prove analytically useful, though not always accurate, to set a definite duration for a particular conflict event.

TENTATIVE PROPOSITIONS ON THE NATURE OF CONFLICT

The implications of social and political conflict might be more easily grasped through suggesting the ways in which various facets of a conflict situation affect one another. Consequently, some tentative propositions concerning the nature of conflict are developed through examination of four significant problem areas. This discussion by no means exhausts all the implications of different kinds of conflict situations; rather, it illustrates some of the important relationships in hopes of stimulating further insight into these matters.

Relationships between Vertical and Horizontal Conflicts

Vertical conflicts involve individuals or groups at different levels of the power pyramid (for example, an elite/mass conflict). They occur primarily over the distribution of power and secondarily over the use of power. Horizontal conflicts involve participants in essentially the same power stratum. Naturally, the more deeply one is involved in horizontal conflicts, the less time and energy will be devoted to vertical conflicts. Therefore, as the intensity of horizontal conflict increases, that of vertical conflict can be expected to decline. The intellectual roots of the maxim "divide and conquer" lie in this proposition. If the subjects can be set against one another, their ability to challenge the rulers will be reduced. Advocates of social change in the United States often point to the latent common interest of poor whites and blacks in changing the existing distribution of power.[15] Effective cooperation, however, seldom has been realized owing to the racial division between the poor and the resultant identification of poor whites with the ruling elites. Similarly, the European colonial powers were able to rule vast areas of Asia and Africa with relatively little resource investment so long as the subject peoples remained divided among themselves.

If, however, the elite is divided, the various factions often attempt to mobilize support from among the masses, though the "masses" may simply be the next group down the ladder of power. In 1957, a faction of the Presidium (now Politburo) of the Communist Party of the Soviet Union, which occupies the pinnacle of power in that country, sought to oust Nikita Khrushchev. Though in a minority in the Presidium, Khrushchev was able to mobilize his supporters in the next collective body in the hierarchy, the Central Committee. This was the first time since the 1920's that the Central Committee played an important role in deciding a critical power question.

On a grander scale, Samuel Huntington argues that mass political parties in Great Britain and the United States developed in a series of stages.[16] Until the nineteenth century, politics remained largely the prerogative of a fairly small elite whose members formed fluid coalitions with one another. These shifting alliances, however, began to harden into factions, and these in turn sought support among lower-level groups, steadily expanding the franchise to include a larger percentage of the population. In the United States, for example, the "founding" political elite split; then the subsequent competition between the two factions and their successor parties contributed to the pressure to extend the vote from a relatively small group of white male property holders to all citizens of eighteen years of age and older, regardless of race, sex, or material possessions.

The reverse of this proposition also appears plausible; thus, as the intensity of vertical conflict increases, that of horizontal conflict tends to decline. When serious challenges are made against an elite's power position, the members usually forget past differences and unite for the common defense of their privileges. As the dominated become more dissatisfied with their inferior positions, the salience of their conflict with the ruling elite tends to reduce their internal divisions to insignificance. Revolutionary ideologies attempt to interpret the world so as to enhance mass solidarity.

The Impact of Mobility on Conflict

Common sense suggests that improving the opportunities for upward mobility should decrease the intensity of vertical conflict. Since the major source of such discord is the unequal distribution of power resources, decreasing these inequities ought to have a moderating effect on vertical conflict.

In this case, however, common sense can be questioned. First, if the total amount of power resources available is seen as constant in size, then any redistribution will be zero-sum (see above): an individual or group could rise only at some other's expense. If the upward mobility of the masses implies the downward mobility of the elite, then the intensity of vertical conflict will increase, not decrease. Even if the total resource base continues to expand, the elite may still resent any lessening of the relative gap between them and the "common herd." Finally, those who benefit from the upward mobility might become less rather than more tolerant of the remaining differential between themselves and the upper classes. The opening of a few avenues of upward mobility may contribute to rising expectations that, if unfulfilled, could produce greater frustration than the original state of deprivation. The effects of feelings of relative deprivation are explored at greater length in Chapter VII.

Downward mobility tends to intensify conflicts among elite factions. If the losers face eviction from their privileged positions, then horizontal conflicts involve questions concerning the distribution of power. But often conflicts within the elite do not significantly affect the basic distribution of power resources and consequently remain fairly civil. Opposing candidates in democratic elections, though competing for one power resource—political authority—usually do not intend to destroy one another's total resource position in the community. Under some circumstances, though, conflicting elite factions may attempt not only to defeat their opponents, but also to destroy them so totally that they will never have the power to raise any future challenge. The defeated, under these conditions, lose not only their authority positions but also all their resources and even their lives.

The history of the succession crises in the Soviet Union appears to illustrate the relationships between the intensity of intra-elite conflict and the threat of extreme downward mobility. Over the past half century, the consequences of political defeat have been steadily reduced in severity. The Bolsheviks seized power through a *coup d' état* at a time when Russia was convulsed with revolutionary upheaval. The new regime was almost immediately attacked and plunged into a savage civil war. Though ultimately victorious, the experience of taking and defending power led the new regime to be rather ruthless in dealing with opponents. After Lenin's death in 1924, the second-level leadership, particularly Stalin and Trotsky, became locked in a power struggle superficially concerned with policy issues (for one, the proper economic policy). But the losers found themselves increasingly isolated and powerless. Trotsky eventually went into exile. Ultimately Stalin, unsatisfied with simply defeating his political opponents within the Communist Party, physically eliminated most of them during the purges of the 1930's. After Stalin's death in 1953, some observers predicted a similar prolonged conflict. The almost immediate arrest and execution of Beria, the head of the secret police, seemed to support this prediction. The subsequent struggle from which Khrushchev emerged victorious, while serious, was not as bitter as that of the earlier era. The defeated factions of the party (among them those of Molotov and Malenkov), though removed from positions of power, remained among the living. Khrushchev's own fall from power in 1964 appeared even more orderly. The Brezhnev faction retired him rather abruptly; he became a political but not a literal nonperson. The final step in the moderation of intra-elite conflict in the Soviet Union will come when the defeated continue to function in public as a loyal opposition and retain some chance of regaining political authority. The existing degree of moderation is, perhaps, a measure of the distance the current regime has come from its revolutionary origins.

The Impact of Legitimacy

Legitimacy works to reduce the intensity and destructiveness of conflict. Legitimacy, as explained in Chapter III, refers to the beliefs of the people as to what is right and justified. Conflict situations are affected in three inter-related ways by the prevailing bases of legitimacy.

First, if most or all in the population view the established distribution of power resources as legitimate, power conflicts will be moderated consider-ably. This type of legitimacy contributes to "elite/mass" integration, because relative positions are accepted as not only inevitable but also just.[17] Legit-imacy reduces the intensity of power conflicts even in situations where great inequalities exist. On the other hand, differences perceived as illegitimate, even though relatively small, can become a source of serious discord.

Second, agreement on the appropriate uses of power resources reduces the intensity of conflict. Legitimacy in this area supports "value integration"; that is, a consensus exists over the ends and means of policy.[18] Intensity declines for two reasons: For one, the broader the consensus, the fewer the areas of disagreement and the less likely that the ones which do occur will be seen as salient. For another, a broad, underlying consensus encourages the development of processes for resolving or regulating the conflicts that do develop (see below). Declining consensus on the purposes of power multi-plies the number of conflict situations and may lead to attacks on the existing distribution of resources as well. Failure to agree on a process of regulating conflict probably will increase the degree of destructiveness, as the partici-pants fail to limit the weapons used in the conflict.

Third, the intensity of a conflict will be lessened if the contending parties recognize the conflict itself as legitimate; that is, they accept both the inevi-tability of the conflict and understand and respect the opposing side's position. This kind of sympathy for an adversary's position reduces the bitterness and hostility that might otherwise be present and encourages compromise. Natur-ally, such feelings are a matter of degree, and belief in an adversary's essential good faith and toleration of another's point of view may be difficult to form and easy to destroy. Insofar as the power distribution is generally accepted and the uses of power agreed upon, respect for another's position in a conflict will be encouraged because of the strong foundation of trust that already exists.

These three propositions can be illustrated by the conduct of "normal" political competition in the United States. The basic distribution of power goes essentially unchallenged, and candidates compete for authority positions within, rather than against, the fundamental political structure. Debates over policies occur, but generally the range of alternatives discussed is developed within a broader ideological consensus. In formulating their programs, both major parties tend to seek the "middle of the road." Competition between them is recognized as not only inevitable, but also as healthy for the political process, as long as it takes place according to the rules and norms defining political civility.

Some radical elements, however, do not accept politics as civil or usual. They reject the prevailing distribution of power and advocate policies and programs that both fall outside the limits of the established agenda and significantly challenge the basic power structure. Since they view the rules of normal politics as supportive of the status quo, these groups do not feel bound by limitations on the weapons used to conduct conflict. Consequently, if feelings of radical discontent spread in the United States, the likelihood of political violence will also increase (see Chapter VII).

The Outcome of Conflict

The relative resource positions of the contending sides and the skill with which they use them obviously affect the outcome of a conflict. The degree to which a conflict is limited and regulated shapes the result (see below). The dimensions of a conflict also have an impact on the outcome. The extent to which a conflict is instrumental in nature influences whether it culminates in the realization of concrete objectives. If the conflicting parties are simply expressing pent-up frustration, the conflict will produce little substantive change (outside of whatever damage they inflict upon each other). As objectives become more definite, so do outcomes. Historically, race riots in the United States were generally expressions of hatred and fear and, as such, produced little change in either attitudes or situations. The ghetto riots of the 1960's, though rooted in the anger of the black communities, were used by some as a platform to demand substantive changes in the status quo. This demand, at least, gave the government some specific issues to address.

Beyond the foregoing, the more emotional the conflict, the more difficult it will be to set up mechanisms of regulation. Most conflicts, of course, are a mixture of instrumental and emotional elements. The extent to which emotions can be soothed by answering instrumental objectives also affects the course and outcome of the conflict.

The degree of change latent in a conflict depends on relative intensity.[19] The more intense the conflict, the more extensive are the changes demanded or resisted. The actual change that occurs is, of course, determined by which side is victorious. In short, radical shifts in power and policy are the result of intense conflicts, but not all intense conflicts produce radical change.

A similar relationship holds between the destructiveness of a conflict and the suddennness of the change.[20] A shift developing over a short period of time will usually be associated with more extensive destruction than an *equivalent* change taking a longer period. Consequently, orderly and relatively nondestructive means of resolving conflicts tend to be rather time-consuming and/or the shifts tend to be moderate. Not all destructive conflicts, however, result in rapid change, for the side advocating change may be partially or totally defeated. Revolutionary conflicts, therefore, tend to be the most intense and destructive form of domestic political discord.

The preceding discussion of the complexities of conflict interaction introduces some problems for analysis. Further complications inevitably arise as specific conflicts, from elections to wars, are subjected to closer examination. What has been set forth, nevertheless, demonstrates that conflicts are not created equal, that they differ dramatically in their causes, courses, and consequences. Specific attention, however, needs to be given to the problem of how conflicts may be regulated.

THE RESOLUTION AND REGULATION OF CONFLICT

Conflict analysts devote considerable attention to the processes for resolving or regulating conflict. *Resolution* and *regulation*, though often confused, refer to two essentially different control mechanisms. In its more restricted meaning, a resolved conflict has been eliminated or solved in some way. Conflicts of limited duration are resolved; in contrast, ongoing, open-ended conflicts are controlled or regulated. Though the distinction between limited- and unlimited-duration conflicts can be somewhat arbitrary, it reflects the fact that some conflicts appear to reach a conclusion, though they may be resurrected at a later date, while others continue, though not necessarily at the same level of intensity. An example of the former would be a war that ends in the defeat of one side, but could start anew once the defeated side recovers its power (an example is World Wars I and II). The latter situation characterizes the ongoing competition between political parties in a democracy, which intensifies just prior to elections.

Conflicts can be resolved in three basic ways:[21] First, one or more of the parties can *withdraw*. Withdrawal does not signify any change in point of view, only that the retreating side has assessed possible gains and losses entailed in continuing the conflict and decided that the risk of the latter outweighs the hope of the former. A second way of resolving a conflict is through *conquest*. In conquest, unlike withdrawal, one party successfully imposes its values on the others, in effect resolving the conflict in its favor.

A final form of resolution occurs through *accommodation*. The process of accommodation takes several forms. First, the value position of one of the parties may change through *conversion* so as to concede the issue to the other side. Thus, Saul was converted from a persecutor to an apostle of the early Christian church. Less dramatic than the process of conversion is that of *compromise*. In a compromise, neither side embraces the position of the opponent, as in the case of conversion; rather, each accepts a second-best position in order to resolve the conflict. A final process of accommodation is that of *arbitration*, whereby the opponents agree to abide by the decision of a neutral party, even though it may go completely against the interests of one or the other. Arbitration sometimes occurs in labor disputes, but a more significant case is that of democratic election. In a sense, the voters become the arbitrator between the contending candidates for office. Compromise and arbitration, when the results are only provisional and not permanent, are also mechanisms of regulation.

The methods of resolution are often not sufficient. In highly interdependent social systems, where people and groups constantly intrude on one another, withdrawal may often be impossible. Conquest, with the levels of destruction likely to accompany it, suggests certain obvious drawbacks. The various means of accommodation are also limited. Conversion is infrequent, and permanent compromise and arbitration are most likely in low-intensity conflicts. These methods may resolve the conflict only provisionally, creating the need for conditions that serve to regulate ongoing conflicts rather than solve them in any final sense.

Successful conflict regulation depends on the fulfillment of at least three conditions.[22] First, the reality and the necessity of the conflict, within certain limits, must be recognized by all participants. Latent conflicts go unrecognized by definition, but even after a conflict becomes manifest, one party may continue to deny its existence. Some industries justify their opposition to unionization by arguing that their workers are contented. They see the unions as the instigators of discontent, rather than as the representatives of one side of a conflict already in the open. Similarly, city officials sometimes refuse to believe that local blacks could harbor any grievances and blame disorders on "outside agitators." Party conflict in the United States and other Western democracies, in contrast, not only is recognized and accepted, but also is considered a vital force in the political system.

Second, the opposing sides of the conflict must be represented by cohesive organizations in a context of mutual toleration. Even after admitting the reality of a conflict, one side may still deny the other's right to exist and attempt to resolve the conflict through conquest. Such attitudes obviously increase the intensity of a conflict. In the early stages of labor/management conflict, for example, management often refuses to allow the workers to organize their own independent unions. If the workers, for their part, attempt to eliminate the owners as a class and seize complete control of the means of production, the conflict may intensify to revolutionary proportions. Accepting the opposing side's right to organize and advocate its interests is a significant step in structuring a conflict.

The mere existence of an environment allowing for interest-group formation, however, is insufficient. The groups themselves must be cohesive and representative. Indeed, once one side has conceded the other's right to exist, it acquires an interest in seeing that the opposing organization is effective, that it actually controls its membership. Therefore, management's desire that the unions with whom they negotiate can guarantee that the contract agreement will be carried out by the union rank and file and that the industry will not be afflicted by wildcat strikes. The absence of effective organizations inhibits conflict regulation, even if the adversaries desire it. The political leadership of some cities hit by ghetto riots during the 1960's discovered that those organizations they assumed to be influential did not represent or influence any significant segment of the black community. The Israelis face a similar problem in their relations with the Palestinians. A number of organizations claim to represent Palestinian interests, and agreements made with one do not imply acceptance by the others.

Third, the conflicting organizations must agree on certain rules and norms, both formal and informal, which provide a framework limiting the conduct of a conflict. These rules and norms help to restrain the destructiveness of the conflict. International conflicts, because of the relative absence of such a consensus, commonly possess greater potential for destructiveness than do conflicts within national political systems, in which such rules tend to be more firmly entrenched. Basically, these rules perform two functions: One is to define the boundaries of allowable coercion, thereby limiting the choice of weapons in a conflict. The government has the primary responsibility in setting and enforcing these boundaries, though general social custom also plays a part. The other function is to set up certain processes by which the conflict is supposed to be conducted and, perhaps, provisionally resolved. Many of these processes are associated with the political system, such as the institutions for making, enforcing, and ajudicating laws. Private groups, however, also devise their own regulating procedures within the general limits defined by the political system.

The effective regulation of conflict requires that the contending groups reach some agreement on the reality of the conflict, the right to organize, and the rules of the game. This agreement must then be reflected in capable organizations, both to represent the conflicting interests and to regulate their interactions. Necessarily, then, these conflicts, whether over power or policy, are not as intense as they might be. Failure to reach this fundamental consensus intensifies any particular conflict and hinders any regulation or resolution except through conquest or withdrawal.

THE FUNCTIONS OF CONFLICT[23]

Conflict appears inevitable as long as resources are scarce and people differ over their distribution and use. Though uncontrolled conflict threatens the social order, some kinds of conflict may prove to be beneficial for the system.

Conflict and Change

Conflict stimulates change, or, reversing the point, change is accompanied by conflict. Under conditions of scarcity, change will usually harm some groups, help others. The former resist and the latter advocate, producing conflict. Insofar as change is desirable, conflict becomes not simply an unavoidable consequence that must be accepted, but also the actual engine of adaptation. Institutionalized forms of conflict, like party competition, are sources of continual, though moderate, change and renewal.

Conflict and Group Cohesion

Conflict with external groups stimulates internal unity and encourages the mobilization of energies. Dissident members may be removed from the association and the boundary lines between groups be more clearly drawn. Without this external stimulus, discipline and coherence tend to decline. Conflict, then, produces unity in social organizations ranging from the family through alliances among nation states. The benefits of response to an external threat are such that political leaders sometimes exaggerate or even create threats in order to foster coherence. As the external threat is seen as diminishing, the motive for internal unity also declines. The fate of the North Atlantic Treaty Organization illustrates this point. When the Soviet threat appeared grave, the N.A.T.O. powers drew close together; as the threat moderated, each began to follow a more independent policy. Similarly, political parties in the United States mobilize the most unity during election campaigns; between elections they often fall into internal bickering.

Generally, internal discipline will increase with the perceived seriousness of the external threat. World War II produced a considerable increase in the unity of the United States as the country moved into a war mobilization status. Lenin imposed a nearly totalitarian order on the Bolsheviks in response to the hostile environment in which they operated. United States political parties, on the other hand, because of the moderate nature of their conflicts, seldom demand a very great amount of discipline on the part of their members, even during elections.

The toleration of internal conflict may actually be a measure of the strength of a relationship. The absence of conflict may be a sign of complete consensus about ends and means; however, it may also be an indication that the parties to a relationship view it as so fragile that the slightest disagreement threatens its existence. This condition can be demonstrated even in two-person relations. When strangers meet, they usually discuss only the most innocuous subjects (perhaps the weather) in hopes of establishing some common basis for interaction. As confidence in the relationship rises, people will accept a wider range of topics and the possibility of disagreements, in the belief that these will not threaten the basic ties between them. Similarly, intolerance of different political viewpoints may be an indication that citizens do not believe that there is any fundamental loyalty uniting them. In this sense, Senator Joseph McCarthy's intolerant "Red scare" of the early 1950's could be interpreted as a sign of internal weakness and distrust among American citizens.

Conflict and the Establishment of New Relations

A conflict relationship is still a relationship. Conflict, then, may bring previously unassociated groups in contact with each other. Of course, a conflict may be quite destructive, but it can also serve as a basis for establishing rules governing the new relation. After the competing parties realize that they cannot resolve the conflict through either conquest or withdrawal, some basis for accommodation and/or regulation must be established. The history of labor/management relations in the United States illustrates this pattern. Several decades of sometimes violent conflict established that neither side could expect to conquer the other; withdrawal was impossible, given the nature of the industrial system, so some grounds of conflict regulation gradually developed. The same process may be at work at the international level with respect to the relations between the United States and the Soviet Union. Attempted conquest through war appears suicidal, and there seems to be no way that the two countries can avoid interaction. Consequently, both countries seem to be tentatively seeking to establish some grounds of limiting the potential destructiveness of their competition. Examples of this activity include the nuclear test-ban treaty, the "hot line," and the strategic arms limitation talks.

In addition to being the first step toward establishing an ordered relationship between opposing sides, a conflict may also produce alliances among individuals and groups where none previously existed. The reason politics often makes "strange bedfellows" is the unifying capacity of a common enemy. The behavior of the Soviet Union during World War II amply demonstrates this maxim, as the Soviets allied first with one of their "demons" (Nazi Germany) and then the other (the capitalist democracies). The crucial test of these relationships is whether they survive the loss of the common foe. They seldom do unless the negative basis of the relationship is complemented by some positive sources of allegiance. Thus, the American colonies in the eighteenth century were able to find some common values for the formation of a "more perfect union" after the common enemy (Britain) had been defeated.

Conflict is unavoidable. When conflict is contained it can become a source of creative change—a vitalizing rather than a destructive force. This chapter surveyed many of the facets of general social and political conflict. The next turns to a more specific issue: Under what circumstances does political conflict become violent?

Chapter VII   Violence in Politics

Behind most political conflicts lurks the threat of violence. A well-integrated political system will be disturbed only infrequently by acts of violence. The vast majority of the population accepts the legitimacy of the prevailing distribution of power resources and keeps within the limitations regulating social and political conflicts. Only a handful of dissidents attack the regime and, consequently, find themselves the target of its repressive force. This happy state of affairs (particularly pleasing to those who benefit most from the status quo) is not inevitable. An increasing number of people may begin to question the justness of their deprived position and may grow willing to express their discontent through violent assaults on the established order. As the number and seriousness of these assaults expands, the regime may find it difficult to pass them off as the activities of a few criminal deviants—violence becomes politicized.

Dramatic outbreaks of domestic violence punctuate the history of this century, from the revolutions in Russia, China, and Vietnam to the internal upheavals plaguing the United States and other Western democracies during the 1960's and 1970's. Violence, always a recognized factor in international relations, seems different and more disturbing when it afflicts the internal operations of a previously stable political order. Consequently, many political analysts attempt to probe into the causes and effects of domestic political violence. This chapter summarizes some tentative conclusions about the nature of political violence, particularly revolutionary violence, the causes of such acts, and some strategies a regime can use to minimize the seriousness of attacks against it. Some specific types of political violence are discussed. Finally, certain justifications and ethical problems concerning violence are examined.

THE MEANING OF POLITICAL VIOLENCE

The idea of violence commonly summons up visions of wanton muggings, murder, destruction, and bloodshed. While not completely irrelevant, these images produce little insight into the nature and purposes of violence. To get such insight requires somewhat greater analytical clarity.

The ability to coerce others, as was noted in Chapter III, constitutes one of the basic power resources in society. Physical coercion consists of those acts intended to damage people or their material-value position, as opposed to simply their psychological state of mind. Psychological coercion and psychological violence undoubtedly occur both as an associated consequence of physical coercion and without it. This discussion concentrates primarily on the coercive acts that have an overt physical dimension. These coercive acts range from the relatively trivial to the devastatingly destructive. The regime, because of its control over the military and police—the major organizations of coercion—usually possesses the preponderance of this resource in the social system. Each individual, though, retains at least some small share which, if used in concert with others, can pose a significant challenge to the position of the regime.

Additionally, the regime attempts to define the boundaries for the acceptable use of coercion in society. In contemporary societies, the legal system serves to delineate the basic boundaries, though custom also continues to play a role. Acts of coercion that *violate* these boundaries can be considered violent, though the boundaries should not imply either that acts of violence are never justified or that all "legal" coercion is justified (see the discussion of the frailties of law in Chapter IV).

Acts of violence become political in nature when deliberately directed at political objects—that is, personnel or structures—and/or when intended to achieve political rather than simply private goals. Political acts, of course, can include private goals as well, for example, personal ambition. This definition excludes acts of violence that accidentally affect political objects (as when a mugger's temptingly prosperous-looking victim turns out to be a senator). Even with these refinements, the definition contains a certain irreducible vagueness, largely because of the shifting nature of the "political." In a highly politicized society, any act might hold some political significance, whereas in a less charged atmosphere it could be considered private. People may also differ over the political significance of a given act. Some imprisoned blacks, for example, claim they are "political prisoners" because the laws they violated protect the interests of the ruling classes in the United States. Others, not surprisingly, dismiss such claims and consider most prison inmates "common criminals." In a highly politicized situation, however, these assertions would be taken more seriously—the storming of the Bastille is viewed as a dramatic political act, not simply as a prison breakout.

Acts of coercion are deemed more or less "acceptable" as they are less or more "destructive." They are more likely to fall outside the acceptability limits of a sociopolitical order as they become more destructive in their impact and are directed at a more radical redistribution of values and resources within the system.[1] Destructiveness is a multidimensional variable including such factors as:

1. *The degree of damage inflicted upon a person's value position.* Death usually is considered more damaging than nonfatal injuries, imprisonment more damaging than a fine, and so on.

2. *The numbers affected by a given coercive act.* Thus, the bombing of a building filled with people would probably be considered more destructive than exploding a similar device in an empty warehouse.

3. *The degree of "due process" in carrying out the act.* In most systems, a severe act of coercion can be imposed on a person in accordance with the laws (for instance, a legal execution).

4. *The proportionality between the damage inflicted and the act to which it is a response.* "Proportionality" is one of the most widely recognized customary limitations on coercion. Thus, most societies recognize a person's right to take a life to protect his own, but to kill a person because of a presumed insult is considered a disproportionate response in many.

Unfortunately, the various measures cannot be easily combined with one another to produce an aesthetically pleasing interval scale of measurement for the destructiveness of various coercive acts. Some rough approximation and ranking can be attempted, however, which may produce an ordinal scale, less sophisticated though still useful.

The end sought by the act of coercion also enters into the appraisal of its acceptability. It is assumed that acts of coercion are usually intended to achieve some end: either to maintain or to alter the prevailing distribution of resources. Alteration can occur through either the creation of a new order or the restoration of previously established one. As the intended change becomes increasingly radical, coercive acts are more likely to fall outside the limits of acceptable coercion, and become acts of violence. The definition of acceptable coercion, then, is not neutral, for it commonly tolerates rather destructive acts that are interpreted as being fundamentally supportive of the status quo (thus, the wide range of "legal" coercion exercised by the state). At the extreme, any form of such "maintenance coercion," no matter how damaging, would fall within the boundaries of acceptability. Most systems, though, place some limits on maintenance coercion, for example, through the establishment of a judicial process providing for certain rights of the accused, limitations on police coercion by prohibiting excessive action against law-breakers, and restrictions on the occasions when an ordinary citizen can "take the law into his own hands." Indeed, a relatively open society not only places limits on maintenance coercion, but also allows some milder forms of redistributive coercion, both creative and restorative. Examples of the latter include industrial strikes which seek to reallocate resources more in favor of the workers. When such overall restrictions exist, three basic types of violence can be distinguished:

1. *Creative or Left Dissident Violence.* Acts of coercion in violation of the systemic boundaries, directed at creating a new distribution of values, a new order. These range from acts of relatively great destructiveness but with little intent of changing the entire sociopolitical order to those directed at achieving large-scale change through mildly (as an illegal demonstration) or intensely (as a guerrilla insurrection) destructive means.

2. *Maintenance or Establishment Violence.* Acts of coercion in violation of societal limits, but which are intended to defend the prevailing order from some form of attack or subversion. Examples include various acts of police violence and community vigilantism in which the presumed offenders are denied their legal rights. This violence can be directed at criminals who appear to be escaping their just due or at various political dissidents of the right and the left who threaten the established order.

3. *Restorative or Right Dissident Violence.* Acts of coercion in violation of the limitations which are aimed at restoring a currently disestablished group to previously held positions of power and privilege. Examples include the counterrevolutionary armies in Russia after the 1917 Revolution and the Ku Klux Klan operations in the South after the Civil War.

Since these three types of violence lie on a continuum of intended change, maintenance violence merges into either form of redistributive violence, and it can become difficult to make completely clearcut distinctions. Nevertheless, the purpose of a violent act must be taken into account in order to gauge its significance for the social and political systems.

THE MEANING OF REVOLUTION

Of all the possible forms of political violence, perhaps "revolution" captures the imagination most easily. This, unfortunately, leads to considerable abuse of the term. Neither the loose nor the restrictive approach adequately captures the meaning of *revolution*. At one extreme occurs the sloppy usage in which the term describes everything from the ouster of one clique of colonels by another to a change in washday detergents. At the other extreme lie the precise, twenty-five word definitions which set down the limits of the concept as if it were describing an object rather than a process.[2] Revolution, on the contrary, should be recognized as a process characterized by a number of interrelated elements, the occurrence of each element being a matter of degree, not a simple present/absent dichotomy. The primary distinguishing components of the process of revolution include the degree and scope of change, the use of violent means, the time factor, and the element of intentionality.

The Degree and Scope of Change

All students of revolutions agree that a revolution must effect a change in society, but some dispute develops over how much change must occur before an upheaval can be accurately identified as revolutionary. Change can be measured along at least two continuous dimensions: degree and scope. Even a profound change, from this perspective, can affect only one individual or group (as did Saul's conversion on the road to Damascus), whereas a relatively trivial change can nevertheless affect an entire country (as did the adoption of daylight-saving time). Consequently, an alteration in the sociopolitical system considered revolutionary should be both significant in degree and wide in scope. Change, accordingly, can have an enormous impact on some subsystem but be too restricted in scope to be a system-wide revolution. A revolution can be either creative or restorative in purpose, as long as it involves a radical shift from the existing order. Obviously, a certain amount of ambiguity affects this indicator, both because change is a matter of degree and because its two elements need not vary directly with one another. Definition of a point beyond which a change can be termed revolutionary must remain somewhat arbitrary.

Violent Means

Most commentators also agree that a revolution must be accomplished through violent means. A relatively peaceful, though profound, change affecting an entire system might be considered "revolutionary" in its consequences, but would not constitute a revolution. The expansion of the electorate in the United States, with the significant exception of the Civil War, is an example of such an evolutionary process of change. A revolution implies radical change implemented through a strategy of violence. Consequently, either creative or restorative violence could be the driving force of a revolution. Maintenance violence, of course, could never be revolutionary.

Short Time Span

Revolution often suggests sudden, as well as dramatic, change. Therefore, some argue that a third criterion for a revolution is that it should occur
over a relatively brief period of time. The Industrial Revolution brought about
significant change and included, at times, considerable violence, but the fact
that it developed over several generations disqualifies it as a "true" revolution. The time factor, however, remains very nebulous, for close analysis of
most revolutions reveals that the preconditions stretch back generations, and
the consequences take decades to unfold. In the case of the French Revolution, one could focus on the spasm of disorder from 1789 to 1793, but the
origins can be traced back to the reign of Louis XIV (d. 1715) and the repercussions lasted at least until the final defeat of Napoleon in 1815. Similarly,
the roots of the Chinese Revolution lie in the first half of the nineteenth
century, and Mao seemed intent on keeping the revolutionary spirit alive at
least through the 1960's. It may be argued that the pivotal period of a
revolution—the time during which the dissidents first seize power—is quite
short, but this criterion too can be misleading. The Chinese Communists
struggled for twenty-five years before defeating the Kuomintang regime and
the Vietnamese revolutionaries fought for three decades to bring their revolution to a successful culmination. Whether a revolution succeeds or fails
depends on the support given and the resistance encountered. Additionally,
the extent of resistance determines whether the dissidents acquire power with
a sudden blow, or *coup d'état*, or must fight over a period of years or decades.
What seems crucial with respect to the time factor, therefore, is that the
revolutionaries *intend* to bring about radical change over as short a period as
possible. They do not intend to wait for the system to evolve gradually.
Whether they are able to fulfill their intentions depends on their own power
vis-à-vis the resistance they encounter.

Intentionality

The final component of a concept of revolution is, perhaps, the most
abstract, yet it remains critical to the understanding of revolution as a purposive sociopolitical act and not simply a random event. This concerns the
intentions of the participants in a revolution, especially those of the leaders.
Accidental change, even though violent, does not qualify as a revolution.
Indeed, intentionality is central to the conception of revolution as a process of
radical change intended to be rapidly implemented through a strategy of
violence. This requirement does not mean that all the goals pursued by the
dissidents have to be thoroughly consistent with one another; rather, that they
have something in mind which differs radically from the established order.

Obviously, the purposes and tactics of a revolution may be more or less comprehensively elaborated—the revolutionary ideology serves this function. Purposeless, expressive violence, no matter how destructive, is not revolutionary.

The foregoing discussion illustrates the complicated nature of revolutionary phenomena. To simplify matters somewhat, three basic kinds of revolution, based on the preceding distinctions, can be identified.[3]

Pseudo Revolution

The term *pseudo revolution* applies to a kind of residual category covering those upheavals that fail to meet all of the criteria. Included under this heading would be the Industrial Revolution, which though significant and sometimes violent was not intended to be a sudden, system-wide shift and which generally occurred within the existing political framework. Also included are violent acts that do little to alter the existing social and political relationships but simply change the personnel who hold positions of authority in the system. Examples include the periodic rebellions in China over 2000 years in which one imperial dynasty replaced another closely resembling it, as well as the factional coups that afflict some of the military juntas ruling many contemporary political systems.

Political Revolution

Violent changes that significantly alter political relationships but leave the underlying social system relatively untouched can be considered political revolutions. The American Revolution, which substantially restructured the political system by eliminating the rule of the British monarchy and creating a constitutional republic, can be deemed a case in point. Despite these substantial political changes, the prerevolutionary social structure underwent little alteration. Many twentieth-century struggles for national independence (in India, Ghana, Kenya, and elsewhere) also are examples of political revolutions. Native elites simply took over political power.

Social Revolution

These upheavals affect basic social and economic, as well as political, relationships. Sometimes they are classified as the "great revolutions," and examples include the French, Russian, and Chinese revolutionary experiences. Whereas political revolutions primarily involve the redistribution of political power resources (authority and legitimacy), social revolutions affect the distribution of other power resources as well, especially economic and status resources.

THE SOURCES OF POLITICAL VIOLENCE

Violence rends the flow of contemporary life. Disturbing events, from domestic crime to foreign revolution, frequently impinge on people's consciousness. Their growing concern stimulates scholarly inquiries into the causes of social and political violence. This section cannot review all the findings and conclusions of these studies, but it can provide an introduction to some of the basic conditions that give rise to violence, especially political violence. Basically, this analysis covers three questions: What causes such dissatisfaction as to incline a person toward "deviant" or nonconformist behavior (deviant from the established regime's point of view)? The person being so inclined, what factors contribute to the choice of political violence as opposed to other forms of deviancy? Finally, under what circumstances is political violence likely to be widespread throughout the system? The answers to these questions must proceed simultaneously on two levels, that of the individual and that of the system. The problem involves how individual dissatisfactions are transformed into system-wide disturbances.

Underlying Conditions—Growing Discontent

Perhaps the real issue is not why there is so much violence, but why there is so little. The vast majority of the human race live in conditions of severe suffering. Even in those countries where people are fortunate enough to receive sufficient material goods, gross inequities of wealth and power persist. Yet most people fail to take up arms against their rulers. One partial explanation for this phenomenon involves the nature of deprivation. Absolute deprivation does not necessarily produce dissatisfaction; rather, this depends on the levels of *relative deprivation*.[4] A person's sense of relative deprivation increases as the gap widens between what he believes he deserves (expectations) and what he thinks he can get (resource capabilities). A group may be so mired in misery that the members expect nothing better. Therefore, levels of absolute deprivation may be quite high while the sense of relative deprivation remains fairly low. In contrast, another group may be objectively well off but hold expectations so high that its resources are far exceeded and its members consequently feel relatively deprived.

The gap between expectations and resource capabilities develops in three basic ways: First, expectations rise while capabilities decline. Some evidence suggests that this pattern characterized several of the great revolutions, when a period of steady improvement in social conditions suddenly reversed, thereby causing a fall in capabilities while expectations continued to rise.[5] A second pattern ensues when expectations rise while capabilities stay relatively constant. Some African, Asian, and Latin American countries appear affected by this trend, as their populations learn more about the wealth and welfare of the rich in their own countries and abroad but see little, if any, improvement in their own lot. This so-called "revolution of rising expectations" probably contributes to many of the urban disturbances in these countries, because urban areas are most likely to include those groups (such as students and unemployed or underemployed white-collar workers) whose education and media contact raise their expectations. Relatively isolated peasants are less likely to be affected by this source of dissatisfaction. The third pattern emerges when expectations remain constant but capabilities decline. This particular source of discontent probably motivates those who engage in establishment and restorative violence. In the case of the former, relatively satisfied sectors see criminal or dissident sociopolitical elements as potential threats to their position and engage in excessive coercion to suppress these challenges. In the latter instance, formerly established groups fight to regain previously held positions of privilege.

The *intensity* of feelings of relative deprivation fundamentally depends on the *degree* to which expectations exceed capabilities and the *salience* of the values affected. A person evaluates some areas of social and political life as being more important than others (see Chapter VI, the discussion of salience). A failure of capabilities to match expectations in these areas kindles greater dissatisfaction than an equivalent shortfall in a less salient sector. Some evidence suggests that for the majority of people in the world, economic concerns are paramount as opposed to other possible issues such as levels of political participation or social status.[6] Not surprisingly, then, mass upheavals are primarily stimulated by economic discontent. The revolutionary leaders of a mass uprising, however, may be more frustrated by their lack of political power than by any sense of economic deprivation. The middle-class origins of most revolutionary elites suggest that their personal economic concerns are not of primary importance (they may, of course, be deeply sympathetic with the plight of the masses). Similarly, elites defending or attempting to regain positions of privilege may be concerned more with questions of political power and social prestige than with economic security. Consequently, excessive emphasis on the economic basis of much popular frustration can obscure other possible sources of discontent.

Obviously, if people's expectations exceed their capabilities in all areas of life, their overall sense of relative deprivation will be quite high. If they retain a sense of efficacy or power in one important area, it may counteract frustrations elsewhere. Indeed, it may lead them to withdraw into that one sector and avoid contact with the other frustrating life experiences.

Two factors contribute to perceived capabilities: an individual's own personal power position and the power of other persons or groups who are considered representatives or allies.[7] Thus, a sense of personal powerlessness may not significantly lower felt capabilities if a person's "representatives" appear strong. Blue-collar workers, though personally weak, may believe that the union is willing and able to protect their interests. The Marxist prediction that the proletariat would not be satisfied until proletarians exercised complete control over the productive process failed to foresee that many workers would accept personal powerlessness because of the apparent efficacy of their unions.

Every system contains some intensely dissatisfied people. In addition to intensity, the *scope* or *extent* of feelings of relative deprivation also influences the actual levels of violence in society. Basically, the scope of deprivation refers to the proportion of the population affected, though the number of identifiable social groups involved is also an important consideration (see Chapter VI). The more widespread the feelings of relative deprivation, the greater the likelihood that some will choose to express their dissatisfaction in a violent fashion, all other things being equal. Beyond simple probabilities, scope of deprivation leads to other psychological and power considerations which may encourage violence (see below). Widely dispersed discontent, however, does not automatically produce extensive political violence. The generalized frustration must become politicized and then violent action selected from among the alternative behavioral responses to discontent; these are the two transforming conditions.

Transforming Conditions—
The Politicization of Discontent

Generalized social discontent need not have any significant impact on political stability, even if expressed violently. Without some political direction, deviant behavior can simply take the form of normal crimes, psychological disorders, and suicide (violence directed against the self). Politicized discontent appears when the deprived blame the political system, its personnel, and its policies for their frustrations, directing their anger at political targets.

Politicization follows inevitably if the area of frustration involves specifically political values, for example, the inability to participate effectively in the political process. Many sources of dissatisfaction, such as that over economic or status values, do not contain an explicit political element; in this case, politicization develops when the deprived hold the political regime responsible for their condition. As the functions of government multiply and its policies increasingly affect aspects of social life ranging from the arts to the economy, more people are likely to hold it at least partly accountable for their problems. Unemployment provides a good example. The citizens in most industrial nations expect the regime to follow policies that insure full employment and, failing to do this, to ameliorate the misery of the unemployed. Economic failure, then, usually produces political repercussions.

Revolutionary ideologies interpret the social world for the disaffected, identify the causes of their troubles, and direct them along a specific course of action. A successful ideology aggregates a wide variety of discontents and focuses blame on a particular political target (the ruling class, the foreign imperialists, or the like). People join revolutionary movements for a variety of reasons, and once the common enemy has been eliminated, the movement may fall apart unless the various participants also share a common vision of the "new order."

Transforming Conditions—
A Disposition to Violence

Discontent, political or otherwise, need not be expressed through violent acts. A person may react passively and behave in an essentially ritualistic fashion, that is, conform to the prevailing norms of social and political conduct though no longer believing them. In other persons, extreme political passivity leads to complete withdrawal from political activity of any kind, conformist or deviant. Still others may be inclined toward a more activist means of expressing their discontent, including violent attacks on the established political order.[8] Whether politicized discontent is transformed into a disposition to political violence depends on the interactions among a number of factors, which are here noted under three headings: physiological capacities, the social learning process, and the intensity of feelings.

1. *Physiological Capacities.* Physiology imposes a direct limit on violent activity. Violence, especially political violence sustained over a long period of time, requires certain minimum levels of physical energy. Revolutions, and for that matter wars and sports, are commonly the work of the young and the fairly healthy. One reason why the utterly abject provide infertile ground for violent agitation is that their bodies, wracked by disease and malnutrition, lack the energy necessary for violent protest.

A more controversial question concerns whether human beings *inherit* different capacities for aggressiveness.[9] Aggressiveness, though, is not equivalent to violence, for it can be expressed through relatively nondestructive and accepted forms of competition and, as such, provides a force for adaptation and creativity. Aggressiveness, though, tends to produce activist behavior, of which one alternative is violence. Some people appear more prone to aggressive responses, and consequently to violence, than do others, but behavior is the product of the interaction of the organism with its environment. Therefore, in order to understand the sources of the disposition to violence, one must turn to the learning experiences of the individual.

2. *The Social Learning Process.* Social learning shapes general behavioral predispositions (see Chapter XI). This learning process, commonly referred to as socialization, can reinforce or inhibit proclivities to aggressive behavior and can direct expressed aggression into relatively destructive or nondestructive alternatives. A person who discovers that violent behavior is an accepted and useful response to frustration may become more inclined to demonstrate political dissatisfaction violently than one who learns to repress aggressive feelings and actions.

The impact of the sociocultural environment on the individual is complicated and seldom consistent. Yet a number of factors that encourage violent expressions of discontent can be suggested:[10]

—Individual learning that reinforces the acceptability of anger and the appropriateness of overt hostility as a response to frustration. In the United States, for example, boys are often rewarded for aggressive behavior and taught to fight for their rights. Girls, on the contrary, are impressed with need to disguise their hostility, behave passively, and accomplish their goals through wiles rather than frontal attacks. Such individual socializing experiences are supported by

—general characterizations of violence as an acceptable and effective tactic in a nation's history. Thus, the United States was created through an act of political violence and preserved through many more. Beyond this creation, the frontier tradition and the Indian Wars present further cases where violence is portrayed as acceptable and/or useful. Historical justifications can be further reinforced by

—the extent to which violence is positively presented in the mass media. Such a general culture of violence could combine with

—individual experiences of past successes through violence or with perceptions of other groups' apparent success through such means, as well as with

—the range of situations in which violence is portrayed as an acceptable response in a culture. Is it only a last resort to counter serious frustrations or is it a possibility in every minor irritation? Finally, resort to violent attacks will be affected by

—the availability of mechanisms of dehumanization.[11] The potentially destructive aggressor must be able to insulate himself from the humanity of his victim. Generalized social prejudices, such as racism, as well as specific ideologies, often serve to characterize the perceived enemy as less than human and deserving of whatever damage is inflicted. In addition, advanced weapons of remote destruction help to isolate the aggressor from firsthand knowledge of the consequences of his actions. Even the handgun is more remote than the club or knife.

3. *The Intensity of Feelings of Relative Deprivation.* Finally, the disposition toward violence depends on the intensity of the feelings of discontent. As discontent increases, so also does the probability that an individual will reach a threshold beyond which destructive action will become a likely response. An aggressively inclined person may be triggered into violence by relatively low levels of frustration. Extremely passive people may never reach a point of frustration intense enough to break down their powerful inhibitions against destructively aggressive behavior. In a system as a whole, as the scope and intensity of feelings of relative deprivation rise, so also will the numbers of people who will be disposed toward expressing their discontent in an actively destructive fashion, other factors remaining constant. As this discontent becomes politicized, political objects will be chosen as targets for the people's anger. Whether the disposition for political violence becomes actualized, however, depends on still another basic condition, a balance of power.

Effecting Conditions—
Regime/Dissident Balance of Power

Despite the existence of widespread frustrations, despite the politicization of this discontent, despite psychosocial conditions that predispose people toward violent responses to frustration, the actual levels of political violence may still be quite low. The magnitude of political violence in a system depends on the relative balance of power between the regime and the dissidents. Violence will be most widespread when both sides are relatively equal in power resources.[12] If the regime controls the vast preponderance of the resources in a system, the dissidents resorting to violence would simply be overwhelmed. If, on the other hand, the dissidents hold a great advantage, they can seize power through a *coup d'état* (revolutionary or otherwise). As the two sides become more nearly equal in power, neither can eliminate the other, and prolonged internal warfare ensues.

As was discussed previously, an individual or group can exercise power by controlling a number of different resources (see Chapter III). A deficit in one resource may be compensated for by the efficient use of another. For example, although the government forces in South Vietnam controlled substantially greater coercive resources than the National Liberation Front, particularly in the early years of the war, the latter compensated for this weakness through more dedicated and disciplined organization. The NLF also successfully challenged the regime's monopoly of political legitimacy resources. Indeed, since the regime generally starts out controlling the preponderance of physical-coercion resources, revolutionary dissidents rely on their ability to organize and direct mass discontent. Whether they succeed in this difficult task depends on pre-existing conditions discussed above, on their own success in focusing dispersed discontent, and, finally, on the regime's ability to implement strategies to deflate the potential for political violence.

REGIME STRATEGIES TO COUNTER POLITICAL VIOLENCE

The political leadership of a state need not stand idly by while conditions that encourage political violence fester and grow. Various strategic options can be followed to lessen the likelihood of outbreaks of political violence. Four of these options are to be discussed: conservative change, manipulation, repression, and ignoring the problem. None of these, of course, is cost-free, for each involves the investment of certain resources and carries with it consequences and risks. Additionally, each must be implemented with some minimum of skill or it can work against the regime itself.

Conservative Change

The first option available to the regime is to identify the sources of discontent and attempt to eliminate them. This essentially consists of raising the capabilities of dissatisfied groups to approximate their expectations.

Since not all dissidents are equally frustrated, it may be possible to "buy off" the moderates and thereby isolate the radicals. Various social-welfare programs introduced by Franklin Roosevelt, for instance, may have been partly responsible for preserving the basic power position of big business in the United States. Similarly, moderate land-reform programs in Latin America and Asia are intended to assuage the land hunger of the peasant classes and undercut the potential for rural revolution. This strategy assumes, of course, that the regime possesses the desire to reform, at least in some measure.

Conservative change entails certain conditions, costs, and risks. First, the leadership must control sufficient power resources to (a) redistribute to those who are dissatisfied while maintaining the support of most of the establishment and (b) control those who remain or become disgruntled. A reformist regime will often be attacked by both the radicals who believe the reforms inadequate and by establishment groups who think the regime's concessions go too far. Second, the strategy presumes that a significant proportion of the dissidents can be satisfied by moderate reforms. Obviously, no regime is going to deliberately reform itself out of power. Consequently, it must impose certain limits on how far reform can go. Limited improvements may not significantly reduce the number of dissidents and may even stimulate more demands; that is, an increase in capability can lead to a further increase in expectation. Traditional rulers who attempt to modernize their countries often discover that the changes they sponsor undermine the basis of their authority. Finally, meaningful reforms cannot be implemented instantaneously, and the regime may lack the luxury of time. In order to succeed, reformist political leadership may have to discover ways of "buying time." For all of these reasons, a regime may be unwilling and/or unable to fully implement a strategy of conservative change and may need to rely to an extent on other alternatives.

Manipulation

Conservative change involves substantive improvement in the lot of the discontented in the hope that this will be sufficient to lower the potential for violence. The strategy of manipulation pursues two different objectives: First, to convince (some might say delude) the people into thinking that conditions are improving without making significant changes. Failing this, the second objective is to deflect the discontent onto targets other than the regime and the order it protects.

The first goal can be achieved through what one political scientist labels "symbolic politics," whereby one sector receives the substance but another wins a symbolic victory.[13] Symbolic politics, if successful, convinces some people that their capabilities are greater than they objectively are. Manipulation can be easily recognized when it consists of overt propaganda containing distorted, exaggerated portrayals of reality, such as that often produced in wartime. More subtle, however, are the deeply held myths of a polity which may produce an overinflated evaluation of capabilities. One survey of political attitudes taken a number of years ago indicated that, at that time, a sizeable percentage of the public in the United States thought they could be politically effective if they wished, but they had never made the attempt.[14] They believed they possessed capabilities that they never exercised. This kind of belief clearly enhances the stability of any established distribution of resources more effectively than does blatant propaganda that can be readily tested against reality (for example, a people are unlikely to believe that their armies are winning glorious victories if bombs continually rain on their heads).

If a regime cannot symbolically inflate the people's capabilities, it may be able to prevent the discontent from becoming focused on itself. Basically, political leaders accomplish this through various scapegoat techniques. A likely "enemy," internal or external, is identified and blamed for all of the people's sufferings. An external enemy can be useful for uniting the people and justifying additional sacrifices. An internal enemy can be used to explain deficiencies in the system that might otherwise be blamed on the regime. Stalin, for example, used the fear of "capitalist encirclement" to mobilize the Soviet population during early five-year plans. Hitler and the Nazis blamed both the German loss of World War I and the economic depression on the Jews, an explanation that prevented many Germans from questioning the failures of the system.

The various aspects of the manipulative strategy contain certain drawbacks. First, propaganda cannot be so far divorced from reality that a people can readily see the discrepancy, for this perception may lead to a loss in regime credibility. Second, legitimacy myths, though more effective than direct propaganda, develop rather slowly and cannot be easily manipulated (see, in Chapter IV, the discussion of the grounds for moral obligation to the state). Third, the tactic of identifying a scapegoat must strike a delicate balance: An external threat must be real enough to convince the population, but not so real as to actually threaten the existence of the regime. An internal scapegoat must also be carefully selected, for scapegoating is an inherently divisive tactic. Again the scapegoat must be believed powerful enough to upset the system, but must not be so powerful in fact as to respond by actually attacking the regime. Finally, all of these various tactics suffer from the fact that they do not cope with the substantive sources of people's discontent. A regime constantly runs the risk that eventually its citizens will reject symbolic rewards and begin to demand concrete changes.

Repression

Even a reformist regime will encounter some dissidents who refuse to be placated by what they see as superficial alterations in a totally unacceptable status quo. Such radicals will simply have to be coerced. Repression may be necessary to gain enough time for long-term reforms to have the desired effect. As a regime becomes less willing or able to reform and as the effectiveness of manipulative tactics declines, more reliance will have to be placed on the strategy of repression, especially under conditions of widespread discontent.

The strategy of repression entails both short- and long-term objectives. In the short run, repression is intended to contain the potential for political violence from becoming actualized; the strategy is to increase the severity and probability of the consequences for engaging in any attack on the regime. Over the long run, an effective strategy of repression may have the paradoxical effect of lowering people's expectations. Initially, repression can be expected to irritate people further, but if they can be convinced that resistance is hopeless and costly, they may eventually despair. Revolutionary activity, it must be remembered, is fundamentally an expression of hope.

Aside from whatever moral objections may be leveled against repression, the strategy also suffers from certain practical limitations. First, it calls for investment in an extensive repressive apparatus. The more repression, the more costly will be the apparatus. Indeed, the cost can eventually strain the resources of the regime. Second, the repressive apparatus itself can become a threat to the survival of the regime. Many third-world leaders discovered to their dismay that using the army to suppress internal dissent often encouraged the military to seize power for themselves. Finally, the strategy of repression, even if consistently applied, fails to solve the underlying causes of discontent. Generally, it buys time for the regime and suppresses those who are irrevocably alienated. Unintelligently applied (for example, if it is inconsistent and haphazard) or insufficiently backed by the required coercive power resources, the strategy of repression may only further anger the dissidents and bring new recruits to their ranks.

Ignoring the Problem

On the surface, ignoring the problem appears to be more stupidity than strategy, closely akin to Marie Antoinette's apocryphal remark dismissing the mass protest over the lack of bread: "Let them eat cake." Deliberately ignoring a recognized problem, however, is different from ignorance of the problem. Every regime must, in fact, decide which problems can be safely put aside for the time being. The necessity for such decisions arises from the condition of limited resources. No regime, no matter how resource-rich, will be able fully to resolve or repress all discontent. Rather, it must seek to aid those sectors central to its survival and suppress those whose dissatisfactions it cannot cure but who possess sufficient power potentially to imperil the regime. Some segments of the population may be so weak, though, that the regime can safely ignore their needs and spend only a minimal effort in repressing what discontent they exhibit. Primary energies, then, are devoted to those sectors whose support or dissent appears more critical.[15] For decades, if not centuries, the problems of blacks in the United States often received such treatment. Recently, though, blacks concentrated in urban areas have demonstrated an expanded capacity for disruption, gaining more attention of both a repressive and reformist sort. The aged poor constitute another group whose needs are largely ignored by the system.

This strategy also runs certain risks. First, a particular sector is assumed to be weak enough to be safely ignored; a mistake in this evaluation can lead to unfortunate consequences for the regime. Second, ignoring problems does nothing to solve them and may even contribute to their growth; a short-run saving may be outweighed by a long-term cost.

No regime relies solely on one of these strategies. Each attempts to develop some kind of maximizing mix. Success in the particular endeavor of minimizing the amount of violence directed against the regime depends on the same factors that determine the results of the general political process: the resources available to the regime and sectors and the skill with which they are utilized. Revolutions overthrow not strong governments and capable leaders but the weak and incompetent.

THE CONTEXT OF POLITICAL VIOLENCE— REVOLUTIONARY WARFARE

The general perspectives on political violence developed in this chapter suggest that such acts cannot be adequately comprehended unless placed in a larger context of social origins and purposes. In order to further illustrate some relationships between violence and a broader arena of sociopolitical behavior, two prominent forms, revolutionary warfare and terror, are briefly examined. Later, in Chapter X, the problem of military intervention receives further attention.

Revolutionary warfare refers to the violent aspects of a general dissident strategy to reinterpret the myths of legitimacy and reintegrate a people into a new sociopolitical order. In recent decades, rural-based revolutionary wars account for the greatest loss of life from internal violence.[16] The violence of the revolutionaries essentially is directed against the old order and its supporting myths, and the outcome is fundamentally linked to the success of the revolutionaries' own reintegrative efforts. Violence by itself may disrupt the old order, but in the absence of a new web of social and political relations, simple anarchy is the most likely result.

Sociopolitical reintegration does not come about automatically. The existing regime must be weak and unable to revitalize itself. Successful revolutionary wars of the twentieth century have been waged against regimes dominated by foreigners (Vietnam, Algeria) or by domestic elites who were inept, disunited, and corrupt (China, Cuba). The existing political authorities can resist and may even receive external support. Often, the result is that the new order must be instituted under stressful conditions. The new, reintegrating myths and relations, moreover, must be relevant and appealing enough to overcome considerable inertia on the part of the people and to galvanize them for revolutionary activity. Consequently, relatively few revolutionary wars have been successful.

By themselves, guerrilla tactics and imitative counterinsurgency are "apolitical." This method of warfare is simply the traditional one used by the relatively weak against the stronger. Isolated from the broader political struggle, these tactics cannot bring victory, or even insure against defeat. Guerrilla war, without the proper sociopolitical environment, becomes strategically naive. In Bolivia, for example, the master tactician Ernesto (Che) Guevara was fairly easily defeated by superior military force. An inadequate social base for revolutionary war made his effort by default almost purely military, and the regime's vastly superior coercive resources determined the result. Revolutionary strategy, in fact, sometimes needs to violate the pure tactical requisites of guerrilla war in order to gain larger political objectives, as was the case with the 1968 Tet offensive in Vietnam.

Generally, the greater the success achieved by the revolutionaries in the efforts to reintegrate society, the more difficult it will be to defeat them through conventional military means. The degree of success can vary. Guevara's failure to create a viable political base in Bolivia probably defines one extreme. The communist insurgency in Malaya during the 1950's occupies the middle range. What success the dissidents had was confined to one ethnic group, the Chinese, and they could make no significant inroads into the Malay community. Even so, it took more than ten years (1948 to 1960) to crush the movement. The Chinese and Vietnamese revolutions exemplify relatively successful attempts at reintegrating the sociopolitical order.

The only way conventional military power can "defeat" a successful revolutionary war is by destroying the social fabric created by the revolutionaries. This approach results in generally genocidal consequences, because the targets cannot simply be the regular military formations but must include the entire population which has been woven into the new order.[17] The United States bombing policy in Vietnam, which identified certain areas as "free fire zones" in which every living thing was defined as an enemy, demonstrates this implication. An authoritarian regime might be able to wage this kind of war to its ultimate conclusion, but a fairly democratic one seems more likely to be afflicted by internal dissent, as was the case in both France during the Algerian War and the United States during the Vietnam War. In consequence, those who wish to continue trying to destroy a revolutionary order abroad will find it increasingly necessary to repress dissent at home. They might even attempt to impose an authoritarian regime, as a right-wing faction of the army tried to do in France.[18]

THE CONTEXT OF POLITICAL VIOLENCE—TERROR

Terror can be provisionally defined as severe acts of violence directed at noncombatants by the contending forces in a political struggle. This definition assumes that noncombatants are distinguishable from combatants, though undoubtedly many borderline cases exist. Nevertheless, one cannot usefully speak of terror under conditions where only combatants are affected (as in an attack on a military position) or in a situation of total war that recognizes no neutral groups. Since terror affects apparently "innocent bystanders," political commentators often condemn it as "senseless." Actually, terroristic political violence serves various purposes, though at a certain cost, and the meaning of a terroristic act cannot be understood apart from its possible functions. Moreover, though dissident terror often receives wide publicity, a regime may also find it useful.

Dissident terror may either be an isolated action or one aspect of a more inclusive strategy of violence. When used as the sole tactic, terror reflects the relative weakness and frustration of the dissident group: the dissidents turn to terror because of their inability to implement alternatives. Terrorism potentially serves a number of functions:[19]

1.   *Release Tension through Action:* Tension release seldom supplies the sole motivation for terrorism. When the position of the regime appears unassailable through direct attack, however, displacing violence onto third parties provides the dissidents with the satisfaction of doing something to lash back at their oppressors.

2.   *Symbolize and Publicize Grievances*: Dissidents, especially in the early stages of their struggle, often use terrorist attacks to dramatize their existence and aims. Through resultant publicity they may begin to convince the uncommitted alienated that they provide a viable alternative to the existing regime.

3.   *Demonstrate Some Coercive Capability*: Terrorism can be intended to demonstrate that the regime is not impregnable, to create doubt about its viability. Indeed, this demonstration could have the effect of further weakening support for the regime because of its inability to provide security.

4.   *Provoke Ill-Considered Responses*: Terrorists often hope that their highly selective irritant acts will prod the regime into an overreaction that will alienate far more people than the original act of terrorism, thereby broadening the dissidents' base of support.

Terrorism can also be used to achieve specific objectives, such as maintenance of the internal cohesion of the dissident movement, reprisals for regime actions, elimination of regime supporters, or the release of captured dissidents. Of course a single act of terrorism may be intended to fulfill a number of the identified objectives.

Terrorist tactics, though potentially useful to a dissident movement, carry certain risks that can limit their effectiveness. First, as is suggested above, if the dissidents are forced to rely solely on terror they probably will not accomplish any positive political objectives. At best, they may so disrupt a regime as to produce a state of near chaos. In the absence of an effectively implemented strategy of reintegration, though, the dissidents will be unable to replace the crumbling order. Moreover, the consequences of terrorism are difficult to predict and control. Such acts can easily alienate potential support and make the population willing to tolerate a strenuous antiterrorist policy on the part of the regime. This, in turn, helps the regime to implement effective repressive policies directed at the dissidents.

The regime, in fact, may be able to mount a campaign of counterterror. Most established systems probably have engaged in some quasi-terrorist acts, for example, the use of excessive police action or torture to repress dissent. A regime can, moreover, use terror as a systematic tactic to achieve broader sociopolitical objectives. The most commonly cited examples of regime terror are those of Nazi Germany and Stalinist Russia, but other cases even prior to the twentieth century have occurred.[20] Regime terror can serve a number of purposes:

1. *Break Down Subregime Loyalities*: If a regime decides to tolerate no competitors for the citizens' loyalties, a terrorist policy can be used to spread so much fear and distrust as to prevent the formation of any horizontal ties among people or groups. Terror atomizes people in their relations with the regime.

2. *Motivate Great Exertions*: In the absence of positive inducements the fear stimulated by terror may substitute for rewards. If significant behavior changes are sought—for example, changing peasants into industrial workers—over a short period of time, considerable violence may be necessary.

3. *Facilitate the Implementation of Programs of Massive Social Change*. Terror may achieve this purpose in consequence of the motivation mentioned above.

4. *Eliminate Potential Opposition*: Terrorist action need not wait until opposition becomes manifest but may be used to strike at any possible source of potential competition. Thus, during the Soviet purges of the 1930's, two of the hardest hit sectors were the officer corps and the apparatus of the Communist Party itself.

5. *Cement Elite Relations*: Elite unity might be enhanced by terror directed at the established cadres. The survivors often owe their exalted positions to the terror which eliminated rivals and created "room at the top." Moreover, all share a collective responsibility for the terror, which may further unify them in guilt.

Regime terror, like that of dissidents, is not cost-free. First, as was noted with respect to any policy of repression, extensive terror requires an expensive and potentially insubordinate police apparatus. Second, terror can cause considerable short-term disruption and inefficiency. The initially weak response of the Soviet armies to the Nazi invasion may have been in part due to the decimation of the officer corps a few years earlier. Over the long run, terror can result in a kind of societal fatigue. Moreover, considerable waste is involved in punishing loyal supporters on the possibility they may eventually compete with the existing rulers. Moreover, the regime will be denied accurate, honest information necessary for correct policy formation because of the slavishness produced by fear. Subordinates will distort their reports in anticipation of what their superiors wish to hear in order to avoid becoming the next victims. Finally, the terrorist dissolution of all ties of trust eventually hinders the cooperation necessary in the coordination of a modern industrial society.

THE ETHICS OF VIOLENT MEANS

Terrorism and revolutionary warfare, because of their extreme nature, commonly raise questions of political ethics. Just because other forms of political violence are more subtle, however, does not mean ethical considerations are not also relevant to them. Consequently, this examination of political violence concludes with a brief review of some of the justifications offered for such acts and a consideration of the value of some nonviolent alternatives.

Political violence causes extensive human suffering. Yet people commonly commit such acts not out of cynical disregard for all moral and ethical principles, but because they believe they are justified: the violence of the aggressor can be violently resisted; the violence of the oppressor can be violently overthrown; the violence of the evil can be countered with the violence of the good. Most people, then, make distinctions among the users of violence and among the purposes for which it is used. The ethical problem resolves itself into one of ends and means.

The overused cliché about the ends justifying the means and its equally inane denial fail to illuminate the dilemmas of political choice. "Means" can be justified only by "ends," but this fact does not mean that every end necessarily justifies any means. The end/means debate disguises two issues: First, some evaluation of the quality of the purposes being pursued must be made. When Hitler decided to eliminate the Jews as a people, the problem involved not simply the means he chose, but also the moral repugnancy of the goal itself. Of course, many of the stated objectives of those implementing a strategy of violence may appear morally ambiguous or even quite desirable, such as the liberation of the oppressed classes. At this point a second issue becomes important: What is the impact of the chosen means on the end?

The question of appropriate means is partly a matter of simple efficiency. It would be unethical to inflict needless destruction if the same goal could be reached at a lesser cost in life and suffering. Unfortunately, political battles usually do not lend themselves to quasi-economic cost analysis, and the tendency is to err on the side of too much coercion rather than too little.

More profound is the argument that violent means must necessarily corrupt the end, no matter how noble. Mankind's political history is littered with the disastrous consequences of good causes perverted by ill-considered violence. The complete pacifist argues that even under conditions of tyranny it would be better for the oppressed to endure rather than violently resist, lest they become as evil as their rulers.

Coercion is evil, especially that which destroys lives, whether within or in violation of societal boundaries regulating its use. Perhaps its use can be justified as the lesser evil under some circumstances. Thus the state rationalizes its use of coercion as a means of controlling lawbreakers so that average citizens can live out their lives in peace. Those who advocate change point to the "institutionalized violence" of the established order as a justification for their own violence in attempting to alter it.

If coercion in general and violence in particular can be justified only as a lesser evil, then certain other conclusions appear to follow. First, violent means can be used only after all other avenues of redress have been exhausted —as a last resort, not a first. Second, careful distinctions must be made among the levels of destruction involved in alternative tactics, and the negative consequences of violence should be minimized. This latter conclusion, in turn, raises the question of proportionality—there should be some equivalance between the value of the goal pursued and the cost involved in pursuing it. Additionally, in considering the cost of a particular strategy, careful consideration must be given to the impact of that strategy on the objective itself. Finally, the question whether any means, including violent ones, can achieve the desired goal must be conscientiously answered. If all these conditions are met, then perhaps violence can be justified as a necessary evil.

Beyond these qualifications, some analysts make a distinction between coercion that consists of direct physical attacks on the person or values of an opponent and coercion that consists of the simple withholding of expected behavior. Gene Sharp, an advocate of what he terms "nonviolent action," argues that all governments depend on the cooperation of their citizens for survival.[21] An oppressive regime, therefore, can be pressured, indeed coerced, into making concessions not through direct attacks on it, but by withdrawing this expected cooperation. Sharp attacks the myth of effectiveness that surrounds the violence of direct attacks and tries to show that noncooperation can be as effective and considerably less destructive.

Two objections are commonly raised against the strategy of noncooperation. First, for the withdrawal of support to work, large numbers of people must be organized to act in a disciplined and coordinated fashion. No doubt, a general strike could bring down a government, but what guarantees that the strike will be general? A strategy of direct attack, in contrast, can be implemented by a small group of conspirators who can operate under the cover of secrecy.

This objection contains some merit, but it oversimplifies the issue. To carry out a revolution through noncooperation would require a mass movement of considerable discipline, but so also would a successful violent revolution. The noncooperation movement, moreover, must necessarily be open and fairly democratic, if the participants are going to voluntarily engage in this kind of action. The violent revolution operates in a context that encourages hierarchical discipline and the creation of a counterelite. Lesser objectives also can be pursued through noncooperation. Many groups occupy strategic positions within the economy and society that enable them to withhold needed services to gain a hearing for their problems. Recent examples in the United States include "normal" industrial strikes, the air-traffic controllers' slowdown, and the independent truckers' refusal to drive their rigs. Admittedly, small groups of terrorists can inflict considerable destruction, but it is by no means clear that they will be any more successful in achieving positive objectives.

The second objection to the strategy of noncooperation raises the problem of regime reprisals: Perhaps in a reasonably democratic system noncooperative means will work, but a more authoritarian regime will simply eliminate the resisters. Who would sit idly by while being violently attacked by the regime? Of course, if the regime is so calloused and coercively powerful that it could freely implement a policy of liquidation, it is by no means clear that a strategy of direct attack on it would be any more successful. Beyond this, no regime, no matter how tyrannical, can afford to destroy all of its citizens. Even Stalin apparently recognized the limits of regime terror, and he encountered *no* systematic resistance. People who refuse to cooperate create certain difficulties for the regime. Since they do not engage in direct violent attacks, the onus of initiating violence must rest with the regime. The image of noncooperating people being attacked by the government is more likely to produce sympathy for the former than the latter. The regime's reprisals can be turned back against it through an act of "political jujitsu," for no ruler can afford to create thousands of martyrs. This possibility is far more unlikely under circumstances where the regime is merely defending itself from violent dissidents.

The strategy of noncooperation, admittedly, is not easy to implement, but neither is a successful strategy of direct attack. The latter, moreover, entails far more destruction and runs a considerably greater risk of corruption of the ends.

Part Three

PRIMARY POLITICAL ORGANIZATIONS

Political relations are not random and amorphous; rather, the vast majority of political acts occurs within various structured environments or organizations. In the United States, analyses of political organizations are often affected by the tripartite division of the government into legislative, executive, and judicial branches. This division is both too narrow and too vague. It is too narrow because it neglects political organizations that are important even though not part of the formal machinery of government. Perhaps the most important of these is the political party, which provides the subject matter for Chapter VIII.

In addition, using the three branches to identify primary political organizations is too vague with respect to the actual operations of government. The executive branch, for example, is far more than a chief executive and a cabinet; rather, its functions are conducted by a vast bureaucratic organization of which the chief executive is merely the tip. Consequently, in Chapter IX, the activities and problems of public bureaucracies are examined.

Legislative and judicial organizations are important and independent political institutions in the United States and other Western democracies, but in the Soviet Union and in many Asian, African, and Latin American countries they lack similar autonomy. If they exist at all, they are appendages of the dominant political party or of the governmental bureaucratic apparatus. Though the possibility of an independent role should not be forgotten, in this part, legislative and judicial organizations are treated only insofar as they relate to the operations of political party and administrative organizations. Later, in Chapter XII, the *processes* of legislation and adjudication, whatever organizations carry them out, are evaluated.

Finally, students of politics need to confront the increasingly active political role played by the military in many countries. Though presumably subordinated to civilian authorities, more and more military organizations are seizing power and ruling in their own right. In Chapter X, therefore, the functions of the armed forces and the causes of military intervention into civilian politics receive some much deserved attention.

The approach adopted in Part Three is broadly comparative in nature. Frameworks

127

are developed to help characterize the operations of political parties, government bureaucracies, and military organizations both in the United States and in other political systems around the world.

Chapter VIII Political Parties

POLITICAL PARTY SYSTEMS

Developing a satisfactory definition of *political party* capable of subsuming organizations as distinct as the monolithic Communist Party of the Soviet Union and the loose conglomeration of allies making up the Democratic Party in the United States is no simple task.[1] A political party can be provisionally defined as a relatively stable coalition among people (and groups) primarily concerned with directly controlling the political authority resources of a system. In short, a party aims to elect, or in a noncompetitive system to select, government personnel and to announce public policy.

This definition excludes fluid, transitory alliances for political gain. Rather, the alliance must be recognizable and endure over time. Perhaps the minimum condition in this regard is whether the coalition has a name or label identifying it to the general citizenry.[2] Interest groups, of course, continue over time and also possess names. However, they do not seek to occupy authority positions, only to influence those who do so through lobbying, campaign support, and the like.[3] If an interest group begins to strive for direct control over political authority resources, it becomes a political party, even though it may appeal only to a very narrow segment of the total population. Examples in the United States of such special-interest parties include the Vegetarian Party and the Prohibition Party.

The extent to which a party succeeds in actually gaining control over positions of political authority depends on the resources at its disposal, the skill with which it manipulates and exchanges them, and the nature of the political system within which it operates. "The nature of the political system" refers both to the competition encountered from other political parties and to the extent to which rival political institutions have succeeded in insulating themselves from direct party control. In contemporary political systems, for example, most officials in the public bureaucracy are very much insulated, being no longer the appointees of the party in power. Consequently, though the majority political party may control the legislative branch and select the top-level administrators, significant political authority lies in the hands of those who occupy supposedly apolitical civil-service positions. In fact, career administrators may become so powerful as to subvert what authority remains in the hands of the elected officials (see Chapter IX).

The amount of competition among political parties relates to the nature of the party system in a country. Party systems can be classified into two basic types and five subtypes.[4]

Noncompetitive Systems

In noncompetitive party systems only one party can legally organize and operate, though conspiratorial groupings may develop outside the established order. In effect, the party is equivalent to the party system. No other parties exist to challenge its control of the political authority resources of the state (though other organizations like the bureaucracy and the military may be a source of competition). Noncompetitive systems can be distinguished according to the amount of internal cohesion and consensus imposed by the central party organization. Although this raises a question of degree, two basic subtypes can be analytically distinguished:

1. *Authoritarian Single-Party Systems*: Authoritarian single-party systems are dominated by a monolithic and usually ideologically oriented political party. Obvious examples include the Communist Party states of the Soviet Union and some of the countries of Eastern Europe. Some noncommunist third world leaders have also attempted to create similar parties, though without as much success. Not only are authoritarian single-party systems highly centralized, but the party also commonly attempts to penetrate and control all other significant groupings in the social system (see Chapter V, the section on the Soviet Union).

2. *Pluralist Single-Party Systems*: Some parties in noncompetitive systems tend to be less rigid and less tightly organized, and ideology plays a declining role in their operations. Their approach to other groups in society tends to be more pragmatic and less domineering. It is even possible that other social forces have as much or greater impact on the party's operations as has the party. In fact, though no legal opposition exists, two or more candidates identifying with the party may compete for the same office. Consequently, significant internal dissent may be tolerated as long as it does not challenge

the primacy of the party. Examples include some African single-party states such as the Ivory Coast and Tanzania, as well as Yugoslavia and possibly Poland.

Competitive Systems

In competitive party systems, as the name suggests, more than one party can legally contest in open elections for control of the available authority resources. One party or coalition of parties holds power while the others make up the more or less loyal opposition. The patterns of victory and defeat occurring in a system suggest three major competitive subtypes:

1. *One-Party-Dominant Systems*: In a one-party-dominant system, other parties are allowed to organize and compete, and they may even hold a minority of seats in a legislature or parliament. The dominant party, however, wins both the majority of legislative seats and control of the executive in election after election for an extended period of time. One-party-dominant systems occur in India and Japan at the national level and also characterized parts of the South in the United States for a long period after the Civil War.

2. *The Two-Party-Dominant System*: The so-called two-party system has always been a somewhat misleading designation, for significant third parties, as well as a welter of minor parties, often compete with the two major parties. The two dominant parties, however, are the only ones to win significant numbers of legislative seats, and they exchange control of the executive. Recent examples include the national political system in the United States and the system in Great Britain, at least between 1935 and 1974. As the experiences of the United States presidential election of 1968 and the British Parliamentary contest of 1974 indicate, third-party movements can develop that prevent either major party from achieving a majority. If third (and fourth, fifth, sixth, and so forth) party challenges continue to be successful, a third subtype develops.

3. *No-Party-Dominant System*: When no party is able to win a majority, then a number of parties must usually come together after the election to form a government. This situation ordinarily occurs in a parliamentary system where the chief ministers of the government must come from parliament, for example, Italy, Israel, and France during the Fourth Republic. A somewhat similar predicament could develop in the United States if no presidential candidate had a majority in either the Electoral College or the House of Representatives, which has the responsibility of electing the President if the Electoral College is deadlocked. A presumptive president would have to forge a coalition of supporters from more than one party in order to win a majority in the House. After he was chosen, of course, his term of office

would not be dependent on a continued congressional majority, as would be the case with a prime minister in a parliamentary system. Considerable debate develops over the origins of a no-party-dominant system.[5] Some tend to blame an extreme circumstance of proportional representation, in which parliamentary seats are divided according to the percentage votes received (thus, a small party receiving 10 percent of the votes cast would be allotted 10 percent of the seats in the parliament). Such a system supposedly encourages the proliferation of minor parties rather than the creation of broad coalition parties. Others argue that pre-existing social divisions determine whether or not one party is able to win a majority. If a broad social consensus exists, proportional representation will not prevent the party representing this agreement from winning a majority and dominating the political system. This latter situation has characterized some of the Scandinavian countries. Thus, significant social cleavages that prevent the emergence of a majority consensus, combined with a system of proportional representation, produce a no-party-dominant system.[6]

This discussion of different kinds of party systems excludes those regimes that have prohibited all political parties (Greece under military rule, Chile after Allende, for example). These non-party systems commonly come about after *coups d'état*, when military and bureaucratic elites hostile to party politics seize power and outlaw party activities. These and other enemies of political parties are further discussed in the final section of this chapter.

TYPES OF POLITICAL PARTIES[7]

Political parties differ in terms of their organization, aims, and impact on the system in which they operate. Eight types of political parties can be analytically distinguished according to the extent of mass participation in their affairs and the primary basis of their organizational identity. Though this typology helps to organize a wide variety of political phenomena, it must be remembered that each type subsumes a considerable diversity of political experience. Additionally, a real-life party may contain elements of more than one type coexisting alongside one another. The basic typology is illustrated in Figure VIII-1, and its elements are explained below:

Participatory Elements

Political parties, as defined here, are relatively recent political inventions. Even in established Western democracies, true political parties can be traced back only about two hundred years. Until the nineteenth century, the fluid coalitions formed by members of the ruling elite to further individual political

Figure VIII-1   A Typology of Political Parties

		IDENTITY ELEMENTS			
		Primordial	*Material*	*Ideological*	*Pragmatic/ Bargaining*
PARTICIPATORY ELEMENTS	*Elite*	Elite Communal	Elite Machine	Elite Believer	Elite Consensus
	Mass	Mass Communal	Mass Machine	Mass Believer	Mass Consensus

advantage are more properly considered factions than parties. As these factions began to solidify into fairly durable groupings possessing recognizable identities, they formed the first political parties. Participation, at least in the early years of party development, remained highly restricted, and so these parties might be called elitist in nature.

Historically, these factions polarized around a core political issue or related set of issues. In the United States, the major conflict dividing the Federalists and the Jeffersonian Democratic Republicans concerned the powers to be exercised by the central government. In Europe, the common reference of factional consolidation involved economic and social issues. First, the competitive claims of the traditional aristocracy and the rising capitalist groups formed the basis for a conservative/liberal split. This division was later complicated by the growing demands of the working classes, which gave impetus to the various European socialist parties. In the twentieth century, many African and Asian nationalist parties began as organizations of native elites demanding from the colonial power greater participation in the internal affairs of the colony. These initial demands later evolved into agitation for complete independence. The political and social conflicts in the United States and European cases are internally divisive and commonly produced two or more parties. Competition with a foreign ruler for independence, however, if uncomplicated by internal concerns, is essentially unifying and generally forms the basis for a single-party system or a one-party-dominant system.

The masses, naturally, are not well integrated into elitist political parties. If they participate at all, it usually is through a patron/client relationship in which the client of an elite patron defers to the latter's political wishes in exchange for his generalized support and protection.[8] Two interrelated factors erode the position of pure elite parties: First, the spread of democratic norms and values throughout a society encourages unfranchised groups to demand a voice in the governing process. The rise of the labor movement in Great Britain before the extension of the vote to the average worker illustrates this kind of pressure. Second, the elite parties, in their competition with one another, attempt to mobilize mass support and often thereby reinforce the diffusion of a democratic culture. A variation of this latter development happened during many independence struggles. The native elites, in their contest with the colonial power, found it imperative to mobilize mass support to counter the claim that the nationalist leaders spoke only for themselves and not for the majority of the people.

The inclusion of the masses in the operations of the political party, however, need not always be associated with democracy. Many authoritarian parties, especially in the communist states, use mass organizations to mobilize the people for developmental objectives. This type of mass participation does not mean that the people freely choose the goals for the achievement of which they are being organized.

The participatory basis of a particular party, moreover, may fail to resolve itself neatly into the elite/mass dichotomy. Some essentially elite parties may have considerable mass followings based on traditional ties of submissiveness to elite status. Alternatively, a party may not attract significant support even though it is clearly intended to be a mass political organization. In these ambiguous cases, the classification must be primarily determined by an evaluation of the essential organizational intent, whether or not the intent is fully realized.

Identity Elements

Party organizations can also be distinguished according to the primary basis of their identity. Identity affects the reasons why people join a party, the purposes which it pursues, and its internal structure and operations. Four essential identity elements can be isolated, though two are most commonly associated only with mass parties.

1. *Primordial Ties*: Certain parties are formed to represent collectivities bound by one or more fundamental or primordial ties, such as race, language, ethnicity, religion, or region. Sometimes, these communal parties address a subnational grouping: for example, a tribal party in a multitribal society, a linguistic party in a multilingual society, and so on. Many nationalist parties, insofar as they attempt to establish a primordial community coextensive with the state's boundaries, can also be seen as basically communal in nature.

People join primordial parties to express solidarity with other members of their community against the claims and demands made by other primordial groups. When such primordial ties are strong they neutralize the impact of other societal cleavages within the community, such as economic class or wealth. The objectives pursued by these parties are essentially indivisible community rewards; that is, they benefit the entire group and not simply individuals within it. These may range from material goods (such as schools, roads, health centers, and other community-development projects) to less tangible policies (such as official recognition of the group's language or religion). An extremely alienated subnational primordial group may even demand the right of "self determination," as the Ibo did in Nigeria, precipitating a civil war from 1967 to 1970.

Primordial parties can be essentially elite affairs, especially in those traditional communities where the majority of the population is largely excluded from decision making. Additionally, if a small minority group dominates the whole sociopolitical system, as the whites do in South Africa, then the party that represents them may be considered elitist, even though it has roots in its own community.

In many instances, the elites will attempt to muster mass support, especially in a competitive situation. If primordial identities are deeply felt, such appeals can prove very effective in politicizing large numbers of people and organizing them for the defense of their community. When the ties are subnational in nature, however, primordial appeals will most likely enhance community solidarity at the expense of national unity. Since World War II, countries as diverse as Canada, Belgium, Nigeria, Zaire, Sri Lanka (Ceylon), and Malaysia have been afflicted by subnational conflict. Similarly, on the international level, nationalistic appeals hinder the growth of world order and unity.

Primordial parties decline in significance as other interests become salient for their members and crosscut, rather than reinforce, communal identities. Differences in economic class, wealth, and political power may eventually undermine community solidarity. Marxists, for example, believe that the common cause of the exploited working classes should eventually foster proletarian unity across primordial barriers. While the supposed international ties of workers have yet to be particularly effective in neutralizing the attraction of nationalism, some subnational primordial appeals seem to have been eroded by the multiplication of social identities.

2. *Material Concerns*: Rapid social change often acts as one of the solvents of primordial ties, solvents that make people available for different kinds of political appeals.[9] In the "space" between the breakdown of communal identities and the establishment of new class, status, and professional interests, a special kind of political party may thrive: the political machine.[10] People are organized into machine politics on the basis of an exchange of short-term concrete material inducements for political loyalty. Generally, machine politics presumes the existence of both widespread political participation and competition. The latter creates the motive for attempting to mobilize support; the former supplies the masses from which support is

mobilized. Though most historical examples of political machines have been mass-based, one could conceive of an elite party organized around the desire for immediate gain rather than any strongly felt primordial or ideological identity.

Machines appear to thrive under certain specific social conditions. First, power should be sufficiently fragmented so as to prevent the rise of a centralized party powerful enough to dictate to the people as opposed to bargaining with them. Conversely, too much fragmentation leads to the rise of independent power domains that will not be susceptible to the appeals of the machine. Second, previously established social ties and identities must be disrupted enough to uproot people and make them available for new patterns of behavior. Consequently, machines commonly operate in rapidly growing urban areas, where they build on recent migrants to the city, whether from the countryside or, in the case of the United States, from foreign countries. The processes of social change, however, should not proceed so far that the people develop new identities with longer-term policy or ideological preferences (see below).

Third, in order for support to be attracted by the immediate material rewards promised by the machine, the people must be poor enough that short-term needs take precedence over longer-term interests. The machine, though, must control sufficient material resources to make the promised payoffs. If the entire system is bankrupt, the machine will not be able to function. Machines will also be hindered by laws that prohibit such direct exchanges (as by the civil-service system that eliminates the patronage positions which the machine distributes to its supporters). Additionally, as the material welfare of average citizens improves and their day-to-day needs are more securely fulfilled, their time frame lengthens to take in issues that the machine cannot adequately address. In United States politics, reform parties that advocate efficiency and honesty in government, as well as the long-run developmental needs of the locality, are usually middle-class in origin. Though political machines are quite fragile because of their dependence on the social requisites that have been set forth, they can serve as an important integrative mechanism during a time of transition.

Machines are typically associated with the urban areas of the United States during the late nineteenth and early twentieth centuries. In this period, immigrant groups (Irish, Italians, and so forth) were readily attracted by the machine's material appeals. Most of these old-time political machines have withered away, but the Democratic Party organization of Mayor Richard Daley of Chicago continued to be powerful into the 1970's. Daley's machine, based on thousands of patronage jobs and black migrants from the South, consistently turned aside all reformist efforts until his death.[11]

Material incentives have played a subordinate role in other types of political parties. Though the Convention People's Party (C.P.P.) of Ghana based its popularity primarily on the communal appeal of nationalism, when it gained power after 1952, it was also able to muster additional support by dispensing government jobs and funds. The acquisition of complete independence in 1957 led to a decline in the appeal of nationalism, and worsening economic conditions in the 1960's limited the material resources of the regime. The C.P.P. was ousted by the military in 1966.[12]

3.   *Ideological Appeals*: Some political parties are organized around an interpretation of the sociopolitical world that transcends any particular primordial tie. These ideologies attempt to provide a reasonably coherent explanation of social reality and, usually, a projection of the kind of society toward which the party strives. People join these parties presumably out of a belief in the interpretation and ideals. Ideological parties integrate their members into a system of belief, and, because of this belief, they tend to be authoritarian in organization and dogmatic in tone. To the ideologues, the most dangerous enemy is not the advocate of the diametrically opposed position, but the heretic who expresses marginal reservations about elements of the dogma.

Parties of believers can be either elite or mass-based, to some extent depending on the environment in which they operate. Thus, Lenin turned the Bolshevik party into an organization essentially of a revolutionary elite, partly in response to the repressive nature of the tsarist state. After seizing power, the Bolsheviks/communists altered their organizational scope to provide for a mass base while preserving ideological purity. In more democratic contexts, such as those existing in several Western European countries, the Communist Party has somewhat loosened its ideological stance in order to compete more effectively in open elections. The dilution of doctrine, if it proceeds far enough, could transform the identity of a party of believers into something approximating the fourth type (see below).

Ideological parties can encounter certain difficulties. The emphasis on doctrinal purity often excludes significant interests. If the party functions in a competitive situation, then its potential base of support may be so limited as to condemn it to a permanent minority position. If the party is in power, ideological exclusiveness allows for no legitimate opposition and may require the exercise of considerable coercion to maintain the party's dominance. Finally, to effectively mobilize society for meeting ideologically defined objectives, the party will require a large dedicated cadre, an effective organization, and possibly the exercise of still more coercion. The nature and implications of ideological politics are further examined in Chapter XI.

4.   *Pragmatic, Consensus-Building Goals*: Parties of consensus differ from primordial and ideological parties in that their basic organizational

stance is inclusive, not exclusive. They attempt to build broad coalitions through bargaining and compromise, rather than dividing the world into we/they dichotomies. Political machines, too, often adopt a fairly flexible, nondogmatic position but differ in the kind of exchanges they make with their supporters. Consensus parties define general policy commitments and promise long-term programs, as opposed to short-term material benefits, as rewards for support.

Cynics might argue that the major reason for supporting these pragmatic coalitions is the desire to be on the winning side. And indeed, some business interests in the United States make contributions to both major parties. This cynical conclusion, however, seems a bit too harsh, for consensus parties often incorporate and moderate the appeals of the other three types of party in an attempt to build a winning coalition. They make overtures to people's primordial loyalties but try to avoid being identified with only one communal subgroup. Their policy promises reflect some common principles, but not ones so rigidly defined as to be doctrinaire. Finally, material inducements are offered in exchange for support; however, these are not the individualistic short-term incentives of the political machine but general programs designed to benefit whole classes of people.[13]

In contrast to the tight organizations characterizing ideological parties, consensus parties usually tend to be more loosely organized because of their attempt to aggregate fairly divergent interests. Consensus politics precludes the leadership from imposing a homogeneous party line on a heterogeneous collection of supporters. Though such parties usually presume competitive political systems, their organizational stance could be adopted by the ruling party in a one-party-dominant system, as well as in noncompetitive systems where the party is pluralist instead of authoritarian.

Though the operations of pragmatic party politics suggest mass involvement in public life, participation may be confined in fact to an elite. In the early years of the United States, the Federalist and anti-Federalist elements were essentially elite parties, though their conflicts were tempered by compromise. Soon these groups began to mobilize support from the steadily expanding electorate. Today, the loosely organized and somewhat contentious Democratic Party provides a good example of a mass consensus party.

Consensus parties possess certain obvious advantages. Different groups can often find a place in the political system, as they cannot do in the situation in which a portion of the population is excluded on class or cultural grounds. Because of the willingness to bargain and compromise, conflicts between or within consensus parties appear more moderate and more easily regulated.

These very strengths, however, may conceal some problems. The ability of a consensus party to function may depend on the absence of serious division in society; the bargaining and compromise to reach consensus occur in politics because an underlying social agreement is already present. A society badly polarized, whether over primordial or ideological differences, can frustrate the attempt to build broad pragmatic coalitions. Moreover, the maintenance of a union of disparate groups may produce political stalemate, as the various competing interests can cancel one another out. Consequently, society-wide problems would be inadequately addressed until they intensified into such crisis proportions as to galvanize these heterogeneous alliances into collective action.

Consensus politics in the United States demonstrates these strengths and these weaknesses. Few significant groups are completely excluded from the political process. Usually one or both parties will attempt to tailor their appeal to fit the needs of emerging interests. Third-party movements generally find that significant portions of their programs will be co-opted by the major political parties.

Though in this way a wide range of interests gains some representation and political conflict is usually moderated, the consequence often appears to be stalemate. The effort at preservation of consensus often results in the various factions being able to veto threats to their special interests (see Chapter V). Because the stalemate must be escaped, United States politics often exhibits something of a crisis mentality, as problems are either blown out of proportion or, even worse, avoided until they actually constitute a crisis.

The eightfold typology displayed in Figure VIII-1 illustrates several ways in which political parties can be compared and contrasted. To flesh out this schematization, the functions performed by political parties and the different modes of performance need to be further examined.

THE PRIMARY FUNCTIONS OF POLITICAL PARTIES

Political parties can contribute in a number of ways to the operations of a political system. The way in which these contributions are made depends on the type of party and party system. In other words, the impact of an ideological party in a noncompetitive system differs substantially from that of a consensus party in the same situation or that of an ideological party in a competitive context. Consideration of the possible effects of political parties can be divided into analyses of their primary functions and the secondary consequences of their activities.

The primary functions performed in at least a rudimentary fashion by every political party that gains control over some authority resources involve participation, recruitment, policy definition, and policy implementation.

Participation

Perhaps the fundamental task of the political party is to structure the participation of its constituency. Political parties commonly operate on four levels, though they differ as to how tightly organized the relations among the levels are.[14] One may see as the top level those individuals who hold public positions as the elected representatives of a party that won at the polls or controls these offices for other reasons; this level might be called the "party in government." The party apparatus, consisting of those members who control the day-to-day operations of the party, makes up a second level. Next are the rank-and-file members, those who identify with the party (usually by paying dues) and who regularly attend party functions but do not hold any official position in the party organization. The fourth and most diffuse level of the party includes its supporters in the citizenry at large.

Political parties can be contrasted according to the way they define their relevant constituencies. Essentially elitist parties define their base of support rather narrowly; in contrast, mass parties direct attention to penetrating and organizing a greater proportion of the population. The central identity of the party also affects the definition of support. Communal and ideological parties usually place clear restrictions on who is qualified for membership, while political machines and consensus parties attempt to embrace as wide a constituency as possible. Communal parties exclude those who fail to possess the key primordial characteristic, whether race, tribe, religion, or the like. Ideological parties relate only to those who have accepted the "faith."

Beyond these four levels, some scholars distinguish among the alternative ways in which ruling parties respond to demands for participation from those currently barred from the political process.[15] *Repression* is the most restrictive response. Established party elites may not welcome the emergence of competitors for their privileges, especially if the party holds to exclusionist communal or ideological identities. Consequently, white-ruled South Africa prohibits the organization of nationalist black political parties.

A second response, commonly chosen by ideological parties that extend their roots into the masses, is to expand participation but do so in a carefully controlled and restricted fashion. This alternative can be called *mobilization*, in that the party wants to draw on the energies released by increased participation as long as they are directed toward ideologically sanctioned objectives. The Communist Party of the Soviet Union is quite concerned with mass political participation, but only on its terms. Organization of an opposition party would not be tolerated.

A third possible response is for the dominant party (or parties) to allow for *partial or full admission* of new groups into the political process, either by absorbing them through compromise and conciliation or by allowing them to organize their own political parties and compete for political authority resources on a more or less equal basis. In fact, few systems are completely open. Even in the more democratic polities, radical fringe elements are commonly excluded from effective participation. In the United States, suspension of equal-time regulations has allowed the two major parties to debate their positions on television without giving minor parties equal access. Many proposals to fund campaigns publicly are similarly biased in favor of the two major parties. Nevertheless, the relative openness of the party systems of the United States and Western Europe can be meaningfully contrasted with the mobilization parties of the Communist systems and the racially repressive policies of the ruling National Party of South Africa.

Recruitment

The second essential function of the political party, that of recruitment, directly affects the party apparatus and the party in government. In a sense, the recruitment function is a continuation of the process by which participation is structured. Despite the relationship between the two functions, the involvement of party or government officials appears qualitatively different from that of the average citizen who merely affirms support for a given party.

The primary consideration in evaluating the recruitment function is the extent to which a particular party really affects the election or selection of government officials. Presumably, every party possesses some interest in gaining control of these authority positions, but parties encounter differing degrees of success. Some minority parties, especially in those systems that do not have proportional representation, may never control any public office. Others may win some legislative seats but never majority control. Even parties in control of a parliament or legislature may be strictly limited in the extent to which they can fill other government positions, especially in the bureaucracy. In past times, the ruling party has exercised more expansive control over political authority resources. In nineteenth-century United States, the so-called spoils system allowed the party dominating the executive branch to dispense a wide array of government jobs among the party faithful. But the steady extension of the merit system in the civil service has meant that the victorious party can directly affect recruitment only for elective offices and for top executive appointees at the cabinet and subcabinet levels. Depoliticizing the bureaucracy clearly serves to limit the recruitment functions of political parties.

Given the range of public offices directly susceptible to party control, a distinction can also be made with reference to the sharing of this control among two or more parties. This distinction involves contrasting *hegemonic* with *turnover* patterns of office holding, though these simply define the extremes on a continuum.[16] The ruling party in an authoritarian single-party system most closely approximates the hegemonic pole, because it controls the recruitment to all important political positions. In a pluralist single-party system, different groups, even though under the same party banner, might compete with one another for office. The one-party-dominant system, where minority parties control some elective offices, is still further removed from the extreme of complete hegemony and occupies the approximate midpoint between the two poles. Competitive party systems (either two-party- or no-party-dominant), where the control of the executive and legislative branches regularly changes hands, approach the turnover pole. Even in these cases, a particular party may continually prevail over its competitors in certain parts of a country. In the United States, for example, both the Republicans and the Democrats dominate the electoral process in certain safe areas. A complete turnover process of recruitment would necessitate that every office subject to party control, either through election or selection, be regularly rotated among the contending parties.

The extent to which parties compete among themselves for the control of the available offices addresses only part of the problem. Also important is the manner by which a party chooses its candidates. This latter aspect in turn, raises questions about the nature of the party organization: Who control it, and how are they chosen? Finally, what people make up the general membership, and how did they become members?

As to the last question, parties may be compared according to the openness of their membership rolls. The members of a wide-open, democratic party are in effect self-recruited: Anyone who so wishes may join, and the membership often reflects heterogeneous backgrounds. Indeed, in the United States, the party's membership is often not clearly distinguished from its constituency in the population at large. At the other extreme, prospective members may be carefully screened before they are allowed to join. The more authoritarian believer parties tend to exercise greater control over the recruitment of members than do either political machines or consensus parties (compare the discussion of recruitment to the Communist Party in Chapter V).

Within the party's general membership are those persons who actually run the party organization. At one extreme are those parties in which officers are largely self-selected; that is, the members who are willing to invest their time tend to fill official party positions. The manner by which officers are chosen at the local party level in the United States resembles this process of self-recruitment. In contrast, the organizations of mass-based believer parties are generally very much bureaucratized and centrally controlled, and this bureaucratic center dominates party activities. Between these extremes are those parties which, though relatively open at the lower levels, become increasingly closed as one moves up the hierarchy. Party organizations in Great Britain appear more tightly disciplined in this manner than do those in the United States. Even under the decentralized conditions prevailing in the United States (some commentators argue that the national political parties are no more than confederations of fifty state parties), recruitment into the higher echelons of the party organization is considerably more restricted than at the local level. Even so, the nominations of Barry Goldwater in 1964 and George McGovern in 1972 demonstrate that a group of grass-roots insurgents can seize control of the central organization from the party regulars, at least for a time.

The final aspect of the recruitment function relates to the process by which the party's candidates for office are selected (of course, in a one-party system, nomination is equivalant to election). As with the other aspects, candidate selection can be placed on an open/closed continuum. In the United States, some candidates are chosen in open primaries, in which anyone who pays a filing fee can get his or her name on the ballot, and all voters, regardless of party affiliation, can vote their preference in either party's primary. Somewhat more restrictive are the closed primaries, in which only registered members can vote in the party's primary. Still more controlled is selection by nominating conventions, these tending to be dominated by party regulars. At the extreme, candidate selection may be completely determined by the elite at the top of the organizational pyramid, without even the trappings of a democratic process. This last approximates the method prevailing in the Soviet Union.

Policy Formation

A third major function commonly performed by political parties is the definition of public policy. The manner in which policy develops, like the other functions, is affected by the nature of the party system and the political party.

The fundamental distinction in this area pertains to the extent of choice among alternative policies and programs available to the citizens. Choice can be limited in a number of ways, some obvious, others more subtle. The most obvious limitation is set by the amount of competition characterizing the party system. An authoritarian single-party system offers a relatively unified party line that tolerates little opposition. Some multiparty systems, such as that in Italy, seem to offer the entire gamut of conceivable programmatic positions. Two-party systems occupy the midpoint on the spectrum of political choice.

Choice, however, can be constrained in more subtle ways. Insofar as party programs reflect societal divisions, the actual differences between or among parties in a highly consensual society may be quite slight. Consequently, the rather widely shared political consensus that prevailed in the United States at least through the mid-1960's tended to propel the two major parties into the middle of the road; their policy differences were more apparent than real. The decay of this consensus under the impact of the Vietnam war and of racial conflict is reflected in the strains placed on consensus politics in recent years, especially within the Democratic Party. In short, significant division produces significant choice, but it also leads to discord and even violence.

But even where a number of parties exist that appear to offer a wide range of alternatives, actual choice is limited by voter knowledge, which in turn depends on the ability of the parties to publicize their positions. Major parties not only can reflect consensus but also can create it. Thus, the eminence they enjoy in one-party- and two-party-dominant systems may be attributed as much to the creative as to the reflective capacity. Minor parties simply lack the resources to gain a hearing.

The fulfillment of the policy-definition function can also be analyzed according to the nature of the programs offered by different kinds of political parties. Party programs can be compared with respect to their ideological coherence and emotional or affective content.

The ideological-coherence variable identifies the extent to which a political program reflects an explicit, systematic, and coherent interpretation of the social and political world. Ideological parties, not surprisingly, score highest in this measure. Primordial parties, in that they celebrate the ultimate meaning of a salient identity, probably rank next on the scale. They interpret the world in terms of threats and supports for this community and formulate programs defending and enhancing the community's position. Pragmatic consensus parties try to avoid dogmatic positions, stating policy vaguely enough to attract wide, and somewhat incompatible, support. This does not mean that pragmatic consensus parties are unprincipled. The attitude of complete expediency, rather, characterizes the political machine, whose concern lies not with the promulgation of long-term policy but with the exchange of short-term incentives for political support.

Party programs often address the passions as well as the minds of their supporters. Consequently, they also may be ranked according to their emotional content. Since primordial parties rest heavily on sociopsychological needs in addition to material desires, their programmatic statements will usually be infused with emotional appeals. Ideological parties, though rooted in a system of ideas, often attempt to engender an attachment to the community of believers as strong as attachments based on primordial ties. The emotional pull of primordial identities often remains strong, as Stalin discovered in World War II. The Russian people appeared more moved by appeals to defend Mother Russia than they were by a desire to preserve the Soviet state.

Pragmatic consensus parties are not beyond emotional manipulation in their policy pronouncements; witness the invocations of "law and order" in recent campaigns in the United States. The affective content, however, is subordinated to the primary goal of coalition building. Consequently, emotional appeals of consensus parties are chosen to reflect a common agreement, whereas those of primordial and ideological parties often take an exclusionist slant. Of all the four basic types of political party, the machine minimizes emotionalism, preferring to conduct politics on something closely resembling a cash basis.

Policy Implementation

Political parties may do more than simply structure inputs (participation, recruitment, policy definition). They also can guide and aid the implementation of government programs (output). Not all political parties are directly involved in the implementation process. One obvious prerequisite is that the party participate in the government. A minority party, controlling no political office, has very limited impact on either inputs or outputs. Moreover, many political parties lack the organizational capacity or interest to take more than a vaguely supervisory role in policy implementation.

Somewhat paradoxically, machines and ideological parties are most likely to acquire an abiding interest in the daily administrative operation, though for rather different reasons. Ruling machines use government goods and services as a major source of political currency with which to pay their supporters. Not only are party workers rewarded with government jobs, but governmental output also will be distributed so as to maximize support for the party. Careful control of output, then, supplies the glue that holds the machine together.

Ideological parties, when in control of the government, can be expected to be quite concerned that their policies be faithfully implemented by the administration. The party could affect implementation in a number of ways. First, and perhaps most important, party loyalists provide an external source of control and evaluation. Bureaucracies often capture the political leadership merely by regulating the flow of information to the top (see Chapter IX). A political party organization, paralleling the government apparatus, can undercut this potential monopoly on information resources. Second, ideological parties often attempt to energize the entire population to struggle for the policy objectives of the regime. The government bureaucracy is unlikely to stimulate such a release of effort, but a highly disciplined and dedicated party

cadre may be able to prod the people into great exertions. Finally, cooperation between the government administrators and the party authorities may
actually enhance the legitimacy of the former (see below).

Extensive involvement in policy implementation places great demands on
the party apparatus and raises an element of risk. Effective involvement
necessitates a complex organization that penetrates as deeply into the social
system as does the governmental bureaucracy it supervises. Moreover, the
people who staff the party organization must be sufficiently trained to perform
their supervisory tasks. Party hacks create several interrelated problems for
the regime. Most obviously, their incompetent interference may seriously
hamper the government's effectiveness and efficiency. Moreover, such interference alienates the administrators, who may passively or actively support
the overthrow of the party regime in favor of one that will allow them greater
independence. Such overthrows have occurred in several Asian and African
states where the political party was not strong enough to resist being ousted by
an aroused military/bureaucratic coalition. Even if they do not provoke
ouster, inadequate skills on the part of the party members may enable the
government bureaucrats to co-opt and control the party, rather than the
reverse.

Creating a party apparatus with the capacity to guide implementation
without damaging performance can be quite costly. To some extent, it requires duplicating talent (as when a government economist must be watched
by someone with sufficient training in economics to be able to evaluate the
former's performance). One way to avoid this wastage is to recruit the
governmental experts into the party. This apparent solution raises questions
of dual loyalties: which way would the person opt in case of a conflict
between administrative and party responsibilities? Despite these potential
difficulties, a party that sets out to significantly reshape society cannot avoid
becoming extensively entangled in policy implementation.

THE SECONDARY CONSEQUENCES OF PARTY ACTIVITIES[17]

Certain secondary effects also flow from the activities of political parties
in a system, especially in the areas of socialization, communication, conflict
management, and legitimation.

Political Socialization

From the moment of birth, an infant begins to learn about the surrounding
social world, and this learning, or socialization, continues until death. *Political socialization* refers to the processes through which a person acquires
specifically political knowledge, attitudes, and beliefs.[18] Although rooted in

early childhood experiences, much of this type of learning occurs after a person reaches the age when he can participate fully in the political life of the community. The socialization process is explored in greater detail in Chapter XI; here it is sufficient to indicate the possible impact of political parties on citizens' socialization.

Every one of the party's primary functions contributes to the political learning process. Consequently, the more active people are in party affairs, the more likely their attitudes and orientations will be shaped by the party. In addition, the more expansively a party sees its role in society, the more deliberately it will proceed in attempting to teach its members. Ideological parties, therefore, tend to be most directly involved in political socialization. This involvement follows from the promulgation of a comprehensive world view to which all members must adhere. Moreover, beliefs are expected to be reflected in "right" action, in terms both of mobilized participation and enthusiastic implementation. Thus, the ideological party attempts to structure both knowledge and behavior.

The primordial party's impact on behavior might not be as comprehensive as that of an ideological party, but it can be more profound. This type of party reinforces and politicizes a salient primordial identity. People learn to carry over into their political activities the same in-group/out-group orientation that characterizes their communities. Machines and pragmatic bargaining parties, because of their more inclusionist and flexible stance, take less of a deliberate interest in political socialization.

Political parties and party systems also have an indirect impact on the political learning of the citizens. By watching how parties interact, and by being affected by their actions, even the politically noninvolved have their expectations and attitudes shaped in some way. Political party behavior is one important source of information about how the game of politics is played in a particular system. The party-related process of socialization, whether deliberately instigated or indirectly learned through experience, in turn molds the effect of the party in other areas.

Political Communication

Political parties obviously shape the content of messages in a political system, primarily in light of their programmatic concerns.[19] Thus, the political communications in a system dominated by an ideological party reflect the prevailing political dogma. The messages given and received by communal parties are colored by the central primordial identity. The messages of consensus parties and machines, on the other hand, suggest their interest in compromise and exchange.

Also important is the impact of the party on the process of communication itself. First, the centralization of the party affects the *directional flow* of messages in the system. In a hierarchically structured, authoritarian party, the prevailing flow is downward, as subordinate sectors and members receive orders from their superiors in the party organization. Alternatively, in a more loosely organized party, the prevailing flow is upward, as the rank-and-file members funnel their messages and wishes up to their popularly responsible officials. In neither case would messages moving in the opposite direction be completely eliminated. Even the most autocratic party leaders must be concerned with acquiring feedback on the performance and morale of their subordinates, just as responsive party officials must make some effort to coordinate and direct party affairs. In any case, the direction of the message flow of the dominant party or parties tends to be reflected in the system at large.

A second aspect of the communications process that may be shaped by party operations is the *penetration* of political messages into society. In some less developed countries, messages emanating from the center often fail to reach the periphery of the society. Obviously, the spread of literacy and the extension of other communications systems, such as the mass media or the governmental bureaucracy, are the critical determinants of the penetration of political messages. The party organization, however, may serve to supplement these other avenues, assuming that it extends beyond the political center. If so, the political leadership may find the party to be a more reliable transmitter of messages, both up and down, than either the media or government administration.

A third area in which the nature of the party may have some effect is in the *definition of the audience* to which political messages are addressed. Communal and ideological parties, as might be expected, tend to define their relevant audience quite precisely according to specific primordial or ideological characteristics. In cases where the ideological party rules the state or when the primordial identity is that of a homogeneous, independent nation, then these parties may direct their messages at the whole population of the political system. Machines and pragmatic consensus parties, however, talk to anyone willing to bargain.

The type of party can also affect the *style* of communications. The content of the message probably impinges more directly on the style than on any other aspect of the communication process. The purpose of the message largely determines the style in which it is communicated. If the purpose is to mobilize and energize support, the style of delivery will tend to be emotional and evocative. If, however, the purpose is simply to inform, the style will be more subdued and designed to appeal to the mind. Very few political messages fall at either extreme of pure emotion or unadulterated information, but the relative mix may change. The more instrumental concerns of the machine and the pragmatic consensus parties reduce the role of emotion in their communications, whereas communal and ideological parties commonly place greater emphasis on the emotional impact of their messages on their followers. The triumph of emotional over informational style can be clearly seen in the mass rallies staged by the Nazis in Germany.

Conflict and Conflict Regulation

Political party activities influence both the nature of conflict and the possibility of conflict regulation in a system. Considerable debate, as was noted previously, swirls around the question whether political parties reflect or create societal divisions. If parties are simply reflections, then they have little independent impact on social and political conflict. If parties create divisions, however, then their behavior is a prime determinant of conflict. Unfortunately the debate is not easily resolved, for parties are neither insulated from the effects of the larger social environment nor completely unable to influence it. Party and society, especially in the area of conflict, are mutually interdependent variables.

Questions of causality aside, the various kinds of parties and party systems suggest different things about the causes and courses of conflict. Both primordial and ideological parties have a somewhat paradoxical effect on conflict. In a competitive context, they exacerbate it; when they are dominant, they repress it. Each consequence follows from the exclusive manner in which they define their identities. Both parties tend to divide the world into the elect and the damned. Such polarization inhibits the development of rules and norms of civility and moderation in a competitive system. Political conflicts with parties of a different ideological persuasion or primordial identity easily become perceived as zero-sum. Little probability exists for compromising doctrinal truth or primordial purity. Conflict intensifies and political institutions begin to disintegrate under the strain. The street battles between Communists and Nazis in Germany prior to Hitler's takeover and the competition among the primordial parties in Nigeria before its civil war illustrate the debilitating effects these kinds of conflict have on political institutions. About the only effective source of moderation is the realization that no competitor can eliminate its rivals or exist apart from them. Recognition of this fact may lead to a gradual acceptance of the others' right to exist.

When a primordial or ideological party manages to secure the dominant position, it commonly uses the power of the state in attempting to resolve conflict in its favor. Opposition parties are proscribed by law, and disagreement with the policy of the ruling party is equated with disloyalty to the state. If the dominant party's position is tenuous, such policies may serve only to

further intensify political conflict. If the ruling party controls the preponderance of the power resources in society, then it may be able to consolidate and
maintain its position indefinitely.

Machines build an organization out of atomization. They thrive in an environment where communal identities have broken down far enough so that
they no longer provide a sufficient basis for political mobilization and where
longer-term affiliations of policy or ideology have not yet emerged. The basis
for agreement becomes short-term mutual advantage. In order to succeed, the
machine must possess some desired resources, mainly through the control of
government operations at some level (for example, in the United States, many
political machines were primarily urban-based). As long as the conditions
persist, the machine can successfully regulate and moderate conflicts among
potentially antagonistic groups (for instance, the black poor and the white
poor). Certain kinds of reformist competition, though, threaten the materialistic foundation of machine operations.

Reformers usually initiate a two-pronged attack on the machine. First,
they strive to pass legislation prohibiting certain practices (graft, patronage)
upon which the machine depends for its incentives. Second, reform parties
direct their appeal at more established class elements who are less attracted by
the rewards of machine politics and who place a higher premium on ideological issues, on long-term policy development, or on what they see as honesty
in government. Pragmatic consensus parties often arise from the collapse of
machines, but ideological or even neoprimordial parties can also develop,
depending on the seriousness of the divisions in society. For a time, however,
the machine can serve to integrate dislocated individuals into the political
system, people who might otherwise be prone to anomic violence.

Pragmatic consensus parties, when dominant in a system, tolerate moderate conflict, both internally and with one another. Both toleration and moderation originate in an underlying agreement on the rules of political competition. As long as this fundamental value consensus exists, the political conflicts that do arise can be regulated and political opposition can be tolerated.
Conflict can intensify if the underlying consensus is seriously challenged.
Consensus parties attempt to prevent such challenges by absorbing new
groups and giving them a stake in the existing order. Still, a salient issue can
develop which will destroy the delicate balance upon which the regulated
conflict of the pragmatic consensus parties depends. Slavery was such a consensus breaker in the United States, culminating in the Civil War.

Legitimacy

The people's beliefs about the essential rightness of a regime and their
moral obligation to it determine the legitimacy of that political order. These

beliefs, in turn, relate to the degree in which the government, its personnel, and its policies reflect cherished political values, as well as to the effectiveness of the system in fulfilling basic needs and expectations.[20] These two components are interdependent: an effective system will become valued, while a valued system will find its effectiveness enhanced. Political parties can affect both the normative and instrumental components of legitimacy.

In some cases, the party claims to be the primary font of legitimacy in the system rather than being subordinated to some "external" source (such as a constitution).[21] Only a dominant party can establish such a claim. Assertion of the claim would most likely come from an ideological party, whose cadres serve as the priesthood charged with the responsibility for interpreting the dogma that justifies the party's position. A communal party can also become the primary source of legitimacy through equating itself with the primordial values it represents. Thus, some nationalist parties have attempted to become synonymous with the idea of the nation. Machines and consensual parties usually do not assert such primacy. They do not incarnate the normative political order; they merely mirror it.

Even when the legitimacy of a political system does not emanate from the political party, other contributions to legitimacy can still be made. Parties, for example, can mobilize and demonstrate mass support for the regime, support that may improve both its instrumental and normative position. Specific groups may be represented in the system through the political parties, and thereby gain an interest in its maintenance. Political parties, assuming they operate in a context of fundamental political agreement, can also aid in the transfer of authority. Without such a basic agreement, support will be mobilized for battle, not for cooperation, interests will be represented at the expense of other groups, and the transfer of authority will become a succession crisis. Under these conditions, the uncivil behavior of the political parties contributes to the decay of a regime's normative appeal and instrumental effectiveness. The result may be that the position of the party system will be seriously challenged or even eliminated by other political organizations, especially the bureaucracy and military.

POLITICAL PARTIES AND THEIR ENEMIES

The power of the political party in the contemporary world does not go uncontested. Even in noncompetitive systems, the ruling party may not be able to establish its authority firmly over other political organizations. In Asia and Africa, many party regimes fell prey to military intervention. In political systems where parties continue to play an important role, their ability to control political authority resources has been significantly constricted.

A party's strength depends mainly on its ability to mobilize support among the politically relevant population of a system (this might be a fairly small percentage of the total population in a country where participation is restricted). In competitive systems this support may be simply demonstrated by the votes received on election day, since this is the way in which the occupancy of certain authority positions is ratified. In noncompetitive systems, the ruling party may be more concerned with frequent demonstrations of support through "right" action, even though maintaining the formality of regular, though uncontested, elections. When popular sovereignty is a potent legitimacy myth, the party's organization of popular support easily translates into control over legitimacy resources. Ideological and primordial parties may also be able to draw on additional legitimacy resources by representing deeply held beliefs and values. Political parties manipulate their primary resources in an attempt to gain control over positions of authority and the other resources controlled by the government. These, in turn, can be used to further increase the popular support for the party, or in other ways consolidate its position.

Three major opponents contest the party's existence and operation, though for rather different reasons. *Traditional elites* oppose political parties because they believe that their established privileges will be threatened by the expansion of participation. Political parties in traditional social settings often undercut existing social structures and change the prevailing power configurations. At times, traditional leaders attempt to adapt party structures to their own purposes, but these essentially elitist organizations cannot compete against more popularly based rivals. They usually succeed only when, through governmental repression, mass participation can be prevented from emerging.

A second source of opposition to party politics comes from the *bureaucratic and managerial elites*, including the military officer corps. These organizations generally place great importance on what they deem efficiency and rationality in the conduct of government operations. Party politics sometimes engenders discord, thereby disturbing the more order-prone administrators. Government bureaucrats may also resent what they view as excessive interference in their affairs by party politicians who implement policies according to criteria of partisan advantage. The expansion of the merit civil service, no matter how justifiable in terms of administrative rationality, eliminates a major building block of political parties: patronage. The growth of administrative prerogatives diminishes the authority resources available to the ruling party or parties. At some point, the military, in alliance with elements of the civilian bureaucracy, may become so frustrated with party politics that they will overthrow the civilian government and proclaim a no-party regime.

A third enemy of political parties is the *populist leader*, even when such a person is allied with a political party. The party, however, often owes its existence to the leader, rather than the reverse, so if the leader is removed, the superficially powerful party vanishes. This was the fate of the Convention People's Party in Ghana after the fall of Nkrumah in 1966. The populist leader accepts the need for mass participation of some sort, but downgrades the role of the party. He desires direct communion with the people, unmediated by any intervening organization. His power depends on his personal popularity rather than on the support organized by an effective apparatus. A consequent decline of party power often occurs in those systems dominated for a time by so-called charismatic leaders. In more technologically advanced systems, the mass media, especially television, may have a similar effect on party viability. A candidate with sufficient funds or talent can utilize the media to bypass the party organization and gain direct access to the voters. Further extension of this trend can seriously limit the political party's primary purpose for existing: to structure participation.

Political parties, therefore, are not the only institutional actors in contemporary politics, or even the most important. Consequently, the next chapters analyze two other political organizations of particular relevance: the government bureaucracy and the military.

Chapter IX Bureaucracy

BUREAUCRACY AND THE STUDY OF POLITICS

The term "bureaucrat" has never occupied a particularly honored position in the political vocabulary of the United States. Certainly the employees of public bureaucracies would choose the more upbeat title of "civil servant" or "administrator." The brilliant pyrotechnics of elected officials and representative bodies often eclipse administrative activities, and bureaucrats usually prefer to work in obscurity. Even reports on the executive branch generally focus on the presidential level rather than penetrating deeply into the day-to-day affairs of the vast national bureaucracy. Yet the actions of large-scale formal organizations, both public and private, increasingly circumscribe the lives of those who live in the United States. Indeed, the preponderance of political acts are probably not legislative or judicial but administrative (though such distinctions blur, for bureaucracies carry out quasi-legislative and quasi-judicial acts). The average citizen comes in contact with members of the ubiquitous public bureaucracies far more often than with his elected representatives, local, state, or national. In this sense, the political process involves even the most apathetic citizen. Since in 1975 the Federal government employed 2.9 million people, and state and local levels an additional 11.5 million, the amount of interaction is not surprising.

Political bureaucracies play an important part in all contemporary national political systems. In France and Italy, these structures provided elements of stability and continuity in the era that followed World War II, offsetting the turmoil in the multiparty national assemblies. The Soviet Union can be reasonably described as ruled by two gigantic, parallel bureaucracies: the Communist Party and the government administration. Some scholars might add a third—the secret police—charged with watching the other two. The operations of bureaucracies are also critically important in the newer states of Asia and Africa. In many instances, the military (a special bureaucracy; see Chapter X) has ousted the political leadership and rules with the assistance of the civilian administrators. In a political environment dominated by bureaucracies, it may become difficult to develop participatory and representative institutions (open political parties, legislative assemblies, and the like).[1]

Even in systems such as the United States, where these more representative bodies continue to carry out significant political tasks, the importance of bureaucratic decision making grows. In part, this tendency is the inevitable consequence of the expansion of government responsibilities which, in turn, enhances the impact of the administering apparatus. The obvious complexity of socioeconomic problems and the programs designed to cope with them also expands the role of the administrator. Policy cannot be specified in any great detail by legislative bodies; rather, fairly broad guidelines are set down, and the administrators of the program are delegated the authority to fill in the blanks. The administrators, in short, take on certain quasi-legislative and quasi-judicial functions. Moreover, some administrators—particularly those engaged in regulatory activities, such as the police—often must select which policies or laws they will execute or enforce, because they cannot implement all of the laws at all times.

Two further consequences result from the complexity of both problems and programs: First, the policy makers become increasingly dependent on expert advice in the formulation of programs. This expert advice commonly comes from the administrative organization(s) responsible for programs in that area. Some observers see this process going so far as to result ultimately in the legislative function being completely taken over by the executive branch. Congress and other representative institutions would serve primarily as overseers of the administration of these programs.[2] But the increasing complexity also implies that the elected representatives will most likely become increasingly dependent on expert advice in evaluating these programs as well. So, whether the elected bodies continue to legislate or simply supervise, their dependency on administrative expertise will grow, perhaps creating a technocratic rather than a democratic system.

Beyond the progressive blurring of the distinction between policy makers and implementors, essentially internal bureaucratic rules and procedures also affect the lives of citizens. As the government touches more daily activities, the average citizen will be confronted more frequently by the necessity to conform with modes of administrative operations: forms to fill, deadlines to meet, organizational environments to interpret. Even the relatively trivial decisions of a low-level clerk may be a source of considerable frustration or benefit.

Analysis of bureaucratic behavior, therefore, is central to an understanding of politics in most national political systems. The preceding observations suggest, however, that bureaucracies are as diverse as the functions of modern government, and the consequences of their activities range from the beneficial to the perverse. In order to provide some guidelines for grappling with this diversity, this chapter summarizes common characteristics of bureaucracies, investigates forms of bureaucratic pathology, and surveys methods for improving their performance.

THE STRUCTURAL CHARACTERISTICS OF BUREAUCRACY

The German sociologist Max Weber profoundly shaped the description of bureaucracy. He believed these organizations to be the epitome of "rational-legal" authority. Although his analysis emphasizes the formal characteristics of bureaucratic organization, it sets forth a useful itemization of some of the common elements of bureaucratic structures.[3]

Formal Traits of a Bureaucracy

1. *Hierarchy*: A bureaucracy is a pyramidal authority structure within which each official occupies a well-defined position in a hierarchy of superior/subordinate relations. Extreme forms of hierarchical organization tend toward centralization, and one person often stands at the apex of the pyramid. Perhaps military organizations most clearly exemplify this structural characteristic. Other bureaucratic organizations may be more decentralized and their authority relations less clearly delineated. Hierarchical organization, nevertheless, remains central to the characterization of a bureaucracy.

2. *Formal Rules*: Formalized rules and regulations define bureaucratic operations. These rules serve three primary purposes: First, they set forth the objective (or objectives) of the organization, thereby directing the activities of the officials toward the accomplishment of certain goals. Although general organizational ends may concern only the higher levels of the bureaucracy, they shape the formal directives addressed to lower levels. Second, the rules differentiate the offices in a bureaucracy, designating their functions and assigning the authority necessary to carry out these tasks. Thus, the rules develop a formal division of labor and assign to each official a reasonably clear-cut sphere of activities. Third, the rules specify the procedures the officials are to follow in carrying out their assigned duties. In brief, these rules help insure continuity in organizational operations and fulfillment of formal goals.

3. *Expertise*: The specified functions associated with each office in a bureaucracy usually assume certain skills on the part of the office holder. For example, secretarial positions necessitate some training and high-level offices

often require extensive education. The organization of expert knowledge enables a bureaucracy to develop and administer complex programs and constitutes a primary source of its power in the political process.

4. *Achievement*: "Achievement" criteria form the basis of hiring and promotion in a bureaucracy; that is, a person must be qualified to fulfill the office to which he is assigned. This requirement obviously follows from the need for expertise. Promotions and appointments based on irrelevant criteria, such as family ties or political loyalties, could result in less competent officials and a subsequent decline in efficiency and effectiveness.* The logical corollary to this formal requirement is the dismissal of incompetent officials. Though maximum utilization of achievement criteria seldom occurs, some minimum standards must be met to guarantee the bureaucracy's survival.

5. *Formal Communications*: The goals, rules, and decisions of a bureaucracy are recorded and preserved. Bureaucracies also gather and systematize the data needed to carry on their operations. This organization of information is another source of bureaucratic power. Additionally, channels of information flow are defined, so that all officials acquire the information they need to carry out their duties. The formal communication system helps maintain the continuity of operations, as well as supply the feedback necessary to evaluate bureaucratic performance.

Informal Traits of a Bureaucracy

The listed elements of formal structure and procedure provide only a partial portrait. Every bureaucracy also contains certain informal structures and processes which can either help or hinder the achievement of formal goals. The informal structures originate in the inability of any rigid specification of patterns of interaction to adequately comprehend either the complexity of the real world or the subjective content suffusing human behavior. Consequently, a bureaucracy also possesses:

1. *An Informal Structure of Authority*: An individual commands authority for reasons beyond the simple occupancy of an official position in a hierarchy. Others may trust and follow him because of his personal qualities and abilities or the power he exercises outside the organization. A person, then, may have influence inside a bureaucracy far in excess of that accorded to his official position. Contrariwise, personal qualities may be such as to

---

Efficiency refers to the cost of operations. One firm is more efficient than another if it produces the same output at less cost or more output at the same cost. *Effectiveness* refers to the degree to which organizational goals are realized. Thus, a bureaucracy may be relatively inefficient, but still be effective, and *vice versa*.

significantly undercut the formal authority of a bureaucratic office.

2. *A System of Informal Processes*: No set of formal rules can anticipate all the situations that even a low-level bureaucrat may confront. Therefore, some room will be left for initiative and personal judgment, and the office holder must develop ways of dealing with situations not covered by the rules. At the adaptive, problem-solving levels of a bureaucracy, this type of latitude is deliberately factored into operations, under the assumption that the officials will attempt to maximize formal goals. In addition to the formal purposes of an organization, however, informal, personal motives also lie behind bureaucratic behavior (the desire for power, money, and so forth).[4]

3. *Informal Criteria for Office Holding*: The performance of a task requires more than the possession of a formal skill. It also involves interpersonal relations. Consequently, a person may be chosen for a particular position for reasons other than, or in addition to, those written down in the job specification. A manager will necessarily evaluate how an individual will "fit into" the interdependent operations of his branch.

4. *An Informal Communications System*: Information in a bureaucracy is transmitted in ways other than formalized reports and memos. Informal channels of communication exist, ranging from "rumor mills" to fairly well-developed personal lines of communication that a bureaucrat may establish to reinforce or crosscut the formal avenues.

At times, informal structures serve to increase the effectiveness and flexibility of a bureaucracy, but they also can subvert the formal goals. Personal authority can be manipulated for individual aggrandizement and may undermine the official hierarchy and lines of responsibility. Discretionary powers can be used for personal gain. Informal job criteria can be used as a cover for prejudice and favoritism and can lead to the appointment of incompetent officials. Informal communications systems can distort information and raise the noise level in a bureaucracy. Consequently, efforts must be made to insure that the informal structures support rather than undercut bureaucratic performance.

THE AMBIGUOUS POTENTIAL OF BUREAUCRACY

Bureaucracies are an important part of a regime's infrastructure, contributing to the accomplishment of a number of essential functions:[5]

1. *Extraction*: In order to develop and implement its programs, a government must have dependable supplies of the necessary resources. Extractive bureaucracies help provide these needed resources, whether men (the Selective Service, the Civil Service), materials (the Internal Revenue Ser-

vice), or information (the Bureau of Labor Statistics, the Central Intelligence Agency).

2. *Regulation*: The complex interdependencies of contemporary socio-political systems require considerable coordination. The regulatory agencies of government help to control the behavior of individuals and groups, thereby minimizing the possibility of serious societal breakdowns. These regulatory agencies include those designed to contain criminal behavior, as well as others that control sectors of the economy in (supposedly) the public interest (examples: the Food and Drug Administration, the Interstate Commerce Commission).

3. *Distribution*: Governments also provide various goods and services to their citizens, and distributive bureaucracies are charged with implementing various allocative programs. As governments adopt more welfare functions, the distributive bureaucracies continue to grow in size and significance (examples: the Department of Health, Education, and Welfare, and the Department of Housing and Urban Development).

4. *Integration*: Through their contributions to the fulfillment of the extractive, regulatory, and distributive functions of a regime, bureaucracies also help the sociopolitical system together through time. Such integration generally requires, beyond this, that some organizations exist to bring about the overall coordination of the bureaucracies engaged in the other three tasks (perhaps a national planning agency) or to defend the system from external threats (the Department of Defense). Even the schools, insofar as they contribute to the development of attitudes supportive of the system, help integrate and perpetuate a sociopolitical order.

Bureaucracies, however, do not necessarily produce such salutary effects, for they can also act as self-serving sectors. Particular bureaucrats or an entire organization may pursue individual or corporate interests that have a detrimental impact on the formal goals defined by the regime, a phenomenon commonly referred to as "goal displacement." A bureaucracy may become disproportionately powerful and place an excessive demand on the government's resources, thereby depriving other operations of needed funds. Finally, bureaucracies can even usurp a political regime altogether and begin to rule in their own right, as would appear to be the case after a number of recent military takeovers. Such potential deviations can be termed bureaucratic pathologies.

BUREAUCRATIC PATHOLOGY

Bureaucratic pathology can be defined as the subversion of the formal objectives of a bureaucracy through the pursuit of subsidiary or even contradictory ends. The concept of pathology in bureaucratic organizations assumes that a bureaucracy has primarily an instrumental value: in other words, that some kind of accomplishment measures its worth. This may be the accomplishment of some externally imposed goal; or it may be the achievement of an internal-operations objective that a superior imposes on his subordinates. (The superior supposedly shapes his objectives according to the strictures of the formal organizational goals.) The organization and its internal operations, therefore, have no inherent value.[6] They are created to serve the clients, whether the general public or the regime. Ironically, the deterioration of beneficial behavior patterns often is the source of a pathological condition, just as necessary cell reproduction running amok causes cancer. The potential for pathology, consequently, is built into the normal structures and procedures of a bureaucracy.

The description of a bureaucracy's behavior as pathological, however, does not constitute a judgment of ultimate good or evil. Such conclusions would necessarily depend on one's evaluation of the formal goals that the pathology undermines. One could wish, for example, that the objectives of Nazi extermination camps had been more effectively sabotaged. Nevertheless, though ultimate value judgments must be reserved, several forms of bureaucratic pathology can be usefully isolated and described:

Rigidity

Bureaucracies, as was noted earlier, operate according to certain explicit, formalized rules. Within limits, these rules produce beneficial results such as continuity of operation, appropriate division of authority, and equality of treatment. Rules, though, are easily ritualized and followed for their own sake; form can triumph over function. This pathological condition may be labeled "rigidity." Overstrict adherence to formal relations and the consequent inability to adapt to a changing environment, the maintenance of meaningless routines, and the punishment of innovative behavior are all symptoms of rigidity.[7]

Rigidity in bureaucratic behavior is most commonly associated with red tape and delays as subordinates, fearful of accepting any responsibility, adhere excessively to rules or pass relatively minor decisions up the chain of command. Since formal rules never anticipate every situation, a well-functioning bureaucracy must be staffed by officials capable of acting on their own initiative to maximize organizational goal attainment. The need to interpret and adapt forms and procedures increases as the environment changes and rules developed for a prior context become obsolete. The failure to adapt or innovate often originates in the desire for security. A bureaucrat is seldom fired for meticulously following regulations, even when these are inappropriate, but failure at innovation carries high risks. Even so, judgmental issues surround bending rules to fit new situations. Excessive initiative on the part of officials can be as disruptive of organizational goals as rigidity is stultifying.

Rigidity also refers to the broader issue of political loyalty. The bureaucratic traditions of the Western democratic states enshrine the value of political neutrality—the concept that a bureaucrat loyally serves the political regime, whether Democratic or Republican, Laborite or Conservative, Social Democratic or Christian Democratic. Whatever the likelihood of this goal being approximated in the rather placid Western systems, it becomes a rather remote possibility in systems affected by more dramatic political change. The Bolesheviks, after seizing power in Russia, confronted a dilemma in which the politically trustworthy cadres were too few and ill-prepared to run the government, and the surviving tsarist bureaucrats were suspect. Consequently, the new regime had to choose between officials who were alternatively Red or expert. The former option could produce an incompetent, loyal bureaucracy, while the latter might increase organizational effectiveness at the cost of political reliability.

A similar problem challenged the newly independent regimes of Asia and Africa when they inherited many officials whose attitudes had been shaped by their experience in the colonial bureaucracy. As in the Soviet Union, the new regimes had to rely on bureaucrats who had not completely adapted to the new order or accepted its values. Just as overconformance to the rules of an organization becomes more serious as the environment for which the rules were designed alters, the problem of general attitudes and loyalties also increases in significance as the regime changes more radically. Fundamentally, then, the impediments to changing deeply ingrained behavior cause rigidity.

Corruption

Officials in government bureaucracies do not perform their functions out of simple public-spiritedness. They are also rewarded with certain material and status incentives. Ideally, the reward system of a bureaucracy should reinforce behavior supportive of organizational goals, but at times these private incentives can become ends in themselves and, thereby, pathological. Corruption in public administration, then, can be simply defined as behavior deviating from the formal purposes of a particular office in consequence of the pursuit of essentially private wealth and status gains.[8] This definition assumes that public role responsibilities can be distinguished from and subverted by such private behavior patterns. This distinction is of relatively recent origin, even in the West. For hundreds of years in many European countries, little difference existed between the state budget and the monarch's personal household budget. Tax collectors commonly kept a portion of the funds they gathered as reimbursement for their services. The sale of state offices supplied a major portion of revenue. Now, presumably, laws set official salaries and other remunerations and regulate the handling of public monies, and public offices no longer go to the highest bidder. Activities previously accepted as commonplace are now defined as corrupt and threatening of organizational goals.

Despite declarations of formal illegality, such actions still occur in many forms:

Favoritism: Officials deviate from the rules in order to benefit friends in various ways.

Nepotism: Officials appoint relatives to office, or reward them in other ways, without regard to their qualifications. (If an organization demands a high degree of internal loyalty, nepotism may actually be a quite effective way of achieving it.)

Speed Money: Officials are bribed to perform duties which they are required to do by law. The term "speed money" refers to the common tactic of deliberately slowing down operations in an attempt to extract an illegal fee from the frustrated client.

Kickbacks: In areas where government funds are being allocated, the official extracts a payment from the client who stands to benefit from the expenditure. For example, contractors might be expected to kick back a portion of payments for their contracts to the officials who awarded them.

Protection: Officials are bribed to "protect" certain illegal activities by not enforcing the relevant laws. Fixing a traffic ticket is a mild form of protection.

Graft: Officials benefit privately from public decisions to which they have privileged access. An official, for example, may purchase land knowing that a proposed highway will raise its value.

Embezzlement: Officials steal state funds or materials.

The seriousness of acts of corruption can range from minor favoritism and petty bribery to the purchase of a city's law-enforcement apparatus by organized crime. The various categories of corruption also overlap with one another; for example, an official may let a contract to a firm owned by a friend or relative. Some analysts argue that, under certain circumstances, corruption may actually be beneficial for the system as a whole. This might be the case in a country where an incompetent government hampers relatively strong and efficient private organizations. Various forms of corruption might then make some space for the more effective institutions to function.[9] In general, though, excessive goal displacement caused by corrupt activities will eventually damage bureaucratic capabilities and undermine legitimacy.

Symbiosis

Literally, "symbiosis" refers to the living together of two dissimilar organisms in a mutually beneficial relationship. In bureaucratic behavior, the concept identifies the tendency for the organizational "solution" to become part of the problem. In many cases, symbiosis takes the form of conflicts between the formal requirements of an office and other roles a bureaucrat may perform outside of his public office. Some conflicts of interest are related to forms of corruption (nepotism, favoritism, and the like), though usually on a more generalized level. For example, some critics have charged that the various government regulatory agencies, like the Federal Communications Commission or the Food and Drug Administration, are manned by persons recruited from and supportive of the industries they are supposed to regulate. When these officials leave government employment, they often return to positions in these industries. Consequently, the regulator and the regulated can form a kind of mutual-benefit association.[10] Nor is this problem confined to the United States. In the Soviet Union, party organs often complain that local party leaders in an industrial firm or administrative branch sometimes join in protective "families" with the management they supposedly watch.[11] Both apparently share an interest in projecting the best possible image of the firm's or agency's performance.

Other forms of symbiosis are more subtle. A bureaucracy, for example, can acquire a vested interest in the continuation of the problem it was created to correct. Basically, officials are naturally reluctant to contemplate the elimination of a task and the consequent irrelevance of the organization on which positions and private ambition depend. Most bureaucracies seldom confront this problem in such stark terms. Many partially avoid the dilemma by being either multifunctional or engaged in controlling an ongoing and essentially insoluble problem (such as national defense). These bureaucracies, however, must still compete for scarce governmental resources and so may be inclined to exaggerate the importance of their operations, while implicitly or explicitly denigrating the activities of competing departments. This form of symbiosis need not imply a purposively dishonest strategy; rather, few bureaucrats can be fully objective in evaluating the requirements of their activities in the context of overall government operations. For this reason, if one segment of the administrative apparatus becomes too powerful, resource allocation can become distorted and other social needs can be neglected as the stronger bureaucracy maximizes its own interests at the expense of the rest of the system. (See the discussion of Imperialism, below).

Inequity

One of the purposes of formalized rules in bureaucratic operations is to insure that similar cases will be treated alike. Inequity occurs when a bureaucracy (or specific officials within it) fails to treat equals equally, where the grounds of equality are defined by the formal rules and/or the requirements for organizational effectiveness.[12] Equity, in this sense, refers not to complete equality but to a kind of equality before the law. Inequity afflicts bureaucracies when essentially irrelevant criteria determine the treatment of either personnel or clients. (These two facets are probably related, for if members of a group are irrelevantly excluded from appointments or promotions within a bureaucracy, they also can expect unfair treatment as clients of that bureaucracy.)

In a limited sense, the various forms of corruption listed above are one source of inequitable treatment. Considerations of private gain on the part of officials clearly lead to unfair treatment of those clients who cannot afford to pay for services which are their right by law. Nepotism discriminates against qualified individuals who fail to meet the irrelevant criterion of a blood tie. Inequity, then, is the other side of the coin of corruption.

Inequity in internal or external bureaucratic operations, however, frequently occurs for reasons other than the desire for private gain. An official may be motivated by certain prejudices which, though of no direct benefit either to him or to his close associates, adversely affect some groups. For example, even after the equal-rights struggles of the past decade, women and members of various minority groups still confront obstacles to their promotion within and fair treatment from certain bureaucracies because of their sexual or racial identities.

Some of the more bitter political conflicts of recent years have been generated by the belief that certain groups dominate the machinery of government and will use it against those excluded from power.[13] In Northern Ireland, many Catholics feel permanently subordinated by a government run by Protestants. The Ibo people of Eastern Nigeria attempted to create the independent state of Biafra because they feared a government controlled by Northern and Western Nigerian groups (Hausa-Fulani and Yoruba). East Pakistan successfully seceded from the Pakistani union after twenty years of frustrated association; one major complaint was that the West Pakistanis controlled the civil and military bureaucracies. Real and perceived inequities, therefore, can do more than limit effectiveness and violate formal rules of treatment; they may precipitate a serious crisis of governmental legitimacy and, ultimately, threaten a system's survival.

Imperialism

Bureaucracies coordinate large numbers of people and material resources in the pursuit of diverse goals. At times, though, organizations may expand in terms of size and diversification beyond the point of efficient and effective goal achievement. Such pathological growth can be called empire building or imperialism. Although imperialism may be motivated by an overt desire for more power (individual or organizational), officials may also be prompted by an exaggerated view of their own or their organization's importance (compare symbiosis). They further can believe that continued expansion is simply a defensive measure against equally predatory competitors.

Pathological growth threatens both bureaucratic effectiveness and the achievement of other societal goals. A number of problems hamper effectiveness. First, when imperialistic drives grip a bureaucracy, the goals of efficiency and effectiveness become secondary to considerations of power and expansion. Second, though no indicators are as clear as are the profit or loss figures of a firm competing in the economic marketplace, one can assume that the phenomenon of diminishing returns will hold for bureaucratic expansion as well—that after some point the additional output brought by the expansion will not offset the cost of producing it. This point, however, may be difficult to establish with respect to noneconomic organizations. Diminishing returns from unrestricted expansion result, in part, from increased costs of coordination and control. The improvement of coordination technology (as by systems of computerized data retrieval and analysis) may enable a given bureaucratic structure to engage in previously "uneconomic" expansion. Even if the growing bureaucracy continues to perform adequately, the expansion can still become pathological if it so distorts the policy-making process that other important functions suffer in consequence of the drain on resources caused by the imperialist bureaucracy. Power, not need, can then dominate the allocative process.

Insubordination

Perhaps the most serious form of bureaucratic pathology occurs when an organization deliberately usurps the authority to which it is formally subordinated. In its early stages, this pathology manifests such symptoms as a proclivity for excessive secrecy and self-protection. As insubordination becomes more extensive, it entails policy sabotage and, finally, supplant-ment, as the presumed bureaucratic servant becomes master.

In a sense, the problem of pathological insubordination underlies the other potential bureaucratic disorders, for it addresses directly the question of control. Generally, the other problems arise from insufficient control. They could be minimized if the political authority had sufficient power to enforce propriety, encourage efficiency, and develop the optimum allocation of resources.

The problem of control, however, is not so simply stated. Two additional complications must be considered. First, the control problem has two phases: the control of subordinates' behavior *within* a bureaucracy and the control of the entire bureaucratic structure by an external political authority. Internal discipline need not imply external subordination, but external control is relatively meaningless with respect to an internally incoherent bureaucracy. The second complicating factor relates to the degree of control exercised, either internally or externally. More control is not necessarily better; indeed, if the controllers are incompetent, it can produce rigidity or even bungling in bureaucratic operations. Within a bureaucracy, a wise superior allows for some initiative on the part of his subordinates; excessive control increases the chances of information overload and the overinvolvement of high-level per-sonnel in minutiae. Excessive control by external political authorities can lead to the harrassment of administrative officials, disruption of internal proce-dures, subversion of standards of operation by political considerations, and a general decline in bureaucratic morale. The political leadership generally lacks the knowledge and skills to intrude into day-to-day administration, even if the political leaders had the time.

Consequently, an appropriate balance must be sought between excessive and deficient control. Figure IX-1 illustrates some of the control problems in various operational contexts. Thus, the information required depends on the level of the organization and the task being performed. A supervisor can have too much or the wrong kind of information, as well as be confronted with a situation in which the necessary data are lacking. Further, relations both within a bureaucracy and between the organization and its political superiors should be characterized by probity and trust, rather than excessive surveil-lance or cover-ups and secrecy. Individual performance should be marked by initiative in accomplishing formal goals, thus avoiding the extremes of rigid-ity or corruption. Consequently, officials should be given the responsibility for decisions in their area, neither being forced to pass all decisions upward for approval nor sabotaging and subverting higher-level policies. In general, too much supervision leads to disruption, while too little increases the risk of usurpation. The appropriate balance contributes to order and effectiveness in bureaucratic operations.

Figure IX-1   Excesses and Defects in the Control of Bureaucracies

Operational Context	Excessive Control	The Golden Mean	Deficient Control
1. Communications Flow	Information Overload	Intelligence	Information Drought
2. Integrity of Operations	Surveillance	Probity	Cover-up
3. Rule Conformance	Rigidity	Initiative	Corruption
4. Decision Making	Overcentralization	Responsibility	Subversion and Sabotage
5. Authority Relations	Disruption	Order	Usurpation

METHODS FOR MINIMIZING BUREAUCRATIC PATHOLOGY

Itemizing the various forms of bureaucratic pathology starkly illuminates the *potential* perversity of bureaucracies. A survey of public administration around the world, however, would reveal relatively few instances of extreme pathological decay, though some abuses exist in every system, in some cases quite extensive ones. Consequently, methods of avoiding or minimizing bureaucratic pathologies deserve some attention.

The problem of keeping the public servant serving the public is a complex one that includes superior/subordinate relations within an organization, as well as the interactions between the bureaucracy and the political authorities. The subsequent discussion focuses primarily on the latter problem.

The relationship between the political authorities and the public bureaucracies is represented in Figure IX-2. Every political system exhibits some concern with strengthening the relations denoted by the solid arrows. First, the political leadership wants to insure that its programs and policies are being faithfully followed by the bureaucracy. Second, they desire effective implementation; that is, that the citizens should receive the desired services or perform the required acts. Even where the "conventional" political leadership has been usurped by a military/bureaucratic regime, the rulers, though bureaucratic in origin, must determine that their wishes are being implemented and that another faction does not emerge to usurp the usurpers.

Most political systems, additionally, allow for avenues of "upward" influence. Even the most autocratic rulers cannot, for example, completely

Figure IX-2   Authority Flows and Public Bureaucracies

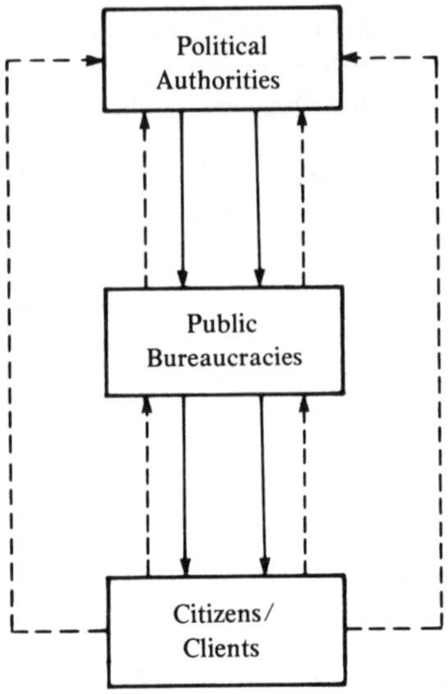

neglect the bureaucrats' claim to expert knowledge. Conceding it, they must accept some bureaucratic input into the policy-making process. The control of knowledge and information, as was noted earlier, sometimes enables the bureaucrats to capture the political leadership without overtly usurping the leaders' position.

In systems of representative democracy, moreover, a citizen presumably maintains some indirect control over the bureaucracy through his direct control of the elected representatives. This statement assumes, of course, that the representatives possess the capacity to exercise control. Some contemporary democratic theorists also emphasize the importance of providing direct citizen access to the bureaucracy, as well as increasing the responsiveness of the elected representatives. Critics note that the benefits of direct access primarily accrue to the economically powerful sectors of society, and these critics assert the need to provide the ordinary citizens with more control over both their representatives and the bureaucracy.[14]

The various strategies devised to promote compliance and effective operations can be analytically divided into structural and attitudinal solutions.

Structural Strategies

Among the structures created to enhance external political control over the bureaucracy are:

1. *Structures to Increase the Intelligence Capabilities of the Elected Authorities*: If the elected authorities have the independent capacity to gather and assess information on a bureaucracy's operations, one major source of bureaucratic power—the control of information—will be counterbalanced. Such intelligence structures help to prevent the capture of the elected authorities by the bureaucracy. In the United States, the General Accounting Office and the Congressional Budget Office exemplify these kinds of structures, as do the professional staffs of various Congressional committees. Often, these units are not sufficiently supported to oversee adequately the huge federal bureaucracy. The Justice Department also carries out investigations of other elements of the federal bureaucracy, providing an alternative source of information to the Chief Executive. Additionally, a growing number of private-citizen groups inquire into administrative activities. Another proposal that could enhance the influence of the average citizen and provide useful information to the overseers of the bureaucracy is to create an independent agency to carry out surveys among the clienteles of various bureaucracies.[15] Such an agency would give the citizen some voice and could supply the political leadership with some information on how the presumed beneficiaries perceive administrative operations.

2. *Structures to Improve the Control Capabilities of the Political Leadership*: Beyond the necessity to gather and assess information is the need to enforce rule conformance and goal attainment. Police and prosecutory administrations carry out this function, along with intelligence gathering. These structures, however, raise the classical political question of who guards the guardians. Often the police are the ones most in need of control. Even when reasonably diligent in accomplishing their mission, moreover, their efforts are essentially negative: They may enforce minimal standards of behavior but do little to encourage maximal performance by the bureaucrats.

Political party cadres, especially in systems dominated by a single party as in the Soviet Union, also contribute to the control capabilities of the political authorities. Unlike the police, the party activists can possibly engender enthusiasm among bureaucrats above and beyond minimal performance levels. Parties, though by necessity bureaucratic, generally operate according to a political calculus of goals and loyalties different from the normal administration; the difference may make them into an effective counterforce. But parties obviously do not automatically perform so beneficially. First, the party members must be dedicated, not simply self-serving opportunists using the party to advance their own careers. Second, they must be sufficiently talented and numerous to parallel and penetrate the entire state bureaucratic structure. In some African political systems, where the party was intended to fulfill this role, necessary numbers of qualified personnel to man both party and government were simply unavailable. Third, as suggested above, excessive intrusion of the party cadres into administrative affairs can be disruptive.

3. *Structures to Improve Citizen Access and Control over Public Bureaucracies*: The structures already mentioned, when effective, primarily benefit the political leadership. One could argue that the citizens in a democracy must have some direct access to and control over the bureaucracy, rather than being forced to rely entirely upon indirect routes through their representatives or upon judicial action. Some encourage the idea of an "ombudsman" system, in which officials independent from a bureaucracy would be given the authority to investigate and redress citizens' complaints about their treatment by administrators.[16] In order to be effective in the context of a large bureaucracy, however, an ombudsman system itself might require a bureaucratic structure.

Citizen review boards constitute another structure for improving citizen control. Such boards, in order to be effective, usually imply another change: the decentralization of administrative services to make them more amenable to community control. These review boards would function as specialized, small-scale, representative bodies, complementing the more generalized structures like Congress and the state legislatures. Not all government services, however, can be decentralized enough to make community control feasible. Among those that might be are education and police services. Local school boards, in effect, already function as avenues of citizen representation, defining policy, hiring top administrators, and investigating parents' complaints. Some activists advocate similar bodies for police affairs, with at least the power to investigate charges of police misconduct. While local school boards are fairly well established, police administrators generally resist instituting similar overseers for their operations. Even teachers (the professional education bureaucrats) have been agitating for more power over school activities and curriculum—power which would usually be taken from the board and its administrative appointees.

If the initial, and reflexive, objections to nonprofessional interference can be overcome, a major political issue still remains: Who is the community? Minorities often feel excluded from adequate representation in bodies ranging from the school board to the United States Congress. Election by majority vote assures this exclusion. Election on the basis of a quota system, through which significant minorities would be guaranteed a minimum representation, leads to the question of who constitutes a "significant group" and may stimulate objections from the majority coalition. Moreover, decentralization down to the level of effective community control of essential services raises obvious problems of coordination and efficiency. The tension between public access and administrative effectiveness, then, is not easily resolved.

4. *Simplification and Automation of Administrative Operations*: Many of the pathologies appear related to the degree of discretionary power given to

the individual administrator and the complexity of bureaucratic operations. If they are, then the simplification and/or automation of bureaucratic procedures could lead to increased effectiveness. For example, police efforts to curb so-called victimless crimes (such as prostitution, gambling, and drug use, though not drug sale) not only take them away from more essential activities, but also contribute to corruption. A realistic reform of criminal law, therefore, might improve police performance. On a grander scale, the bureaucratic mess of the welfare system could be eliminated through a guaranteed minimum income for all citizens. This apparently simple program could be administered through the Internal Revenue Service and could replace a welter of existing programs. This proposal prompts energetic opposition, including that from the bureaucrats whose jobs might be eliminated, but it does exemplify the type of simplification that might be attempted. The monetary controls manipulated by the Federal Reserve Board perhaps illustrate the ideal of a relatively simple instrument with wide-ranging effects on the economy that would require a massive bureaucracy if directly administered.

Proposals for simplification, however, can be deceptive. Bureaucratic rules, as was noted earlier, always have been intended to make operations automatic. Yet rules have proliferated and discretionary authority has been delegated as the rarefied simplicity of the formal programs confronted the complexities of the actual world. All such regularized procedures are based on the assumption that the cases treated by the bureaucracy will be similar. Significant differences must be managed either by making the rules more complex, thus allowing room for individual interpretation, or by committing an injustice through treating unlike cases in an identical fashion. For example, the guaranteed minimum income would have to take into account differences in the cost of living around the country, or else be biased against groups living in certain regions (for instance, New York City). This alternative requires that the program be made more complex.

Attitudinal Strategies

The structural controls and proposals discussed above are meant to be illustrative, not exhaustive. Often they raise new problems along with solving others and are not sufficient to guarantee optimal administrative performance. Ideally, the political authorities desire to have the bureaucrats *naturally* act in an efficient, effective, and loyal fashion, doing so because they have internalized attitudes conducive to high levels of performance. Attitudinal mechanisms for improving performance are not mutually exclusive of structural ones, for the structure within which one works shapes attitudes, though not always in expected ways.

Various means of bringing about attitudinal change include:

1. *Manipulation of the Rewards*: Basically, people internalize behavior patterns for which they have been rewarded. This fundamental proposition of behavioral psychology, though its statement here is oversimplified, identifies an underlying mechanism of behavior change—the manipulation of rewards.[17] This tactic, however, must cope with some difficulties: First, individuals may respond differently to the same rewards; thus, one might readily accept a material inducement while another might view it as an insult. Second, behavior that is viewed as inherently valuable—as its own reward—may prove especially difficult to change. Third, a regime may simply lack the resources to alter effectively the pattern of rewards. Fourth, all the consequences of a particular change are nearly impossible to anticipate. Finally, since qualitative changes in attitudes and behavior are hard to measure, they tend to be neglected for more quantitative standards of performance.

Some of these problems can be illustrated in an area of concern to most students: good teaching. Rewards at large universities (promotion, salary increases, tenure) are primarily given on the basis of success in scholarship. Good teaching, when it occurs, is largely done for its own sake, that is, for the teacher's own sense of satisfaction. Insofar as time spent on teaching or meeting with students cannot be allocated to research and writing, "too great" a concern for students can have a detrimental effect on an instructor's career. Despite student protests and administrative exhortations, there is little incentive for professors to alter their priorities until the basis for rewards changes. When, however, schools make an effort to reward good teaching, another problem develops: Though everyone may agree that good teaching should be rewarded, much less agreement exists as to what constitutes good teaching. As in other bureaucratic contexts, activities that can be quantitatively measured (number of publications) tend to displace more intangible and subjective standards of performance.[18]

Despite such complications, every regime relies on a reward mix of some sort—wealth, status, ideological values—to encourage the desired behavior. How well it utilizes the resources at its disposal will be a large determinant of whether bureaucrats act in furtherance of the public interest.[19] Perhaps the optimal solution, from the perspective of the political authorities, would be to have administrators who act effectively and loyally, not because they desire some external reward, but because they wish to be loyal and effective. These selfless public servants are difficult to produce, as is indicated by the corruption and waste that characterize so many bureaucratic organizations.

2. *Changing of Role Definitions*: A bureaucrat's definition of his role in a organization partially shapes his behavior. Consequently, those directing government administration attempt to shape that definition in a way that will maximize performance. A basic problem arises when the bureaucracy changes and takes on new functions but individual officials fail to adapt. Thus, some

bureaucrats in Asia and Africa, initially trained to function in the law-and-order orientation of colonial bureaucracies, found the activist, development-oriented policies of the new independence regimes alien. Their original role definitions were no longer compatible with the new administrative functions. Comparably, in the United States, a policeman can no longer be simply "a badge and a gun," but also must be a criminal psychologist, lawyer, social worker, and expert in community relations.

Simply altering the pattern of rewards may change role definitions and develop new perspectives. Training and retraining programs can provide needed skills. Educational programs may be particularly useful when the desired changes are relatively limited and technical. More drastic shifts in social and political goals may necessitate altering predispositions and prejudices that extend beyond an official's role in a bureaucracy.

3. *Consciousness-Expanding Programs*: Significant retooling of bureaucratic minds requires more dramatic efforts than normal training programs. These efforts, such as sensitivity training and encounter-group therapy, generally aim to reduce prejudices and increase the official's empathy for those with whom he deals. Therapeutic sessions of this sort have been used to break down racial stereotypes and improve relations between officials and black communities in the United States.

On a more expansive level were the forced role reversals of the Chinese Cultural Revolution, when factory managers were forced to work on the assembly line and government officials were sent to the fields. These were intended to break down the status barriers between superior and inferior and to create in the more privileged leaders a better understanding of the position of the masses. A similar mechanism is at work when a criminal-court judge puts himself in jail for a week or when welfare officials try to live on a welfare check for a month. These reversals help expand the consciousness of the bureaucrats, and though tried relatively infrequently, deserve serious consideration.

The democratizing implications of attitudinal changes clearly depend on the content of the change. Increasing an official's understanding and sympathy for his client's position would probably give the client more influence over the administrative process. Just retraining the bureaucrat to more effectively carry out his job need have no such consequences; such programs could simply make him a keener instrument of an autocratic political leadership.

The discussion of methods for containing the pathological potential of public bureaucracies is not exhaustive. The impact of interest groups on bureaucratic operations has been barely mentioned. The effect of political socialization on the general citizenry and specifically on those who become civil servants has not been discussed, though the political learning process will be analyzed in Chapter XI. Moreover, the analytical distinction between structural and attitudinal "solutions" is somewhat artificial, for in practice, they cannot be so easily distinguished. Structural change helps create new attitudes, and attitudes not structurally supported will probably decay rapidly.

This chapter investigated why bureaucracies are useful instruments to a political regime and how they can turn on their wielder and subvert the ruler's purposes. The implication has generally been that such subversion is "bad" and that ways of preventing it should be sought. Such conclusions, as noted above, must ultimately rest on the value placed on the activities pursued by the political authorities.

Chapter X   The Military: A Very Special Bureaucracy

Politics, Thomas Hobbes remarked three hundred years ago, is like a game of cards in which the players must reach an agreement on which suit is trump. Failing to come to a consensus means that "clubs" become trump.[1] In contemporary systems, the armed forces control most of the clubs. When rival political factions are unable to establish the rules for the game of politics, the military often becomes the final arbiter of their conflict. Consequently, though military organizations share many characteristics with the civilian bureaucracies, the decisive role they play in the politics of many states earns them special attention.

Like other public bureaucracies, the military is commonly seen as an instrument of ruling groups external to it. It can make substantial contributions to the survival of a political order, but like other bureaucratic instruments, it can also subvert or even replace the external governors. Both the positive functions and the negative potential need to be examined. Beyond these, the levels and causes of military intervention into civilian politics deserve investigation, as does the compatibility of military values and institutions with democracy. These and other issues are probed in this chapter.

A NEEDED INSTRUMENT . . . AND ITS LIMITS

Every regime finds the military a necessary instrument of rule, for reasons both directly concerned with as well as only loosely related to the military's control of physical-coercion resources. Even assuming the military is not behaving pathologically, however, its contributions are still limited and somewhat ambiguous. Nevertheless, the positive functions of the military in society and polity should not be underestimated.[2]

1. *Defend against External Enemies*: The military is primarily justified as a means of defending the state from external attack. While true to an extent, this somewhat pious declaration should not obscure the use of the military as an instrument of national aggrandizement. After all, if some countries did not use the military aggressively, others would not need it for defense. The military in carrying out its national-defense obligations may influence the regime to adopt a "militaristic" and belligerent position *vis-à-vis* its neighbors. An equally cogent case, however, can be made that the military leadership, though constantly emphasizing the need for preparedness, usually wishes to avoid actual warfare, which only consumes the carefully marshalled men and equipment. Some countries, of course, face no identifiable external enemies, yet still maintain armed forces. To do this need not be a case of extravagant expenditure, for the military can also perform useful tasks in the domestic sphere.

2. *Preserve Internal Unity*: When all else fails, the military can hold a country together by force. Naturally, the consequences of this last resort are not pleasant to contemplate, but most regimes will accept the cost and forcibly resist dismemberment or revolution. The ability of the armed forces to preserve national unity depends on the extent to which they are insulated from the conflicts afflicting the society. If the military reflects social cleavages, then its injection into the conflict merely escalates the level of destructiveness. The military, itself, can split and bring on a condition of internal war, as was the case in both the American and Nigerian civil wars.

3. *Symbolize National Independence*: The armed forces can also be used to symbolize national independence and purpose. Control over the military was the last symbol relinquished by the European powers as they granted independence to their colonial wards. The armed forces, moreover, provide a major element in the pageantry of the modern state. But military symbols of political ideals, though significant, cannot fully replace more profoundly relevant myths of legitimacy and norms of political behavior. In any case, the efficacy of the military as a symbol of national unity depends on the perceptions of the people. If the armed forces are believed to be dominated by one subnational group at the expense of others, they will come to represent division and oppression rather than unity. In East Pakistan (now Bangladesh), the West Pakistanis dominated the garrison army and local citizens viewed it more as an occupying force than as a source of national pride.

4. *Train Citizens*: Military training does more than simply forge a fighting machine; it also provides an avenue for citizenship training. The very fact that people are inducted into military service means they confront an institution that exposes them to a larger political identification. One justification for universal military service for both men and women is that it dramatically emphasizes the obligations of all citizens to the national political order.

Furthermore, training usually includes a measure of political socialization, as the recruits are taught about the purposes of the state and presumably learn to identify with its objectives. Aside from training, a provincial recruit may become somewhat more cosmopolitan in his judgments of others simply through associating with people from all over the country.

These consequences, however, are neither inevitable nor wholly beneficial. The military, as is noted above, might be under the control of one sectional interest, which would reinforce subnational rather than national identities. The specifically political indoctrination included in training is often jingoistic and chauvinistic. It prepares the soldier to be more of a *subject* than an active political *participant* (see Chapter XI). The stress placed on rank, deferential attitudes, and highly structured behavior may make the military experience irrelevant for more fluid civilian political and social roles.

5. *Provide Job Training*: Military experience can improve the veterans' ability to participate in modern economic activities. First, certain values which enhance performance may be imparted, such as self-discipline, evaluation of others on the basis of achievement, and relation to others according to the specific requirements of the task to be performed rather than incidental characteristics. Military service can also teach basic literacy skills where these are deficient. Finally, modern military operations require more sophisticated tasks than simply following orders and firing a gun. A soldier—man or woman—may receive job training that is applicable to civilian life—a mechanic is a mechanic, whether civilian or military. The soldier may also get training in administrative skills. But these economic spillover effects are limited. Not all military education transfers into the civilian economy. Even when it does, one must still ask whether conventional educational institutions might not be able to give this training less expensively and more effectively.

6. *Support Economic Development*: Military expenditures may be justified as a means to economic development and prosperity. Marxists even argue that a capitalist economy requires war both as a stimulus and as a way of consuming surplus production. Actual warfare, though, can be catastrophic for the economies of both victors and vanquished. Whatever economic benefits flow from military expenditure accrue most rapidly under conditions of constant preparation for war, not of actual conflict. In this case, the defense industry thrives, jobs are provided, and the civilian economy enjoys the secondary benefits of military investments. Military personnel can even be directly used for developmental tasks, like road building.

Unfortunately, the benign economic consequences of large defense expenditure are more apparent than real. First, they assume that a government has a domestic arms industry to support. But only the largest military powers have; most countries must import most of their weapons, thereby diverting foreign-exchange reserves from other needs and subsidizing not their own economies but those of the arms suppliers. Even when domestic producers are available, the economic value of defense expenditure can easily be overestimated. Strictly speaking, the output of the weapons industry has no direct economic value; that is, arms neither produce future wealth, like machine tools and other forms of investment goods, nor improve present well-being, like food, clothing, and other consumer goods. Of course, the secondary economic benefits from the workers' wages and managements' investments are important. From an economic perspective, though, it would be more beneficial to take the money spent on arms and use it for direct consumption or investment. Over the long run, continued military expenditures contribute to inflation, consume scarce resources, and distort economic investment. Military organizations are only marginally engaged in development projects like road building. Most soldiers are, in fact, economically idle. Military investment, therefore, is better justified on political, rather than economic, grounds.

MILITARY ORGANIZATIONS AND BUREAUCRATIC PATHOLOGY

The armed forces, though important to any regime's survival, can also behave pathologically, and often do so with peculiar military twist.[3]

Rigidity

The military, more often than other bureaucracies, is attacked or satirized for its tendency to ritualize rules and regulations. Rigidity is usually demonstrated in the proliferation of red tape, which to some extent afflicts all bureaucratic operations. The military's primary task—the organized application of massive physical coercion—can suffer a deadly result from rigidity, especially in the areas of tactics, strategy, and political loyalties.

Tactical and strategic rigidity can be summed up by the cliché about generals always fighting the last war. At times, this inability to adapt to changing circumstances leads to the repression of innovative thinkers. Both General William Mitchell's advocacy of the importance of air power and Admiral Hyman Rickover's drive for a nuclear navy met considerable opposition. Some scholars argue, however, that the important role of technology in World War II made the defense establishments of most countries more open to technological innovation.[4]

Strategic rigidity can have more serious consequences than technological conservatism. Thus, the French assumption in the 1920's and 1930's that the next European conflict would follow the trench-warfare pattern of World War

I prompted the construction of the world's mightiest trench, the Maginot Line. This defense was easily outflanked by the highly mobile German *Blitzkrieg*. Similarly, the battle experience of World War II left the French (and the Americans) unprepared for the guerrilla insurgency in Vietnam.

Finally, the inertia of bureaucratic operations may hinder military adaptability. One military analyst argues that the Vietnam War lasted so long because:

> Once involved, commitments begot larger commitments, and careers required defense of positions previously taken. The self-interest of many civilian and military bureaucrats coincided, resulting in organizational inertia. For example, military officers in the field had reason to make their reports unrealistically optimistic; as advisors or commanders they were held accountable for what happened in their districts. Future advancement depended on *successful* tours of duty in Vietnam.[5]

Consequently, though civilian bureaucratic rigidity produces frustration and inefficiency, military rigidity can directly cause the loss of thousands of lives.

Rigidity also raises questions of political loyalties, especially in systems that enshrine the principle of civilian supremacy. As with bureaucracy in general, rapid and radical political change will probably strain the military bureaucracy's ability to transfer loyalty from one regime to another. Old, well-established beliefs and expectations may find little support in a revolutionary context. The Chilean military, for example, was ultimately unable to accept the Marxist regime of Salvador Allende. Such inflexible political attitudes then contribute to another pathological disorder: insubordination (see below).

Corruption

Military bureaucracies handle millions (and in some cases, billions) of dollars worth of materials and make allocative decisions that mean the difference between prosperity and bankruptcy for many enterprises. Consequently, extensive opportunities for corruption exist. The pursuit of personal enrichment at the expense of organizational goals seems to increase during wartime. The most recent case of widespread corruption in the United States military occurred during the Vietnam War when large amounts of financial and military aid provided lucrative opportunities for unscrupulous profiteers. Unlike some of the other pathologies, corruption in military organizations does not appear to have a unique military stamp on it.

Symbiosis

The symbiotic pathology takes two major forms in military behavior. The first involves the relations between the weapons manufacturers and the defense establishment, commonly referred to as the "military/industrial complex." Though the phrase arises out of the United States political context, all major military powers probably have similar coalitions. Certainly, the military needs to insure a reliable source of supply. The dependence of defense industries on public budgetary decisions, however, raises the possibility that military allocations may be justified in terms of industry's economic needs rather than the defense requirements of the country. Thus, some critics suggest that the controversial F-111 contract was awarded to General Dynamics because the company was in financial trouble, not because its aircraft design was superior.[6] The movement of high-ranking officers from the military into corporate positions also raises the suspicion that a mutual-benefit association may displace national interest as procurement officers become concerned with future job possibilities.[7]

The economic dependence of the defense industries and the institutional perspective of the military establishment lead, in turn, to a second form of symbiotic pathology, that of a possible vested interest in the problem itself. Thousands of military careers and tens of thousands of defense-related jobs would be threatened by an incontrovertible lessening of the external threats to the nation's security. Consequently, military spokesmen possess a built-in tendency to exaggerate the military needs of the country. In part, this attitude arises because an error in judgment about a potential enemy's intentions and capabilities could be disastrous, wherefore military strategists tend to "hope for the best while planning for the worst." Though such conservatism may be understandable and, within bounds, necessary, the resources of any system are limited. The political leadership must face the difficult problem of evaluating the military's requests in light of the other needs of the society. The weighing of the military's demands is made more difficult by the proclivity of the armed forces to equate their institutional interests with those of the nation-state.

Inequity

Pathological inequity afflicts a bureaucracy when distinctions are made among people according to criteria that are irrelevant to the fulfillment of the formal goals of the organization. Military bureaucracies, like their civilian counterparts, can manifest this pathology in many ways, from the trival to the significant. The problem reaches its most serious proportions when the armed forces are perceived by one segment of the community as essentially the instrument of a rival element. This problem commonly develops in a society riven by serious class or primordial divisions. When the military becomes a mechanism for internal repression rather than external defense, it can contribute to conditions encouraging either civil war or revolution.

Imperialism

The symbiotic pathologies that affect military operations can evolve into a pathological growth syndrome—empire building or imperialism. At some point, the growing size and influence of the armed forces will begin to have a serious negative impact on other social and political institutions and goals. Some scholars fear that the constant threat of war and revolution will encourage the growth of a garrison state in which all other social values come to be sacrificed to the needs of the "specialists on violence."[8] Although this extreme has been approached in only a few countries like Nazi Germany and Stalinist Russia, the potential remains so long as large military establishments demand substantial support from the regime. Excessively powerful military organizations discourage the maintenance of an open political process, distort the direction of economic growth to suit their own material needs, and limit the activities of classes or institutions that might prove to be effective competitors for public monies. Ultimately, an imperialistic military bureaucracy may even overthrow the civilian political regime; this possibility goes from imperialism into the pathology of insubordination.

Insubordination

Military organizations demonstrate insubordination in a very dramatic fashion—the *coup d'état*. This pathology can also occur in a more subtle ways, including insubordination within the military organization, as well as the subversion or elimination of external civilian authority. The latter problem seems to be the more serious. In any case, military intervention into the political process takes many forms short of a *coup*, some of which are a legitimate and necessary part of the civilian political process:[9]

1. *Participation*: The armed forces, both as an organization of skills and expert knowledge and as an advocate of national-security needs, have a rightful role to play in political decision making. Military representatives can appeal to both the minds and the emotions of the civilian leadership in presenting their position, just as do the other participants in the policy process. Two considerations arise with respect to such legitimate involvement. First, the line between acceptable advocacy and unwarranted pressure is not easy to establish. Second, the boundary usually works both ways; that

is, not only should the military's political role be limited, but the civilian leadership also should refrain from excessive interference in the internal operations of the military. Indeed, "political meddling" often provides the military with an excuse to intervene in civilian politics as a defensive reaction (see below).

2. *Sabotage*: The involvement of the military in civilian politics, even when falling short of overt intervention, may be more injurious. Unwilling to openly challenge the policies of their civilian superiors, elements of the officer corps may try to twist them through subversion and sabotage. In its milder forms, sabotage may simply take the shape of an appeal to a higher authority—for example, to another branch of government or to the public. In the United States, the heads of the various service branches have used their connections with sympathetic congressmen in an effort to undermine positions defined by their civilian superiors in the defense department. Soviet Field Marshal Georgi Zhukov, the hero of the battle of Berlin, drew on his popular appeal in an attempt to advance policies opposed by Nikita Khrushchev; he was removed from his position as defense minister. General Douglas MacArthur lost his position as commander of the United Nations forces in Korea for somewhat similar politicking.[10] A more serious form of sabotage develops when officers simply violate policies with which they disagree. General John D. Lavelle's private air war, in opposition to the suspension of bombing of North Vietnam, is a recent example of this type of sabotage.

3. *Pressure*: Disgruntled military commanders may not be satisfied with simply undercutting disagreeable policies after the fact. They may wish to intervene more "positively" to insure their desires will be met. The first method of overt intervention uses implicit and explicit threats to shape government policy. Consequently, though the civilian regime remains in power, it does so only with forbearance of the military, knowing full well that insufficient attentiveness to military interests will probably bring about a *coup d'état*. Military concerns may range from relatively straightforward material demands to quite broad social and political policies. Only a small step separates making such threats from carrying them out. In fact, for the threat to be credible, the power to act on it must be periodically demonstrated.

4. *Interim Rule*: If the military establishment decides that its threats are insufficient to guarantee appropriate civilian behavior, it may be led to still more dramatic intervention. Though reluctant to assume power indefinitely, the military may overthrow the regime, act as an interim caretaker government in an attempt to "clean up" politics, and then turn power back to a "purified" civilian leadership. These interim "purification" regimes have taken power in places as various as Argentina in 1955 and 1962, Turkey in 1960, and Ghana in 1966. Subsequent failure of the new civilian regime to

meet the military's expectations can contribute to the most extreme form of intervention.

5.   *Indefinite Rule*: In many cases, the military junta formed after a *coup* may settle in for an indefinite period of rule, the ruling officers being so suspicious of civilian motives and capabilities that they have no intention of relinquishing power in the foreseeable future. Often the inclination toward indefinite rule takes shape after a disillusioning experience with recivilianization. The military in Burma seized power in 1958, returned it to the civilians in 1960, and came back in 1962 as indefinite rulers. Similar patterns have developed in Ghana and Zaire.

The discussion of the levels of intervention into politics oversimplifies the problem to some degree. The military, for example, need not intervene as a unified entity; any intervention, from sabotage to indefinite rule, may be undertaken by only a faction. In most cases, moreover, the post-*coup* regime is actually a military-civilian coalition, as the talents of the civil service are usually drawn upon for the new order. The new leaders may retain their military character or attempt to civilianize themselves by abandoning their uniforms, adopting a more political stance, and developing broader institutional supports. Some of these complexities can be amplified by reviewing the causes and consequences of military intervention.

THE CAUSES OF MILITARY INTERVENTION[11]

In recent years, the *coup d'état* has become a major means of transferring political power. Such European countries as France, Greece, and Portugal, as well as dozens of Asian, African, and Latin American states, have experienced successful *coups* or attempted *coups* since the 1940's. The record suggests that even those countries where civilians seem in firm command, such as the United States, Great Britain, and the Soviet Union, may not be immune from this form of political violence. The cycle of civilian institutional decay and military intervention has been attributed to a variety of factors. This section develops a framework or model to organize and summarize many of the elements that appear to affect the level of intervention. Although the model focuses primarily on intervention in or against a civilian regime, it also is useful for understanding factional military movements against a ruling junta.

The levels of intervention, as defined above, range from acceptable participation to displacement and extended rule. The level of intervention is determined basically by the interactions among three factors: the intensity of military frustration, the scope of this frustration, and the nonmilitary strength of the civilian institutions. A strong civilian regime may be able to restrict a very frustrated military to vague mutterings and occasional sabotage. Alternatively, a weak regime may be ousted for relatively trivial grievances by a faction of the military. The three interacting determinants of level of intervention now require exploration and analysis.

The intensity of military frustration seems best explained by reference to feelings of relative deprivation; that is, the degree to which the military is denied its expectations, needs, or deserts that it perceives the civilian regime as capable of providing. The scope of frustration refers to the extent to which these feelings of relative deprivation are shared throughout the military structure. The scope of frustration affects the relative force position of the conspirators *vis-à-vis* the regime—the extent to which they control or at least neutralize the major physical coercion resources of the regime (regular military, militia, police). Capability for intervention depends on relative force position and scope of frustration. But nonmilitary power resources also exist, and the civilian regime can draw upon these to offset the superior force position of any potential group of conspirators. These primary and secondary relationships are illustrated in Figure X-1 and elaborated below:

Sources of Military Frustration

Frustrations can mount in three major areas of expectation: professional, material, and sociopolitical.

1. *Expectations Concerning Professional Integrity*: All military organizations possess at least a minimal code of organizational integrity, that is, a conception of their prerogatives and responsibilities. Military men desire to preserve control over their internal affairs. Violation by civilian rulers can stimulate military counteraction. Consensus on where the boundary lies and adherence to it by both sides are important components of continued civilian rule.

Organizational integrity, however, often involves more than internal authority. The military also has a conception of its appropriate role in the political system. The creation of paramilitary formations outside the regular chain of command can be interpreted as challenging this position and can increase the frustration of military personnel. Furthermore, the armed forces may view themselves as political actors in areas beyond normal military concerns. This problem is further examined below.

The professional desires of specific individuals within the military organization can also be frustrated, and the anger produced can be directed both at other members of the organization and at the overarching system of civilian authority. A common cause of individual dissatisfaction arises from the

Figure X-1   The Causes of Military Intervention

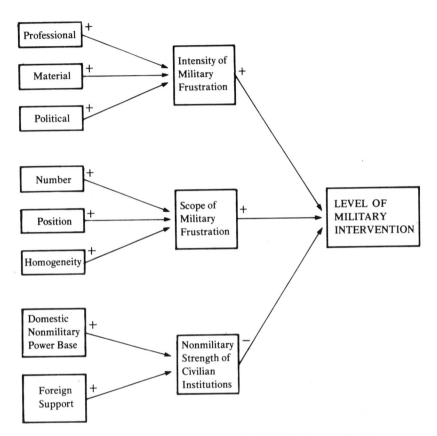

Note: A plus sign (+) denotes positive association; a minus sign (–) denotes a negative one.

contraction of opportunities for promotion. A particularly destabilizing sequence has proceeded in many states that gained their independence since World War II. An initial expansion of the paths of upward mobility, resulting from the withdrawal of the foreign officers and the enlargement of the forces, preceded a leveling off and subsequent decline in the possibilities for advancement. Indigenous senior officers, moreover, often had come from the ranks of the old colonial army and were not as well-trained or educated as many of the newer members of the officer corps. Junior officers, under these conditions, came to feel that their way to the top was blocked by less competent individuals. Consequently, relatively satisfied senior ranks found themselves ousted along with the civilian order by a *coup* of middle- and lower-echelon officers.

2. *Material Expectations*: Of a more concrete nature are the military's expectations concerning their proper share of the economic resources of the state. In a positive sense, these expectations involve the equipment deemed necessary to provide for a respectable force capability, as well as salaries and other benefits. Negatively, the defense establishment may be concerned with the ability of political competitors to increase their share of the economic pie at the expense of the military. As in the case of promotions, a period of increase followed by a relative decline seems to be a particularly frustrating sequence, *if* expectations continue to rise. Expenditures on the military in many newer states expanded rapidly around the time of independence, but then leveled off, contributing to a frequency of *coups* a few years after independence. Though halting short of outright ouster, the military organizations of some countries make it quite clear that failure to provide what they deem appropriate arms may be a cause for more vigorous intervention. Civilian regimes usually respect the threat.

Sometimes military intervention is motivated less by frustration caused by the organization's material position than by the welfare situation of individuals within it. Troop mutinies and other disturbances are frequently provoked by low pay, poor living conditions, or the loss of previously held benefits.

Professional and materialistic motives, though sufficient to cause some interventions, are generally not enough to sustain them over time. An intervention stimulated primarily by material desires is unlikely to form the basis for indefinite rule. These concerns, though, are sometimes coupled with more diffuse military expectations concerning the operations of the whole society.

3. *Sociopolitical Expectations*: Professional expectations, as is suggested above, may include a concept of the role of the armed forces in society, and material desires may affect attitudes toward competitors for economic resources. Apart from immediate military interests, these concerns can easily lead to some generalized expectations about how the political process ought to function. Underlying these expectations is the degree of attachment to the principle of civilian supremacy. The stronger this norm, the more intense other frustrations will have to be to offset the inhibitions against interference.

In addition, a highly developed ethic of military professionalism probably hinders the formulation of a well-articulated system of general social and political beliefs. Ironically, civilian use of the military as a weapon in domestic political struggles erodes professionalism and often serves to coalesce the political opinions of the military. The expectations concerning the appropriate exercise of political authority are commonly related to the military's own operational code of efficiency, order, and national purpose. The free-wheeling and sometimes corrupt style of civilian politics may appear unseemly at best and disastrous at worst. Post-*coup* rationalizations commonly recite a litany of civilian errors, ranging from corruption and waste to threats to national unity.

The military's developmental expectations tend to be rooted in their perceptions of the kinds of economic investment which support a strong military posture. Military professionals usually favor a self-sufficient economy biased toward heavy industry and weapons manufacture. Moreover, they sometimes oppose social changes that mobilize new groups who threaten the military's privileges and resources.

The military's self-image may extend beyond that of guardian of external and internal security. The role of protector of the political order can evolve into that of ultimate arbiter of political life—a kind of armed supreme court. This tendency can be further complicated by the military's equating its own corporate interests with those of the nation. In short, the military supreme court is inclined to decide constitutional issues in its own favor.

In addition to all other components of frustration, the political ambitions of some individual officers should not be overlooked. Organizational perspectives and frustrations may well be intertwined with a need for personal aggrandizement. Unfortunately, the role of private desire is difficult to assess, for, like other public figures, the leaders of a *coup d'état* disguise these needs with declarations of public spiritedness.

The intensity of frustration, as argued in earlier chapters, depends on the importance or salience of the values, the number of values affected and the size of the gap between expectations and capabilities in these areas (see Chapters V and VII). As frustrations mount, especially if professional frustrations are reinforced by discontent in other areas, the level of military intervention in the political process will increase, other things being constant. "Other things," of course, are seldom constant, and they must now receive some attention.

Scope of Military Frustration

The scope of the feelings of frustration affects the capability for intervention and may have an indirect impact on intensity as well. Three interrelated aspects of the problem of scope need to be considered.

1. *Number Frustrated*: Most simply defined, scope refers to the number or the percentage of the total population who feel deprived. Obviously, frustration may be more or less widely shared. Conditions may be such that only a few isolated elements believe it necessary to intervene; whereas, under other circumstances, discontent may be widespread throughout the military. Estimation of the numbers affected must be rooted in a careful analysis of the

sources of frustration and their differential impact on the armed services. Eliminating the fringe benefits for officers may have little direct impact on the enlisted men, but a general cut in pay will disturb the entire organization. The extent to which certain patterns of civilian behavior frustrate the military depends on how widely contrary norms and values are shared within the armed forces.

The number frustrated influences the relative force position of the conspirators *vis-à-vis* the regime; that is, it affects the likelihood that some elements of the military may rise to defend the civilian order. Widespread discontent need not imply that a sizeable percentage of the armed forces actually participates in the act of intervention; the nonparticipants may assume a stance of "benign neutrality." Also, the fact that discontent is not widespread is not a guarantee against intervention. A small but intensely disaffected faction may be willing to accept high risks in order to eliminate the cause of its dissatisfaction. Whether the faction succeeds depends on factors other than the simple numbers involved.

2. *Position of the Frustrated*: The scope of frustration as measured by numbers may not be particularly significant. Some account must also be taken of the ability to intervene effectively in civilian politics. This capability seems related in part to the position of the conspirators in the organization and in part to the type of intervention contemplated. *Legitimate participation* essentially depends on rank: whether or not a particular officer has the authority to speak for the organization or possesses the credentials to give expert advice. Though policy makers may listen to the complaints of an enlisted man, the major military participants in "normal" politics are officers of the highest rank, like the chiefs of staff.

Even the lowliest private, however, can commit *sabotage*, and widespread discontent in the lower ranks may be demonstrated in this fashion. Again, some account must be taken of rank, for an alienated officer may be in a better position to engage in serious sabotage than the average enlisted man. However, officers at the highest rank may not be effective saboteurs, as they are too closely watched by their civilian superiors. Rather, it is those officers somewhat further down the chain of command and relatively insulated from direct civilian supervision who may be able to disregard the orders of the regime (and, for that matter, their commanders) with relative impunity.

Pressure, too, can arise from all ranks. Widespread frustration among the enlisted men can lead to a mutiny as a means of redressing their grievances. Again, position, as well as numbers, must be considered. The prime determinant of the effectiveness of pressure depends on whether the threat of intervention is credible. Some elements of the armed forces may be better able to make a plausible threat because of their capability for intervention.

The ability to actually *overthrow* the civilian regime hinges on whether the instigators are in a position to control the necessary coercive power resources. At the most general level, the various branches of the armed forces differ with respect to this capability. Both the navy and the air force are under certain obvious difficulties in seizing and holding the geographic centers of political authority. Both of these branches can threaten damage—warships and airplanes can shell or bomb presidents' palaces—but they cannot easily translate this ability to damage into any ability to control. Not surprisingly, therefore, the army, because of its capacity to occupy land, plays the major role in most *coups d'état*. If the civilian leaders could choose how to distribute discontent among the three services, they would be wise to allocate the greatest share to the less dangerous branches. This motivation, in fact, may lie behind the division of the military budget in some countries: if the regime lacks the resources to keep everybody happy, it concentrates on those in the best position to overthrow the government.

The military need not act as a cohesive body in overthrowing a regime; indeed, a few armored units are often all that is required for the initial seizure of power (consolidation, though, depends on acceptance by the noncommitted sectors of the armed forces). Some individuals, then, may be in a better position to plan and carry out a *coup*. Officers controlling units near the capital city can more easily act on their discontent than those stationed in more remote areas, as can commanders of attack units in contrast with those less involved with the direct control of weapons.

Some speculation also centers around the ranks of colonel and major, which seem prominent in many military overthrows. Generals may be too isolated from the men on the line to be able to organize an attack, and those below the rank of major may not control enough troops to succeed in their attempt. Though these considerations are not without value, the lowest rank for successful intervention of this type depends on the level of force necessary to overthrow the regime—regiment, platoon, even squad. Noncommissioned officers overthrew an unpopular military regime in Sierra Leone, and two lieutenants nearly accomplished the same objective in Ghana.

The ability of the conspirators to influence others, the access they have to the weapons of the military, and their relative proximity to the centers of political power, all influence their capability to intervene. Therefore, the frustration of those who occupy strategic positions in the military hierarchy has an impact on the quality of the scope of discontent and, thereby, on the likelihood and level of intervention. Since no necessary reason exists why all the elements of the armed forces should be equally frustrated (or content) at any given time, a skillful regime may be able to balance one sector off against another. This tactic raises the problem of military unity or homogeneity, the third, and most complex, aspect of the scope problem.

3. *The Degree of Homogeneity*: Disunity in the armed forces has a complicated impact. The greater the homogeneity, the greater the chances that the military will respond to frustration as a coherent organization. Heterogeneity, on the other hand, can lead to the compartmentalization of discontent. Disunity among the military enables the civilian leadership to play factions against one another and maintain the allegiance of some elements in the hope of counterbalancing the coercive power of the discontented. These tactics, though possibly effective, run a grave risk: Favoritism aggravates the frustration of the deprived sectors, and the gains in terms of limited scope may be lost through the increased intensity of the deprivation felt by those who are excluded.

No military organization is completely unified. Cleavages occur along a number of lines: hierarchical, functional, political, and cultural (or primordial). Conflicts among the ranks, or hierarchical cleavages, are not easily manipulated by the regime. Senior officers, often promoted by the political leadership, may be quite loyal, but such advancements may only further alienate junior officers in a position to attack the government. Alternatively, regular soldiers loyal to a populist regime may refuse to follow the orders of their interventionist officers.

The functional rivalries among or within the branches may be more easily manipulated. The regime, as noted earlier, may try to secure the loyalty of one branch and hope that its loyalty will be sufficient to discourage the others from political adventurism. Some leaders have attempted to reduce the coercive power position of the regular military through the creation of special units, "people's militia," or paramilitary police forces. The organization of such irregular forces, however, could trigger a *coup*, as the action both further exasperates the military and provides an incentive to act before the counterbalancing force becomes too powerful.

Hierarchical and functional conflicts are, to some extent, inevitable, but political and cultural ones are generally discouraged because they can seriously hamper the effectiveness of the military organization. The pursuit of a politically or culturally homogeneous military in a divided society, however, may be a source of considerable discontent if certain segments of the population come to see the military as the tool of the dominant group. Trying to achieve ethnic balance can be equally destabilizing. Granted, a civilian leader may be able to rely on the support of one cultural faction, but the appearance of this type of alliance can further strain the loyalty of the other factions. Political alliances, in which the civilian regime allies with and supports those elements that appear to share its ideological identifications, can have the same ambiguous effect. Finally, if one cultural or political faction overthrows the government, the chances of a counter *coup* by another become quite great.

Nonmilitary Power Resources of the Civilian Regime

Physical coercion may be the power resource of last resort, but others exist which the regime may control to offset the superior force position of the military, regardless of the intensity and scope of frustration. The level of intervention is determined both by the strength of the attackers and the weakness of the regime. Even fairly intense military discontent can be contained if the leadership controls a sufficient power base apart from the military. If it lacks a well-developed domestic power base, a regime can be bolstered by foreign support.

1. *Domestic Nonmilitary Power Base*: Military intervention need not be enthusiastically supported by the general citizenry to succeed; civilian apathy and resignation are probably sufficient. Insofar as the civilian order is *actively* supported by the populace, militarism encounters a hostile response. As the citizens' alienation increases, however, they become more sympathetic to the elimination of the old regime. If there are extensive divisions among the governing elites, these diminish the capacity of the regime to defend itself from excessive penetration or overthrow. Factionalism within the government can develop along the same lines as that in the military: functional (for example, bureaucratic vs. political elites), political, and cultural. These cleavages can set one elite faction against the others, and even encourage them to seek out allies in the military. This course of events increases the destructiveness of domestic conflict. Only a united elite, moreover, can successfully manipulate divisions in the military.

The nonmilitary resource position of the regime largely determines its ability to minimize or deflect citizen frustration and maintain internal unity. Primary among these alternative resources is the control of the myths and symbols of political legitimacy. Continued frustration will eventually erode the value of this resource, but some time may be bought through its use. Both military and civilian discontent can be countered if the regime can retain this fundamental mantle of legitimacy. But the civilian leadership is placed in an especially precarious position if the military happens to have partial command of legitimacy resources, as when the armed forces plays a critical role in the formation of the nation-state through a war of national liberation.

Economic resources provide a second source of nonmilitary strength. An expanding economy can reduce the material deprivation of both the military and the civilian sectors. Other types of frustration may also be diminished. For example, people may become more willing to tolerate government inefficiency and corruption if enough wealth exists to spread around. A country beset with economic problems, by contrast, appears more susceptible to military intervention.

Information resources also enable the regime to structure public opinion and, more importantly, penetrate into the conspiratorial activities of dissident military groups.

A major nonmilitary resource lies in the organizational capabilities of the regime. The bureaucracy, as discussed in the previous chapter, sometimes is an unreliable instrument of the political leadership. A large, disciplined, and loyal political party, however, can do much to shore up a government pursuing unpopular policies. The ouster of some single-party regimes in Africa (Ghana, 1966; Mali, 1968) reveals that in some cases the party is no more than a paper structure unable to resist the intrusion of the military.

2. *Foreign Support*: A regime lacking in domestic power resources may still be able to resist significant military intervention. Foreign support can make up a deficit in a number of areas. Foreign military aid can reduce the frustration caused by the regime's inability to equip the military in a satisfying fashion. Economic aid can support an ailing economy. In a crisis, foreign military intervention can prop up a threatened civilian order. Usually assistance of this sort has been associated with the suppression of guerrilla insurgencies, but, at times, external patrons have preserved a regime from its own military. Examples include British assistance to Tanganyika (now Tanzania) to suppress a troop mutiny and French intervention to quell an attempted *coup* in Gabon, both in 1964.

Foreign support, of course, need not flow only to the regime in power. Covert assistance may be directly or indirectly given to the military conspirators by an interested foreign power. Since World War II, both the United States and the Soviet Union have been implicated in this kind of attempt to subvert the viability of established governments. Merely signaling that the current regime is in disfavor is sometimes sufficient to undermine the power position of the incumbent political leadership and encourage those considering intervention.

A CASE STUDY OF INTERVENTION: GHANA 1966

The utility of this framework for analyzing the factors affecting the level of military intervention would be best demonstrated through systematic, cross-national comparisons of a wide sample of cases. Although such an extensive study cannot be undertaken in this context, a brief examination of the background of one *coup d'état* can illustrate some of the relationships identified by the model.

Ghana, under the leadership of Kwame Nkrumah and the Convention People's Party (C.P.P.), gained independence in 1957. At first, the civilian regime appeared strong: the economy was prospering, the C.P.P. was the dominant political party, and Nkrumah, as the leader of the national independence movement, possessed considerable popular appeal. Yet nine years later, while journeying abroad, Nkrumah was ousted from power and the vaunted political organization of the C.P.P. withered overnight. Why did the military intervene, and why was the Nkrumah regime unable to resist this intervention?

Military Frustration

Elements of the officier corps had become increasingly dissatisfied with Nkrumah's rule, especially after 1960 when the regime became more authoritarian. With respect to professional status, these frustrations arose from Nkrumah's tendency to interfere in what many officers believed to be the purely internal affairs of the military. He attempted to balance off divergent tribal interests, bypass formal lines of communication, and infiltrate the army with security police. He also sent a large group of officers to be trained in the Soviet Union, a move that raised the suspicions of those who received their training from the British. Perhaps most important, he tried to set up a militia to counterbalance the regular armed forces. In time, the leaders of the *coup* (a colonel and a major) expressed suspicion of the top-level commanders whom Nkrumah appointed.[12]

With respect to material standing, the armed forces suffered from the pattern followed in many newly independent countries: an initial expansion was followed by a relative decline (see Table X-1). The spending on defense and foreign relations peaked in 1961-1962 when about 12 percent of total expenditures were devoted to this area. In the next year, the relative share of this sector fell. After the 1966 *coup*, this decline was sharply reversed. In fact, one general justified the high level of expenditure on the military because "owing to the neglect of our armed forces in the past, it has become imperative to re-equip the entire army to make it justify its existence."[13]

A major factor inhibiting intervention was the fact that the British-trained officers had been introduced to the Anglo-American code of civilian supremacy and apolitical military professionalism. Such norms are not easily transplanted from one culture to another, however, and whatever strength they once had was eroded by Nkrumah's injection of the army into domestic political battles with his enemies. Moreover, many officers became disgusted with the growing corruption and authoritarianism of the civilian regime, as well as its apparent mismanagement of the Ghanaian economy.

Scope of Military Frustration

The degree to which the entire Ghanaian officer corps shared the frustrations outlined above is difficult to assess directly. The *coup* itself was

Table X-1　Spending on Defense and Foreign Relations
as Percent of Adjusted Total Expenditure*

Year	Percent
1955-56	3.4
1956-57	5.6
1957-58	7.4
1958-59	7.0
1959-60	7.8
1960-61	11.2
1961-62	12.0
1962-63	10.0
1963-64	9.7
1965	10.4
1966-67	11.2
1967-68	14.3

*Based on: Peter C. Sederberg, "National Expenditure as an Indicator of Political Change in Ghana," *The Journal of the Developing Areas*, 7 (October 1972), pp. 48-49.

Note: Absolute levels of expenditure continued to rise, but much of this increase was negated by the rate of inflation. Also, percentage shares indicate how the military was faring in competition with its competitors in the government or a portion of public monies.

engineered by middle-level officers who moved their forces from the northern part of the country to the capital city, Accra, under the guise of a practice maneuver. Most of the other elements of the armed forces and the police supported the conspirators after the initial blow appeared successful.

Nkrumah did try to divide the military in an effort to break up its monopoly of coercive resources. His program to create a militia had proceeded only far enough to irritate, but not to counterbalance, the conventional military forces. His Soviet-trained presidential guard resisted the *coup*, but lacked the power to defeat it. As an "after-the-fact" judgment, it is obvious that the scope of the discontent was widespread enough to guarantee the success of the intervention, though this should not be construed as evidence that all of the military supported the *coup* with equal enthusiasm.

The Nonmilitary Strength of the Nkrumah Regime

Nkrumah would not have been overthrown had it not been for the weakness of his base of political support. Among the factors that contributed to this weakness were:

1. *The Decline of Nkrumah's Personal Appeal*: Nkrumah's popularity has been largely based on his role in winning independence for Ghana. After 1957, the potency of nationalist appeals declined, and the politically relevant groups in Ghana became more concerned with the distribution of power resources among themselves rather than between them and Great Britain. Nkrumah's effort to substitute the ideals of socialism and pan-Africanism for the decaying symbols of nationalism failed to generate much domestic enthusiasm.

2. *Economic Weakness*: The Ghanaian economy was seemingly on the verge of collapse. The real growth rate was nil, inflation was rampant, and many consumer goods were in short supply. Moreover, the economy was further encumbered by profligate government spending, inefficient state-owned industries, and a growing foreign debt.

3. *Repression*: Another factor was the increasing authoritarianism of the Nkrumah regime. Opposition political parties were proscribed and many opposition leaders were either in prison or forced into exile.

4. *Corruption*: The corruption of the regime alienated the general public, as well as many military men. The ostentatiously displayed wealth of those in favor with the regime further narrowed Nkrumah's base of support.

5. *Political Neglect*: The C.P.P., which had been a fairly effective organization in competing with the British in the 1950's, was allowed by Nkrumah to waste away in later years. In part, this neglect was the result of his preoccupation with the affairs of government. In addition, since the party's dominant position was guaranteed by law after 1960, it faced no opposition to generate internal vitality and consequently grew flacid.

The foreign supporters of Nkrumah's regime were not able to compensate for its internal problems. Although he enjoyed friendly relations with the Soviet Union and other communist countries, the value of these was canceled by the hostility of the United States government. Increases in Soviet aid were negated by a decline in Western assistance, and, in any case, aid programs were mismanaged. If anything, the ties with the Soviet Union increased the fears of conservative elements within the military. Immediately after Nkrumah's fall, the United States gave economic aid and recognition to the new military regime.

THE CONSEQUENCES OF MILITARY RULE

To oust a decaying regime is relatively easy; to create a viable political order is considerably more difficult. Military training, which emphasizes the organization and utilization of physical coercion, is ideally suited for a quick blow against the state. Unfortunately, the training is much less relevant to the complex tasks of governance faced after the initial triumph. In most cases, the problems encountered by the new military rulers are precisely the ones which contributed to the intervention in the first place. Indeed, the military's reputation for honesty and efficiency may be rapidly tarnished after its leaders confront the problems and temptations that led to the downfall of their predecessors.[15]

Military elites often favor a sanitized, apolitical form of politics, imposing order rather than engaging in the more demanding tasks of bargaining and conflict management.[16] Though the imposition of order may be welcome after a period of decay, it is not a sufficient condition for institution building. The desire for stability undisturbed by partisan politics usually means that military regimes stunt the development of participant and representative political institutions. The common pattern followed after a successful *coup* includes the prohibition of all party activity and the severe restriction, if not complete abandonment, of the responsibilities of legislative assemblies. If the new leaders intend to serve only as an interim government, they may lift the ban on civilian political activity, but only so long as it conforms with new rules and regulations. A junta which settles in for an indefinite rule may attempt to sponsor the growth of supportive participant institutions, but such regime parties often remain only vehicles for the mobilization of mass affirmation.

The military also suffers certain liabilities in the area of policy definition and implementation. As was argued earlier, military intervention is often prompted by relatively narrow professional or material concerns. Under these circumstances, the new rulers are unlikely to have a well-conceived, positive program for the country (beyond, of course, improving the conditions of the military).[17] Consequently, the period of military rule may resemble a holding pattern in which no new social or economic initiatives are undertaken. Sometimes, military perceptions of civilian autocracy, corruption, and incompetence motivate takeovers. Even these broader concerns remain largely negative; the conspirators merely wish to eliminate what they see as reprehensible practices, but possess no objectives to guide their actions beyond this point. Admittedly, some officers hold, or develop after the fact, specific ideas on the direction the country should follow, but even these tend to have a technocratic bias.

Whether or not the ruling junta sets forth a positive program of development, the military generally lacks the skills to carry out day-to-day administration, much less initiate significant new projects. The limitations on the military's administrative capabilities commonly lead to *de facto* alliances with top civilian bureaucrats, even though the bureaucracy may be partly responsible for the conditions that contributed to the *coup* in the first place. Bureaucratic personnel may find the organizational perspective of their nominal military superiors quite compatible with their own. Military ministers, moreover, may be more easily captured by bureaucratic expertise than were the preceding civilian politicians.

Ironically, the fact of intervention makes both the continuation of the new military regime and the reestablishment of civilian politics very problematic. The limited political and administrative skills of the military regime are not always sufficient to cope with the problems that contributed to the decline of their civilian predecessors. Moreover, the successful *coup* establishes a precedent that encourages other discontented and ambitious officers to try their luck (some observers also argue that a similar contagion can spread from one country to another). A cycle of *coup* and counter-*coup* becomes probable when the ruling junta represents only one faction of the military.

Recivilianization also meets certain obstacles, though a frustrated military regime may welcome the opportunity to relinquish power. Some military men, however, discover they enjoy the exercise of power and forget their promises to return to civilian politics. In any case, they may fear reprisals from the reinstated civilian groups who lost because of the *coup*. And above all, they may believe the civilian politicians will simply resume their bad habits if returned to power. Even if the military withdraws despite all these objections, the example has been set and the threat of future *coups* remains— the intervention level shrinks only to that of pressure.

Occasionally, a talented and politically skillful leader, who happens to be an officer, may use the armed forces as a vehicle to power. Such men, like Ataturk or Nasser, tend to send the military back to the barracks and are better able to make the shift to more diffuse political roles. The attempt of a military ruler to civilianize himself often leads to a concern with the creation of a political base independent of the armed forces. Because the leader is already in power, the process of institution building tends to be from the top down. Consequently, the last stage, if it gets that far, is the extension of institutional roots into the populace at large. Often these efforts remain essentially elitist affairs, with no real penetration into society. The process is the reverse when a political leader tries to build an organization with which to gain power, in that the roots of popular support are established first. The military *cum* political leader does not face insurmountable barriers in institution building, but the most important stage is also the most remote. Failure to create or reinvigorate civilian institutions probably means that subsequent succession to top authority positions will be determined by the military.

Ghana illustrates most of these tendencies. After the fall of Nkrumah, the new military junta immediately allied with the higher-level bureaucrats in order to administer the state. The policies followed were generally conservative, designed to correct the excesses of the Nkrumah years rather than to make any major developmental initiatives. Although slow but steady progress was made toward returning power to a civilian regime, it was a political process purged of the supporters of the old order. The reintroduction of civilian rule in 1969 proved to be only an interlude, for in 1971 another *coup* occurred. These latest military rulers settled in for what appears to be a period of indefinite rule.

MILITARY ORGANIZATION AND DEMOCRATIC POLITICS

The armed forces pose a problem for every civilian regime, and even for a military junta. They occupy a particularly ambiguous position in a democratic political system. Obviously, no existing government is a perfectly representative democracy, much less a pure one (see Chapter V), but a number do enshrine general principles of popular participation and political and personal freedom. The extent to which these rather diffuse principles are realized in practice affects the level of tension existing between the political order and the military organizations. This problem can be examined by isolating the values typically espoused by the military professional and investigating some of the difficulties encountered in establishing a defense organization compatible with democratic ideals.

Values

Samuel Huntington, in an eloquent section concluding his major study of civil/military relations, contrasts the worst of American individualistic pluralism with the purest embodiment of the military spirit:

Just south of the United States Military Academy at West Point is the village of Highland Falls. Main Street of Highland Falls is familiar to everyone: the First National Bank with venetian blinds, real estate and insurance offices, yellow homes with frilly victorian porticos, barber shops and wooden churches—the tiresome monotony and the incredible variety and discordancy of small town commercialism. The buildings form no part of a whole: they are simply a motley, disconnected collection of frames coincidentally adjoining each other, lacking common unity or purpose. On the military reservation the other side of South Gate, however, exists a different world. There is ordered serenity. The parts do not exist on their own, but accept their subordination to the whole. Beauty and utility are merged in gray stone. Neat lawns surround compact, trim homes, each identified by the name and rank of its occupant. The buildings stand in fixed relation to each other, part of an overall plan, their character and station symbolizing their contributions, stone and brick for the senior officers, wood for the lower ranks. The post is suffused with the rhythm and harmony which come when collective will supplants individual whim. West Point is a community of structured purpose, one in which the behavior of men is governed by a code, the product of generations. There is little room for presumption and individualism. The unity of community incites no man to be more than he is. In order is found peace; in discipline, fulfillment; in community, security.[18]

All efforts to portray "typical" characteristics tend to oversimplify—no real person conforms exactly to the postulated traits. Nevertheless, Huntington's evocation suggests several major elements of the professional military ethic:[19]

1. *Nationalism*: The military professional views the nation-state as the focus of his ultimate loyalty since the armed forces are charged with its defense. The assumption that the military organizations of other states adopt similar orientations makes the possibility of war an accepted fact of existence, a potential outgrowth of the inevitable clash of national interests.

2. *Order*: Professional military personnel tend to have a strong positive orientation toward order. Though the attitude characterizes all bureaucracies, military institutions seem to place special importance on hierarchical relations, obedience, and functional specialization. Individual desires must be strictly subordinated to the requirements of the organization.

3. *Puritanism*: The demands of military discipline lead to a necessary stifling of impulsiveness. The military code emphasizes the value of self-sacrifice (heroism) and suspects tendencies toward the free expression of emotion.

4. *Power*: The hierarchical organizational environment and the nature of the military's obligations produce a positive orientation to power. Individuals are compared in terms of their relative rank in power structures. Cross-national competition to improve the national power position is intrinsic to military behavior.

5. *Pessimism*: Constant concern with the "calculus of coercion" produces a pessimistic view of human nature and an acceptance of the need to use force in political and social relations.

6. *Activism*: The military occupation discourages the development of profoundly introspective inclinations. Rather, the characteristic stance is one of externally projected activism—the "can-do" mentality.

The virtues of the military ethic are undeniable, especially in regard to the mission with which professional soldiers are charged. Yet these values, whatever their contribution to the effectiveness of military operation, oppose some of the basic assumptions supporting a democratic political process. The military's fealty need not be to democratic ideals; indeed, these principles may be seen as hampering the fulfillment of the mission of maximizing the security of the country. Democrats may be patriotic, but they are not, first and foremost, nationalistic. Rather, they see certain principles and procedures of governance as the major concern, not the nation-state, *per se*.

Democracy, insofar as it stresses individualism, liberty, and popular participation in political decision making, can be somewhat disorderly. Rather than hierarchy and obedience, equality and self-responsibility dominate the democratic citizen's perspectives. The democratic belief in individual freedom, in turn, encourages self-expression, producing a diversity of life styles and a plurality of norms. Democracy tolerates, within limits, somewhat deviant subcultures, as well as a wide range of opinion. Democratic culture, therefore, can offend those with a strong need for order and a single definition of appropriate behavior.

Power relations in a democracy, though inevitable, are de-emphasized. Human beings are believed to be naturally cooperative, and the role of power in general and force in particular can be minimized in social and political life. Citizens relate to one another on bases other than that of relative position in some salient power ranking. The belief in individual freedom and fulfillment reflects a fundamental optimism about the perfectibility of human beings and their ability, under most conditions, to live in harmonious diversity. This belief is carried over into the international realm, where wars are not assumed to be inevitable and preparation for war becomes not wisdom based on a realistic evaluation of human nature but a self-fulfilling prophecy which causes what it purportedly seeks to avoid.

In principle, a democratic system should be able to tolerate the military ethic, within limits. The reverse, however, is not true. The military ethic, if it becomes too strong, will displace democratic virtues. The problem for a democracy, then, arises in establishing a military organization that provides for the continuation of the system, both in terms of protection from external threats and the survival of the domestic values being protected.

The Organization of Defense

The crucial political dilemma of the United States involves whether the world-wide role of a great power can be harmonized with domestic democratic ideals. The obligations of the former necessitate the maintenance of a large standing military and nurture the growth of an overriding obsession with national security. The global patterns of competition raise the risk of military involvement and magnify the importance of national preparedness. The economy becomes increasingly geared to armaments production, and the political processes are distorted by the need for security. The government cloaks its operations from the eyes of its own citizenry on the rationale that to do otherwise would simply benefit possible enemies. Since the government still depends, in part, on the consent of the governed, unpopular policies, however well justified in terms of global interest, can undermine the people's confidence. Popular discontent, then, may force the abandonment of policies that the leadership believes are in the country's global interests. Realization of this possibility encourages officials to manipulate public opinion, to lie, and otherwise to subvert democratic procedures, all in pursuit of the national interest. At best, therefore, the role of a great power does not support the continuation of domestic democracy; at worst, it destroys it.[20]

But as a matter of reality, the world is imperfect, and a democratic country must provide for its own defense, which in turn requires a military organization. The United States, however, is not simply defending itself. Rather, it protects worldwide interests as well, many of which have little relevance to democracy. These may be justified on other grounds, but their existence distorts the internal political process. Ideally, in times of peace the military organization of a democracy should be kept very small—a mere nucleus of the wartime defense force. In war time, the system should be protected by a citizen army that voluntarily rises up to defend the state. This ideal, of course, is never perfectly realized. In all of the major wars of the United States (Civil War, World Wars I and II, Korea, and Vietnam) conscription has been necessary to fill the ranks of the armed forces. Moreover, the small peacetime standing army meant that the country was unprepared for the two great wars of this century.

The incongruity of small military organizations and great-power politics was recognized after World War II, and the government opted for an international role. This undertaking led to the largest peacetime defense budgets in the history of the country and the introduction of the peacetime draft. The draft, however, was inequitable in its impact, because the burden fell most heavily on the lower-middle and lower classes; it was also in violation of democratic proscriptions against "involuntary servitude." Involvement in an unpopular war, probably an inevitability given the country's international commitments, intensified the disgust with the draft and helped to bring back the all-volunteer army.

The volunteer organization, in the context of the country's international obligations, may be even more suspect from a democratic standpoint. First, the salaries required to attract volunteers enormously increase the cost of national defense. In fiscal year 1975-1976, about 58 percent of the defense outlay went to cover manpower costs. And even with the high pay levels, the lower classes and minorities are still overrepresented in the military—a peculiarity which suggests that the system is being defended by those groups which benefit *least* from it. And inevitably, the presence of a large military organization, isolated from the pressures and values of civilian life, raises the specter of an armed "state-within-a-state," primed for intervention into domestic politics.

A small military establishment appears most compatible with a democratic political system, but the United States cannot return to the pastoral isolation of the nineteenth century. If a large military structure is necessary, then perhaps it should be based on a universal and equitably applied system of military obligation for both men and women (as always, in a democracy alternative service should be available for conscientious objectors). Every social class and power group should be proportionately represented throughout the armed forces, including the combat units.

This alternative is not without problems. It could lead to the total militarization of society, though this is unlikely if terms of service are relatively short. On the other hand, this plan definitely civilizes the army, making it a more unwieldy weapon. The fact that all power strata are proportionately involved may make the political leadership less able to commit military forces without widespread domestic approval—a consensus that could rapidly dissipate in contact with rising casualty figures. One benefit, however, may accrue: The need for domestic support for foreign engagements may encourage the government to take the citizenry into its confidence and begin to build consensus through truth and discussion, instead of manipulation and distortion.

International involvement and the consequent infiltration of security concerns into every level of national government operations, as well as the effects on the definition of social and economic purposes, place democracy under siege. Whether a balance can be struck between global entanglements and democratic ideals will determine whether the United States survives as both an independent state and a democratic polity.

Part Four

POLITICAL VALUES AND POLITICAL POWER

Politics involves more than a crass struggle for power resources. Power must be used, and the ways people choose to use the resources they control are affected by their values. Political activity, then, is "value-saturated." In order to understand what is going on, therefore, some account must be taken of the political participants' perspectives and purposes. Where do they come from and what form do they take?

The problem of political values can be approached in a number of ways. In Chapter XI, the method of analysis is essentially sociological in nature. The idea of political culture is introduced as a means of describing the common political orientations of the people of a particular society. Culture is then distinguished from the more explicit and systematic statements of political beliefs known as ideologies. Finally, the process through which values are learned, or socialization, is examined.

The values and norms of behavior that support a social system are never perfectly learned by all of its members. Some deviation may be tolerated, but certain limits are generally defined and enforced by the political authorities. These values and norms, then, become law. In Chapter XII, the nature and functions of legal systems are outlined. In addition, the ways in which norms are translated into laws—problems of legislation, adjudication, and enforcement—are discussed.

A more philosophical approach is adopted in Chapters XIII and XIV. In political discussions, various concepts like *freedom*, *justice*, and *equality* are used with abandon. Not only do these terms mean different things to different people, but, depending on how they are defined, they may not be completely compatible with one another. These two chapters, in an effort to help clarify the difficulties in value choice, investigate some of the implications of four primary political values: freedom, order, justice, and equality.

Chapter XI Political Culture, Ideology, and Socialization

Stereotypes abound in people's characterizations of one another. Germans are seen as disciplined and authoritarian, the English as reserved and status-conscious, the Japanese as clever and hard-working. Sometimes these sweeping classifications, though grossly oversimplified, are harmless enough, serving as handy "recipe knowledge" for admittedly complex situations.[1] When shaped by hatred and prejudice, however, stereotypical descriptions become twisted into a justification for evil.

The assumptions underlying the types developed in the everyday world also motivate a major area of social scientific inquiry. Certain collectivities of individuals can be seen as sharing basic attitudes, beliefs, and orientations, so much so that they form a group distinct from any other. In short, they possess a common culture. Discovery of the major components of a community's culture reveals some of the roots of the members' behavior and forms a primary basis of generalization in the social sciences.

Culture is an inclusive category, encompassing all the social acts and objects held in common, ranging from language, history, and art to shared values and beliefs. Political scientists, while not ignoring the larger cultural milieu, concentrate on those aspects which seem to have political implications —aspects which together might be called the *political culture*.

Within the generalities of a community's political culture exist the more systematic and intellectualized *political ideologies*, and these also interest many political analysts. Finally, political scientists wish to know how a shared political culture comes about. How do people learn, or fail to learn, the content of a particular political culture or the principles of an ideology? This learning process is usually referred to as *political socialization*. The problem of political socialization links the concerns of this chapter with some of the prevailing themes of this book, for the control and manipulation of the socialization process has profound implications for the nature and exercise of power in a political system.

POLITICAL CULTURE

A political culture "consists of the system of empirical beliefs, expressive symbols and values which defines the situation in which political action takes place."[2] Three analytically distinct components are comprised in it:[3]

1. *The Cognitive Dimension*: What do people know, or think they know, about the operations of the political system of which they are a part? The scope of this knowledge extends from a general recognition of the existence of the system to extremely detailed information about particular policies and personalities. The information people believe to be true may be very inaccurate. One of the basic objectives in a study of political culture, then, is to determine both the quantity and the quality of a populace's knowledge of politics.

2. *The Affective Dimension*: This dimension refers to the feelings prompted by the political system, whether love and respect, indifference, or fear and revulsion. Feelings are dependent on knowledge, for people cannot emotionally relate to that of which they are unaware.

3. *The Evaluative Dimension*: The combination of knowledge with feelings produces conclusions and judgments about the operations of the political process. Thus, a person who sees the government as an alien and oppressive force is likely to judge its policies quite harshly.

Discussions of the parameters of a political culture commonly focus on national political systems. Although the nation-state appears to be the primary political community in the contemporary world, other levels ought not be ignored. The worldwide communications web and the consequent dissemination of knowledge and values may be contributing to the emergence of a global culture that includes some political implications. The almost universal acknowledgment, if not actual implementation, of certain democratic, social-welfare, and modernization ideals may be signs of this world culture.[4] Conversely, some struggling countries are composed of peoples who have little or no knowledge of the national system of which they are presumably a part and who, therefore, cannot really be said to share in the national political culture.

Even in countries with established records of continuity and national identity, attempts to generalize about the political culture will necessarily obscure considerable diversity. In the United States, for example, many people are ignorant about the nature of the political process, though others are quite well-informed. Among those who possess at least some knowledge, there exists considerable variation in their feelings and judgments about this information, as is demonstrated by the divisive politics of the 1960's and 1970's.

Consequently, discussions of the political culture of the United States generally refer to those characteristics that appear to be widely distributed among the population. Even deviant subcultures may share some values and beliefs with the other members of the political system. Many radicals in the United States, though rejecting all or part of the social and political order, still think of themselves as Americans. Others, like the members of some black-separatist movements, appear more thoroughly alienated from the prevailing loyalties of the national political culture. In a stable system, the basic elements of the three dimensions set forth above will be supportive of established institutions and procedures, and any identifiable subcultures will at least be compatible. Increasing disaffection and consequent negative evaluations among sizeable factions of the population can lead to growing political discord.

A fundamental problem in the study of culture and its political implications is to establish some means of identifying and comparing cultural types. Perhaps the most ambitious efforts are those of some sociologists to define the basic frameworks of knowledge that dominate different sociopolitical systems.[5] Contemporary managerial capitalism, for example, is under the sway of technical knowledge; that is, the form of knowledge concerned with the manipulation of the social and material worlds for what is assumed to be some advantage. The pre-eminence enjoyed by this form of knowledge means that those who possess it exercise great power within the society, economy, and polity. Concerns about political and social relations are reduced to problems of appropriate means, and the supposedly free area of scientific inquiry becomes subordinated to the goal of improved techniques. This culture can be contrasted with the feudal order in which philosophical-theological knowledge was ascendant and the Roman Catholic Church and its clergy served as the primary social and political framework of the age.

Some political scientists devise more specifically political classifications of national political cultures, through the careful analysis of public-opinion surveys and also of the political impact of broader cultural dispositions. One of the most influential of these studies identifies three basic types of political culture according to the nature of cognition prevailing among the citizens: parochial, subject, and participant:[6]

Parochial Political Culture: The definition of *parochial* depends, in part, on the systemic level chosen for analysis. Assuming, as is usually the case, that the national system is the level selected, then a parochial subculture would exist in a community so isolated from national political life as to be ignorant of the very existence of the nation-state, hence of the structure and operations of its institutions. Naturally, such total ignorance means that the affective and evaluative dimensions are irrelevant with respect to this level. Certain tribal groups in the Amazon jungles and perhaps others in some remote areas of Africa offer the purest examples of parochial political cultures. Less extreme, but still parochial, are those people who, though dimly aware of the existence of a national political order, believe it to be remote and largely inconsequential to their lives.

Subject Political Culture: Subjects are well aware of the national political system and its importance to their lives. However, they perceive themselves mainly as passive bearers of burdens and recipients of benefits. Subjects relate to the political system primarily in terms of governmental outputs. They possess little knowledge about how policies are made and do not see themselves as active participants in political decision making. The lack of input knowledge and influence, however, does not necessarily mean that the subjects hold strong negative feelings toward the government. They may take pride in its accomplishments and feel that their needs and expectations are being adequately met.

Participant Political Culture: In a participant political culture, the citizens not only see themselves as the objects of governmental outputs, but they also are aware of how policy is made and see themselves as active contributors to its development.

Subjects and participants can demonstrate three basic affective/evaluative positions with respect to a national system.[7] Under conditions of *allegiance*, the political knowledge of the citizens is accompanied by generally positive affective and evaluative orientations. *Alienation* means that negative feelings and judgments pervade the politically aware population. Under circumstances of *apathy*, what is known about the political system encounters only indifference.

This simple typology cannot adequately classify contemporary national political cultures without considerable refinement. Essentially, every system is a mixture of parochials, subjects, and participants, as well as the faithful, the disgruntled, and the unconcerned; however, the relative proportions differ. For example, a classic survey of political attitudes in the United States, Great Britain, Germany, Italy, and Mexico indicates that the United States and Great Britain contained significantly greater numbers of people holding "participant" attitudes than the other three countries. In the United States and Great Britain, for example, 75 and 62 percent of the respondents believed they could affect national regulations. In Germany, Italy, and Mexico, the figures were 38, 28, and 38 percent respectively.[8] Patterns of allegiance and alienation also differed markedly from country to country.

Another complication arises from the fact that many individuals exhibit a mix of all of the orientations. In certain areas of political life they feel informed and influential, while in others they may be simply subjects. Even relatively knowledgeable citizens may be ignorant of some elements of the political system. In addition, feelings and evaluations are unlikely to be completely equivalent for all facets of political life. Some people, though alienated from parts of the system, remain attached to others.

A final problem concerns the amount of change in the population's general attitudes and beliefs over time. Sometimes political cultural change is seen as a process of political modernization. As the national system increases its capabilities, more and more citizens move from parochial to subject and, finally, to participant political orientations. This movement, though, can be uneven and need not inevitably produce a participant political culture. Indeed, the movement may be in the opposite direction, at least from participant back to subject, or even complete withdrawal into political parochialism. The surveys indicating strong participant attitudes in the United States were taken in the late 1950's and early 1960's. More recent evidence suggests that large numbers of people have become negative about their ability to participate effectively in the national political process. Attitudinal changes of this sort mean that initially adequate statements about the nature of a political culture are subject to obsolescence.

IDEOLOGY—FORM AND FUNCTIONS

A few years ago, some American social scientists, with not a small degree of satisfaction, greeted the "end of ideology"—a phrase chosen to represent the trend toward political moderation and the decline of extremist belief systems.[9] Modern "postindustrial" societies, by supposedly resolving most of the fundamental conflicts spawned by industrialization, were believed to introduce an era in which a broad consensus on ends would reduce most political debates to ones over means (see the discussion of managerial capitalism, above). Ideology, from this perspective, implies dogmatic and scientifically false social and political belief systems. This definition, however, is too restrictive. Recent political conflicts in the United States and elsewhere in the world suggest, in any case, that the end or decline of ideology may have been prematurely celebrated.

Other treatments of ideology merge it imperceptibly with the more amorphous concept of political culture.[10] All people are seen as learning certain mental "sets" that are used to interpret the world and structure their responses. Admittedly, the idea of political culture refers to the basic attitudes and dispositions toward politics held by a community, but to equate culture with ideology is too imprecise. Politically aware and active individuals go beyond vague inclinations and orientations and develop more explicit systems of political belief. These systems can be labeled ideologies.

Ideologies, then, can be considered part of the more inclusive and diffuse political culture of a system. Some articulate the prevailing norms and beliefs, while others define the felt needs of deviant subcommunities. Not all people advocate an ideology in this sense, though those politically active citizens who follow a course of action related to consciously held and developed principles possess at least the rudiments of one. An ideology, then, can be defined as an action-oriented sociopolitical philosophy. More elaborately, ideologies are :

Explicit: An ideology is an explicit statement of beliefs. A person may absorb the biases and dispositions of the prevailing norms and values and act on them, but never really examine and state the reasons for his preferences and behavior. Ideologies, even in simple, mass-consumption, sloganeering form, overtly articulate the bases for political behavior.

Coherent: The explicit statements set forth a relatively coherent, consistent, and fairly comprehensive interpretation of the social world. These interpretive efforts provide an ideology with a descriptive, or quasi-scientific, foundation. It may be that the goal of comprehensiveness and coherence leads to rigidity and dogmatism, and that the followers grasp an ideology as a source of psychological security in a terrifying, complex world. It appears more reasonable, however, to view different ideologies as more or less flexible and open to revision in confrontation with social reality. Even Marxist analysis continues to thrive and develop, despite its apparent rigidity in the Soviet Union.

Value-Oriented: Ideology is more than an explicit social analysis; it also sets forth a system of social and political values. Some analysts conceive of ideologies as being primarily revolutionary in intent, consisting of a critique of the existing order and a vision of the "brave new world" of the future. This viewpoint also seems too limited, for formal ideologies can also justify the status quo. In fact, as the Soviet experience demonstrates, what was once a revolutionary ideology can, after the revolution, become a central support of the new establishment. Perhaps establishment ideologies are not as prominent, because in a stable system most citizens learn supportive attitudes without recourse to systematic rationalizations. In a newly constituted order, however, explicit ideological justifications play an important role in legitimizing the regime.

Action-Oriented: Ideologies go beyond diagnoses of right and wrong in the political world; additionally, they generally define the actions necessary to preserve or correct this world. These "tactical" considerations are usually combined with emotional appeals intended to move people to take appropriate actions.

Many people fail to examine their political beliefs and are passively molded by the pervasive influence of the prevailing political norms. Others search for a more explicit rationale for their political actions, and for them an ideology can have an appeal and serve certain functions:

1. *To Explain the Nature of the Social and Political Worlds*: Ideologies fill a need to know. For the alienated, a revolutionary ideology identifies the causes of their discontent and outlines a strategy of change (and hope). The philosophical systems underlying more sophisticated ideologies appeal to intellectuals searching for some truth. Establishment ideologies provide a systematic justification for supporting the prevailing order and preserving the current distribution of privileges.

The nationalist ideologies that furnished the intellectual basis for a multitude of twentieth-century independence movements explained the plight of the inhabitants in terms of their inability to control the social, economic, and political institutions of their territories. Similarly, Marxist analysis discovered the source of the workers' deprivation in their separation from the control of the means of production. After independence, the role played by the new native elites in the national liberation struggles was used to justify their control of positions of social and political power. Similarly, the role of the Communist Party in the Revolution, as well as the presumed ability to interpret the basic forces of history, explains prominence of the party elite in the postrevolutionary state.

2. *To Provide a Framework of Ideas and Values for a Community of the Faithful*: Sometimes ideology has been described as a "political religion," in that it performs many of the communal functions of a religion, though it usually has no other-worldly characteristics.[11] Thus, an ideological belief system provides a source of security and identity for the psychologically uprooted. As the basis for a community of believers, an ideology serves as a potential source of political legitimacy. Ideological emphasis on the establishment of a community of believers can be seen in nationalist appeals to the "people" and in Marxist evocations of worker solidarity throughout the world.

3. *To Order and Motivate Political Action*: An ideology, because it provides a relatively systematic statement of political priorities, aids decision making. Objectives are defined; certain avenues of action are outlined or rejected. Further, the emotional content of an ideology is intended to inspire the believers to strive for the designated objectives, whether they be ones of preservation or change.

This function can be demonstrated by the popularizations of various ideological systems. The slogans of nationalism ("Seek ye first the political kingdom, and all else will be given unto ye"), Communism ("Workers of the world, unite! You have nothing to lose but your chains"), and New Left participatory democracy ("All power to the people!") succinctly state the primary purposes in a manner designed to compel action.

Certain strains, tensions, and ambiguities, however, may accompany ideological politics, especially when an ideology becomes closed and unbending in its interpretation of the world. All ideologies claim relevance, but their analyses will always be, in some ultimate sense, incomplete, misleading, and even false. An "open" ideology will be capable of revision and development in response to contradictory evidence. The evolution of "liberalism" from *laissez faire* to welfare capitalism over the past two hundred years illustrates such a change. The more inflexible ideologies will increasingly substitute ritualistic incantations for meaningful analysis. Some ideologies might be so irrelevant that reasonable examination would suggest abandonment. Certain critics suggest that contemporary liberalism, despite its revisions, has reached this point.[12] Additionally, a particular ideological interpretation may prove to be singularly unconvincing to the vast majority of the population of a country (socialism, for instance, in the United States), because it appears to oppose major elements of a well-established political value system. Under these circumstances, the ideological "priests" may find themselves without a congregation.

Ideologies also tend to stimulate expectations, perhaps beyond the ability of the leaders to fulfill them. These make problems for a revolutionary ideology that continues unable to bring the revolution to pass. Ironically, the problem can become even more serious if the revolution actually succeeds but fails to deliver all the presumed benefits. For many of the countries that gained independence with ideologically inflated expectations, the winning of the "political kingdom" was followed by little save intractable problems and inevitable disappointments. Nor do establishment ideologies escape this problem. Though intended to justify the status quo, they often present a rather idealized version of the existing system. When people who have absorbed the ideal confront the blemished reality, considerable disillusionment may result.

Finally, ideological politics can heighten the intensity of political conflicts. In part, this exacerbation results simply from the levels of activity common to ideologically motivated citizens. After all, if people are uninterested and uninvolved in political life, they are unlikely to participate in many political conflicts. Additionally, ideologies, because of their comprehensive nature, can politicize many aspects of human behavior, thereby multiplying the potential areas of conflict in society. Continuing the analogy between ideology and religion, the definition of a community of believers by necessity excludes some people. The more extreme the ideology, the greater the likelihood that the world will be divided into friends and enemies, with very little room for neutrals between the opposing forces. As ideologies become more dogmatic and rigid in style, the possibilities for pragmatism and compromise decline.

Despite these potential problems, ideological formulations seem inevitable as long as people participate in political action on the basis of a reasonably coherent and explicit statement of principles and justifications. A strong ideological consensus can lead to the absorption of the basic tenets of an ideology into a less self-conscious prevailing political culture. Political behavior can then increasingly reflect these unexamined preferences, rather than a deliberately formulated ideological system. For example, the principles of the American Revolutionaries, defined in a multitude of pamphlets and documents in the eighteenth century, have been transmuted into the dominant norms of the political culture of the United States. This kind of transformation can, in turn, contribute to a decline in ideological conflict because of the nearly universal and, in a sense, automatic acceptance of the ends and means of political action.

IDEOLOGY—CONTENT

Ideologies address many of the same fundamental issues, but, obviously, they arrive at substantially divergent conclusions. These differences can be largely explained by the contrasting answers given to some of the basic questions that engage the attention of philosophers and ideologists alike. These questions cannot be definitively answered through scientific analysis, for they transcend science and move into the realm of value preferences. We shall explore six among the implicit or explicit concerns of any comprehensive ideology.

What Is the Nature of Human Beings?

The question of human nature appears to be susceptible to a scientifically grounded answer that would be acceptable to all. The primary debate, however, revolves around an issue that is metaphysical rather than scientific: Are humans naturally "good" or "evil"? The response to this query influences the evaluation of the operations of society and government. If people are by nature inclined to the "good," then the problems that exist in the world are the fault of imperfect and corrupting social and political institutions. If, on the contrary, people are essentially egotistical and malicious, then society serves to restrain these natural tendencies to "evil." The former view leads one to favor social reform; the latter encourages conservatism.

This apparently abstract debate actually underlies many contemporary policy disagreements. In the discussion of the nature and causes of crime and its prevention, environmentalists stress the corrupting effects of the circumstances in which the criminal was raised—poverty, broken families, inadequate opportunity—and advocate programs of rehabilitation for the criminal and reform for the environment. Conversely, their more pessimistic opponents tend to hold the criminals individually responsible for their actions and emphasize more effective controls of deviant behavior (such as reinforced police forces). Prisons are viewed more as institutions to protect society than to rehabilitate the criminal.

A second human-nature problem with profound implications involves the extent to which people are assumed to be naturally equal. Again, this question seems susceptible to scientific investigation, but even if certain characteristics can be empirically established, they do not determine what value conclusions should be drawn from them. Ideology, it must be remembered, is both evaluational and analytical. The assumption of natural equality is the foundation for guarantees of equal rights and responsibilities in a political order. The opposing assumption of *politically relevant* inequality leads inevitably to the conclusion that some are better suited to rule than others (see below).

One of the more recent incarnations of this controversy is the Women's Liberation movement, whose advocates deny that the biological differences between men and women should serve as a justification for social and political discrimination. Another provocative natural-equality issue concerns the political implications of genetically based differences in intelligence and other inherited traits. It is scientifically undeniable that people do inherit different genetic packages and that some are more "gifted" than others. What science cannot decide is how society should reflect these differences, if at all. Ideologies, however, do decide whether for political and social purposes people should be considered equal to one another.

What Is the Nature of the State?

The view of human nature adopted by an ideology probably determines its basic tone and direction. More specifically political themes are also woven into ideologies. The philosophical assumptions concerning the nature of the state are of particular importance in shaping attitudes toward it.[13] Organic theories hold that the state is a kind of living organism whose existence and needs take priority over the concerns of the individuals who compose it. The origins of the organic state are almost mystical in nature, emerging out of the immemorial traditions of the people and reflecting their collective soul. Contrary to organicism, *instrumentalist* theories see individuals as standing prior to the state, which serves as an instrument to meet their needs. According to some instrumental theories, such as those of John Locke and the United

States Constitution, the state is formed by the consent of all the members. Other instrumentalist theorists, like Marx, see the state as the tool of only one part of the population. Each of these positions involves far more than a simple scientific conclusion about the actual beginnings of a particular regime. Rather, they determine the basic philosophical attitude toward the nature of the political community.

What Is the Relation of the Citizens to the State?

Assumptions about the origins of the state affect the definition of the citizens' relation to it. If an ideology adopts an intrinsically organicist position, the requirements of the state take clear precedence over the needs of the members. Citizens' lives have meaning only through the fulfillment of their appropriate functions within the organic order. To consider the individual as existing apart from the state would be meaningless. Government, then, tends toward a form of benevolent despotism.

If, on the other hand, the state is conceived as a instrument of the citizens, then the meaning and purposes of the state derive from the needs of individuals. Moreover, if the state is merely an instrument, it can, therefore, be altered by its members to better suit their purposes. The major issue to be determined in an instrumentalist ideology is whose interests are being served: those of a ruling class, of the majority, or of all the citizens?

Who Should Rule the State?

In some sense, every political ideology revolves around the issue of who *should* govern, though the answers given relate to the preceding positions. If people are believed to be inherently unequal and the state is considered a kind of social organism, then some members would be better suited to perform the "higher functions" of the body politic. Organic ideologies, therefore, usually identify a ruling group who, by their "natural" superiority, have a right to rule. If humans are assumed to be naturally equal, at least for the purposes of governance, there can be no intrinsically qualified ruling class. If a particular faction happens to dominate the state, its position is illegitimate and a target for change. A belief in politically relevant inequality can be combined with an instrumentalist notion of the state. In this case, the strong, or naturally gifted, will be seen as ruling in their own interest and defining the nature of legitimacy. This is the position attributed to Thrasymachus in Plato's *Republic* (see Chapter VI). If an ideology espouses the ideal of political equality, it faces a significant problem in organizing political participation so as to achieve this goal (see the discussion of democracy in Chapter V).

What Are the Functions of Government?

The essential issue in defining the appropriate tasks of government involves the extent to which they are to be limited. Organic ideologies place no theoretical limits on the authority of the government, though certain practical ones may exist. Liberal, instrumentalist ideologies define an inviolable sphere of private rights. In eighteenth- and nineteenth-century liberal doctrines, this ideology demanded economic as well as political noninterference. A well-ordered society was one governed by a minimalist state whose primary task was the preservation of order. In the more activist doctrines of welfare liberalism, core political rights of the individual restrict the power of the government. Instrumentalist ideologies, however, need not limit state power. Some aim at the complete transformation of the society, which though justified in terms of the benefits ultimately produced for the population, places few if any restrictions on state power in the period of transition.

What Is the Relation of Truth to Politics?

Ideologies are sometimes considered to be absolutist belief systems; that is, proponents of a particular ideology believe they possess the ultimate truth about politics. Organic ideologies certainly tend in this direction, and "political truth" assumes an almost mystical nature, knowable only by the chosen few. Some instrumentalist ideologies, such as Marxism, also assert that they embody certain ultimate truths, but they are of a rationalistic, quasi-scientific nature. Again, only the gifted few demonstrate the perception to see the "true" nature of reality. Even presumably absolutist ideologies may be open to some revision, depending on the extent of their infallible characteristics. They may, for example, consist of rather vague "first principles" which leave considerable room for interpretation.

Other instrumental ideologies are not absolutist in nature, even in this limited sense. Rather, political truths are always considered to be partial, and all people are equally entitled to search out and formulate their own views. A plurality of value positions can exist, encouraging value relativism and tolerance of different viewpoints. At the extreme, this relativism deteriorates into an inability to make any kind of evaluation among alternative political value positions, all of which are considered equally valid.

IDEOLOGIES—COMPARED

An ideology includes more than a philosophical discourse on these six questions. The principles, by themselves, do not constitute a program of action, so a major portion of most ideologies is devoted to isolating the appropriate strategy and tactics with which to achieve or defend these principles. Yet the basic thrust of an ideology will be molded by the answers given to these problems. Chart XI-1, Patterns in Ideological Principles, sketches out the essential positions of three global ideologies of the twentieth century—Fascism, Communism, and Liberalism. This brief schematization greatly abbreviates the complexity of each ideology, but it serves to illustrate some of the basic contrasts among the three.[14]

The appeal of all three ideologies has declined in recent decades. Fascism, particularly the Nazi variation, was discredited by the horrors committed in its name during World War II. The authoritarian bureaucratization of the Soviet state and the emergence of competitors for the Marxist-Leninist mantle tarnished communism's image. The domestic failures of American liberalism in the areas of racism and poverty, as well as the international revulsion against the Vietnam War, compromised the promises of this ideology. The decline of these global ideologies has produced something of a vacuum, currently filled by a plethora of liberation movements, nationalisms, and socialist variants. Whether one or more new global ideologies will emerge out of this morass in the next few decades remains problematic (see Chapter XVI).

POLITICAL SOCIALIZATION—FUNCTIONS

Infants do not emerge from the womb singing national anthems or defending ideologies. These general identifications and specific principles are learned through a process called *socialization*. The relevant content of socialization includes the entire substance of a culture. Political socialization refers to that special subset of general learning which has identifiable political content or implications. Since political socialization is part of a larger whole, it reflects more general cultural learning. Political philosophers from the time of Plato have recognized the importance of socialization both for the continued stability of a political order and for the ability to change it. The educational policies of every contemporary state echo this ancient philosophical concern.

Political socialization can serve several basic objectives, though it is most commonly associated with *preservation*.[15] Through "proper" socialization, attitudes and beliefs supportive of the existing system can be passed from generation to generation. In a national political system, preservative socialization contributes to the formation of a common national identity, expectations about the nature of the political institutions, and the kinds of behavior deemed appropriate for different political roles (citizen, bureaucrat, elected official). Understandably, those who wish to alter the system in some way view the conservative consequences of socialization as a major obstacle to reform or revolution.

Chart XI-1   Patterns in Ideological Principles

Basic Problems	Fascism	Communism	Liberalism
1. Nature of Man	Masses are basically irrational: swayed by passions of race and nation. Naturally unequal.	Potentially rational, but consciousness shaped by role in the productive process and may be distorted. Naturally equal, but might need guidance of those with understanding of historical laws.	Basically rational and cooperative. Morally autonomous and equal.
2. Origin of State	The mystical embodiment of the people's collective soul. Transcends individual members.	Creation of the class controlling the means of production. State withers away in the classless society of pure communism.	Creation of all citizens who freely consent to subordinate themselves to law.
3. Relation of Citizens to State	Complete subordination. Individual has no claims against state. Stresses corporate nature of state where each has a role to play. State is the purpose for individuals' lives.	State is instrument of the needs of the ruling class. For subordinated classes, relation is coercive in nature.	Citizens' needs are prior to the state, which is their instrument. Citizens retain certain fundamental rights. Relation is consensual in nature.
4. Who Should Rule	Masses fit only to follow. Small elite fit by nature to rule. Emphasizes role of great leader. Rulers responsible not to people, but to nation's "destiny."	Ultimately, no one has right to rule over anyone. Tends to discourage leadership principle, but sanctions authoritative role of Communist Party.	All possess right to participate in governing process. Efficiency requires selecting some for authoritative roles, but these remain responsible to people.
5. Functions of Government	No theoretical limits. Purpose is to control the components of corporate society to insure fulfillment of state objectives. International struggle to insure nation of rightful position necessitates preparation for war.	Instrument of class coercion. If controlled by proletariat, it is used for the transformation of the social base to bring about pure communism. Thereafter, it has no purpose and withers away.	State not concerned with realization of collective objectives; rather, it facilitates realization of individual goals. Legitimate sphere of state activities is limited.
6. Truth and Politics	Value absolutist. Truth embodied in the state, but is of an essentially irrational nature. Reflects soul of the nation.	Value absolutist. Truth embodied in doctrine claimed to be scientific and rationalistic in nature. Reflects underlying laws of history and society.	Value relativist. Truth always partial. Reasonable men can reach different conclusions. Requires toleration of divergent views.

In a completely static and surprise-free society, preservation would be the sole function of social learning. Most contemporary social systems undergo constant change, and their citizens continually confront new situations to which they must adapt. Socialization contributes to this *transformation* in a dual fashion. First, people can learn how to cope with the novel situations they encounter by altering their expectations and adopting new skills and norms of conduct. Thus, a peasant who migrates to a large city must learn how to survive in the new environment and fulfill a function within an urban-industrial economy. This example typifies one of the most significant periods of adaptive socialization; that is, the massive transformation from agricultural to industrial societies. Alternatively, people may learn new values and expectations and then strive to transform institutions to fit these new values. Reformers and revolutionaries are most concerned with this kind of resocialization, for through this method they can foment the kinds of disgruntlement needed to change society.

Through the inculcation of totally new political identification, socialization can even help to *create* a political order where none before existed—a function related to transformation, but more ambitious. The need to create, in effect, a new political culture has been especially pressing in some of the African states. The national boundaries of these systems were drawn during the European scramble for African colonies in the late nineteenth century, and they reflect the requisites of great-power politics rather than any internal African logic. The independent African states, by retaining the colonial boundaries, often include groups who experience little loyalty to the presumptive nation-state. These governments, therefore, place considerable stress on a socialization program meant to contribute to the creation of an inclusive national identity. Of the three possible purposes of socialization, creation is the most challenging and, in many cases, time consuming. Many states have already endured civil wars (notably Nigeria, Zaire, Sudan, Ethiopia) because of their inability to overcome subnational identities. Once the transformation or creation process has succeeded, the new identities help to preserve the new order.

Despite the adaptive and creative functions, socialization seems to be most commonly considered from a preservative perspective. Investigators delve into the ways in which a system maintains itself through time. Disruptive behavior is attributed to "breakdowns" in the socialization process. This approach, however, can be misleading, for whether a particular pattern of behavior constitutes a breakdown depends on one's point of view. From the individual's standpoint, there is no such thing as a breakdown—everyone is socialized into something. Only after the objectives of socialization have been selected can one speak of breakdowns. The choice of objectives obviously depends on one's values. A revolutionary may view the failure of workers to recognize their class interests as a breakdown in transformative or creative socialization.

POLITICAL SOCIALIZATION—PROCESSES

Learning starts at the moment of birth, if not before, but it does not begin with a *tabula rasa*, a blank sheet. Rather, socialization occurs within the context of a genetic and social inheritance. The genetic traits of the infant are the more fundamental and controversial of the two contextual givens.[16] Some traits are obvious and undeniable, though often their impact on subsequent learning cannot be fully anticipated. Basic physical or mental characteristics, for example, limit the adult roles a person might be capable of fulfilling and structure the intervening learning experiences. A man of slight build will be unable to be a linebacker in professional football, no matter what his other talents, while another of limited intelligence would make an unlikely nuclear physicist. Beauty may be only superficial, but a child who inherits physical features thought beautiful in a particular culture will have a life experience profoundly different from that of one viewed as ugly. Similarly, in a society in which roles are distributed on the basis of sex, this accident of gender will significantly affect subsequent learning.

Somewhat more controversial is the degree to which certain behavioral and personality dispositions are biologically inherited. Considerable evidence suggests that introvert/extrovert behavior may have substantial genetic roots. There may also be genetic contributions to the capacity for aggressiveness, as well as to forms of mental disorder such as schizophrenia. Again, the presence or absence of these traits can have a substantial effect on subsequent socialization.

Perhaps the most intensely disputed question concerns whether certain of these genetic traits are distributed randomly throughout the human race or skewed according to certain groupings, such as sex, race, or ethnicity. Thus, some suggest that males dominate the political processes in most societies because they are biologically inclined to organize into groups to pursue collective goals.[17] This position is not acceptable to those who believe that women have been socialized to be nonpolitical and to accept home and hearth over the struggle for power. An even angrier reception greets those who argue that whites, as a group, tend to score better than blacks on certain kinds of intelligence tests because of inherited ability.[18] Again, opponents attribute racially based discrepancies to differences in socialization and the environment, rather than heredity.

Whatever the scientific answers to these disputes, qualifications must be added with respect to genetic makeup. First, though genes may designate certain givens, they do not completely determine outcomes. A person develops through a complex interaction between nature (heredity) and nurture (socialization), and individual growth never becomes final. Second, social institutions do not have to reinforce "natural" characteristics; rather, they can be designed to compensate for what are decided to be deficiencies. Just as a hemophiliac can be given the coagulants necessary to prevent bleeding, other kinds of genetically based traits can be compensated for in subsequent socialization.

The second set of contextual givens also occurs as a consequence of birth —in this case social inheritance as opposed to biological.[19] In brief, the social circumstances into which a person is born will often shape all subsequent learning experiences. This expectation is partly a phenomenon of opportunity. A child of wealthy and high-status parents enjoys substantially more privileges and options than one born into poverty. Beyond the matter of opportunity lies the broader question of perspective. Lower-class children are not simply economically deprived—their class position affects the environment in which they live and the kinds of people with whom they are likely to associate and thereby has an impact on attitude formation. At the extreme, poverty can lead to dietary deficiencies that can stunt the development of the brain.

Socialization, then, may start with birth, but the direction it will take has already been partially charted. Early learning, moreover, is not specifically political in nature. Rather, the infant begins to discover the nature of its surroundings and how to cope with them. Language and other social skills are acquired, and basic personality and intellectual characteristics are further developed. Some of this essentially nonpolitical learning, though, can have an indirect impact on the formation of political attitudes later in life.

Freudian analysis, in particular, stresses the importance of early childhood experiences for adult social and political behavior. Political activity has been seen as an attempt to displace an essentially private psychological problem into the public realm and thereby solve it.[20] One analyst, for instance, sees revolutionary behavior as a way of working out resentment against paternal authority and privileges by attacking the political authority of the state.[21] One reason why the participants in radical movements are generally in their late teens and twenties is that this is the time when conflict with paternal authority becomes most intense because of the need to form one's own identity apart from the family.

Freudian analysis need not be fully embraced in order to concede the potentially important political consequences of early socialization. The general development of the personality can also shape the course of later political attitude formation. A child who learns to be dogmatic, rigid, intolerant of ambiguity, and submissive to authority will probably develop political attitudes and affiliations substantially different from those formed in one who tends to be more tolerant, flexible, and self-responsible. In addition to personality formation, early childhood learning contributes to the development of intellectual attitudes and skills which determine children's ability to interact with their environment and control it.

The first specifically political learning appears to involve the recognition of some fundamental political identity, such as being American, French, or Chinese.[22] In some countries, this primary political identity is subnational in nature, a fact which contributes to later political problems. As children grow older, their political knowledge becomes more detailed and complex, moving from the recognition of basic political authority figures (such as the president and the policeman) to recognition of fundamental political institutions and affiliations (such as Congress and political parties). Knowledge about particular candidates and policies is not acquired until relatively late—usually beginning with adolescence.

Of greater importance for the system is how a person feels toward the acquired knowledge. Some research suggests that in the United States many children initially carry over to political authority figures the warm feelings they possess for family authority relations, but other research has not found strong support for this hypothesis.[23] Young grade-school children, especially of the white middle class, generally hold positive images of the president and other political authority figures. Older children and young adults begin to demonstrate somewhat more skeptical, or rather perhaps realistic, views of the political process, reflecting their greater knowledge. Other studies indicate that children from deprived environments develop more negative attitudes earlier than their advantaged peers.[24] It may be, moreover, that due to the disillusioning experiences of Vietnam and Watergate, children are starting to learn negative attitudes at an earlier age than a decade ago.

Another central problem in understanding socialization concerns the extent to which early socialization can be altered by subsequent learning.[25] Generally, it appears that dispositions learned in the first few years of life are quite difficult to change, but that socialization continues to add on further layers of detail and elaboration. Though the core personality and intellectual proclivities may condition political learning to some extent, it must be remembered that specifically political learning of even the most basic sort probably does not begin until ages three or four. Elaborate political knowledge and opinions are added later and continue to evolve throughout life. Feelings of national identity are probably the most difficult to change. To leave the country of one's birth requires a significant psychological break; nonetheless, millions of immigrants to the United States were able to make this change, though they often retained much of the old country in their new setting. To switch party affiliations is obviously not as difficult as changing national affiliations, and it is even less difficult to alter opinions about particular government policies and officials.

Interestingly, the seriousness of deviant political behavior declines in a similar fashion. It is most serious to betray one's country, and violation of the norms governing the political process, though less grave, is also often considered a crime. To change one's mind about supporting a particular candidate or program is viewed as normal politics, except in those authoritarian systems in which the leader and his policies are equated with the integrity of the nation-state.

Whatever the durability of different levels of political affiliation and values, there can be no doubt that political learning continues throughout life.[26] One reason the socialization process is never complete arises from the inability to anticipate correctly all the attitudes and behavior that may be associated with political roles encountered at a later time. Early socialization cannot fully prepare the child for adult political roles. Social and technological changes also require new ways of coping. Geographic and social mobility increase the chances that people will encounter situations for which prior socialization did not prepare them. Beyond all else, the existence of a plural society with a variety of groups espousing different values creates a further need to respond and adapt. The more rapid and radical these changes are, the greater will be the strain on the learning capacity of the population.

Another socialization problem arises when a person receives inconsistent or even contradictory messages about the nature of the social world. School civics programs commonly portray the system in very positive terms, but these may contrast with the children's experience. A classic case of inconsistency is that between the image of the helpful and friendly policeman contained in primary school readers and the ghetto children's actual encounter with law enforcement in their neighborhood. The multiplicity of socializing agents (see below) is the fundamental source of this problem. Inconsistency means that the socialization process is not one of simple accretion of attitudes and information, but may be accompanied by considerable psychological tension. Ultimately, the ambiguity produced by inconsistent messages may lead to an attempt to reduce this tension by withdrawal from or rebellion against one of the sources.

POLITICAL SOCIALIZATION—AGENTS[27]

People learn their attitudes and beliefs from innumerable encounters and experiences throughout their lives; nevertheless, a number of particularly important socializing *agents* can be identified and briefly examined:

Family

Almost all of a child's early socialization occurs through the agency of the family, primarily the parents. The child's world, at least for the first two years, is almost totally circumscribed by the immediate family, which also retains a central position for many of the later years as well. The most significant contributions of the family, especially at this early age, are not specifically political in nature, but they could influence later political learning. Among the indirect contributions to the later formation of a child's political identity are the following:

1.   The development of *intellectual inquisitiveness and achievement motivation* can be encouraged or stunted by the home environment.[28] Parental overprotection or authoritarianism tends to discourage the child's early exploration of his surroundings and the consequent development of problem-solving abilities and self-confidence.

2.   Early experiences with parental authority appear to shape general *attitudes toward authority relations*, including those in the political system. Often this connection is seen in terms of the formation of "authoritarian" or "nonauthoritarian" personality traits.[29] Subject and participant political attitudes seem ultimately rooted in the nature of the family structure.[30] Positive or negative feelings toward societal authority figures, as noted above, may also be related to a child's early experiences with familial authority. Rebellion against the parent may be carried over into political arena. Ironically, some evidence suggests that the student disturbances of the late sixties and early seventies were caused, in part, by the disillusioning contrast between warm, personalistic, and liberal family environment and the rather depersonalized and imperfect world encountered by the students as young adults.[31] Early socialization, in fact, did not prepare the children for the imperfections of the outside world.

3.   The development of *attitudes of trust and openness* is also partially related to early socialization. Erratic parental demonstrations of affection and disdain tend to make children fearful and suspicious of their surroundings, which seem to be totally beyond their ability to control.[32] Fearful and suspicious parents, of course, can directly communicate these attitudes to their children.

Parents also transmit certain specifically political messages. Party identification in the United States is commonly passed from parents to their young, though the labels are initially devoid of content. Later, more detailed political preferences and prejudices may be transmitted. The parents of student protesters, for example, tended to be significantly more liberal than those of nonactivists, though not as radical as their children.[33]

The consequences of the family's near monopoly on early learning are quite important for the political system. Usually, the family is thought to be essentially conservative in its impact, at least insofar as the parents are deeply concerned with providing the basic tools necessary if their children are to survive in society. Such a general conclusion does not mean that the family plays no role in the production of "deviants"—both social and political. Clearly, early learning need not be the basis for "perfect" citizenship. Deviance, from the established order's perspective, can be deliberately produced (obviously, radical or alienated parents can intentionally communicate their disaffection with the system), but it more likely results from ignorance of how different parental behaviors affect socialization and from the inability to control all the variables—genetic and environmental—that act on a child. The decentralized, dispersed nature of family socialization in most political cultures means that those attempting to manipulate the socialization process encounter obvious problems of coordination and control.

School

The formal educational system, the second major agent of political socialization, can be more easily controlled than can the family to achieve community objectives, at least insofar as the curriculum can be structured according to certain goals. The course of study followed from primary school through college includes some specifically political content. In the early years, the tendency is to portray the system in very positive terms—a portrait that will most likely contrast with the messages of other agents, as well as with adult political experiences. Courses in college generally take a more critical look at the system's operation, though most are still fundamentally supportive. Indeed, critical acceptance may be more stable than naive optimism which leads to inevitable disappointment. In any case, what few true revolutionaries exist on college faculties are usually under heavy pressure from school and community officials.

The school, like the family, can also make an indirect contribution to the students' political socialization. Like the home, the school environment manifests a basic authority structure. The nature of student/teacher interaction may affect the development of attitudes and expectations about other authoritative relations. The more authoritarian political cultures are usually characterized by both authoritarian family structures and authoritarian student/teacher relations.[34] In contrast, a classroom situation in which pupils are encouraged to participate actively in the learning process may contribute to the formation of more "democratic" attitudes. But a conflict between the school structure and the values it teaches, or between the school and other agents, may be another factor contributing to some of the student rebellions against educational institutions.

The school system, as a significant agent of socialization amenable to state control, is often suggested as a means for achieving specific political objectives. Unfortunately for these schemes, the school's participation in direct political socialization does not appear especially effective in altering basic dispositions, though it can reinforce and build on existing ones. This limitation does not seriously affect an established political system in which other agents can be largely depended on to transmit fairly supportive orientations. In countries where the government is attempting to forge a new national identity out of a multitude of subnational loyalties, the difficulty in countering preschool socialization can have serious implications for political stability.[35]

Peer Groups

Relations with peers, or equals, are a third major socializing experience. Associations with peers begin with early childhood friendships and continue through adult relations with friends, co-workers, and avocational associates. Peer relations tend to be less hierarchical than those within the family or the school, though rather interesting authority structures often develop in teenage gangs or organized peer groups. Peer groups can challenge, more effectively than the school, the primacy of the family in the life of the growing youngster. The opinions of peers become especially important in adolescence, when children usually attempt to develop identities independent from the family. As with other agents, the amount of direct political socialization that occurs through the agency of childhood peers is probably not great, at least in the United States; children usually have more important concerns than political affairs. The peer affiliations of later years may include more overt political content. In authoritarian political systems, like the Soviet Union and China, the potential of peer associations is clearly recognized, and the state makes an effort to control the content of peer socialization through the creation of a multitude of government-sponsored youth groups.

The indirect political impact of peer relations can be quite significant. Since peers provide a substitute for the warm, interpersonal relations of the family, they may be able to erode commitments made under parental influence. The generally liberalizing effect of a college education seems at least as much attributable to peer associations and pressure as to formal institutional experiences. Often the "liberated" norms expressed in a college milieu are abandoned when the graduate assumes a position in a more conservative social nexus.

Peer groups, however, are not always a means of change; in fact, in most cases they serve to reinforce existing predilections. Most people seek out friends who support rather than challenge their beliefs. Peers apply tremendous pressure for conformity to group norms and can be conservative in consequence, if the group accepts the established political culture.[36] Even students who join groups espousing values contrary to those of their parents can be seen as searching for ways to state their own identity.

Secondary Associations

Social relations include more than family and friends. Most people also occupy positions in various kinds of more highly structured groups, such as labor unions, churches, public or private bureaucracies, political parties, and the like. These also serve as agents of political socialization, especially for adults. Role occupancy in these organizations requires the fulfillment of certain responsibilities. New members may not at first know these behavioral norms, but they soon learn them.

As with the other agents, the learning that occurs need not be directly political in nature, though whether it is so clearly depends on the type of organization. If someone joins a political party or is elected to political office, the subsequent political learning is direct and substantial. Other organizations relegate political affairs to a subsidiary position. Still, apparently nonpolitical organizations like churches or labor unions can play some role in political value formation.

Secondary groups also contribute to the general social growth of their members, as do other agents, and this growth can affect political behavior. Again, these experiences will be mainly reinforcing of established inclinations, as people seek out affiliations or jobs compatible with their preferences. But people often do not have the luxury of choosing their groups, and some may find themselves in organizational settings contrary to their preformed preferences (like unwilling draftees in the army). In this context, they must either learn to adapt or face considerable social and psychological conflict.

Mass Media

The mass media play a crucial role in the later political socialization of most citizens in advanced societies. After the person attains a certain level of interest and awareness, the media become a major source of political information. Nor is their socializing function confined to information transmission. As was discussed in earlier chapters, how the news is defined—what stories are emphasized or ignored—structures how people think about matters political. When choice of media messages exists, people usually select those sources which confirm their predispositions. Few deliberately seek opposing views.

The relevance of media as agents of political socialization has been generally restricted to the later development of children and adults. Obviously, one has to be able to read before newspapers or magazines have much impact. Also, basic levels of cognitive development are necessary before a person seeks out political information from the media.

This argument, however, takes into account only direct political socialization. Television, in particular, plays a growing role in the general learning of the very young. Though they probably do not absorb many specifically political messages, pre-school children experience an array of sensations that may shape subsequent political attitude formation and behavior. The remarkably successful program "Sesame Street" teaches more than numbers and the alphabet. Early lessons in racial integration, social tolerance, manners, and friendship are included as well. Other consequences of a television culture may not be so benign for early development. Commercial television attempts to socialize children into an instant-gratification consumerism at a rather young age, not to mention continually exposing them to dramatizations of violence. Even if television fails to produce the "global village" predicted by media prophet Marshall McLuhan, its total impact on socialization has yet to be delineated completely.

CULTURE, SOCIALIZATION, AND POWER

The most subtle and effective way of controlling people's behavior is to induce them to want to act in the desired fashion. This kind of control is the promise of socialization, *if* all the participating agents can be bent to such a purpose. Some social analysts, like psychologist B. F. Skinner, argue that all significant social acts are learned responses to certain situations and are in a sense, predetermined. People do not choose to act in a particular manner; rather, they behave as they have been taught through a learning process that is essentially a complex form of conditioning. Thus, the critical question concerns the control and content of the conditioning process; freedom becomes an illusion.[37]

If all social behavior consists of learned responses to environmental stimuli, then, in principle, it would be possible to design socialization so as to produce the desired response. Presumably, a society free from the current discords could be deliberately constructed in this way. Accepting this line of reasoning implies that the regime, or someone, must exercise far more control over socialization than is currently acceptable in the United States. The advocates of such a program point out that people are equally socialized in a less structured environment, but in this case the agents are uncoordinated, contradictory, and self-serving. The problem, then, is reduced to the alternatives of random socializing and socializing directed at the achievement of some consistent set of social goals (presumably, one's preference here would be largely determined by prior socialization). Not surprisingly, for many critics such a program summons up images of *Nineteen Eighty-Four*.

Some more substantive criticisms also can be directed at the total faith in socialization control. It tends to ignore, or understate, the impact of the organism on learning. In part, social behavior appears genetically based; if it is, then, socialization must necessarily be limited to a given set of genetic possibilities. More importantly, a debate revolves around the issue whether learning is best conceived according to a stimulus/response (S-R) model or whether the organism mediates the process and affects the ultimate response (S-O-R). Proponents of the S-O-R position point to the unpredictable impact of an individual's memory and associative powers on the interpretation of a particular stimulus.[38] Any individual's unique biocognitive capabilities may affect responses in ways unanticipated by the S-R model, especially in nonhabitualized, problem-solving areas of behavior. Total control, like that envisioned by the perfect socializers, would probably require methods of manipulating the inner organism, as well as structuring the environment. This manipulation might be accomplished through either chemical or electronic means.

Despite these limitations, control of the educational process remains a primary power resource. The diversity and number of the participants in socialization means that this resource is fairly widely, if not equally, distributed. Powerful groups and the regime can exercise considerable influence over the entire society through the manipulation of the media or the school system. Moreover, the established power structure of a society indirectly influences other socializing agents, like families and peer groups, by defining the "reality" to which these groups must adjust. Dissident factions, then, face substantial difficulties in overcoming this kind of inertia, unless people are sufficiently disgusted with the status quo to be available for countersocialization.

The more authoritarian regimes, especially those intending to bring about a major social transformation, are usually not satisfied with direct control of only the media and the school system. They need to penetrate into the primary socializers, like the family and the peer group. In the Soviet Union, for example, some efforts have been made to place very young children—under two years of age—into full-time state-controlled care centers where the early socialization can be more carefully monitored by the authorities. In addition to regulating schools more closely than is common in the United States, the Soviets also attempt to control out-of-school peer-group activities through such organizations as the Little Octobrists (ages 8 to 11), the Young Pioneers (ages 9 to 15), as well as the Young Communists (late teens and twenties). Unlike the Scouts in the United States, these groups are closely supervised by the regime. All significant adult associations are also closely guided. This degree of control both requires and contributes to the continuation of a great concentration of power. Despite all these efforts, the Soviet state has been unable to eliminate social deviance, either criminal or political—something of a tribute to the stubbornness of the human creature.

The control of social deviance raises another problem for political analysis: that of law, or when behavioral values and norms are authoritatively enforced.

Chapter XII Values, Law, and Power

THE PARADOX OF THE LAW

In Franz Kafka's novel *The Trial*, a man who comes seeking admittance to the Law finds his way barred by a gatekeeper.[1] Indeed, the guard warns the man that even were he to force his way past the first door, he would confront a series of gates and guards, each more powerful than the one before. The keeper, however, allows the man to wait on the chance that he might be admitted at some later time. Days, months, and years pass, but still the man is denied access. Finally, as he is about to die, he beckons to the guard and gasps one final question: "Everyone strives to attain the Law. How does it come about, then, that in all these years no one has come seeking admittance but me?" The guard replies, "No one but you could gain admittance through this door, since this door was intended for you. I am now going to shut it."[2]

The parable can be interpreted in a number of ways in the context of the novel, but here it serves to represent a primary paradox: The law commonly is viewed as remote and inaccessible to the average citizen. Its meanings are manipulated by the ritualistic incantations of lawyers and judges. People seeking the presumed protection of the law cannot penetrate its mysteries and must depend on those trained in its intricacies. The law does not guarantee justice, or even that the immediate interests of the client will be served. Yet, despite the law's inaccessibility, the claim is often made that the intended purpose of the law is to serve the needs of the people and not those of some obscure clique of legal high priests.

The paradox of the law may not be impenetrable; perhaps, it can be pierced and some understanding gained of the role of law in society. In order to do this, a number of questions need to be addressed. First, what is meant by "law"? What is the relationship between the laws of a society and the

231

values and norms expressed in the political culture or in particular political ideologies? Second, how are laws made? Where do they come from? Law making, however it occurs, can be called the *legislative* process. Third, what happens when actual behavior clashes with that prescribed by the laws? What happens when the laws themselves conflict with one another? These questions require an investigation of the processes of *adjudication* and *enforcement*. Finally, what happens when strongly established values are inadequately protected by existing laws? The failure of law can lead to private "law making" and enforcement.

LAW IN SOCIETY

People possess certain values and expectations concerning appropriate social and political behavior. When these values and norms are extensively shared, it is possible to speak of a common sociopolitical culture. If the shared values and expectations prevail in a specific society, they make up the dominant culture (see Chapter XI). In any stable social system, laws emanate from and tend to reflect the dominant cultural values, though this reflection is not perfect.

A widely shared consensus about a social value or norm of behavior is not, however, in and of itself, a law. To be a law, a social norm must be authoritatively defined as binding regardless of the immediate preferences of the affected individual or group (compare the definition of authority in Chapter III). Many aspects of the dominant culture, perhaps most, are not this binding; that is, certain values and orientations may prevail in a society but are not enforced. Deviant values, accordingly, will be tolerated, at least within certain limits. For example, a particular style of dress may be predominant at any given time in the United States, but the variety of dress tolerated is fairly wide. Legal limits, though, do exist, like the ordinances prohibiting public nudity. Now people may agree or disagree with this regulation of behavior, but whether they agree or not, the legal norm binds their behavior.

Law, defined in this fashion, is closely associated with the idea of enforcement. If a norm is widely shared though not imposed upon the minority whose preferences dictate different behavior, it can be called a *social convention*, but not a law.[3] Identifying enforcement as a distinguishing characteristic of legal norms seems straightforward enough, but it creates two further definitional problems. First, enforcement may be more or less effective. Lawlike statements may be promulgated by those with the appropriate authority but may be largely ignored by the affected population. These statements are laws *in form*, not *in fact*. Often-cited examples include the failure of prohibitory laws to discourage significantly the consumption of alcohol or marijuana. Alternatively, some norms may be lawlike in their effect but have no formal legal status. In this case, compliance may be forced, but the enforcer lacks the authority to do so (see the discussion of vigilantism, below).

Enforcement, true enough, is always a question of degree; even the most vigorously enforced law may allow some deviants to escape unpunished. A formal law, to be a law in fact, must be backed by continuous enforcement reasonably effective in deterring nonconformance and punishing that which does occur. This distinction makes it possible to recognize and analyze norms that possess a lawlike form, even though not effectively enforced. In international law, for example, certain norms may be recognized as binding on all international actors, even though no effective organization for enforcement exists.

A second definitional problem remains: What constitutes enforcement and who carries it out? A restrictive definition of the law argues that enforcement involves the threat or use of physical force imposed by an ongoing organization created for that purpose—the state.[4] Therefore, law cannot exist in "stateless" societies, such as those of some primitive tribes who possess no clearly articulated political system; nor, for that matter, can law exist in the international system in the absence of a world government. A less restrictive definition recognizes the possibility of enforcement measures short of physical force (for instance, shunning), as well as voluntary adherence to unenforceable laws and communally sanctioned self-help in the absence of a formally organized enforcement apparatus.[5]

No matter how the enforcement process is conceived, whether the formal legal norms are effectively binding depends in large part on the strength of the social consensus underlying them. In every society, no matter how stable, the dominant value system is opposed by countervalues.[6] Often these countervalues are represented through deviant subcultures, although individuals simultaneously may possess values both supportive of and counter to the established order. The more powerful the countervalues become, the more difficult it will be to enforce established legal norms through any means or mechanism. Formal laws will be ignored, and pressure will build for their revision.

Despite the fact that effective law depends upon the support of a broad social consensus, the very existence of law indicates that the consensus is not perfect. In this imperfect situation, law potentially can fulfill a number of functions:

Provide Justice: Ideally, the legal system is supposed to produce justice through equitably balancing competing claims and conflicting values. In fact, perfect justice is never attained and is difficult even to define (see Chapter XIV). Nevertheless, though legal systems are commonly condemned as mere facades serving to protect the interests of the powerful, the existence of legal standards binding upon all citizens offers at least the possibility that the claims of the weak will gain some hearing. The longevity of any regime depends, in part, upon its ability to make a plausible claim that its rule is just.

Regulate Conflict: An effective legal system, whatever its contribution to justice, also provides a means of regulating conflict. It does this by establishing a common mechanism for resolving disputes among citizens.[7] As was discussed in the analysis of social conflict (Chapter VI), successful regulation depends on the acceptance of some rules of the game.

Restrict Behavior: A function somewhat related to conflict regulation, laws also serve to define the range of acceptable behavior. This definition may be more or less restrictive—the laws of a "closed" society would tolerate a far narrower range of behavior than those of a more "open" system. The restriction of behavior helps "to make human actions conform to predictable patterns so that contemplated actions can go forward with some hope of achieving a rational relationship between means and ends."[8] Predictability, it is acknowledged, need not be associated with justice (see the discussion of order in Chapter XIII).

Promote Change: Generally, the impact of the law is taken to be essentially conservative in nature. Certain characteristics of some legal systems (among others, reliance upon custom and the role of precedent) can produce a somewhat conservative bias. Laws, however, can also be used to promote social change and support innovative behavior.[9] This function is related to the presence of countervalues that can grow strong enough to affect the development of the legal system. Under such circumstances, various laws may aim at changing previously accepted behavior patterns. Recent examples in the United States include legislation in the areas of civil rights and protection of the environment.

Legitimate the Political Process: The rituals of the law, despite the frustrations they often provoke, nonetheless can contribute to the legitimacy of the political system. The belief that there is a regularized and potentially predictable process through which certain norms are made legally binding helps to soften the harsh realities of power and manipulation that necessarily constitute part of the political process.[10]

So far, laws have been discussed as if they were relatively equivalent social norms, sharing the characteristic that they are authoritatively defined as binding regardless of immediate preferences. In fact, a number of different levels of law can be distinguished. At the highest level are broad moral principles defining the ideals of justice that underlie the legal system. Sometimes these principles are referred to as natural law and are presumed to be universally applicable and discoverable by anyone capable of exercising "right reason."

At the next level are certain customs, which though not codified or formalized through any regularized political process, may still possess the authority of law. Many customary norms, if not most, fall into the class of social convention rather than law, but some, especially in legal systems that have developed in the tradition of the English common law, have legal status.

Sometimes deriving from custom, but often formalized in a written document, is constitutional law. The constitution provides the formal rules governing basic political relationships and the conduct of political affairs. As such, it serves to restrict government, although such restraints are often only in form and not fact.

The general statutes and policies of the government are promulgated within the presumed framework of the constitution. These laws can be further distinguished as to whether they create criminal or civil restraints. The former deal with behavior to be prohibited (for instance, murder), whereas the latter regulate normal relations among citizens (such as contracts, economic regulations, and domestic relations).

Finally, at the most specific, law consists of the decisions affecting particular individuals made by judicial and administrative bodies. This level of law makes the greatest impact on the daily life of the average person. Yet the higher levels of the law should not be ignored. Specific decisions occur within a context largely defined by the more general levels of the law. This definition of context, however, differs from legal system to legal system and can be compared and contrasted in a number of important areas:

1.   *The Balance of Process versus Result*:[11] Every system of law is concerned both with *how* something is done (process or procedure) and with *what* is done (result or substance). The relative emphasis given these concerns differs in differing systems. In the United States, one often hears the complaint that criminals escape justice due to legal "technicalities." Insofar as this view is accurate, it indicates that the legal process, which is designed to protect the rights of the accused, takes precedence over what might appear to be a socially desirable result (the conviction of "obviously" guilty criminals). In other political systems, especially those representing a highly developed ideology, the politically desirable result will be produced regardless of what procedures might have to be ignored.

2.   *The Balance of Individual versus Community Interests*: Somewhat related to the problem of process versus result is the question of whose needs take precedence in the legal system—the individual's or the community's. These interests, of course, need not be viewed as completely antagonistic, but neither are they completely compatible. The community, for example, cannot rely on voluntary donations to collect the necessary economic resources from the citizens but requires a tax system backed by the threat of coercion. The

concern for legal processes is often associated with the desire to protect the individual from the arbitrary exercise of state power. Substantive results, however, may be biased in favor of either the individual or the community. Libertarians, for example, advocate eliminating a whole package of governmental regulations that have been implemented to promote the general welfare (such as safety devices on cars or business regulations).

3. *The Balance of Stability versus Change*: Law, as was agreed above, can function not only to conserve but also to alter existing norms of behavior. The extent to which the legal system is used as a deliberate instrument of social engineering constitutes another basis for comparison. A political regime influenced by a revolutionary ideology is likely to perceive the legal system as just one of several means of promoting social change. Regimes that view the existing order as something to be defended will use laws to protect established values and preserve the distribution of power.

4. *The Degree of Impartiality*: Legal systems can be contrasted as to whether certain groups or classes receive preferential treatment under the law. A legal system is impartial to the extent "to which there is an effective application of a formula distributing values on bases equally accessible to all."[12] Marxists commonly argue that capitalist systems develop laws solely to protect the propertied classes. In contrast, the ideologically motivated law of communist states tends to favor, at least in form, the interests of the proletariat.

5. *The Degree of Challengeability*: Legal systems differ in the extent to which they provide effective opportunities to challenge decisions.[13] This difference relates, in part, to the relative balance between process and result. A system emphasizing process is likely to provide an elaborate procedure of appeal through which the decisions of lower courts can be reviewed. Certain substantive results of law, especially constitutional law, also may open some indirect avenues of redress. The political rights of free speech and assembly allow for the creation of a political base from which to pressure for changes in the laws.

The nature and functions of law in society, then, are complex but not incomprehensible. Understanding of the law can be further enhanced by investigating the processes through which norms become law and are applied —questions of legislation, adjudication, and enforcement.

LEGISLATING: HOW NORMS BECOME LAW

Not all the norms of the dominant culture acquire formal legal status. Nor do all the formal laws perfectly mirror the prevailing social values. Opinion can change faster than formal laws, and legal development can lag behind shifts in social values. Moreover, since laws can be used to alter as well as to support the status quo, legal development may leap ahead of the established norms of behavior. Consequently, an interpretation of the legal order should include a discussion of what norms become law, how they become law, and why. The process through which certain norms become binding is called *legislation*.

In contemporary Western democracies, the legislative process, not surprisingly, is often associated with legislatures—the supposedly independent structures, like Congress or Parliament, that have the authority to consider and pass general policies and statutes. This association, while convenient, is misleading. On one hand, legislatures, where they are active and independent, do more than simply legislate. On the other, legislatures do not possess a monopoly of the authority to make laws for a society.

Legislative bodies can make a number of contributions to the functioning of the political system. A comprehensive catalog would include:[14]

Law Making: Legislatures play a part in the development of both statutes and policies. In many countries, including the United States, they also contribute to the creation of constitutional law. Legislatures, however, are not the only political structures that can make laws.

Representation: In carrying out their responsibilities, legislators generally represent the interests of various groups and individuals in the political system. Karl Deutsch identifies four different conceptions of how legislators might represent interests.[15] First, they could be a true *sample* of their constituency in their "opinions, personality, and circumstances." This idea assumes a very homogeneous constituency. Therefore, sample representation tends to be functional in nature; that is, the constituents are members of a functional group, like industrial workers or farmers, rather than accidentally associated in a geographic district. A second concept of representation is that of *messenger*, in that the representatives vote exactly as they have been instructed by their constituents. This instruction could come from a majority or even a plurality of the citizens and thus does not assume homogeneity. Third, legislators can be seen as *trustees* of the people's best interests, drawing upon their presumably superior wisdom to make the proper decision, regardless of the opinions of their constituents. In the fourth concept, legislators attempt to act as *brokers*, making bargains and compromises among the various interests of their constituents.

Interest Aggregation: Legislators do more than simply articulate the interests and opinions of their constituents. They also must work with one another in order to develop general policies and statutes. For them to succeed in doing this, the diverse interests of the social system must be aggregated or combined in some way, so that generally acceptable decisions emerge. The more bitterly divided the legislature, the more difficult it will be for the members to fulfill their aggregative role.

Supervision and Surveillance: A fourth function, and one that may be more significant than that of making laws, is the supervision of the activities of the executive bureaucracy. Legislatures can investigate allegations of bureaucratic wrongdoing and review the expenditures of public monies. The successful performance of these tasks, as was noted in the analysis of bureaucracies (Chapter IX), requires considerable resources of both time and expertise. The relative paucity of these resources often undercuts the potential importance of legislative supervision.

Political Socialization: The operations of the legislature also affect the political education of the citizens. Whether this learning is accompanied by positive or negative feelings depends, in large part, on the effectiveness of the legislature. A reputation for incompetence, inefficiency, and corruption can detract from the legitimacy of political institutions.

Though legislatures can make a contribution to the formation of laws, they are by no means the only participants in this work. Many political systems do not have legislative bodies. In other systems, they are often inhibited by executive power. Even in those countries possessing fairly strong traditions of independent legislatures, the significance of their role in law making has suffered a decline.[16] The usual explanation for this decline is the growth in the power of executive bureaucracies.

The executive bureaucracies of modern democratic systems have been able to aggrandize themselves at the expense of the legislatures for a number of reasons. In part, the growth of executive power is a consequence of the inability of the legislature to cope with the volume and complexity of legislation required in the contemporary welfare state. Greater reliance, therefore, has been placed upon the organized skills and information of the bureaucracy (see Chapter IX). In addition, many western democracies, including the United States, seem afflicted by increasing social divisiveness, making it more difficult for legislatures to aggregate interests and to develop a consensus on goals. These problems, in turn, damage the prestige of legislative assemblies and culminate in a growing tendency for executives to assert emergency powers for dealing with what appears to be a crisis situation. At the extreme, the implementation of such emergency powers can take the form of a *coup d'état*, eliminating the legislature altogether.

Even where legislatures continue to play an important role, other agents also participate in law making. The most diffuse of these other participants is the citizenry at large who, through direct referendums, can make law. Legislatures are primarily involved in the development of broadly construed statutes and policies. In the absence of independent legislative assemblies, general legislation and even constitutional changes will come from the executive bureaucracy.

Judicial and administrative organizations apply these general statutes and policies to specific cases; their application is itself a form of law making.[17] Some scholars even argue that only when a general law has been applied to a specific case can a law be said to have been made (see below). Bureaucratic organizations also make their own rules of internal operation that are lawlike in their effect. The law-making process spreads even further, since the enforcement of the decisions of the executive bureaucracy or the judiciary is a form of legislation, inasmuch as a decision not to enforce is possible.

Whoever the participants in the legislative process are, the significant question concerns what norms are made into laws. In general, laws will reflect the values of the dominant culture, though the presence of powerful countervalues may bring presssure for change. Moreover, the dominant value system is not likely to be fully consistent or unambiguous. Even if it were, different people among those who benefit from the status quo could disagree on which norms should become law (thus, one might disapprove of homosexuality but still believe that private relations between "consenting adults" are not an appropriate area for state regulation).

Nor is it simply a matter of the powerful dictating which norms are translated into laws.[18] Only if power were highly concentrated would this explanation be of much utility. Multiple sources of power exist in society, and even in relatively authoritarian systems the distribution is somewhat dispersed. Consequently, the process of law making requires bargaining among a variety of involved power holders. Differences of opinion, combined with the dispersal of power resources, means that the legislative process will necessarily involve some conflict. The more serious the value divisions and the more evenly power is divided among the contenders, the more severe the conflict is likely to be. At the extreme, differences of opinion over the content of the laws are expressed through revolutionary civil war (see Chapter VII).

The creation of laws, as we know, seldom degenerates into a completely unrestrained power struggle. The existence of prior laws, as well as other commonly shared values, usually guarantees a certain degree of civility. Conflict over the definition of specific statutes and policies occurs within a framework of basic constitutional law regulating the conduct of such disagreements.

Beyond the restraints the laws themselves place on the law-making process, certain practical limits exist as well. Whatever a faction's power and preferences, only finite changes can be legislated.[19] The changes possible in the area of private behavior may quite great (if sufficient power is available to the regime to enforce the law) though not unlimited. The constraints are more severe in social and economic questions where factors beyond the control of any single political agency are at work. Thus, it is difficult to legislate the behavior of the natural elements that affect the success of a country's agricultural policy or the actions of other nations whose decisions might affect the world market for the crops raised. The closer a regime pushes to the limits of the possible, the more costly it will become to legislate change.

In the light of the earlier analysis of power relationships in society (Chapters III through VII), the process of law making can be seen as a complex form of power brokerage.[20] Competing groups attempt to influence those who have the political authority to make laws for a particular system. They can use all the power resources available in society—economic wealth, status, information, physical coercion, and, most certainly, organization. How these resources are brought to bear depends on the formal and informal regulations governing bargaining relations. Among the major methods of manipulating power resources to affect the legislative process are the following:[21]

1. *Lobbying*: Lobbying refers to the process by which a group organizes to put pressure on legislators and administrators to make the desired decision. The method assumes, therefore, that the independent interest-group organizations are legally tolerated. Examples in the United States include professional associations like the American Medical Association, public-interest organizations like Common Cause, and the political arms of economic organizations like trade unions and manufacturers' associations. The resources generally most valuable to a lobby are economic wealth (from which, perhaps, to make campaign contributions), information (from which to make a persuasive case), and organization (by which to turn out a disciplined block of voters).

2. *Behind-the-Scenes Bargaining*: The open pressure tactics legally tolerated may not seem sufficient to accomplish the desired objectives. Even those systems that allow lobbies to organize and operate usually regulate their activities (for instance, by outlawing bribery or limiting campaign donations). Consequently, interests may move behind the scenes to pressure key decision makers. Some of these activities, as when privileged access is granted to high-status individuals, may not be strictly illegal. Others, like secret bribery or covert threats, usually are illegal. Useful resources include money (the ability to bribe), privileged information (possibly for blackmail), or coercive power (the ability to make a credible threat).

3. *Propaganda and Public Relations*: In addition to directly influencing legislators and administrators, interest groups may attempt to shape public opinion in favor of their positions. (As with lobbying, it is assumed that such activities have at least a degree of legal toleration. In the absence of constitutional guarantees, interest groups could be denied access to the mass media by the government.) Informational and organizational resources are central to the success of this tactic, especially with respect to the ability to use the mass

media. When allowed, most interest groups will mount extensive advertising campaigns, as have the utilities and the oil industry in recent years, to present their case to the public.

4. *Special Relationships to Political Parties or Bureaucratic Organizations*: Some interest groups have close ties with a particular political party or branch of the executive bureaucracy, and they are in this way able to influence the legislative process. Examples include the relationship between the trade unions and the Labour Party in Great Britain and, to a lesser extent, between organized labor and the Democratic Party in the United States, or the ties between the defense industries and the Pentagon. The major issue with respect to this technique is who controls whom. In some countries, especially those dominated by a strong single party, the interest groups are mere appendages of the party organization. This avenue of influence, to be meaningful, requires that the interest groups possess some autonomy. In competitive party systems, this independence is commonly the result of a group's ability to organize the vote for its associated party.

5. *Direct Representation*: Functional representation, through which certain interests are directly participate in legislative and administrative bodies, provides a fifth avenue of influence. Interest groups often demand direct representation in governmental activites that specifically affect their well being. It has become common, for example, to include labor, business, and sometimes consumer representatives on boards regulating wage and price controls. The utility of direct representation depends on the independent power base of the interest group *vis-à-vis* the others so represented and on the authority of the institutions of direct representation.

6. *Violence*: A group that cannot successfully employ any of the other methods may be able to use the threat of violence to gain some measure of influence. Even the apparently powerless may be able to cause enough disruption to make more powerful groups take notice and respond. The urban riots of the 1960's, to some extent, helped to give blacks in the United States a greater voice in community affairs. Clearly, the use of violence is a resource of last resort, for it is at least as likely to lead to repression as to a more positive response. Moreover, the widespread use of violence as a means of influencing the legislative process is a sign that the legal system itself is breaking down.

ADJUDICATION AND ENFORCEMENT: WHEN NORMS CONFLICT

If legislation refers to the process by which social norms become law, then no necessary relationship exists between legislatures and legislating. Executive bureaucracies, courts, and even the people at large may participate in law making. Legislatures, from this perspective, have no unique function to perform in a political system. Nor, for that matter, do the courts. Some more authoritarian regimes dispense altogether with a meaningfully independent court system. Yet judges and the judicial system, even when relatively circumscribed by other political organizations, can help to carry out a task necessary in any system that has recognizable laws. This function is *adjudication*—deciding whether behavior conforms with the practices mandated by the law.[22] Adjudication also involves deciding among laws or legal interpretations when they conflict.

In a sense, adjudication is a special form of legislation, in that judicial decisions are binding regardless of preferences. Sometimes adjudication is distinguished from legislation by the argument that judges do not make, but rather discover, the law.[23] Legislation predates the judicial process, which simply involves identifying the correct legal standard and deducing the appropriate decision. This viewpoint often accompanies a strong emphasis on process over result.

This rationalist notion of adjudication is countered by the position of the legal "realists." They argue that not only do judges and courts legislate, but also that until they make their decision, laws do not exist with respect to the persons affected. Only the sources of the law—legal statutes, custom, judicial preferences, and so forth—exist prior to the decisions. As Jerome Frank states, "Law is made up not of rules for decision . . . but of the decisions themselves."[24]

Both the rationalist and the realist perspective on adjudication seem too narrowly conceived. The former denies, in the face of much contrary evidence, any creative or discretionary role to the courts, or to whatever other political authorities participate in adjudication. Judicial realism, however, goes to the opposite extreme in asserting that only specific decisions concerning particular persons should be considered law. Indeed, if the major premise of this position is accepted, it would seem that the realists do not carry their argument far enough. After all, courts cannot enforce their decisions. The action that really affects lawbreakers is that of the enforcement bureaucracy. The logical consequence of this line of reasoning is that only the enforcers, typically the police, make the law—rather an oversimplification. A more balanced and comprehensive view of the legislative process considers the definition of general statutes and policies, specific decisions as to conformance and conflict resolution, and enforcement as stages in the law making process.

The courts are both more and less than sole and solely adjudicators of legal conflicts. They are less, because other political authorities, such as certain regulatory boards and legislative committees, are also involved in adjudication. The courts, moreover, can participate in other phases of the legislative process as well. Although judicial decisions involve specific cases, they can, at the same time, make general rules. Decisions of the Supreme Court, in particular, are seen as covering all related cases, not just the one being pleaded. The decisions concerning the right of the accused to counsel affect all defendants in criminal cases, not just Gideon, Escobedo, and Miranda, the three men whose appeals were heard by the Court.[25]

At times, courts also become involved in the administration of decisions. Some judges in the United States, acting under the principle of "one man, one vote," have not only declared certain state election practices illegal, but also have taken an active role in defining new ones. Federal courts have also participated in the administration of school-desegregation decisions.

The legislative process, then, subsumes three relatively distinct phases: general legislation, adjudication, and enforcement. Separate structures—legislatures, courts, and administrators/enforcers—appear to conduct these three phases. But actually, each structure can be involved in the other two phases to some degree. Division of the authority to legislate among these three structures, therefore, may seem likely to produce duplication, contradiction, confusion, delays, and inefficiency. To eliminate these problems, the entire legislative process could be centralized into a single, hierarchically organized structure. In this way, redundancy might be reduced and overall coordination improved.

These tempting gains in efficiency, though, would most likely be purchased at a cost in individual liberty and governmental responsiveness. The division of legislative responsibility among a number of relatively independent structures prevents any one of them from acquiring a monopoly of this important political authority resource. Moderate competition among these structures, moreover, may help to encourage responsiveness of each to the people.

The decentralization of legislative authority is indicated by a number of factors. First, do legislative and judicial structures exist, even in form? If they do not, then the legislative process is totally dominated by the executive bureaucracy. Second, do the people retain some legislative authority, if only indirectly through the power to elect office holders? Third, how independent, in fact, are the separate structures formally involved in the legislation of laws?

Relative independence is suggested in a number of ways. First, the procedures by which people are chosen for office in each of the structures should not be controlled by one of the others. If the selection, retention, and promotion of the officeholders in one structure are dictated by another, then legislative authority would actually be centralized. For example, if the members of the legislative assembly and judiciary of a country serve only at the will of the executive bureaucracy, they are unlikely to make an independent contribution to the development of law. The control which the Communist Party of the Soviet Union exercises over all governmental offices approximates this condition. In contrast, the members of Congress are elected separately from the President in the United States. Moreover, the selection and promotion of individuals throughout most ranks of the bureaucracy, because of civil-service reforms, is no longer dictated by elected officials. Members of the federal judiciary, though nominated by the President and approved by the Senate, serve terms of office largely independent of either.

A second contribution to independence requires that all the structures should be involved in the authoritative legislation and enforcement of laws. In many countries, this condition is circumscribed by the power of the executive bureaucracy to rule by decree during a "state of emergency." The executive, moreover, usually possesses the authority to decide when such an emergency exists. Legislatures and courts, though still in existence under these circumstances, find themselves bypassed by the executive structure that has centralized all the legislative phases under its control. The usual justification for this centralization is that threatening circumstances require swift, effective action not possible under more decentralized conditions. Conversely, the more the power to rule by executive decree is restricted, the more independent the other structures are.

The degree of structural independence is suggested by the extent of each structure's power to overrule actions taken by the others. If one structure can veto the decisions of the others but not have its own subject to any review, then legislative authority is actually centralized. Authority is more decentralized when the actions of each structure are subject to review by the others and, under certain circumstances, can be overruled. The power of the president to veto acts of Congress and the power of Congress, if sufficient majorities exist, to overrule a veto provide an instance of such a reciprocal check. The power of the Supreme Court to declare laws unconstitutional might appear to make it the supreme legislator. National and state legislatures, however, retain the authority to change the Constitution through amendment.

The virtues of a decentralized legislative process can be transformed into vices if carried too far. Effective legislation and enforcement under conditions of relative structural independence require a high level of cooperation among all the participants. Attempts at aggrandizement, bitter ideological rivalries, or covert efforts to pervert and sabotage formal statutes and policies all paralyze the effective development of law.

PRIVATE "LEGISLATION":
THE PHENOMENON OF VIGILANTISM[26]

In every society, some people will believe that the laws are not providing an adequate defense of the established order. If sufficiently frustrated, these people may even be willing to resort to violence, not to change dominant system of values but to defend it from what they see as dangerous threats. The perceived failures of the formal legislative process, in short, may prompt private "legislation" and enforcement. The use of violence to defend the prevailing order from some form of attack or subversion can be called establishment violence or vigilantism (see Chapter VII).

Vigilantism, commonly characterized as "taking the law into one's own hands," tends to produce images of rowdy cowboys lynching an unfortunate horse thief. But in fact, the phenomenon is not confined to any one time (the nineteenth century) or place (the American West). Rather, vigilante acts can occur in any society where (1) the dominant cultural value system is being challenged in some way, and (2) some limits exist defining the acceptable use of coercion to defend the established order.

In addition, vigilante activities are more various than simply the spontaneous reactions of an outraged citizenry. Many of the more significant vigilante events of the United States frontier were carried out by relatively well-organized groups that maintained their operations over an extended period of time. Indeed, if the laws governing the use of coercion in social relations are binding upon the rulers as well as the ruled, then certain acts of police violence (such as "third degree" interrogations) can also be considered vigilante in nature.

If the laws generally reflect the values of the dominant culture, why is it that some citizens may come to engage in vigilante violence? The answer seems to lie in the limits placed on authoritative legislation and enforcement, especially in a relatively open society, as well as in the needs of the vigilantes themselves.

The existing legal system may come short of providing a sufficient defense of the status quo for a number of reasons. First, not all the norms of the dominant culture are translated into law. Therefore, certain "deviant" values and behavior will not be subject to criminal sanction even though they flout conventional beliefs. Examples might include the expression of unpopular political opinions or unusual sexual practices. Potential vigilantes believe that the law should restrict behavior in these unregulated areas, and in the absence of legislation they may act on their own.

A second source of frustration develops if the existing laws are not vigorously enforced. The enforcement phase of the legislative process, the one that translates laws in form into laws in fact, can be undermined in a number of ways. Sometimes the official enforcement apparatus lacks the resources to penetrate effectively into remoter area of the country, as was the case on the United States frontier. Sometimes, as has occurred, effective enforcement can be frustrated by indifference or corruption. Citizens of black and other minority communities sometimes charge that the police do not really care about the level of crime in their neighborhoods. Sometimes the frustration is ascribed to legal restrictions on the use of official coercion, like the laws requiring due process and protecting other rights of the accused, which are seen as handcuffing the police while unleashing the thugs.

A third factor may contribute to vigilante violence. In some societies, including the United States, the legal system itself has become a source of value change. As was stated earlier, the dominant culture is not static and homogeneous; rather, new values can emerge and grow strong enough to use the legislative process to force some behavior change instead of protecting established behavioral norms. Vigilantes, resisting such change, can come to view the state as not simply ineffectual but as an actual enemy. Vigilantism under these conditions borders on reactionary violence.

These three factors in combination broaden the range of values and behavior that will be manifested in social relations. Vigilantes resort to violence in an effort to restrict the range of behavior, seeking to make it more predictable and keep it in closer accord with their own values. The failure of existing law to sufficiently restrain behavior to the satisfaction of potential vigilantes, however, is not a sufficient explanation for their resort to violence.

Vigilantes do not respond to perceived threats in a vacuum. Other factors mediate between the frustrating experiences and their violent response. One of these is the extent to which a particular culture condones violence as a useful and justifiable response to frustration. A culture of violence, of course, supports the excesses of both dissident and establishment violence (see Chapter VII). On the other hand, a culture that discourages overt expressions of hostility reinforces more passive responses to frustration.

The actual levels of vigilante violence will also be affected by the ability of the regime to defend the boundaries defining the acceptable use of coercion. One might expect that a government unable to adequately enforce formal laws or one whose legal system does not define a consistent position on the norms to be upheld would be less able to contain vigilante violence than a regime that defines a consistent position on the range of tolerated behavior, whether liberal or restrictive, and defends it through vigorous enforcement.

Vigilante violence, though easily condemned, has a somewhat ambiguous impact on legal and institutional development. When laws exist in form but not in fact, vigilante action may be a short-term substitute for a regularized system of law enforcement, until the regime increases its coercive capabilities or the people better internalize system-supporting values. Law enforcement that is both effective and protects the rights of the accused, moreover, tends to be quite costly and often ponderous. Establishment groups who feel seriously threatened by increasingly brazen criminal elements may be unwilling to accept either the costs or the delays involved in an institutionalized system of law enforcement, preferring vigilante self-help.

The potential costs of vigilantism are obvious. When successful, it brings only order without law. In many cases it fails to provide even order. Law, it can be argued, should impose limits not only on the average citizen but also on the enforcers. These are precisely the kinds of limitations the vigilantes are often trying to evade. Obviously incompatible with a regularized legal system, vigilantism may also sabotage the very order it seeks to guarantee. Vigilantism can become worse than the behavior it aims to suppress. Vigilante punishments tend to be disproportionate; the innocent have little protection; and quite often quasi-criminal elements are attracted to the movement, where they have a semilegitimate avenue for the expression of their antisocial tendencies. In addition, when law-enforcement officials are the ones participating in the acts of vigilante violence, what moral validity the formal system of laws retains may be diminished.

Vigilantes do not always direct their wrath only at those engaging in criminal activities. Their targets, as noted above, can include those who express deviant social or political values, but who are not, strictly speaking, committing crimes. The growing demands of deviant groups for increased power and representation may exceed the capacity of the established institutions either to meet or suppress them.

During such times of expanding demands, the adaptive capabilities of the dominant institutions are severely tested. Failure to cope can culminate in collapse and, ultimately, the reintegration of the people into a new sociopolitical order. Vigilantism, insofar as it retards these demands, may buy time for the established institutions to increase their capability to absorb or restrict the challenges. A partial redistribution of values which will satisfy at least the more moderate of the dissidents while not seriously alienating core establishment groups requires time to effect.

Social-control vigilantism might succeed in imposing quiescence on disruptive elements and in this way help to prop up threatened institutions, but it can do little to aid the process of adaptation. Successful adaptation requires that at least some of the deviant values be woven into an altered fabric of social and political relations. The most that can be accomplished through a strategy of coercion, vigilante or otherwise, is that the deviant elements may sink into despair and withdraw from the confrontation with the proponents of the established value system. Such a result would constitute preservation, perhaps, but not adaptation.

Moreover, the suppression of social groups who represent countervalues involves certain clear risks. An erratic and uncoordinated series of vigilante attacks on these groups may simply serve to increase their sense of alienation. In the absence of meaningful reform, the likelihood of dissident violence in the future could rise, and the established order might find itself under even more severe attack.

The self-appointed legislation and enforcement of the vigilantes, therefore, cannot be dismissed simply as pathological. These activities may make some contribution to the survival of the dominant system of social values. Granted, the established order does not deserve automatic defense, for it inevitably contains substantial elements of injustice and perversity. Behavior norms and patterns counter to the established system, however, also are not inherently acceptable, for many are as perverse and destructive as the worst aspects of the status quo. A just legal order must reflect the needs of all its citizens—the needs of some to restrict the range of tolerated behavior, as well as the needs of others to express contrary values and behave in novel ways. In this dilemma, perhaps, lies the tragedy of all human legal systems.

Chapter XIII Primary Political Values: Freedom and Order

POLITICAL VALUES AND POLITICAL CHOICE

Meaningful political participation involves decision making. Intelligent decisions, in turn, assume the existence of sufficient information on which to base a judgment and the existence of some criteria, values, or goals to guide the choice. Political values, in order to provide the needed guidance, must be sufficiently elaborate to define an applicable set of social and political priorities. Only then will the participants be able to select from among the available alternatives the course of action most in accord with their preferences.

This idealized process is seldom approximated by ordinary citizens. The shortfall results, to a great extent, from two obvious practical limitations. First, most people confront relatively few significant political decisions—in part because of the unequal distribution of power existing even in democratic countries, which concentrates most decisions in the hands of relatively few. Many, though, fail to take full advantage of the participatory opportunities available to them. Decision-making situations are often anxiety-producing, and some people would rather avoid the dilemmas of choice, preferring to have their actions determined for them. Such "escape from freedom" may be a primary basis for the survival of authoritarian systems.[1]

A second practical barrier to intelligent participation involves the amount of information available to the participants. "Rational choice" is often defined in terms of value maximization; that is, rational decision makers will choose the course of action that gives the largest return in terms of their values, whether material or metaphysical. Perfect value maximization, then, requires knowledge of all the available options and their consequences. Even the most knowledgeable decision maker lacks complete information, and the average political participant functions in a miasma of ignorance. The best that

249

can be hoped for in this regard, perhaps, is what two political scientists have called "optimal ignorance."[2] Rather than strive for total knowledge about a situation, a maximizer would stop at that point where the value of an additional unit of information falls below the cost of acquiring it. This point, however, though clear in the abstract, may be quite difficult to determine in areas of concrete choice. In any case, those who control other significant power resources will be better able to acquire needed information than the resource-poor.

In addition to surmounting these external, practical impediments to intelligent participation, an internal conceptual requirement must also be met: The decision makers must know their own minds. Intelligent choice depends on the self-conscious development of personal values—for without such development, the grounds for a decision will be unclear and probably ill-conceived. Political ideals like freedom, order, equality, and justice are often invoked to justify particular actions; so often, in fact, that they have deteriorated to the status of clichés. Yet the frequency of their use should not obscure the complexity of their meanings. Perhaps these general principles could provide criteria for choice, but only after their implications have been specified. Each of these values, however, has multiple facets that may not be entirely compatible with one another. Consequently, two people may advocate "freedom" or "equality" but draw substantially different conclusions about the proper course of public policy. These core political values, moreover, may not be wholly consistent with one another. To maximize one within a political system may entail sacrificing the others. Thus, intelligent decisions require that the value bases for judgment be specified, that the implications of each value be understood, that inconsistencies between or among multiple values be recognized, and that some resolution or trade-off be attempted.

This chapter and the next will investigate some of the common meanings and ambiguities of the four primary political values mentioned above: freedom, order, equality, and justice. All four are interrelated, but for ease of analysis they have been split into pairs. This chapter revolves around the compatibility between freedom and order, while the next is fundamentally concerned with questions of distribution—equality and justice. The definition of each, of course, impinges on all the others, and the final section of the next chapter attempts to recapitulate some of the possible interconnections. Finally, power questions provide a pragmatic dimension to the more abstract philosophical discussions. Problems of value choice and maximization cannot be realistically considered apart from a configuration of power relations.

A preliminary examination of political value problems does not presume to give definitive answers to questions that have intrigued political philosophers for millennia. Rather, it pursues a more modest objective: to identify some of the complications that attend forming a conscious system of political values and moving beyond ignorance and prejudice in the area of political choice. What each person ultimately decides remains his or her own individual responsibility.

ISSUES IN THE MEANING OF FREEDOM

Historically, the appeal of freedom has been great. Nations have fought for it, scholars have debated it, constitutions have institutionalized it, and individuals have defended it. On the bleaker side, tyrants have often limited it, and countries have lost it. Despite the turmoil instigated in its name, however, the precise meaning of *freedom* for its advocates is not always clear. Several pivotal problems include the reality of "free will," the various definitions of freedom, and the relation between freedom and order.

The Problem of Free Will

The question of free will lies at the center of any discussion of freedom, for unless in some fundamental sense human beings have the capacity for real choice, subsequent discussion of freedom becomes largely meaningless. If human action is predetermined, then both morality and freedom are illusionary. Morality requires that people can really choose between good and evil, for if behavior is determined then to do good merits no praise and to commit evil deserves no blame.

Determinism may be of two types: remediable and irremediable. The former recognizes that although people possess the capacity for choice in principle, external constraints may be such as to deny it in fact. One could presumably elect to die rather than submit to an externally imposed tyranny, but the extremity of this decision hardly qualifies it as the best example of a person freely choosing between alternatives. This type of determinism, since it is not complete and is based on external factors, can be changed. Indeed, one could argue that the primary goal of the struggle for freedom is to eliminate or minimize such restrictions on the ability of people to shape their own destiny, for good or ill.

Irremediable determinism does not simply place choice in chains; it denies its reality. Behavior is seen as predestined to follow a certain course, wherefore choice is only apparent, not real. Though free will would seem necessary for any conception of individual moral responsibility, some religious sects have asserted that one's salvation or damnation has been predestined and that the individual can do nothing to alter this ultimate consequence.[3] The religious debate over the reality of free will primarily results from the apparent paradox between the Almighty's precognition of all that will happen and the assertion, nonetheless, of the reality of free will for people in the temporal sphere.

In this more secular age, doctrines of irremediable determinism adopt less metaphysical forms. Individual behavior is seen as the inevitable product of prior learning—humans have no choice but to behave in the manner that they have been taught through a continuing process of reward and punishment (see the discussion in Chapter XI). On a somewhat grander scale, laws of historical evolution are believed to be such that individual decisions are meaningless, for macro outcomes are inevitable. Consequently, though people may appear to have choice in their individual lives, their decisions have no impact on the primary thrust of history.[4]

The proponents of free will, understandably, hold different views of human volition and historical progression. History, rather than being deemed an inevitable evolution or cycle of macro events, is viewed as the product of individual desires and decisions, many of which are misguided or "evil." A major concern of those who focus on the indeterminacy of human action is how to insure "right" or "moral" choice. Liberal theorists usually argue that most people will freely choose the correct course if they recognize it—that imperfect knowledge leads to misbehavior. The need, then, is for enlightenment, and the liberals' stance is basically optimistic and progress-oriented. For religious liberals, human reason, guided by the teachings of the church, insures the selection of the proper path, the path in conformance with God's law. Secular liberalism places great emphasis on education and on the operations of the "enlightened self-interest" of reasonable men and women as the guarantee of social welfare. This position supports a negative conception of freedom as the absence of restraint (see below).

Those more conservative theorists who accept the reality of free will believe that humans are fundamentally flawed and that if left to their own devices will tend to choose prideful and selfish alternatives. Therefore, the "right" way must be imposed—an attitude which aims to place external constraints on the exercise of free will, ironically affirming its reality while attempting to restrict its exercise. This position tends to be pessimistic, paternalistic, and biased toward stability. These conservative fears about the likely consequences of the free exercise of human will incline the proponents who entertain them to favor a "positive" view of freedom as self-perfection (see below). Between these two faces of freedom, it may be possible to stake out a third position, which sees freedom as action.

There remains in any event the question of which stance on free will is correct. No definitive answer can resolve the tension, for the sensations both of free will and of determinacy are part of human experience. The notions of cause and effect, whether in the natural or social sciences, depend on the idea of determination. One's view of past events is shaped by a sense of inevitability. What has happened cannot be altered, and to speculate "what if" is a logical fallacy in historical inquiry.[5] Turning to the future, to the "yet to be completed," does give the feeling of possibilities, of the meaningfulness of choice. Even the natural sciences have abandoned absolute cause-effect notions for theories that include elements of indeterminacy. Perhaps the contradiction between the two positions can never be fully resolved, and it is necessary, as Carl Friedrich suggests, to live with the paradox of free choice and causality.[6]

Freedom as the Absence of Restraint

One prominent concept of freedom considers it in a negative sense: that freedom is the absence of restraint.[7] Simply put, this type of freedom aims to remove all obstacles to people's doing what they wish. Though usually individualistic in emphasis, it has been expanded to collectivities through the principle of national self-determination.[8] This perspective on freedom commonly stresses human rights and liberties, whether "inherent" or assigned through some political compact. These rights circumscribe a sphere of inviolability within which the individual can do as he pleases. At the extreme, this position asserts that there should be no external limits on the sphere of inviolability. The function of the political system, if it has a function at all, is to insure as far as possible that everyone has the opportunity to do what each desires.

A moment's reflection, however, immediately qualifies this objective, for the absence of restraint for one person could easily result in tyranny for another. Therefore, the goal is often redefined as the maximization of individual freedom insofar as this does not interfere with the freedom of anyone else. Unfortunately, this principle, though often restated (as in "my freedom to swing my arm ends where your nose begins"), fails to add much clarity to the situation. It merely regresses the problem back one step to the determination of what constitutes interference.

The difficulty in establishing the limits of interference arises from the fact that the "inviolable sphere" of human liberty is something of a conceptual fiction which is interpreted differently by different people. It suggests a view of society as a collection of impenetrable balls, each encasing an individual citizen. Society, however, can also be conceived as a complex web of interdependencies, with each citizen being defined as a point of connection among numerous relationships. Both of these idealizations exaggerate, but the second serves to point out the difficulty in discussing noninterference if each person is viewed as an inseparable part of a wider context. The absolute principle of noninterference is reduced by necessity to a consideration of the degree of "acceptable" or "tolerable" interference compatible with the idea of freedom as the absence of restraint.

This rather abstruse problem can be concretely illustrated by reference to the controversy surrounding the First Amendment protection of freedom of speech. The amendment reads as follows:

> Congress shall make *no law* respecting an establishment of religion, or prohibiting the free exercise thereof; or abridging the freedom of speech, or of the press; or the right of the people peaceably to assemble, and to petition the Government for a redress of grievances. (*emphasis added*)

Taken literally, this is about as absolute a statement of an individual liberty as exists in the world's political documents. "No law," as the late Supreme Court Justice Hugo Black argued, means *NO law*, which seems simple enough. The application of this apparently straightforward dictum, however, has become encrusted with complications because of the interconnections of the social web. First, most libertarians concede that the absolute right of individual free speech must be limited so that all can enjoy it; that is, one does not have the right to shout down an opposing argument.[9] Second, at some point speech can become an act that damages another person (interferes with his freedom), for example, libel and slander. It seems justifiable to prohibit such speech.[10] A third, and more nebulous, limitation arises when the exercise of free speech comes into conflict with the state's right to preserve the public order (see the next section). At times, the Supreme Court has ruled that speech can be limited only when its exercise constitutes a "clear and present danger" to the public safety, as when a demagogue attempts to foment a riot in a volatile situation. Other Court decisions have applied a looser doctrine, allowing suppression if the speech has a "tendency" to lead to disorderly acts, even though the danger is not clear and present.[11] The so-called "bad tendency" test could be used to quash any opinion with which the established authorities disagree.

Each of these criteria attempts to delineate boundaries for the acceptable exercise of a right which appeared to be an absolute. Logically, there are very few clear-cut limits on how far the government could restrict free speech under the justification that its exercise interferes with the rights of others or the obligation of the government to preserve public order. Probably the only speech which does not potentially interfere with anyone else is that without an audience. Consequently, to say that citizens are free to say or write what they please as long as they do not interfere with others' freedom is to say very little indeed. The hard question involves how much interference and what kinds of limitations on liberty are compatible with a free society. What is more, if these kinds of arguments can be marshalled for restraining the exercise of a relatively intellectual freedom, it would not be too difficult to develop similar justifications for restricting various kinds of actions.

The nature of restraints on freedom can be interpreted more broadly than the direct denial of what are assumed to be absolute liberties. All the citizens in a country may be free to express any opinion they wish, but those who have control of, or access to, the media seem to be "more free," or at least to have more resources for exercising their freedom. Thus, the freedom to act without formal, legal restraint does not mean the same to the poor as it does to the wealthy.

Consequently, people, in the absence of appropriate means, may be unable to take full advantage of formally constituted rights. A broad interpretation of freedom as the absence of restraint, therefore, could well strive to provide sufficient power resources to every citizen, so that all could fully enjoy "the blessings of liberty."[12] At this point, the goals of freedom would begin to merge with those of equality. Such a merger generates certain problems, for in order to give the deprived the necessary means to exercise their formal freedom, it may be necessary to restrict the freedom of the more advantaged. So again, the question arises: How far can the freedom of some be limited in order to provide or maximize freedom for others? Other tensions between freedom and equality will be examined in the next chapter.

Somewhat paradoxically, freedom as the absence of restraint is, in a sense, compatible with behavioral determinism. A determinist could imagine a society in which people could do whatever they desired, but what they desired would be the subject of prior conditioning. External restraints would be unnecessary because of the effectiveness of the internalized ones. The experience of freedom under these conditions would be something of an illusion.

Freedom as Self-Perfection

The essentially negative nature of the concept of freedom as the absence of restraint is countered by the "positive" thrust of the concept of freedom as self-perfection:[13] One is free to do only what one ought. People are not free to commit error; rather, they are free only to act in the "proper" manner—to aim at some good. This idea may seem innocuous enough, until one attempts to define the positive goals of human action, the goods. What commonly occurs is that in the dominant community the norms supporting the existing distribution of power and reflecting the preferences of the powerful are accepted, whereas the norms that question the establishment are declared to be misguided and are not tolerated. Not surprisingly, radical dissidents adopt precisely the opposite attitude: Their views must be allowed to prosper, while those of the dominant community should be repressed.[14] In both instances, freedom is viewed as not extending to behavior that is considered repugnant.

People who refuse to accept the consequences of freedom as the absence of restraint generally imply a positive notion of freedom in their condemnations of "unbridled license." Thus, freedom may be supported only if it is "responsibly exercised," a phrase which usually means "exercised in an acceptable manner through the pursuit of certain goals."

This positive notion of freedom influences the continuing debate over pornography.[15] The courts have generally held that the First Amendment does not protect pornographic materials, a position which is quasi-positive in nature, in that the "quality" of the content is considered a relevant criterion in applying the law. The advocate of freedom as the absence of restraint would argue that no restrictions should be placed on the reading (and by extension, viewing) matter of adults, regardless of the content. Once the courts have excluded pornography from the protection of the First Amendment, they necessarily face the problem of defining what constitutes pornography. Early efforts developed the standard of "redeeming social value"—that is, if the work under consideration has some "value," then its sexual material can be tolerated. This positive freedom sentiment, however, proved to be rather vague. The Supreme Court found itself, in a potentially unlimited series of cases, to be the prospective ultimate tribunal for evaluating "social value." Recent decisions tend in the direction of allowing local authorities greater discretion in deciding what is obscene in their communities. The contradiction in applying an essentially positive notion of freedom in the interpretation of a clearly "negative" liberty has yet to be resolved.

In some sense, the problem is one of tolerance. How far are the people or the government willing to tolerate opinions and behavior that deviate from conventional standards? Freedom as self-perfection, in effect, "tolerates" only that which meets a certain standard. This practice, however, is not really toleration at all, for one does not really tolerate that with which one agrees. Moreover, toleration implies that the tolerator could do something about the disagreeable actions or opinions but deliberately chooses to do otherwise.[16] In short, helplessness is not a sign of tolerance. The idea of freedom as the absence of restraint, then, implies a considerable degree of toleration from one and all.

Freedom limited to only those actions which are deemed appropriate may strike many as not really being freedom at all. Notwithstanding the intrinsic appeal of guiding people to do good and avoid evil, this rationale has been used to justify paternalistic and even repressive policies. It is an idea of freedom unable to accept fully the implications of free will—that human will cannot be said to be completely "free" unless people can choose the "wrong" direction as well as the "right." Pushed to the extreme, freedom as self-perfection justifies "forcing people to be free," that is, using coercion to structure the proper behavioral response.

Freedom as Political Action

A third concept of freedom, lying between the negative and positive positions described above, can also be defined. Freedom can be seen as "acting freely."[17] It is not simply being able to choose, but choosing. Unlike the concept of negative freedom, it implies deliberate action, not simply the absence of restraint. In this limited sense, the concept of freedom as political action contains a certain positive element—citizens must act on their freedom, not simply sit on it. It is unlike the concept of freedom as self-perfection, however, in that the proper course of action is not pronounced. The act of choosing is central, not the precise content of the choice.

Freedom as political action goes beyond freedom as the absence of restraint in another respect as well. It emphasizes the *public* nature of the actions, whereas negative freedom usually stresses the private lives of the citizens. Certain negative liberties, such as those guaranteeing free speech and assembly, are necessary but not sufficient conditions for the existence of this type of freedom, which depends on people *using* their liberties to participate actively in public life. As one advocate of freedom as political action put it: "Politics is the public actions of free men; free men are those who do, not merely can, live both publicly and privately. Men who have lost the capacity for public action, who fear it or despise it, are not free, they are simply isolated and ineffectual."[18]

This belief in the primacy of public action can be traced back to the ideals of the Greek *polis* or city-state of 400 B.C. In Athens, men were considered not completely free, indeed not fully human, unless they participated in the public life of the *polis*. As the Athenian statesman Pericles stated:

> Here each individual is interested not only in his own affairs but in the affairs of the state as well: even those who are mostly occupied with their own business are extremely well-informed on general politics—this is a peculiarity of ours: we do not say that a man who takes no interest in politics is a man who minds his own business; we say that he has no business here at all.[19]

Similarly, Hannah Arendt argues that when Jefferson included the rights of "life, liberty, and the pursuit of happiness" in the Declaration of Independence, he had something more in mind than simply private, self-regarding happiness. Rather, he wanted the citizens of the new country to experience "public" happiness, something quite distinct from the protection from arbitrary interference in their private lives. Public happiness consists of being a "participator in the government of affairs."[20] Americans, Arendt believes, have neglected the pursuit of such public happiness.

Appealing as freedom conceived as political action appears, it, too, is not without some problems. Carl Friedrich notes that there may be a particular tension between participatory freedom and the independence of private life.[21] One way of increasing participatory freedom is to expand the sphere of public activities. The contemporary welfare state, for example, engages in much more social activity than its nineteenth-century predecessor. In a sense, therefore, the significance of freedom as political action has also increased. Correspondingly, there has been a decline in the individual's private independence. Ultimately, one could conceive of a situation in which all social action becomes a matter of public decision and the sphere of private independence dwindles to zero. Just as the concept of freedom as political action modifies the concept of freedom as the absence of restraint, it also may need to be limited.

Freedom to Create

The different meanings of freedom discussed so far have all dealt, in one way or another, with choice among existing alternatives: Free will concerns the problem of whether people have the capacity of choice in any meaningful sense. The concept of freedom as the absence of restraint focuses on the elimination of restrictions on people's ability to choose. The concept of freedom as self-perfection addresses the issue of correct choice. Finally, the concept of freedom as political action emphasizes the act of choosing. Carl Friedrich observes, however, that it may be possible to go beyond existing alternatives and create a new option. One way in which the concept of freedom can expand is by widening the range of choice through innovation and invention.[22]

The conditions that encourage creativity in either the private or public realm are imperfectly understood, though they seem rooted in the ability of gifted persons to give free rein to their imaginations. The constraints on imagination can be culturally imposed, as when communal values discourage any kind of nonconformity in ideas or action. Similarly, prevailing power holders might deliberately discourage activities that threaten to undermine their established positions. Thus, traditional elites not only oppose the formation of new political organizations (such as political parties) that present a direct political challenge, but they also may be hostile to apparently nonpolitical social and technological innovations (such as industrialization) that could lead to a redistribution of power in society.

Freedom to create, though distinct from other forms of freedom, appears to require a minimization of restraints and the ability to act on the new ideas. Thus, one can reasonably argue that the several concepts of freedom, while not identical, should be fairly highly correlated with one another—where freedom as the absence of restraint and freedom as action are present, so also will be creative freedom and vice versa. In addition, the freedom to create implies the ability to do the totally unexpected and, therefore, affects order in society.

ISSUES IN THE MEANING OF ORDER

Appeals to the value of order punctuate recent political campaigns in the United States. The specter of ever-escalating crime rates, combined with racial strife and campus conflicts, produced a willingness in many citizens and their representatives to support measures reinforcing police power. This strengthening of the forces of "law and order" ranged from the acquisition by local police departments of paramilitary weapons (machine guns and armored cars) to limitations of criminal suspects' rights through recent Supreme Court decisions. Nor are these concerns unique to the United States. Other political systems, when afflicted by disruption and violence, have granted considerable power to those who promise to recreate order. Indeed, it could be that order is the primary political value. All the other goals of political life, such as freedom, equality, and justice, seem possible to pursue only when order exists. This does not mean that the realization of other values follows automatically upon the imposition of order; rather, order is a necessary, but not sufficient, condition for their maximization.

This conventional wisdom regarding the value of order fails to examine fully either its meanings or its implications. It may be that order, plausibly defined, is not a necessary condition for the maximization of other values and may even be antithetical to their realization if pushed too far. Before this possibility is investigated, some of the various meanings assigned to order must first be explored.

Order as the Absence of Overt Conflict

One "commonsense" meaning of *order* places it in opposition to *conflict* in society. Social and political conflicts are viewed as the sources of disorder, wherefore an orderly society must strive to eliminate all vestiges of overt conflict. One critical issue is how the conflictless society comes into existence. Conflict may diminish or disappear if the participating groups in society have basically compatible interests. Or instead, conflict may not be manifested because of the failure of a disadvantaged group to recognize how its interests clash with those of more privileged elements of society. In the Marxist model, this type of ignorance explains the quiescence of the proletariat before the growth of class consciousness. Still another possibility is that overt disagreements can be coerced into nonexpression by the superior power position of one side, thereby creating the appearance of a conflictless system.

Each of these three possibilities results in order as the absence of overt conflict. Clearly, the quality of this order is substantially different in the three cases. Though a society characterized by a significant compatibility of interests on the part of all the members may support the growth of other political values, the other two cases offer no such promise. It is difficult to imagine how freedom, equality, or justice could be fostered in a social order that either manipulates or coerces conflict out of existence.[23]

Order as Harmony

Some of the more noxious implications of the concept of order as the absence of overt conflict can be avoided by stressing that only a value consensus is the basis for true order. The vision of a completely harmonious society exercises strong appeal over the minds of citizens, especially during periods of serious discord. In these visions, other values also thrive, as citizens pursue their activities in complete accord over the ends and means of society.[24]

Unfortunately, dreams of complete social harmony, though they may illuminate the shortcomings of the existent world, really avoid the problems of order and disorder in current social and political systems. Conflicts, or disharmonies, inevitably develop over both power distributions and social purposes, but to evaluate all of these as examples of disorder ignores the great differences among types of conflict (see Chapter VI). Consequently, just as defining order as the absence of overt conflict seems too broad, limiting its meaning to complete social harmony appears too restrictive. Rather, one must inquire whether the conflicts that are endemic to all social systems could be conducted in an "orderly" fashion.

Order as Adherence to the Law

The common incantation "law and order" implies that there is a connection between the two. If the people obey the laws of the land, which are designed to structure their relations along certain lines, order will prevail. These laws could conceivably guarantee complete social harmony, but they need not. The legal order might simply limit the weapons that can be used to express social conflict, as well as establish ways to regulate or resolve it. In this regard, Carl Friedrich defines an "orderly arrangement" as one in which the use of coercion in the attainment of political ends is kept to a minimum.[25]

The concept of order as law, however, begs the question as to the origins of the law. Is law a reflection of some immutable truths that are assumed to govern human societies? Medieval philosophers like Thomas Aquinas argued that human law in order to be binding must reflect the precepts of natural law—principles assumed to be so basic that they could be recognized by all those capable of exercising reason.[26] A regime based on commands in violation of these precepts would not be an order at all, but a tyranny, a system of violence. Human law might supplement and elaborate natural law in providing for orderly social relations, but not subtract from it.

The development of legal positivism has generally replaced this metaphysical interpretation of law.[27] Rather, law is conceived of as situationally specific; each culture's law reflects the peculiarities and preferences of a particular time and place; what is lawful or unlawful in one culture may not be so in another. The more cynical "positivist" interpretation views law as simply the system of rules that the powerful foist upon the weak. These rules could structure conflict and minimize violence in society, but they certainly do not reflect any ultimate good. Rather the "good" defended by the laws is the interest of the ruling classes.

A less cynical "positivist" perspective sees law as essentially consisting of the formalized statements of the customs and values of the members of a common culture. Insofar as cultures differ, so also will notions of what is lawful. If an agglomeration of individuals shares few values and standards, it becomes correspondingly more difficult to establish formal rules governing their interactions.

Liberals and conservatives generally differ on how easily a lawful order can be extended or altered. Conservatives see a common culture developing slowly through a gradual accretion of tradition. They therefore consider it unwise to tamper with established patterns in order to pursue revolutionary schemes, no matter how attractive they appear in the abstract; new law, unsupported by customary inclinations, will prove to be a futile exercise.[28] Certainly, the failure of Western-model constitutions to take root in Asia and Africa, where they were largely unsupported by tradition, tends to support the conservative position. Legal development since independence in these areas has generally paid greater regard to local customs.

Liberals, on the other hand, see the relation between formal law and underlying values as more dynamic and reciprocal. Consequently, though customary proclivities may support the law, law can also be used to change these attitudes. Law, therefore, can be used to bring about orderly reform. Though liberal optimism seems excessive with respect to the postcolonial experience, perhaps because this involved establishing basic law, it has proven more justified in cases where the constitution is generally accepted and reforms take place within this fundamental legal order.

This different attitude toward the role of law can be seen in the reactions to civil-rights legislation in the United States over the past two decades. Conservatives often argued that laws against discrimination were impractical, because law could not be used to change the human heart. Conversely, liberals answered that law could alter overt behavior, and hearts would follow after. The significant success achieved by antidiscriminatory legislation, though not unmixed, is probably attributable to the fact that most Americans remained loyal to the underlying legal system.

Whatever the source of law, if all the citizens in a society recognize and comply with it, orderly social interaction will most likely result. Nevertheless, this proposition does not really identify the nature of order, only what might produce it. In fact, recognizing and obeying law is not the only cause of order in social relations. Like the other two definitions, order as adherence to law defines the concept in terms of what is presumed to be a desirable social condition (as the absence of conflict, or as the presence of harmony), rather than isolating the psychological basis of the perception or order.

Toward a Psychological Definition of Order

The unanticipated disorients people, whether it consists of the vicious attack of a midnight mugger or simply of behavior that deviates from stereotypical expectations. Order, then, exists when people are able to develop stable and accurate expectations about one another's behavior.[29] *Disorder* basically means surprise, though the nature and consequences of the surprise may vary considerably. Even presumably pleasant surprises can be a source of social disruption and cause considerable psychological strain. Some research, in fact, suggests that significant change in a person's life, whether an improvement or not, increases both psychological tension and even susceptibility to illness.[30]

Order defined in these terms does not preclude the existence of conflict from an orderly society, as long as that conflict develops along expected lines. The reason why adherence to the law produces order is just this: People conduct their affairs, whether conflictual or consensual, according to commonly recognized rules. Complete harmony of purpose and perspective, obviously, would also engender stable and accurate expectations, but so might a regularized system of coercion. Habitualized behavior is a major contributor to order in a system, as people can anticipate that others will automatically react in specific ways to particular stimuli (for instance, drive on the right side of the road).

Some amount of order is necessary for the functioning of any social system, but the value of that order—whether it is judged "good" or "evil"— depends on the application of some external standard. It seems very dubious, therefore, that order *qua* order is the ultimate political value, for without considerable qualification any expectation would then be acceptable as long as it were accurate and stable. The inmates of a concentration camp, for instance, lead very orderly lives, but most would probably be willing to accept a little disruption rather than tolerate complete regimentation. The evaluation of any particular order reduces to issues of kind and degree, and, in the final judgment, rests on the extent to which that order *facilitates* the realization of other values. Perhaps the most problematic area in this regard concerns the relationship between the various concepts of freedom and order as stable expectations.

FREEDOM, ORDER, AND POWER

Freedom and order are sometimes considered to be polar opposites. The concept of freedom as the absence of restraint, for example, often produces images of people following their momentary whims and engaging in wild behavior unrepressed by the shackles of society. A society without restraint is portrayed as approaching social if not moral anarchy. The concept of freedom as political action also appears to increase the likelihood for disorder. Conventional political wisdom suggests that extensive participation in a country with a large and untutored populace will make the process of governance unwieldy and erratic. An orderly political process is generally thought to require a certain concentration of power to facilitate decision making and provide the necessary social coordination. Even democratic societies must create representative bodies and bureaucracies to provide for order and efficiency in government. Sometimes, the dissemination of accurate and comprehensive information is perceived as a threat to the integrity of the government by the bureaucrats who cloak their activities under the mantle of national security or organizational efficiency.

In addition, the freedom to create is obviously a source of disorder. By definition, such inventions and innovations are unexpected and initially disturbing. In time, of course, people can adjust to the new pattern or process. Authoritarian regimes usually restrict the amount of political experimentation allowed, for it is intrinsically disruptive of the status quo. The most dramatic and disruptive act of creative politics is revolution, and such attempts to create a new web of social and political relations will cause disorder throughout the system.

Only if freedom is defined as self-perfection does it seem to escape the tension with order. If people are "free" to behave only in the prescribed manner, and all other actions represent the illegitimate vestiges of deviant tendencies, then freedom and order can indeed be completely compatible. Of course, as was noted earlier, the concept of freedom as self-perfection appears to be something of a contradiction.

The simple dichotomy of freedom vs. order, though indicative of a potential conflict, actually obscures the complexity of the interaction between the two values. In the everyday world, as opposed to the realm of philosophical discourse, the relations between freedom and order are mediated by considerations of power. Free will holds little meaning for the person who is not free to carry out his will because of the lack of sufficient means. Freedom in terms of the absence of restraint can mean both protection from external interference in one's life and freedom from resource constraints on one's desires—both of which require power. Creative freedom and the exercise of freedom as political action also necessitate a certain level of resources to bring the concepts into being. The expansion of participation or the dissemination of information about the political process both mandate a distribution of these key power resources. Even the concept of freedom as self-perfection raises questions about the means that facilitate appropriate behavior. Freedom requires power. In fact, in a sense, freedom is power: power to protect oneself from undue interference and/or to translate preference into action.

The "enabling" capacity of power resources, however, has another aspect. The control of these resources permits persons or groups to have an impact on their environment. These resources, in effect, can be used to impose a preferred order. In this way, one person's freedom and orderly expectations can become others' nonfreedom and possible disorder. If the latter have sufficient power to resist but not enough to realize their own preferences, then the freedom and order of both parties can decline. The distribution of power becomes the link between freedom and order. A concentration of power leads to freedom for the few and order, at best, for the many. A dispersal of power leads to anarchy. The only apparent way out of this dilemma is through a consensus among citizens about how they prefer to behave. They must freely choose not to disrupt one another's lives, because only through civic moderation can a limited freedom and order co-exist for all citizens. All this, of course, assumes that the sensation of choosing is not an illusion. If free will is simply another of humanity's self-deceptions, then the problem of freedom and order is simply reduced to one of creating an automatically supported order rather than one externally imposed.

The maintenance of order in society, whether through the power of the few over the many or that of the majority over the minority, or the cooperation of each with all, tends to support the existing distribution of power. Change is disorderly, and the more significant the change, the greater will be the disorder. The evaluation of the desirability of a particular order, therefore, generates questions not only of freedom but also of equality and justice. Freedom, too, insofar as it requires some power resources, leads to similar inquiries into problems of equality and justice. Some of these are discussed in the next chapter.

Chapter XIV   Primary Political Values: Equality and Justice

The inevitable scarcity of desired power resources generates distributive conflict. Disputes over ethical principles delineating a *legitimate* distribution of resources also proceed from the same conditions of scarcity. If supplies of a valued resource were sufficient, issues of equality and justice would decline in salience. Unfortunately, the realities of this imperfect world insure that these two values will be of paramount importance in political discourse.

Equality and justice are intimately related. Once the circumstances under which humans should be treated as equals have been identified, the basic contours of justice also emerge. Alternatively, principles of justice, once agreed upon, determine the manner in which citizens should be treated—whether as equals or according to some norms which distinguish among them.

These two values are also interconnected with those of freedom and order. The link between equality and freedom can be seen in the drive for equal rights and liberties. The idea of *equal* rights is relatively new. Liberty is an ancient value, but was usually defined according to a person's station in society. Thus, the rights and obligations of a noble differed from those of a free commoner. The first significant, programmatic coupling of the goals of liberty and equality (that is, an ideology) developed during the American Revolution.[1] Hannah Arendt argues that in subsequent revolutions (from the French through the Russian and Chinese) the desire for equality grew to overshadow that for liberty and often tended to snuff out liberty in the name of equality.[2] On the other hand, as was suggested in the previous chapter, the distribution of power resources affects the extent to which a person can take advantage of formally guaranteed rights. Consequently, the potential effects of freedom and equality upon one another are likely to be as complicated as the interrelations between freedom and order.

Similarly, the concept of justice prevailing in a society affects not only the

265

definition of what constitutes a legitimate distribution of resources, but also the evaluations of both freedom and order. Indeed, one could put forth a persuasive claim that justice is the most important of all the values which guide political choice. The establishment of a just system solves the problems concerning the nature and limits of freedom, order, and equality.

This hierarchy, however, tends to understate the extent to which the other political values can affect ideas of justice. To paraphrase the language of scientific causality, justice is not the independent value and the others dependent ones; rather, all are mutually interdependent. In order to clarify some of these problems, the next two sections will briefly examine alternative ways of viewing equality and justice. Finally, the conclusion, though not proclaiming any definitive answers, sets forth a number of the major problems relative to all four political values.

ISSUES IN THE MEANING OF EQUALITY

Equality, like freedom and order, is a question of degree—people can be more or less equal to one another. Often, definitions of the ways in which persons are, or should be, considered equal for political and social purposes are really attempts to limit how far the principle of complete or "perfect" equality should be carried.

Moral Equality

". . . all men are created equal . . .," Jefferson holds in the Declaration of Independence. By this phrase he does not seem to mean that men are equal in political, social, and economic power, nor that they are born with equal talents and capabilities. Rather, he is apparently asserting that in some fundamental sense all human beings are *moral* equals. Although Jefferson argues that this truth is "self-evident," historical experience belies this conviction. Not only have people repeatedly behaved as though their fellows were members of some lesser species, but political philosophers also have often attested to the reality of moral *inequality*. Plato asserted that certain men and, interestingly for a classical philosopher, women were best suited by nature and training to know and appreciate the idea of the Good. In the *Republic*, he devised a myth that some derived their natures from gold, others from silver, and the vast majority from iron and brass, symbolizing the innate inequality of humans.[3] Even his more moderate and in some respects democratic student Aristotle believed that some were suited by their natures to be slaves.[4]

Belief in the moral equality of all humans received its major impetus from the Christian idea of equality in the eyes of the Creator. This metaphysical conception of ultimate equality has no *necessary* implications for other possible forms of equality. People still may be endowed with different talents, and they may legitimately control unequal amounts of political and social power resources ("the powers that be are ordained of God.").[5]

In recent centuries, specifically religious conceptions of man have gradually given way to more secular, humanistic notions. The belief in equality before God, for example, has been partially transformed into a generalized assertion of universal human dignity.[6] This form of moral equality can also be largely independent of any specific social and political inequalities that characterize social relations. Moral equality, whether religiously or humanistically inspired, however, does imply that people should treat one another with a certain fundamental respect, despite their rank according to other criteria. Assumptions of human dignity, moreover, may facilitate the development of other ideas of equality with more direct implications for the constitution of the social order.

Equality before the Law

Equality in the eyes of God presumably will affect the decisions rendered on the day of "final judgment." Equality before the law affects the process of judgment in a more mundane and immediate fashion. This principle presumably assures that laws are defined in such a way so that no person or group is singled out for preferential or detrimental treatment. The laws should apply to all people equally. The most general issue in the area of legal equality is whether the rulers, as well as the ruled, should be equally subordinated to the laws of the land. The evolution of constitutional government is the history of the struggle to subordinate rulers to some fundamental law.

More particularly, legal equality assumes that all citizens, regardless of their station in society, should be treated equally by the courts. The use of precedent, the rules of evidence, and the right of every defendant to an attorney are elements of the United States judicial system designed, in part, to insure that each case will be judged on its merits and not on the personal qualities of the people involved.

Legal equality, whether in the broad sense of subordinating the political authorities to constitutional limitations or in the particular meaning of guaranteeing equal protection of the law to all citizens, encompasses the idea of moral equality but appears not to require any further efforts to reduce other social discrepancies. This appearance, however, may be somewhat deceptive, for despite the formal incarnation of principles of equal treatment, the powerful still benefit more from the law's "equal protection." Laws may be framed in universally applicable terms (for example, a general definition of burglary or vagrancy) but still be designed to defend the interests of the established classes from the challenges of criminal or radical groups. The legal system in the United States, for example, deals far more harshly with offenses against private property than with offenses against the public welfare (for instance, theft vs. pollution). To some extent, this emphasis is reversed in the Soviet Union. One could argue that for the laws to protect everyone equally, all must have an equal stake in the order that the law defends. This stake may not require complete social and economic equality, but a cursory survey of the condition of deprived groups, both in advanced nations and in the developing countries, suggests that a considerable redistribution of power resources would be necessary to achieve this condition.

The legal system, moreover, does not deal with offenders in an equivalent fashion. The relatively rich and powerful in the United States can afford to take full advantage of all the benefits and protection afforded by the system, including going free on bail, hiring the best attorneys, and utilizing all the possible appeal routes. Poor and even middle-class defendants lack the resources to pay for equal protection. They often languish in jail awaiting trial, accept a less-qualified court-appointed attorney, and are unable to appeal their conviction to a higher court. Equality before the law, therefore, cannot be seen in isolation but must be evaluated in a context of wider social and political relationships.

Political Equality

A third form of equality involves the extent to which citizens carry equal weight in the political process. As such, it subsumes and goes beyond considerations of moral and legal equality. Clearly, the amount of influence a person exercises in politics is a matter of degree, and perfect political equality could be approximated only in a pure participatory democracy. Even under these conditions, certain personal qualities may give some individuals greater persuasive power than others. Obviously, representative democracies will fall even shorter of this ideal.

An intensive drive for political equality and against aristocratic privilege began with the American and French Revolutions and continues to this day. This quest for political equality became intertwined with issues of freedom, especially insofar as it was thought necessary to guarantee certain political rights to all people in order to provide for their voice in the political process.

Political equality also presumes a kind of limitation on freedom—people are not free to create privileged positions that place others at a disadvantage. Moreover, the extension of political equality, while increasing the "total" liberty in the system, could well decrease the liberty of particular elements; the expansion of political liberties to a wider segment of the population may constitute a dilution of the freedom of those who occupied advantageous positions before the change. This ambiguous consequence raises an obvious question of justice: Is it justifiable to sacrifice the lesser number for the benefit of the greater proportion of the population? This problem is discussed further in the section on justice.

The goal of political equality begs another question. Though political power can be more widely dispersed through the expansion of formal political rights (such as the right to vote), these measures still fail to guarantee citizens an equal weight in the political process. In part, this failure is simply a result of the organization of a large-scale society. To facilitate efficient and effective governmental operations, it seems necessary to assign significant political authority to relatively few people. Even if these officials remain responsive and ultimately accountable to the general citizenry, they still must be considered more powerful politically. The apparent need to provide for a division of political labor identifies an area of tension between greater equality and effectiveness.

A problem in addition to that of who directly controls political authority resources in a system is the matter of which individuals and groups wield indirect control over the political authorities. As the exchange analysis of power resources suggests (see Chapter III), those who control other power resources will be able to use them to gain access to and influence over the political authorities. Consequently, political equality involves the problems of who has the direct authority to make political decisions and of who is able to exercise greater indirect control over this policy formation and implementation. The drive for greater political equality, therefore, eventually raises the question of whether it might not require increased socioeconomic equality as well.

Socioeconomic Equality

The most comprehensive form of equalization would aim at the redistribution of all significant power resources so that everyone shares equally in their control. In principle, at least, the programs of the modern welfare state are intended to create greater socioeconomic equality by establishing a floor below which society will not allow its members to slip. The programs of the welfare state are often financed by graduated taxation through which, in theory, those who earn more pay a larger proportion of their income in taxes.

The equalization produced by these welfare policies, however, is of a quite limited sort. The objective of perfect socioeconomic equality could be approximated only in a communist (though not necessarily Marxist) society. Many classical utopian thinkers (Plato, More, Bellamy) envision an ideal social order in which nearly all share equally in the total resources of society.

Another possible solution to this problem would be to increase the supplies of all significant resources so much that absolute differences in the amounts controlled would diminish in significance. Questions of socioeconomic equality appear to decline in intensity in a bountiful society in which resources continue to expand. Severe scarcity, combined with no-growth, increases the probability that any attempt at redistribution will provoke intense conflict.

And striving to maintain an established distribution, in the face of growing frustration among the deprived, also might undermine order.

The possible interactions between order and equality are not the only ones of significance. Any attempt to redistribute socioeconomic resources will necessarily have an impact on freedom as well, since power enables the one who has it to act on the freedom that may otherwise be only theoretical. The potential freedom of those who benefit from an equalization will be enhanced, while those who lose from the reallocation may find their former freedom limited as well. As with the expansion of political equality, efforts to redistribute social and economic power resources raise questions of justice.

Notwithstanding the popular appeal of the value of equality, however defined, a cynic might doubt whether human beings truly desire real equality. Rather, people wish to bring down those whom they perceive as more advantaged than they; but of course they desire to maintain the advantages they hold over others. The drive for equality, from this perspective, is rooted in envy and only operates one way—to one's own benefit.[7] Very few are so self-sacrificing that they would give what they have to the poor in order to promote greater socioeconomic equality.

Equality of Opportunity

The most ambiguous form of equality is that mandating equal opportunity for all citizens. What this entails and implies is seldom clarified. Usually equality of opportunity seems to require the elimination of all "artificial" barriers to the full realization of one's "natural" abilities. As such, it resembles a form of freedom—the absence of restraint. Certainly some attractive social policies have been justified by the goal of equal opportunity, among them the elimination of more obvious discrimination against women and ethnic and racial minorities. Notwithstanding these apparent advances, the meaning of equality of opportunity raises some rather interesting questions:

1. How does one distinguish between an "artificial" barrier and the consequences of different "natural" abilities? Of course, extreme cases of overt discrimination can be recognized and certain inherited traits could be considered "natural." Some forms of discrimination are quite subtle, however, while the implications of different inherited abilities cannot be always extracted from their interaction with the environment.

2. Insofar as people do have different abilities, then equality of opportunity would result in the creation of a kind of "natural aristocracy." There does not seem to be any compelling reason why society should institutionalize such an order. The opposing extreme, that of handicapping those who are favored by their genetic inheritance, seems even less acceptable. Novelist Kurt Von-

negut imagines a society in which the beautiful wear masks, the strong and graceful have weights attached to their limbs, and the intelligent have electronic devices implanted in their ears to disrupt their thoughts.[8] One potential escape from this dilemma raised by the goal of equal opportunity would be to aid the disadvantaged rather than handicapping the gifted. This solution, though, does not eliminate all the problems with the concept of equal opportunity.

3. What types of "artificial" barriers to self-realization should be eliminated in the name of equal opportunity? Some groups may appear to suffer because they are barred from certain neighborhoods, schools, or jobs, but the fundamental problem may be their lack of power resources. Just as the powerful possess, in a sense, greater freedom, so also do they have access to greater opportunities. Equal opportunity, then, seems to suggest the need for equal power. A related aspect of this problem is created by efforts at compensatory, or reverse, discrimination. If, for example, a particular school or employer admits people on the basis of talent rather than any irrelevant criteria such as race or sex, it may still be maintaining an artificial barrier if certain groups have been denied adequate preparation because of their ethnic, economic, or sexual background. Consequently, many favor compensatory programs under which members of socially disadvantaged groups are accepted even though they are less qualified than other candidates. Not surprisingly, those who have been rejected believe they have been denied their legitimate opportunity. A thorough effort to eliminate all artificial advantages and disadvantages could well require massive social change which, in equalizing opportunities for all, would restrict the previously held opportunities of some while expanding those of others. This consequence, again, strongly suggests the need for some standard of justice to evaluate such a policy.

4. Assuming that opportunities can be equalized so that all can fully realize their natural potential, what happens over time? If humans are differently endowed, the gifted in a system of equal opportunity will eventually rise to the controlling positions in society. After the rise, their natural abilities would come to be reinforced by "artificial" social power resources. Under a system of perfect equality of opportunity, these resources would give them an unfair advantage over others unable to secure control over equal amounts of power. Consequently, the equalization of power resources would have to be constantly renewed, so that the natural aristocracy that arises out of a system of equal opportunity would not degenerate into an artificial one. High inheritance taxes are an example of a type of policy designed to reduce the unearned advantages of the children of wealthy parents. Comprehensive attempts of this sort could result in continuous social disruption because of the constant redistribution programs and could destroy initiative, as people would not be allowed to retain the fruits of their accomplishments. Some balance

must be struck between these values and that of equal opportunity.

5.   Finally, one might question whether people desire equal opportunity any more than socioeconomic equality. As in the prior case, a skeptic might argue that though most people are sympathetic to proposals to eliminate others' advantages, they are not willing to sacrifice their own. In addition, a system of perfectly equal opportunity implies mobility downward as well as upward. Many might find themselves less protected from failure than they would like. Even worse, in a system of truly equal opportunity, the only fault for failure would lie in one's own inadequacies. There would be no convenient scapegoats—real or imaginary—to blame. People might find this kind of self-knowledge difficult to accept.

The popular facade of equal opportunity, therefore, disguises a thicket of problems. There appears to be no intrinsic reason why the process of equalization should be limited in any way, but the extreme of complete equality challenges other political values, such as freedom and order. It seems reasonable to assert that some trade-off among the competing claims of contradictory goals must be found; however, how is this balance to be defined? The debate over this question concerns the meaning of justice.

ISSUES IN THE MEANING OF JUSTICE

The obvious solution to political value conflicts is to do what is right and just. Justice is sometimes considered the primary political virtue because of its presumed ability to mediate among other value positions. Principles of justice supposedly reveal the answers to such recurring questions as how much freedom? order? equality? All that needs to be done is to come to agreement about definition of the principles of justice. This agreement, regrettably, has not proven easy, for, justice, like the other values previously discussed, has been assigned a number of meanings, none of which offers completely unambiguous guidelines for value choice.

Politics has been popularly defined as the process that determines who gets what, when, and how.[9] In a sense, principles of justice indicate who *should* get what and how. Thus, justice is concerned with the distribution of power resources in society. Perhaps the most commonly invoked principle was first enunciated by Aristotle: Equals should be treated equally, or to "each according to his deserts."[10] As Aristotle was quick to point out, difficulties emerge in the attempt to define the criteria by which people are to be evaluated. Democrats argue that it should simply be the fact of free birth (and, all people are born free and thus equal in our society); oligarchs favor wealth as a measure; and "aristocrats" prefer the principle of excellence.[11] Aristotle advocates a modification of the excellence principle, asserting that those who contribute equally to the well-being of the community should be given equal recognition and reward. Apparently, he thought that coming to an agreement on what constitutes "civic excellence" would be easier than it has proven to be in most historical political systems or, for that matter, most political philosophies.

Paternalism

One of more frequently invoked principles of distribution asserts that some persons are best fit to rule, and they should control at least the political authority resources in a society. Plato, the classical proponent of this view, argues that one should no more entrust the power of the state to amateurs than one would the navigation of a ship or the treatment of the sick. People differ in their capacity, and justice consists of each doing the task for which he or she is best suited. Injustice develops either when people attempt to rise above their proper station in life or fail to accept fully the responsibilities incumbent upon them.[12] Plato believed that the just political community would be governed by those few individuals who, through a combination of inborn talent (recall the myth of metals cited above) and rigorous training, are able to discern the Good and to formulate policy accordingly.

In a sense, platonic paternalism is echoed by the advocates of technocracy, who often tend to reduce politics to the selection of the most appropriate means for the maximization of already agreed-upon ends. The average citizen, from this point of view, lacks the capacity to evaluate the available alternatives. Interestingly, though Plato would concentrate authority resources under the control of his rulers, he would not reward their superior service with great wealth. Indeed, they would live in a communal equality apart from the rest of society, for Plato believed that wealth would lead to the corruption of the "philosopher kings."[13]

Most people would agree that if a select group of superior individuals truly possessed the capacity to know and choose the Good, then they should be allowed to rule without interference from lesser mortals. Paternalistic justice, therefore, rationalizes significant inequality, limits the political participation of large segments of society, and sanctions an order within which each performs his or her appropriate function. The form of freedom most compatible with this type of justice is that of self-perfection: One is free to do what one ought.

Many people, of course, are unwilling to concede that others possess such excellence, though they may believe themselves to be so endowed. The fundamental assumption of paternalistic justice, therefore, is not universally recognized. Indeed, Aristotle and others argue that Plato may have been drawing a false analogy in equating moral and political expertise with that of the technical world.[14] Though experts may prepare the feast or guide the ship, it is the guests who judge the quality of the meal and the passengers who choose the destination of the voyage. Experts should be drawn upon for their special skill, but perhaps the citizens should be the final judge of the quality of their lives in the state. This reasoning suggests a second principle of justice—to provide the greatest happiness for the greatest number.

Utilitarianism

The basic premise of utilitarianism is that humans seek, and are their own best judges of, happiness.[15] An individual pursues whatever course of action appears to guarantee the greatest happiness or, more pessimistically, the least pain and suffering. The condition of maximum happiness or minimum pain is considered to be "good." Admittedly, people may be mistaken about what will bring them happiness; for example, a hedonist might abuse his body in pursuit of physical pleasure, when more moderate habits would actually produce greater well-being. Such a qualification, though, does not, in the utilitarian's view, invalidate the assumption that people pursue happiness and consider success in their endeavors good.

By extension, therefore, the good society is the one that provides the greatest happiness for the greatest number. A just distribution of resources, rights, and privileges is one that guarantees the maximization of happiness. Utilitarian justice, in contrast with the paternalistic variant, holds that humans are essentially equal and tends to some majoritarian form of democracy. Its principles have been used to validate the elimination of vested privileges and inequalities which, though they give happiness to the few who enjoy them, deny a greater measure of happiness to those who are deprived. Utilitarianism, then, seemingly solves the problem whether one person's freedom or resources can be reduced in order to increase those of another, or whether a certain degree of order can be sacrificed to increase freedom: Yes, if the change increases total happiness in society.

Utilitarian justice compensates for some of the difficulties intrinsic to paternalism, but creates a new set of problems. Some of these difficulties are essentially technical/conceptual in nature. To speak of the greatest happiness for the greatest number assumes that some means of measuring and comparing happiness exists. Happiness, however, is a subjective state of mind. Perhaps one could simply ask if people are happy and strive to maximize the number answering in the affirmative, but this solution ignores ideas of degree or quality. Plato noted that the principle of maximizing happiness without regard to quality could well produce a city of pigs.[16] Further complications arise when problems of degree are included. Two people may be happy, but one could be happier than the other. How is this difference to be measured and compared? Efforts to devise measures of quality and degree appear to give ambiguous results, to say the least.

More importantly, the use of the utilitarian principle of individual choice as the criterion for social decisions could lead to the rationalization of great evil. Individuals may act so as to maximize their own welfare, however they see it, but to assume that a group or a society should do likewise is to consider it as an individual writ large. This assumption easily justifies the oppression of minorities. If every person is assumed to have *independent* worth, then some cannot be sacrificed to benefit the whole in the same way an individual may discipline his body to improve his mind. Utilitarian justice could conceivably be used to justify the elimination of the Jews in Hitler's Germany, if such a move increased the total sum of happiness in the country. Granted, utilitarians would probably deny that such an outrageous policy could increase total social happiness, but granting the denial does not solve the conceptual ambiguity inherent in the social-maximization principle. Indeed, one could plausibly argue that no rational person would submit to a system of justice in which the individual might be oppressed in the name of the general happiness of the people.

Justice as Fairness

John Rawls, a critic of the utilitarian theory of justice, argues that an appropriate method for discovering the basic principles of justice is to imagine what fundamental rules rational human beings, unaware of any vested interests, would choose for governing their relations.[17] Utilitarianism, because it could well treat the minority as a means to the greater happiness of the majority, would be rejected. Reason dictates that all would desire to be treated as ends. Consequently, a rational conception of justice must provide for certain basic protection for all citizens.

Second, the rules of justice should establish the contours of a legitimate distribution of resources. The participants in the formulation of the fundamental rules of justice would have a presumption of complete equality. They would recognize no *prima facie* reason why some members should enter into the association with more resources than the others. Any subsequent development of inequalities must, therefore, be in accordance with principles acceptable to all—both to the beneficiaries and to the disadvantaged.

Rawls argues that the two principles of what he terms "justice as fairness" meet these requirements:[18]

First Principle: Each person is to have an equal right to the most extensive system of equal liberties compatible with a similar system of liberty for all.

Second Principle: Social and economic inequalities are to be arranged so that they are both: (a) to the greatest benefit of the least advantaged, consistent with the just savings (see the next paragraph) principle, and (b) attached to offices and positions open to all under conditions of fair equality of opportunity.

The basic liberties (freedom of thought and of person and equal political rights), therefore, cannot be restricted for some unless it is demonstrated that this limitation is necessary for the equal exercise of liberty by all (for instance, certain norms to govern the exercise of free speech so that all can exercise this right). The second principle asserts in effect that any social or economic inequality that fails to benefit the least advantaged is unjust. One example of a justifiable inequality might be the giving to a doctor of a material incentive to work among the poor. Other doctors earning enormous incomes by treating the psychosomatic ills of the wealthy would be enjoying an illegitimate reward. The "just savings principle" refers simply to the necessity to put aside a portion of current wealth to provide for the future survival of a just society (in other words, investment). A savings rate beyond that necessary to maintain the current standard is justifiable only if it mitigates the lot of those bearing the burden.

Equality of opportunity, as discussed above, can have a number of implications. Rawls, in discussing "fair" opportunity, adopts a broad view of the requirements of this principle.[19] First, there must be formal equality of opportunity; that is, no legal barriers against certain individuals or groups. Second, the principle requires that the impact of class and status differences should be minimized. Rawls also believes that fair opportunity mandates mitigating the effects of the "natural lottery." He sees no reason why principles of justice should institutionalize unequal opportunity caused by accidents of birth.

The justice-as-fairness doctrine rejects paternalistic justice because of its denial of equal rights and its acceptance of the consequences of the natural lottery. It rejects utilitarianism because of the tendency to treat some citizens as means to others' happiness, rather than as ends. This principle, if applied to most contemporary social systems, would eliminate significant inequalities as not truly benefiting the deprived or as being in violation of citizens' fundamental rights.

Although the justice-as-fairness doctrine seems rather convincing in the abstract, it cannot be applied easily to the concrete. For example, as examined in the previous chapter, it is difficult to determine the ways in which the freedom of some can be legitimately restricted in order to maximize freedom for all. Second, every privileged group claims that its advantages are to the ultimate benefit of everyone concerned. Even though this claim may be challenged, it is by no means easy to demonstrate that any proposed redistribution works to the benefit of the least advantaged. It also appears that those in the middle are somewhat neglected by this scheme. One could imagine a situation in which the very rich might work for the benefit of the very poor at the expense of the middle classes.

Finally, the question of time is a problem. If any inequalities are justified as truly benefiting the deprived, when, exactly, are they supposed to accomplish the benefit: immediately, in short run, in the long run? Certainly, one could argue that the concentration of wealth and other resources may be needed for a considerable time in order to transform the economic structure for the betterment of all. The industrialization of the United States took more than a century and caused enormous hardship but ultimately raised the standard of living of nearly the entire population. Similarly, the forced mobilization of the Soviet industrialization program wreaked havoc for a generation but created considerable wealth. Are inequities lasting for more than a generation justifiable? If not, then the bases for long-term projects become tenuous. If so, then it becomes easier to justify the perpetuation of inequality by reference to some vaguely evident "trickle-down" theory according to which the poor eventually gain something for their years of suffering.

Relativist Justice

The argument for justice as fairness, as well as those for paternalism and utilitarianism, attempts to establish basic principles that are universally applicable. But in fact, it must be observed, all these concepts are essentially Western in origin, from Plato and Aristotle through Rawls. What seems self-evident to a Western philosopher may not occur to a citizen of another culture. Therefore, a fourth approach to the problem of justice is to accept the fact of cultural diversity and define justice accordingly.

Carl Friedrich adopts such a view. He argues that an act or decision is just "when it involves a comparative evaluation of the persons affected by the action, and when that comparison accords with the values and beliefs of the political community."[20] This definition accepts the possibility that different communities could hold somewhat dissimilar values, and an act considered just in one might not be so evaluated in another. It explicitly links justice with all the other political values prevailing in a system.

Although this statement avoids the ambiguity of dubious absolutes, it substitutes the equally problematic condition of cultural value variation. Contradictory values, moreover, may be held by the members of the same political community, or an act may be in only partial accord with the prevailing principles of justice. Friedrich maintains that the "most just act" is one in accord with the greatest number of values and beliefs after adjusting for their "intensity."[21] This solution appears rather mechanical and does not provide a very satisfying means of adjudicating a conflict between two equally appealing values. By overstating the extent to which the meaning of justice is dependent on other values, this approach nearly eliminates the independent role of justice in resolving inconsistencies and contradictions among rival political and social values. It also minimizes the possibility of making evaluations of conceptions of the just in different communities.

Possible Universals

The diversity of human values, in the relativist view, results in a variety of conceptions of the just (which, though not identical, need not be in complete opposition either). Some scholars believe that despite the potential for variation, certain principles will be common to all conceptions of justice. Among the universal postulates commonly mentioned are:[22]

1. *Treating Assumed Equals Equally*: Treating equals equally is the basic assumption of Aristotelian justice. The criteria for defining equality may change from culture to culture.

2. *Generality of Community Standards*: If justice is defined according to the prevailing standards of a political community, it would be unjust arbitrarily to abandon those standards and apply other standards in judging different cases. Once a community has defined justice, that definition is the one that should be generally applied.

3. *Truth*: In judging an act or person, it is necessary to base this judgment on the facts of the case. People should not be falsely accused and convicted.

4. *"Ought" Imples "Can"*: The requirements of justice must take into account the necessities and limitations of nature. It is unjust to require behavior which is, in fact, impossible.

These principles, and possibly some others, appear to characterize every conception of justice worthy of the name. The extent of compliance with such norms could be used to evaluate a number of different systems comparatively, despite diversity in other cultural values. Closer examination, however, reveals that even these presumptive universals can become rather vague in application. For instance:

1. Treating equals equally and treating like cases alike is fine, once two cases are indeed determined to be alike. The bases for defining equality must be set forth and applied. No two individuals or cases are identical, and one can nearly always make an argument that "extenuating circumstances" allow for special consideration. Pleading temporary insanity (or possession by evil spirits in other cultures) can be seen as a means of gaining a judgment different from that applied to other perpetrators of the same offense. Certain questions about the norms used to determine equality can also be raised: Are they consistent? Are they exhaustive? Are they universally accepted within the political community? Replies in the negative mean that further difficulties afflict the application of the equality principle.

2. Justice demands that standards be applied according to the facts of the case. "Factual" truth, however, is not quite so absolute as it might appear.

Rather, relevant data are selected from a potential universe of information by those making the judgment. What is considered of relevance may not be identical for every observer and will be affected by cultural values. For example, in some traditional societies people believe in the reality of an unseen spirit world. The evaluation of what appears to Western eyes to be an ordinary and innocent event may take on sinister, supernatural overtones in these cultures. A brush against the shoulder may be cause for violent reprisals, if the person touched believes he has just been cursed with impotence.[23] Even without considering the complication caused by belief in the reality of spirits and demons, the facts of a case will often support more than one interpretation. Which interpretation is chosen will be partially affected by the preferences of the observer. Human beings are as much rationalizing as rational creatures, and people tend to select those facts that conform with their predilections.

3.   Certainly, no meaningful conception of justice would require action that is impossible. But what is meant by "impossible?" The issue is not a simple either/or—possible or impossible—rather, one of a range of difficulty. At what point of difficulty does a demand become unjust? The extreme case may be easy enough to determine, but the vast range of alternatives before the limits on the possible are reached creates special problems of interpretation. Again, the impact of different cultural perspectives affects the definition of the possible. A belief in the efficacy of magic, for example, adds a whole dimension of possibility lacking in more secular and empirical world views.[24]

DILEMMAS OF POLITICAL CHOICE

This and the preceding chapter have introduced some of the difficulties in interpreting the meaning and consequences of four major political values— freedom, order, equality, and justice—which are often invoked to aid or validate political choice. Each was examined critically, not with the intent of promulgating ultimate answers to the challenge of value choice, but with the goal of illuminating some of the inherent ambiguities. Among the dilemmas implicitly or explicitly raised are the sixteen groups here to be enumerated:

1.   *In what sense, if any, are human beings free to choose?* Or is human behavior predetermined by biological and environmental factors? If the sensation of free choice is an illusion, would it be a desirable illusion to maintain? (If, of course, all behavior is predetermined, one's response to this and other questions would simply be the product of heredity and prior learning.)

2.   *What is the meaning of "freedom"?* Is it freedom "from" or freedom "to," or some mix? Is freedom a matter of degree? If so, how much freedom should exist?

3.   *Who is to be free?* How does the freedom of one person affect that of others? In what ways, if any, must the freedom of each be limited in order to insure freedom for all?

4.   *How is potential freedom actually used?* What are the power requirements for a meaningful exercise of freedom?

5.   *Do people really desire freedom insofar as it means making decisions for themselves?* Or do most people desire to escape from the responsibility of choice and have others resolve their dilemmas for them?

6.   *What is the meaning of "order"?* Is order a matter of degree? If so, how much order should be present in a society? How much order is required for governmental effectiveness? To what extent are conflict and order compatible?

7.   *Whose order?* What is the impact of the distribution of power resources on the nature of order in a system?

8.   *What are the relationships between freedom and order?* Is a certain amount of order required for freedom? Does freedom disrupt order? Does freedom interfere with effectiveness? If so, what is the best trade-off?

9.   *What is the meaning of "equality"?* To what extent are the various forms of equality (moral, legal, political, socioeconomic, and equality of opportunity) dependent on one another?

10.   *Is equality a matter of degree?* If so, how much equality is desirable?

11.   *To what extent is equality required for widespread freedom?* Does the expansion of equality limit the freedom of some? If so, to what extent is such a limitation justifiable and desirable?

12.   *What is the impact of "natural" inequality (that is, of accidents of heredity) on both equality and freedom?*

13.   *Do people really desire equality?* Is the desire for dominance stronger than the desire for equality? To what extent are unequal rewards required to provide needed incentives for socially desirable activities?

14.   *What is the meaning of "justice"?* How is the definition of the just related to the meanings assigned to other values held by a political community? Is the meaning of justice completely relative to the culture considered, or are there some underlying universal norms? If so, what are they, and how are they interpreted and applied?

15.   *What is the impact of justice on the other political values?* Is it ever just to limit freedom? Equality? Order?

16.   *What is the impact of the distribution of power on the definition of justice?* Do the powerful define justice in such a way as to rationalize their own privileges? Alternatively, does the conception of justice limit the exercise of power in society?

Every conscientious participant in politics will have to grapple with these and other enigmas and come to some conclusions that he or she believes to be best. Continuous and rigorous examination of one's value preferences may never produce completely satisfying solutions—and, indeed, this condition may be for the best, as complete satisfaction would lead to dogmatism—but it will contribute to intelligent and informed political decisions. Living with the conflicting requirements of a number of apparently attractive goals may produce a certain level of cognitive tension, but this tension is a vast improvement over the smug complacency of uninformed prejudice.

In the coming decades, the peoples of the world will confront choices of greater import than any ever before encountered in human history. The efforts to cope with, to manage, and to survive these challenges will be partly political in nature, involving both power and values. In the final part of this book, Chapters XV and XVI, the problem of the future is examined with regard both to how it is studied and to the range of possibilities open to humanity.

Part V

THE FUTURE OF POLITICS

Social scientists, despite efforts to distinguish themselves from historians, study past events. On the basis of prior experience, they hope to construct frameworks of analysis and explanation that will illuminate the present as it unfolds. Some social scientists, though, are not satisfied with doing this. Rather, they argue that the social sciences should be explicitly and directly concerned with studying the future. These scholars, sometimes called "futurologists," admit one cannot know *the* future, but they believe systematic analysis can distinguish among "alternative futures" and thereby guide policy making in the direction of a "preferable future." In Chapter XV, the reasons for the growing interest in "future studies" are explored. Additionally, the more important methods commonly used to study the future are critically examined.

A more speculative approach is adopted in Chapter XVI. Four alternative futures are briefly described. These are not intended to exhaust all the potentialities of the present, but they illustrate the range of possibilities available to humanity. In the second part of the chapter, the politics plausibly associated with each future is described. The politics of future building will largely determine the nature of the future. The responsibility for these political choices, however, falls on the present generation.

Chapter XV   "Studying" the Future

THE END OF THE MODERN AGE—A SPECULATION

The contemporary world seems to be riding on a rising curve of unpleasant surprises. Good things (like the automobile, DDT, nuclear power) are turning out to be bad, and bad things (like the long-term consequences of nuclear war, the exhaustion of earth's resources) are even worse than feared. The strange ways of modern living, one sociologist has observed, have not been around very long, perhaps two hundred years, and may not prove viable much longer.[1] Indeed, there are numerous signs that certain limits to modernity exist, increasing the likelihood and necessity for a major social transformation.

The Limits to Material Growth

Modern social and economic systems are founded on ever-expanding levels of material production and consumption. When this trend has been temporarily reversed in the past, as it was during the Great Depression, the change has caused grave global, social, and political instability. Yet the ability of the earth to sustain these growth rates is clearly finite.

The most commonly recognized limit is that on population. The rapid expansion in the world's peoples is primarily attributable to innovations in health care and sanitation that have decreased infant mortality rates and lengthened life spans, as well as to modern agricultural techniques that have enabled the globe to support the new billions. One must question, however, whether further increases in food production will be able to keep pace with population. Currently, the world's population is growing at approximately 2 percent a year, which means that it doubles about every 35 years. At that rate, one scientist estimates that there will be standing room only by the year 2585.[2] If the human race had been growing this rapidly a million years ago, when the world's population is estimated to have been around 125,000, it would have taken only a little over 500 years to reach the 1970 population of 3.5 billion.[3] This unprecedented rate of population growth does not seem indefinitely supportable, given the earth's agricultural potential. Something will have to control it. Already, "automatic" mechanisms of controlling population are beginning to take over—one is called famine, another plague.

It seems obvious that men and women could choose to limit the number of their children to two or fewer per couple, but this deliberate choice involves certain fundamental value changes. Many population-control programs have failed to produce the desired effect. Population growth rates have declined significantly in some of the more advanced industrial states, but this success merely raises questions about another limit to growth—that on levels of material consumption.

The problem of what is called overpopulation actually has two components. The first, and more obvious, is the numbers explosion occurring in many African, Asian, and Latin American countries. The other is the consumption explosion that characterizes the industrial countries of the world. Limiting numbers will be insufficient, if the levels of per capita consumption continue to grow. The inhabitants of the United States consume on a per capita basis an estimated 30 to 35 times as much as the people of India. In terms of the burden on the world's resources, therefore, the United States has a population equivalent to about 7 *billion* Indians.[4] Continuing increases in the levels of per capita consumption, even if the world achieves zero population growth (ZPG), will lead to the rapid depletion of available resources.

Finally, the capacity of the global ecosystem to absorb the polluting by-products of continued growth in population and production is also limited. At some point, the levels of environmental poisons will begin to limit or even force a reduction in both population and production. In order to avoid eco-collapse, patterns of living that waste resources and multiply pollutants must be altered.

Admittedly, the limits on material growth appear most susceptible to a technological adjustment. Technological optimism, in fact, is one of the underlying attitudes of the modern age. Technological advances have been relatively steady over the last several centuries, helping to postpone the fulfillment of the original doomsday predictions made by the nineteenth-century economist Thomas Malthus. This advance, though, has not continued over a longer time span, and it would seem foolhardy to assume that it can be maintained for the indefinite future. On the contrary, the rate of technological innovation may also encounter certain limits.

The Limits to Technological Innovation

The modern world and the modernization process are based upon a sophisticated technological infrastructure—a foundation which is, in one critic's view, both the unique excellence and the tragic flaw of the modern age.[5] The effects of technology are part of the problem, and to rely on more technology to correct the effects of earlier innovations suggests a treadmill phenomenon which cannot be sustained forever. Instances of the technological treadmill abound, but two will suffice to suggest that modern social systems may even be falling behind the consequences of their own technologies.

The first of these cases involves the problem of feeding the world's population. Population growth, it must be recalled, is itself a result of improved technologies. In order to fill the multiplying mouths, more food must be produced per acre. Increased land productivity depends in large part on the use of nitrogen fertilizers. Increasing fertilization, however, encounters diminishing returns; that is, each additional unit of fertilizer produces an ever smaller increment in the total crop. The enormous amounts of fertilizer, moreover, begin to pollute streams and rivers.[6] Some evidence even indicates that as the nitrogen fertilizer combines with oxygen it produces nitrous oxide, which is converted to nitric acid in the atmosphere. Nitric acid, in turn, attacks the ozone layer which protects the earth from the sun's ultraviolet radiation.[7] A significant increase in ultraviolet exposure could have a deadly impact on both plant and animal life. Thus, one technology (artificial fertilization) devised to help cope with a problem created by another (improved medical and sanitation techniques) may, in turn, be contributing to an even more serious problem.

The area of energy offers another critical example. Modern life styles require enormous amounts of energy. An early nonanimal source of energy— wood—was clearly inadequate, so technologies were devised to exploit the fossil fuels of coal and oil. These technologies supported the growth of energy-consuming technologies (for one, the automobile); in turn, their growth led to pressure being placed on the readily available reserves of these fuels. Recognition that oil and even coal supplies are limited encouraged investigations into alternative energy sources. Nuclear power is touted as a major energy source of the future. But apart from the risks of power-plant malfunctions and the theft of nuclear fuel, reactors produce large amounts of radioactive wastes that remain "hot" for millenia. No way of safely disposing of these wastes has yet been devised. Consequently, the Atomic Energy Commission, in 1974, proposed to build a temporary storage facility in the *hope* that a technological solution to the waste problems would be found in the next few decades.[8] This progression suggests that modern societies may be falling behind on the technological treadmill.

The treadmill effect is linked to another potential limit on innovation, the ability to anticipate the undesirable side effects of new technologies. The more rapidly the treadmill turns, that is, the faster technological innovations are introduced, the more difficult it becomes to predict and assess all their consequences correctly. New inventions can have enormous impact, as the effect of the automobile on American society attests. Given the increasing complexity of the contemporary technostructure, an undesirable side effect that goes unanticipated or unrecognized may have devastating consequences. Right now, Americans are paying for the failure to control the introduction of the horseless carriage.

Some doubt must also be cast upon the capability of even the most research-and-development-oriented society to maintain a continuing expansion of scientific and technological knowledge. Economist Kenneth Boulding argues that an "entropy trap" may exist in which the "stock of knowledge will be so large that the whole effort of the knowledge industry will have to be devoted to transmitting it from one generation to another.[9] Even if this ultimate limit is not reached, it appears plausible that the ever increasing demands of maintenance and transmission will begin to reduce the amount of scarce resources that can be devoted to primary research.

In addition to this specific trap, it is evident that the costs of innovation are steadily increasing. The inventions of previous centuries came relatively cheaply, but now billions of dollars must be invested in a vast, organized effort to keep pace on the treadmill. Technological innovation, therefore, encounters more limitations than those of the human imagination. At some point, the economy of the world may simply become unable to afford technologies that are theoretically possible.[10]

Finally, some account must be taken of the ways in which scientific reductionism and technological determinism impoverish human existence.[11] The rhythms of life have been replaced by the rhythms of the machine. Rather than undulating to the sun and the seasons, people pace their lives to the beat of the clock and the assembly line. Nor can much hope be held out for the liberating effects of the new information technologies, for just as the industrial age shackled the body, the cybernetic age seems on its way to shackling the mind. Certainly, one cannot be particularly sanguine about the increased capacity for surveillance and control which the new information systems bestow on large-scale organizations. From a humanistic bias, one has to wonder whether the human spirit will perpetually tolerate the constraints of scientific method and technological rationality. There are other ways to knowledge and other sides to life.

The Limits to Modern Social Relations

Contemporary social and political organizations are also manifesting signs of strains that raise doubts about their continued viability. In part, these strains are the result of problems generated in the scientific and technological areas. One might well consider whether modern institutions will be able to survive the "little demons" of inflation, pollution, and resource shortages. Even if these demons are cast out for a time, they may well return with others more powerful than they—famine, ecocollapse, and world war—that will certainly destroy the social order as presently constituted.

Even without the effects of the other problem areas, modern social organizations and relations appear to possess certain intrinsic limits. Perhaps the most basic of these is the impact of secularization and the pluralization of values. The spirit of scientific rationality has infused the modern social vision with a skeptical acidity destructive of earlier religious belief systems. Though traditional religions have declined in appeal, the suffering and death which they sought to explain still remain.[12] The frantic pursuit of material pleasures and the exaggerated pride in the accomplishments of the scientific mind constitute attempts to screen off the death and suffering with an ineffectual curtain of escapism or "rationality." The more perceptive have penetrated this curtain and concluded that the human condition is one of existential absurdity. Millions in the modern nations are pursuing a bizarre array of presumptive religions ranging from fundamentalism through Eastern mysticism to the occult and Satanism. Not surprisingly, none of these "solutions" has proven to be very effective.

If modern man has lost God through secularization, he has also lost his fellow man through the alienation caused by organizational gigantism and the decline in primary relations.[13] The compartmentalized and segmented nature of contemporary social relations, dominated by the requirements of organizational rationality, serves as a barrier against human interaction on the basis of whole selves. The forces of mobility (occupational and geographic) further isolate people from one another. Primary relations within the family and among friends have become more and more depersonalized, partial, and transitory. The occupational demands of many organizations are, in large part, responsible for the deterioration of these primary bonds. Even if humans can survive in such an emotional vacuum, they certainly cannot thrive with fundamental social needs thus thwarted. Again, many people attempt to find fulfillment of these fundamental needs through psychoanalysis, T-groups, and encounter sessions. Such efforts are merely palliatives treating, as do so many "cures," the symptoms rather than the disease.

Finally, the pace of change, technological and social, imposes another cost: human obsolescence. The slower rate of change in traditional societies places a premium on the wisdom of experience, and one's value increases with age. In a context of rapid change, this process is reversed; value declines with age. In an order that abjures the obsolete and does not wish to be reminded of death, the aging find themselves cast out onto a rubbish heap. The tendency to depreciate human lives as one would a machine is not an attractive aspect of modernity.

Ironically, the movement to ZPG and increased longevity is likely to raise the average age in many countries, further emphasizing the contradiction between the social requisites of modernity and human needs.

Taken individually, perhaps none of these problems is insoluble or even inevitable, but, like modernity itself, these limits seem to come in "packages." They cannot be dealt with in a piecemeal fashion. Contemporary political institutions, already shaken by economic crisis, can well collapse and be replaced by unstable tyrannies. Continued efforts to manage the manifold problems through ever-expanding technique, instead of through significant social and value change, seem likely to exacerbate rather than cure. Refusal to recognize the "limits" to modernity can lead to a catastrophic collapse. The alternative to catastrophe may be a steady material decline, coupled with widespread social and political pathologies—a long and painful whimper rather than an apocalyptic bang. Certainly, the primary goal of the politics of the future must be to avoid these fates.

THE NEED TO "STUDY" THE FUTURE

Every conscious action includes a prediction of the future. Even a mundane act such as crossing the street is founded upon one or more projections about the future position of oncoming traffic, as well as the purpose for crossing the street in the first place. The success of public policies also depends on the accuracy of implicit and explicit assumptions about the future. In the early autumn of 1974, for example, the economic policy of the Ford administration was predicated upon the presumption that inflation would remain the critical economic problem, at least for the rest of the year. Unemployment, unfortunately, rose at an unanticipated rate, and considerable doubt was therefore cast upon the validity of the policies founded on the original forecast.

A number of factors appear to be stimulating a growing interest in the futurist component of social and political decisions:

1. *Change and the Pace of Change*: In a static society, the "shape of things to come" poses no great conceptual difficulties. The future can be safely assumed to be much like the present, barring natural calamities. But when the pace of technological and social change quickens, as is characteristic of modern societies, the present no longer provides an accurate portrait of the future. Ironically, as it becomes more difficult to assess the future, it also becomes more important to do so. As was suggested in the preceding section, the accurate anticipation of all the consequences of new technologies could modify the ways in which they are utilized. Doubts about the value and fears

of the risks of the supersonic transport, for example, persuaded Congress to stop funding its development.

2. *The Increasing Magnitude of the Impact of Change*: Human devices, both technological and social, have vastly increased in sheer power, so that their misuse can cause unprecedented destruction. Whereas early agricultural techniques might destroy the fertility of a tribe's territory, contemporary levels of pollution can well threaten life on the planet. Wars between ancient states caused great suffering, but modern thermonuclear weapons raise the specter of global "overkill." Governments have always tried to control the lives of their citizens, to some extent, but recent developments in the biological, genetic, and psychological sciences produce the possiblity of *total* control. The sheer magnitude of the impact of material and social innovations for good and ill provides another motivation for deliberate efforts to evaluate the course and consequences of projected developments.

3. *Increasing Interdependence*: Related to the problem of magnitude is the growing interconnectedness of the world. One reason why the effects of a particular innovation may be so great is the difficulty in isolating what happens in one part of the world system from the rest. Therefore, planning for the future by a particular nation state must take into account the actions of all the other actors in the international system. Failure to take account of probable actions of other participants can easily negate too narrowly construed policies, as the 1974 oil embargo so forcefully demonstrated.

In a literal sense, of course, one cannot *know* the future when developing current policies.[14] Although the future implications of contemporary technologies can be examined, it is obviously impossible to judge the effects of inventions that have yet to be conceived. Similarly, though the consequences of current policy decisions may be identifiable, it is impossible accurately to anticipate decisions that have not yet been made or even conceptualized. Indeed, because of the incredibly complex ramifications of any given action, it is often difficult to predict the full implications even of that which is known. Apparently trivial or idiosyncratic events often have momentous impact. "Futurologists," by focusing on basic trends, often overlook the unique incident that ultimately undercuts the predicted course of events.

The further ahead one attempts to predict, the more important uncertainty factors become. As one critic puts it, the most common prediction is persistence—real qualitative changes are difficult to anticipate.[15] In a sense, futurologists look to the recent past in the hope that it will act as a mirror reflecting time ahead and thereby guide their steps as they walk backward into the future. Like an effort to steer a car by using only the rear-view mirror, futurist studies become less useful as the speed increases and as the road changes directions more often. Yet even such imperfect steering is preferable to driving blind.

Apart from seers, prophets, and astrologers, then, few futurologists claim the ability to predict specific events. Rather, the objective is to sketch out *alternative* futures, each of which expresses potentialities seen in the current situation. Naturally, these alternatives may range from the remotely possible to the very probable and from the repulsive to the highly desirable. Attempts are also made to estimate relative probabilities and to identify *preferable* futures.

Whether a particular alternative future becomes an actuality depends, in large part, on what people decide to do now. Projections can be either self-fulfilling or self-defeating. A forecast of economic recession, for example, may induce consumers to cut back spending and businesses to reduce investments, thereby producing the predicted economic downturn. In contrast, this prediction could prompt the government to take certain remedial steps, such as lowering the tax and interest rates, in an effort to stimulate the economy and thereby defeat the forecast. Depending on which of these two responses is stronger, the prediction of recession would be self-fulfilling or self-defeating.

This example illustrates the importance of defining alternative futures, not so much for predicting *what will happen* in the future but for identifying *what should happen* in the present if undesirable alternatives are to be avoided. After the possibilities have been delineated, intelligent policy making should work to decrease the chances of the "negative" futures, while enhancing the probability of the "positive" ones. This objective, of course, begs the question of how it is determined which alternative futures are preferable. The answer necessarily involves setting goals for society and is uniquely political in nature. Whose preferences will be reflected in the policy-making process? The simple answer is, "Those of the powerful." Only persons with sufficient power resources to participate in political exchanges can influence the course of public policy and the shape of the future. The politics of the future, therefore, involves a number of issues: (1) What are the various methods of projecting alternative futures? (2) What are some of the alternatives, positive and negative? (3) By what process, or nonprocess, will one alternative become the future? These issues are discussed in the remainder of this chapter and in the next.

METHODS OF FUTUROLOGY

Futurologists draw upon a number of methods, ranging from the impressionistic to the apparently scientific, in defining alternative futures.[16] Among the more important are: free speculation, scenarios, polling techniques, attempts to identify basic social forces, extrapolation of trends, and simulations.

Free Speculation

Since the early modern era, scholars and artists have been interested in the promise of the future. This interest was generally expressed through imaginative speculations, often fictional, giving rise to two literary subgenres: utopian and science fiction. Among the authors commonly associated with imaginative speculation are Jules Verne, Edward Bellamy, and H. G. Wells in the late nineteenth and early twentieth centuries, and more recently Kurt Vonnegut, Arthur C. Clarke, B. F. Skinner, Aldous Huxley, and George Orwell.

Most of their speculative works appear in retrospect to be quaint or even absurd, though often entertaining. Some few, however, have proven remarkably prescient, though accuracy in prediction often depended as much on luck as on any valid insight. Attempts to project the technologies of the next century have proven the most hazardous, for truly innovative discoveries are impossible to anticipate except through pure luck.

Fictional speculations, however, can serve several important functions, especially when focused on human behavior rather than on the specifics of technology. George Orwell's *Nineteen Eighty-Four* (first published in 1949) is a powerful speculative work, though not in the sense of describing a future technology accurately and not because anyone takes it as an accurate description of what the world will be like in the year that is its name. Rather, it presents a chilling examination of the human capacity for evil and tyranny.[17] Thus, fiction can help the reader to imagine the possibilities in the human situation. It is a good means of identifying preferable (or in the case of *Nineteen Eighty-Four*, repellent) futures that may expand awareness beyond conventional opinion.

Scenarios

Related to free speculation, though somewhat more systematic, is the scenario, or "future history." Instead of simply describing a future state of affairs, the scenario writer tries to provide a plausible sequence of related events which move from the known world to a future state. In this sense, scenarios are possible histories of the future. This approach combines the imagination of free speculation with the more intellectually rigorous requirement of a plausible argument of how the imagined "future" could come about. Scenarios are a dramatic way of illuminating possible directions of change, as well as the dynamics of the process of change itself.

Many scenarios outline how certain calamities could occur. Herman Kahn, for example, has developed future histories on the causes of World War III and the ways in which it could be fought.[18] Paul Ehrlich, in a scenario entitled "Eco-Catastrophe," delineates a course of events and decisions that lead to the end of life in the oceans by 1979.[19] On a more positive note, sociologist James Cooke Brown, in his utopian novel *The Troika Incident*, describes how the peaceful and bountiful world of 2070 arises out of the impoverished and war-torn globe of the 1970's.[20]

Scenario writers are not seriously predicting a specific series of events. They are simply attempting to demonstrate how a particular future might evolve out of the contemporary world. As such, scenarios can provide policy makers with some idea of the types of actions to take or avoid to produce a specific future. In this fashion, future histories are an advance over the free-flying imaginings of pure speculation.

Polling Techniques

A third method involves polling experts in a particular area of knowledge on what they believe to be possible developments in their field.[21] Polling methods could presumably be applied in most any area of expertise, but they are most commonly used in various scientific and technological fields. The more sophisticated of these studies involve repeated, anonymous polling, feedback, and evaluation through an intermediary until some kind of consensus emerges. A sample of experts, then, might be asked to specify the likely developments in their field in the next five, ten, and twenty-five years. The results would be compiled and then returned to each expert for reactions and revisions. This process could be repeated until no major revisions occur. Finally, the experts could also be polled for their opinions on the consequences of the forecasted event, and whether these effects would be good or bad.

Polling techniques seem to be an improvement over the two previous methods in respect to scientific "rigor." First, the frailties of the individual speculator are minimized, as a large number of qualified people are involved in the formulation and revision of the forecasts. Second, the repeated pollings and feedback give the impression of a more systematic approach to the definition of alternative futures.

Polling, however, is not free from criticism. Despite the appearance of scientific validity, the result of a compilation of opinions is still an opinion. Second, reliance on expert opinion can lead to the concentration on the specific to the detriment of the general. Polling techniques, unlike either free speculation or even scenarios, fail to provide any sense of the whole fabric of future possibilities; rather, they focus on one specific thread. Despite the forward thinking they undoubtedly encourage, polling techniques cannot discover or assess the impact of inventions that have yet to be conceived.

Identifying Social Forces

Attempts to be both systematic and comprehensive often resort to the identification and analysis of basic social forces that are assumed to determine, or at least condition, the nature of the future. These social forces, or "laws," have been formulated in a number of ways:[22]

1. *Structural Certainties*: If institutional patterns are well established, then certain kinds of behavior can be projected over time, regardless of the individuals who perform institutional roles. Thus, one can predict that presidential and congressional elections in the United States will take place every four and two years respectively. Moreover, the ways in which these two institutions function between elections are also governed by structural characteristics. Of course, some so-called institutions are quite fragile and may wither away in a brief time. Inevitably, even well-embedded institutions decay, as some do in the United States, and their formal structure becomes less useful in predicting behavior.

2. *Structural Requisites*: Although futurology deals with alternative futures, not all conceivable alternatives are equally probable. Some may demand certain preconditions that are difficult to fulfill. Identification of the structural requisites of each alternative, while not necessarily isolating the precise path taken, can simplify the selection of probable paths by eliminating those for which the preconditions are absent. To give a rather extreme example, the poverty-stricken African country of Chad is unlikely to industrialize in the foreseeable future because it lacks the resources, population, infrastructure (transportation and communications systems), and sociocultural values associated with industrialization.

3. *The Overriding Problem*: Some systems confront a problem so grave as to affect all other aspects of their behavior, the problem thereby becoming the primary determinant of the future. The overriding-problem mode of analysis does not specify the exact course of the future, but it does narrow the possibilities, as does the structural-requisites analysis. Whatever happens will have to be a response to this problem. The need to preserve national unity has been an overriding issue for many third world nations (among them Nigeria, Pakistan, Zaire). Not every system is confronted by such a problem, though it may be that the energy requirements of the advanced industrial countries will be their overriding problem for the remainder of the century.

4. *The Prime Mover*: Some social analyses have attempted to isolate what they believed to be the "prime mover" of social change. Marxism is the most famous of these theories, arguing that the mode of economic production is the basic source of change in society and determinant of history. Other analysts have assigned the role of prime mover to specific technologies. Marshall McLuhan, for example, sees the nature of the medium of communications as being basic to the structure of social relations.[23] Society has been fundamentally altered as the dominant means of communication changed in progression from the printing press to the radio and most recently to television.

5. *Sequential Development*: Many theories postulate that social and

economic change occurs in a specific sequence or stages. Again, Marxism provides one of the better-known theories of developmental stages, arguing that the mode of production (the prime mover) passes from primitive communism through slavery, feudalism, capitalism, and socialism, finally culminating in advanced communism.[24] Whether this sequence must be followed, or whether one or more of these stages might be skipped, is one of the livelier areas of debate in twentieth-century Marxism. Similarly, capitalist economist W. W. Rostow has devised an alternative theory of the stages of economic growth, arguing that industrializing economies pass through five distinct stages: (1) the traditional society; (2) preconditions to take-off; (3) the take-off into self-sustained growth; (4) the drive to maturity; and (5) the stage of mass consumption.[25] As with Marxist theory, the necessity of passing through these five precise stages can be questioned.

6.   *Recurring Patterns*: A final approach sees social systems or cultures repeating a given cycle. Whereas in the post-Renaissance Western world the dominant image of change has been linear, before the seventeenth-century and in other cultures essentially cyclical theories of historical movement have held sway. A simplified version of one of these cycles posits that human societies are fated to pass through successive ages of gold, silver, bronze, and iron. More recently, twentieth-century social philospher Pitirim Sorokin has proposed a theory of the "creatively recurrent" development of Western culture.[26] He recognizes that cultural systems never perfectly replicate earlier ones; rather, they share certain fundamental characteristics, though each does so in its own creative way. He sees Western society as oscillating between two primary cultural types—the *Sensate* and the *Ideational*—though mixed systems also have occurred. (See Table XVI-1.) Sorokin argues that the twentieth-century is experiencing the twilight of the most recent Sensate era, and that out of its ashes will rise a new Ideational cultural system (see the discussion in Chapter XVI).

Most of these endeavors to isolate basic social forces suffer from the same problems. With the possible exceptions of the cyclical and sequential theories, all are simply predicting persistence. Like many of the other futurist methodologies, they cannot aid in the anticipation of qualitative change. But if the identification of the basic trait is accurate, it will limit the range of the likely, if not conceivable, futures.

More importantly, these basic-social-force theories tend to be unicausal in emphasis, stressing only one factor, whether it be a structural characteristic, a prime mover, or an overriding problem. While some factors will certainly be more important than others, adequate explanations of social change are more often multicausal in nature. Despite these difficulties, efforts to identify and assess the impact of supposedly basic social forces lead analysts into questions of social dynamics that are sometimes slighted by other futurist methodologies.

Trend Extrapolation

The method of trend extrapolation is related to the projection of basic social forces, but is usually more specific in focus and mathematical in technique. Although any projection from the past into the future could be considered trend extrapolation, in this case the methodology is limited to those instances in which the trend can be quantified in some manner. Consequently, these extrapolations are most frequent in such areas as population growth and patterns of distribution, resource usage, and economic growth (see Tables XV-1 and XV-2).

Table XV-1   Extrapolated GNP for the Year 2000
(1968 dollars with no allowance for inflation)

Country	GNP per Capita in 1968	Average Annual Growth Rate of GNP per Capita (1961-1968) (% per year)	Projected GNP per Capita in the Year 2000
China	90	0.3	100
India	100	1.0	140
USSR	1,100	5.8	6,330
US	3,980	3.4	11,000
Japan	1,190	9.9	23,200

Note: The accuracy of the projection depends on whether the 1961-1968 rate of growth can be sustained for the years 1969-2000.

[Based on D. Meadows, *et al.*, *The Limits to Growth*, pp. 42-43.]

Table XV-2   Trends in Resource Usage

Resource	Known Reserves	Projected Growth Rate of Consumption	Estimated Years before Resource is Exhausted	Estimated Years with Five Times Known Reserves
Aluminum	1.17×10^9 tons	6.4%/yr.	31	55
Iron	1×10^{11} tons	1.8	93	173
Coal	5×10^{12} tons	4.1	111	150
Natural Gas	1.14×10^{15} cu ft	4.7	22	49
Petroleum	455×10^9 bbls.	3.9	20	50

Note: The accuracy of these projections depends on the accuracy of the projected growth rate of consumption and the growth in the world's reserves.

[Based on D. Meadows, *et al.*, *The Limits to Growth*, pp. 56-59.]

The accuracy of forecasts based on extrapolations depends on how easily the trend can be changed (a quality sometimes referred to as its inertia), and how far into the future the trend is projected. A high-inertia trend can change considerably if given enough time. Even a short-term projection of a low-inertia trend may prove faulty. Trend analysis, then, like many of the other methodologies discussed, is a predictor of persistence.

One way in which the anticipation of change could be aided by trend extrapolation is through combining it with certain assumptions about the structural requisites for the trend's continuation. Thus, the population-growth trend depends on, among other things, adequate supplies of food (a structural requisite). If one assumes that the total amount of arable land is fixed and the average productivity has an upper ceiling, then, at some point, population growth must cease. Similarly, if quantities of a certain resource (say oil) are limited, then trends in resource usage must eventually alter as the resource is depleted. The tendency for trends eventually to encounter structural limits is one of the primary reasons why some futurists argue that the general trend of continued material growth cannot be maintained indefinitely.

Simulations

The most technically sophisticated method for constructing alternative futures is through the use of simulations, or simplified models of real-life situations. Though the multitude of variables affecting social and political systems cannot be freely manipulated, the various elements of the simulation can be altered and the effects on the whole model assessed. The value of a simulation is only as good as the analogy on which it rests. All simulations are simplifications of the problem being simulated. If they were not, there would be no point in using them. The fundamental question is whether the important relations are adequately represented in the simulation.

Various types of simulations are used to anticipate the future. Mechanical simulations, such as studying the behavior of a scale model of an airplane in a wind tunnel, are common means of evaluating new designs. Games in which individuals play at being decision makers in an international crisis are sometimes drawn upon to gain some idea of how a real crisis might evolve. Finally, mathematical models representing real-world relationships are constructed and manipulated, generally with the aid of computers. The value of computerized simulations lies in their ability to handle relatively complex systems involving numerous variables and masses of data.

One of the more controversial attempts to use a computer simulation to examine alternative futures is reported in *The Limits to Growth*.[27] In this study, the authors describe their attempt to develop a model representing the dynamic interactions among several key elements of the world ecosystem:

population, resources, land productivity, capital, and pollution. Key relationships were specified and equations representing them devised. Where possible, the calculated relationships were checked against the existing data and modified if necessary. Then the questions were put—the values of the various components were altered in order to gauge the impact on the entire "world model." The purpose of this exercise was not so much to predict inevitabilities as to identify the probable consequences of certain patterns on the world system.

The basic conclusion of the authors is that continued growth in population and industrial output per capita cannot be supported either by the earth's nonrenewable resources or by its carrying capacity for pollutants. Moreover, technological innovations to control pollution, recycle materials, increase agricultural productivity, and discover and utilize new reserves would only delay the final collapse by a few decades. Only when combined with a general weakening of the growth forces in population and industrial output per capita until zero growth is approached could the world system reach a stable equilibrium.

Not surprisingly, the world model has been attacked as being a faulty analogy to the real world.[28] Critics have argued that the simulation is based on insufficient data, that the basic assumptions underlying its equations are inaccurate, and that it fails to represent adequately either the role of technology or the capacity of the system to change. In short, the simulation is not a simplification but an oversimplification of real-world interactions. Regardless of these criticisms, the "limits to growth" model represents an ambitious effort to draw upon computerized simulations in constructing alternative futures.

This chapter began with a speculation that the modern world system was coming to an end. It did not, however, specify the content of the postmodern era. A number of alternative futures can be sketched which, though by no means exhaustive, illustrate the range of possibilities available to humanity. These are explored in the final chapter.

Chapter XVI

The Politics of the Future

CONSTRUCTING ALTERNATIVE FUTURES

Future I: Pathological Decline

Current problems could grow into an interlocking set of socioeconomic, political, and ecological disasters, sending the human race sliding into oblivion.

Socio-Economic Crises: Changes in the global climate and current population levels are already generating pressures on the world's food supplies, causing near-famine conditions in parts of South Asia and Africa. Further population growth, coupled with poor global weather conditions, could create massive food deficits culminating in death by starvation for millions. Food-exporting countries, primarily the United States, could well become both unwilling and unable to meet the needs of deficit countries by giving away food increasingly needed at home or for income-producing export. Such a policy could embitter desperately poor nations, who might begin to contemplate extreme measures to force a redistribution of world wealth.

The industrial countries face an economic crisis of their own. Resource shortages, both real and manipulated, could further increase the inflation/recession twist. A collapse of the international monetary system brought about by the massive shift of the world's liquid assets from the industrial to the oil-exporting countries could trigger a world-wide depression. Weaker economies, like those of Britain and Italy, might go completely under, while stronger ones would be placed under severe strain. Due to worsening economic conditions, domestic social tensions could increase and crime and disorder spread as the norms governing social interaction erode.

Political Crises: The growing economic dislocations and the accompanying social disorder would place enormous pressures on existing political institutions. Previously established norms of political civility might decay, and political conflict might become more violent. Governments would grow more unstable and subject to overthrow. Military intervention, even in the supposedly immune Western democracies, could proliferate. Economic depression could encourage the rise of radical, mass movements, producing further disorder, which, in turn, would make more people willing to turn to authoritarian rule that promises at least some minimum amount of social and political peace. The trend to authoritarianism would be reinforced by the apparent need for stringent state controls to manage the crumbling national economies.

The international political system would reflect the chaos prevailing within the nation states. Individual states, struggling to maintain their own economic position, could implement "beggar my neighbor" economic policies which serve only to deepen the global depression. Finally, a poor country, reduced to a point where it feels it has nothing more to lose, might get control of a few nuclear weapons and use nuclear blackmail in an effort to force a redistribution. As an alternative, the United States could intervene militarily in the Middle East, causing the world to totter on the brink of thermonuclear war.

Ecological Crises: Even if the world manages to avoid perishing in a nuclear conflagration, ecological disasters could pose no less a threat to human survival. The demand for food would lead to increased soil fertilization and intensification of agriculture. Short-term increases in food production, however, might be bought at the expense of the atmosphere's ozone layer that protects the earth from excessive ultraviolet radiation. Skin cancers could multiply. The life cycle of plants might be altered. Previously established crops could begin to fail, and mass starvation could threaten even former food-surplus areas. With this eventuation, the last vestiges of civil order would vanish.

Coupled with the crisis of the atmosphere could be the crisis of the oceans. The scramble for food may lead to massive overfishing. Whole species could be eliminated, while others, though not destroyed, would be fished out. Worse still, the delicate ecosystem of the oceans finally might be irreversibly damaged by decades of petrochemical pollution. The oceans could begin to die.

This combination of crises may be somewhat improbable; yet, no single one of them is impossible, and the likelihood that at least one will occur appears quite large. This brief scenario, though, defines the worst possible future. The extent to which this future is avoided is largely dependent on how closely elements of the other futures are approached. The most conventional hope for avoiding pathological decline is the search for a technological remedy or "fix" for some or all of the above problems.

Future II: A Technological Fix

"The country that put a man on the moon in less than a decade can solve the problems of the cities, of pollution, of energy." This common refrain reflects the expectation that some kind of technological fix can be found for most, if not all, of the problems projected in Future I.[1] Past efforts, like the Manhattan project to develop the atomic bomb and the Apollo moon program, are cited as examples to be imitated in dealing with the problems of population, pollution, and energy. Indeed, in some instances like population control, the technologies are already available. What remains to be done is to utilize them.

Advancing technology could solve many of the problems of resource scarcity.[2] Innovations might lower the cost of exploiting known reserves. "New" resources could be brought into use to serve instead of those growing scarce (as aluminum has served in many uses that would have demanded steel or copper save for the technological innovation that facilitated the commercial extraction of aluminum from bauxite). Technology could find interchangeable applications for known materials (as paper and glass and plastics and various metals used in making containers). Technology could also improve the efficiency of resource-consuming industries (as through recycling). Indeed, the rising prices of raw materials should be viewed not with alarm but as a mechanism necessary to encourage such developments.

The provision of a cheap, nonpolluting, plentiful source of energy appears to be the primary requisite for the stabilization of contemporary socioeconomic systems. If sufficient supplies of energy are readily available, many of the other problems seem less intractable. With enough cheap energy, deserts could be made to bloom, food and minerals could be extracted from the oceans, and the poverty of many of the underdeveloped nations could be ended. At the very least, time could be bought in which to deal with other problems. Neither nuclear nor thermonuclear power seems to offer a good solution, for both raise grave problems of pollution—the former of radioactive wastes and both of thermal pollution. The development of commercially exploitable solar energy offers, perhaps, the best hope for a long-run solution to the energy problem.

Physicist Gerard O'Neill promotes another very ambitious fix for many of the earth's problems—the colonization of space.[3] O'Neill tries to demonstrate that with the technology already available and at an annual real cost no greater than the Apollo program, huge satellites could be constructed in space. If the effort were begun in 1975, the first colony for about 10,000 people, could be completed by 1988. By the year 2008, satellites 32 km in length and 3200 m in radius could be built. These would be so large that they would have their own weather and landscape (rivers, hills, and small mountains), as well as artificial gravity supplied by rotation. Most of the material to build these would come from the moon and the energy from the sun. Each satellite would produce its own food. O'Neill has even devised simple and efficient means of transport among the satellites and between them and the moon. He calculates that with an Apollo-scaled effort, the expanding number of satellites could absorb all of the earth's annual population increase by about 2050 and actually begin to reduce global population after that (assuming a continuation of the 2 percent annual growth rate). O'Neill's proposal, then, is a multipurpose "megafix" potentially solving in one bold stroke the problems of population, pollution, resource shortages, and energy.

The future to be achieved by way of the technological fix is substantially a continuation of life as lived in the quarter century after World War II. A project on the grand scale of the colonization of space could conceivably bring the consumption/production patterns of the postwar industrial countries to many of the poorer peoples of the world, but this change would nevertheless be more of an expansion of one aspect of the present rather than a qualitative change. The primary purpose of efforts to discover and implement technological fixes is to avoid the cataclysms of Future I on one hand, but to maintain contemporary patterns of life and thought on the other.

The technological approach tends to slight the sociocultural dynamics of the current plight of the human race. Even accepting the idea that the solutions outlined above are technologically feasible, one must still confront the problem of how to implement them. Something as apparently straightforward as population control demonstrates little success after a decade of work, despite the availability of appropriate technologies. If these relatively simple programs flounder, it seems highly unlikely that the existing national and international systems have the capacity to undertake the massive population relocation required by the O'Neill project.

Technological innovations, moreover, have the definite tendency to create new problems while attempting to correct for the old—the treadmill effect discussed earlier. Technological solutions also are often piecemeal in nature and ignore the systemic context within which they must work. Consequently, though the careful implementation of certain technological fixes may be a necessary condition for the avoidance of Future I, it might not be sufficient. At the very least, massive demands will be placed on the political process (see below). Many of the technological solutions, ranging from population control to pollution abatement, may not work at all except through the threat (and exercise) of state coercion. Indeed, if Future I is to be avoided, it may even be necessary to abandon some of the primary values and orientations of modernity.

Future III: A Cognitive Fix

As the crises of the modern age grow more severe, there could be a turning away from the basic cognitive and normative attitudes that underlie modernity. Since this turning would be intended to counter the pathologies intrinsic to modernity, it might be surmised that a so-called counterculture provides an alternative. The counterculture present in society, however, is really a grab bag of traits and values rather than a meaningfully integrated alternative system. Certain elements, admittedly, offer clues to the nature of a truly *counter* culture, and these groupings are symptoms of the discontent with conventional modernity. Other aspects, though, are deeply rooted in the contemporary scene and reflect its materialism and value diversity. Some, like the drug culture, seem to be efforts to achieve stupefaction more than enlightenment—a response, but not an alternative, to the contradictions of the modern age.

Pitirim Sorokin, in his *Social and Cultural Dynamics*, defines a meaningfully integrated cultural type that would provide a cognitive fix for the discontents of the age. Modern sociocultural systems exhibit the general traits Sorokin associates with the *Sensate* cultural type. *Ideational* culture, though, appears to correct a number of the excesses of modernity identified earlier. See Chart XVI-1 and the discussion that follows.

1. *The Limits to Material Growth*: The drive for continually increasing material output, the consequent depletion of resources, and destruction of the environment are rooted in an acquisitive, Sensate culture that stresses the ultimate value of the pursuit of physical pleasures. An Ideational culture would discount these pleasures, emphasizing in their place transcendental absolutes. It would encourage self-abnegation. Freedom, Sorokin suggests, depends on the extent to which the individual can fulfill his or her desires.[4] Sensate freedom, since it encourages the multiplication of material wants, reinforces the exploitation of the environment to meet these wants. Ideational freedom would encourage the minimization of material desires, which, in turn, would lessen the impact of human activities on the environment.

Kenneth Boulding notes that the realization of a no-growth economy which would place a minimum burden on the world ecosystem depends on the ability to identify with a community extending through time as well as through space.[5] The modern, Sensate mentality, however, stresses flux and transience, a bias that contributes toward a tendency to discount the future in making calculations of profit and loss. Not surprisingly, this attitude produces a profligate pattern of resource usage. Ideational culture, characterized by absolute and unchanging values, would seem more likely to encourage a generalized identification with posterity.

Overpopulation appears at least in part related to cultural mentalities as well. One irony of the techniques of Sensate medicine and sanitation is that their implementation has produced a tremendous increase in world population. New birth-control techniques alone are not sufficient to halt this growth,

Chart XVI-1   Summary of the Primary and Secondary Traits
of the Ideational and Sensate Mentalities

Main Elements	Ideational	Sensate
1. Reality	Ultimate reality eternal and transcendental.	Ultimate reality material and empirical.
2. Main Needs and Ends	Spiritual.	Richly sensate.
3. Method of Satisfaction	Mainly self-modification.	Mainly modification of external milieu.
4. Worldview	Being; lasting value, indifference to transient values, imperturbability; relatively static.	Becoming; transient values; full sense of life, joy, and grief; dynamic, endless readjustment (progress, evolution).
5. Power and Object of Control	Self-control; repression of the sensual man.	Control of the sensate reality.
6. Activity	Introvert.	Extrovert.
7. Self	Highly integrated, spiritual, dissolved in ultimate reality; sensate world an illusion; anti-materialistic.	Highly integrated, dissolved in immediate physical reality; materializes all spiritual phenomena; cares for body; sensual liberty and egoism.
8. Knowledge	Develops insight into spiritual phenomena and experiences; education and modification of inner life.	Develops science of natural phenomena and technical invention. Emphasis on technology, medicine, sanitation—modification of man's physical actions.
9. Nature of Truth	Based on inner experience, mystical; concentrated meditation, intuition, revelation, prophecy.	Based on observation, measurement, experimentation with exterior phenomena, mediated through senses; inductive logic.
10. Moral Systems	Absolute, transcendental, categoric imperatives; everlasting and unchanging.	Relativistic, hedonistic, utilitarian. Seeking maximum sensate happiness; morals of "enlightened" egoism.
11. Aesthetic Values	Subservient to main inner values, religious, nonsensate.	Secular, created to increase joys and beauties of a rich sensate life.
12. Social and Practical Values	Those which are lasting and lead to the ultimate reality; all else is valueless or nearly so, particularly wealth and material comfort; principle of sacrifice.	Everything that gives joy of life to self and partly to others, especially wealth and comfort; prestige based on the above; physical might tends to become "right"; principle of enlightened egoism.

[Based on Pitirim Sorokin, *Social and Cultural Dynamics*, pp. 37-39.]

for they simply allow women to decide how many children to have—a decision that may or may not produce zero population growth (ZPG). Population control depends on making individual choices that result in the desired collective consequence. In times when humans were fewer in number, "increase and multiply" might have been the collectively responsible decision. Under conditions of overpopulation, however, responsibility dictates the opposite course. "Enlightened" egoism seems to be an inadequate basis for obedience to such responsibility. In fact, when people of Sensate cultures do decide to limit the numbers of their children, it is usually because the cost prevents them from realizing other material pleasures. The consequent social benefit in terms of a lower rate of population growth is more than lost through the rise in the level of per capita consumption.

Ideational values, however, could provide a foundation for accepting responsibility to the community as it extends through both space and time. Decisions as to the number of children would reflect shared absolutes, rather than the unpredictable whims of "enlightened" egoism. The positive consequences of the limitation on numbers, moreover, would not be negated by a subsequent rise in personal consumption.

2. *The Limits to Technology*: The modern Sensate mentality sees the modification and manipulation of the external environment as the primary means of satisfying its goals. This attitude defines the uses to which science and technology are put. Such an orientation, though, is clearly ill-suited to cope with the problems that the technological imperative itself raises. If the rate of innovation cannot be sustained, upon what reservoirs of knowledge and behavior can Sensatism fall back? Probably on none, for the only way a technologically dependent age can cope with the problems created by technology is through still more technology. As this contradiction grows too severe, there may well be a growing need to revise radically the relation of human race to its environment.

The Ideational mentality could provide an alternative to Sensate interventionism. By denigrating material pleasures and stressing self-control rather than environmental control, an Ideational culture would lessen dependence on technological capacity and would reinforce the importance of other ways of knowing and coping. This change would not necessarily mean that existing techniques would be abandoned; rather, the pursuit of material means of control would become secondary to other and immaterial goals. The need for, and the consequent pace of, technological innovation would slow down. This slower pace would allow for a better understanding of all the consequences of innovation. Above all, an Ideational world view would consider human beings in terms of absolute, transcendent values, and people would less likely be subordinated to the needs of a technostructure.

3.   *The Limits to Modern Social Relations*: Sensate skepticism and moral relativism have undermined traditional religions; but hedonism, utilitarianism, and faith in technological progress are proving to be inadequate substitutes. As this situation becomes more intolerable, people could turn away from the promise of Sensate reality and seek a faith better able to succor them through times of trouble. As the material conditions of Sensate societies worsen, the pressure to find some nonmaterial source of comfort will grow even more intense. The spiritual paucity and physical crises of the Sensate era, therefore, could produce a situation ripe for the introduction of an Ideational faith. This faith could fill human existence with meaning and provide the foundation for a new community of believers.

The Ideational future also promises to reunite humanity through the new community. No longer would people be alienated from one another; rather, all would be united in a quest for the enrichment of their inner lives. The value of a human life would no longer be determined by reference to its contribution to the functioning of the technostructure, but rather by absolute and unchanging categoric imperatives.

Future IV: The Ultimate Evolution

The three alternative futures sketched above concentrate primarily on contemporary problems and gaze forward perhaps two generations. A fourth alternative casts back to the origins of the universe and looks forward to an *omega* point—an ultimate end. This appears in the evolutionary philosophy of Pierre Teilhard de Chardin.[6]

Teilhard, who was both a priest and a scientist, synthesizes science and metaphysics into a vision of evolution not only of physical forms but also of consciousness. He proposes that one can understand the current plight of humanity only by seeing it as an integral part of the overall evolutionary process. According to Teilhard, the evolution to a higher form of consciousness develops through four basic stages:

Stage 1.   *Geogenesis*:   The origins of the physical universe. Consciousness, insofar as it can be said to exist at all, is extremely rudimentary.

Stage 2.   *Biogenesis*:   The leap to life. The basic distinguishing characteristic is reproduction.

Stage 3.   *Psychogenesis*:   The leap to self-consciousness. The key characteristic is reflection, the capacity to know you know.

Stage 4.   *Noogenesis*:   The leap to collective consciousness. This is the stage which Teilhard sees the human race is now entering. The fundamental trait is the growth of self-awareness as a species.

For Teilhard, then, contemporary traumas are simply part of the movement towards this final new leap in awareness. The creation of a collective consciousness involves the combination of two apparently contradictory forces—collectivization and personalization. The growth of the former can be seen in exaggerated form in the rise of twentieth-century totalitarianism. The latter is demonstrated by the emphasis on the individual in Western liberal societies. Each force, by itself, is incomplete and distorted—noogenesis requires that they be synthesized. In consequence of this synthesis, the union of individual consciousnesses into a collectivity will not destroy, but instead will fulfill, the individual. Just as love between two people unifies them without eliminating the personality of each, so the collective consciousness that Teilhard sees evolving out of the modern world will repeat, through the energy of love, the paradoxical feat of personalizing through unification.[7]

Assuming Teilhard's alternative future to be an accurate perception, then the other futures can be subsumed by it. Although he believed in the inevitability of this evolutionary thrust toward greater consciousness, he never assumed that it would be easy or come without great suffering. Though he would deny that the human race will destroy itself, he would see the crises of Future I as part of the process through which humanity becomes aware of itself as a species. World wars, the energy shortages, and the economic crisis are leading to greater recognition of global interdependence. Teilhard also believed that the human animal could not be viewed apart from the physical universe. Thus, he developed an ecological perspective similar to that which environmental problems are now forcing on larger numbers of people.

The technological advances of Future II also fit well with Teilhard's argument. Cybernetics, the expanding information technology, despite the ways in which it can be abused, clearly contributes to collectivization and growing unity. Improvements in communications and transport are drawing the peoples of the world closer together, whether they like it or not. The trip to the moon, in fact, may ultimately be more important for the pictures of earth as a small beautiful island floating in the void than for any scientific data brought back. These pictures, more than any other single image, drive home the point of the species unity.

Even Future III, which foresees Western culture as moving toward ideational forms, can be absorbed into Teilhard's vision. Noogenesis cannot simply involve one or the other cultural disposition; instead, both must be combined and fulfilled. The superconsciousness would deny neither the individual nor the collective, neither the physical world and its pleasures and pain nor transcendental truth and mysticism. All forms of partial truth, all partial values, would be combined into whole truth and comprehensive values.

John David Garcia, in *A Moral Society: A Rational Alternative to Death*, accepts much of Teilhard's argument that the basic thrust of evolution is toward expanding consciousness.[8] Unlike Teilhard, though, Garcia is not optimistic about continued progress in this direction. He denies that the rise of collective awareness is inevitable, stating that it can come to pass only if people deliberately set about working to expand their awareness—individual and collective. Instead of doing this, most people are pursuing happiness, a course that will lead to declining awareness and to the ultimate death of the human race. Garcia's preferred future is as cosmic as that of Teilhard, but he believes that the probable future resembles Future I.

If Garcia is correct in arguing that the preferred future must be consciously built, then his view leads back to the question: By what process will the future be made? What are the politics of future-building?

THE POLITICS OF FUTURE-BUILDING

The range of alternative futures available to the world is already somewhat limited by events in the present and the past. Decisions have already been made, nonrenewable resources have been used, and options have been closed. This narrowing does not mean that the future has been completely determined, for there is still a role for choice, which means a role for politics—the process by which decisions for the whole system are made. Each of the futures outlined above is characterized by politics most likely to produce and accompany it.

Future I: The Politics of Greed

The choices most likely to create and sustain Future I are self-serving ones—the politics of greed. Fault does not lie solely with the individual, whether citizen or leader, because the social setting within which people function encourages selfish behavior. Environmentalist Garrett Hardin calls this setting and the greed it encourages "the tragedy of the commons."[9]

A commons system exists whenever an environment is owned and utilized by a group, but the proceeds of the utilization go to the individual members. Hardin illustrates the consequences of this system through a simple parable. Suppose ten dairy farmers each graze ten cows on a common pasture. Suppose also that this pasture has a carrying capacity of one hundred cows; that is, if one more cow is introduced, the total amount of milk produced will actually decline slightly, because of over grazing.

If the pasture were equally divided into ten plots among the ten farmers, it would be irrational for any one of them to add another cow to his plot, for he would bear the entire cost of overgrazing. If the whole pasture, however, is held in common, the overgrazing cost of any single farmer's adding a cow would be shared by everyone, but the benefits would accrue only to him. Consequently, even though "social costs" outweigh individual benefits, the private profits going to the greedy farmer outweigh his individual costs.

Therefore, when the pasture is held in common, it would be "rational" for the profit-maximizing farmer to add the eleventh cow, even though "society" suffers. What is more, it would be rational for each of the other farmers to do the same thing, until the pasture is irreversibly damaged. If one farmer takes the long-term view and does not add extra cattle, he will in effect be punished for his restraint and be victimized by his unethical associates. As long as a single farmer places personal gain over the general welfare, the pressure will be intense for the others to follow suit in order to protect themselves over the short term.

The implications of this parable may seem rather remote, until one realizes how much of the world "commons" is being used in precisely this fashion. Perhaps the clearest examples are with regard to the use of the air commons and the water commons. The social costs of pollution are not imposed only on those who create the pollutants, but are shared by all. The benefits, however, accrue directly to those who use the waterways and atmosphere as their sewers. Even the individual automobile owner has not fully absorbed the entire social cost of the pollutants produced by his car. The fact that air and water are being used as commons for individual profit produces many of the problems outlined in Future I.

The population problem, Hardin believes, also may result in part from the "commons" mentality.[10] The right to decide to have children rests primarily with the individual, but, more and more, the responsibility for supporting those children is carried by the entire society. The modern welfare state pays for a growing proportion of everything from basic necessities like food, clothing, and shelter to education and health care. World-wide, populations that would have otherwise been decimated by famine have been sustained through international aid. While such welfare and aid measures may be justifiable from a humanitarian view, the separation of rights from the responsibilities they imply may well make the population problem worse.

Nor is the problem simply one of the internal functions of national economies. The behavior of the members of the international community displays many of the same tendencies. Overfishing and the pollution of ocean space are two cases of individual states pursuing self-regarding interests at the expense of the global commons. Patterns of resource use in which short-term profits are made at the expense of long-run needs may be another case. Even interstate competition and the enormous annual investment in armaments could be seen as a manifestation of this mentality. Every state believes that it must invest in defense so long as a single country exists that might take advantage of a disarmed world for purposes of national aggrandizement.

The tragedy, then, is that the policies that could well produce the global irrationalities of ecocatastrophe, economic collapse, and world war are "rational" from the point of view of the individual decision maker. The politics of greed and fear lead to the future of pathological decline.

A traditional solution to this problem has been to divide the commons up so that each decision maker bears the full cost of his or her choices. This division would presumably encourage a politics of responsibility, rather than one of greed. Some of the key commons areas, however, like the seas and the atmosphere, cannot be so divided. Moreover, the elimination of welfare programs that protect people from some of the consequences of their actions would not be humane. Most of these programs are primarily intended to protect people from social forces beyond their control, as well as from themselves.

Hardin believes that the only way out is through "mutual coercion mutually agreed upon."[11] Just as modern governments cannot operate on voluntary donations, but require mandatory taxation, so also must the use of the commons be governed by mandatory regulations. Already, some national governments are moving in this direction by imposing fines and other penalties on polluters and requiring that antipollution devices be installed on cars and factories. National authority, though, is insufficient, for there is a need for a world overseer who will insure that the global commons is not abused. The chances for such an international political authority appear, at this time, to be relatively remote, though some interim treaty agreements might be made among sovereign nation-states.

Future II: The Politics of Technological Innovation

Future II, an alternative to pathological decline, depends on the success of another type of politics, that of technological innovation. Technologies to meliorate, or possibly solve, some of the crises of Future I are unlikely to develop spontaneously. Rather, the future of the technological fix depends on the political process successfully performing a number of critical tasks: (1) definition of the problems most susceptible to a technological fix; (2) assessment of the alternative possibilities available in terms of their costs and benefits; (3) support of research and development into promising areas; and (4) implementation of the optimal technology.

Stated in this way, the politics of technological innovation appears to be relatively straightforward. Each step, however, presents some challenging political problems.

1.   *Defining Problems Susceptible to a Fix*: The politics of this alternative future may fail right at the initial step in the decision-making process.

Since resources are limited, not every conceivable problem can be addressed. Consequently, a set of priorities must be established. But how will these be set? The existing domestic political process essentially identifies the salient needs of the politically powerful sectors of the population. The international system functions in a somewhat similar manner. The needs and interests of groups who lack the power to assert them go underrepresented when social priorities are set.

Even when a common problem is identified, competing interests will still define it differently. The population problem exemplifies the effect of differing perspectives. The wealthy nations see it as a question of the burgeoning numbers in the "third world" countries and, consequently, advocate technologies to control population growth. Representatives of the poorer nations see this definition as a way of passing the entire burden onto them, while wealthy nations continue their patterns of profligate consumption. Similarly, conservation groups in the United States condemn the techniques of Japanese whalers which are bringing the whale to the brink of extinction. The Japanese, who lack the sources of animal protein available to Americans, tend to see the problem somewhat differently. Before a technological fix can even be developed, therefore, some consensus must also be reached on the dimensions of the problem for which a fix is to be attempted.

2. *Assessing Alternative Technologies*: Once the problem has been defined, then the possible solutions must be evaluated in terms of their costs and benefits. In the past, such assessments have been most commonly undertaken by those organizations that wish to exploit particular technologies.[12] The frame of reference of these groups, obviously, is not going to be entirely unbiased. Thus, critics argue that the Atomic Energy Commission has consistently underestimated the risks of nuclear power-generating facilities. One critic goes so far as to suggest that the government create an agency to serve as a "devil's advocate" in the public debate over particular technologies.[13] This agency would attempt to present the worst possible consequences of implementing a particular technological solution. In this way, the presumed costs and benefits of a technology could be more clearly recognized.

This proposal assumes, of course, that costs and benefits can be assessed, at least in principle, once the appropriate administrative organization is created. Aspects of a particular technology, though, may not be easily measured and compared with other alternatives. Where quantitative measures exist for part of the cost (or benefit), they may be overemphasized at the expense of more qualitative dimensions of the impact.

In addition, some costs and benefits may go unrecognized or may be given little weight because of "the lack of effective constituencies informed and influential enough to inject diffuse and poorly articulated interests into the decision making process."[14] Especially for the more qualitative dimensions of the costs and benefits of technological options, calculation is as much a political as a methodological problem. Where no valid quantifiable measure of impact exists, the evaluation often depends on the relative power position of those affected by the technology. For example, if environmentalists had not been able to organize substantial opposition to the supersonic transport, the decision whether or not to support its production would have reflected only the interests of those groups who touted its presumed benefits (jobs, export income, national prestige). The go-ahead decision would not mean the environmental costs of noise and air pollution would disappear, only that the adversaries concerned about them lacked the power to get them factored into the assessment process.

3.   *Financing Research and Development*: Assuming that a technology is judged to be a useful corrective to an existing problem, it must then enter the next stage of the political process—resource allocation. Whereas the assessment process involves the relative merits of alternative fixes, the problem of financing entangles the program in the entire texture of political debate. The resources needed for a technological development must be evaluated in comparison with all the other demands made on the government's limited funds. When one is speaking of the tens of billions of dollars required by an ambitious fix on the scale of O'Neill's satellite proposal, the relevance of limited resources becomes quite clear.

Again, this problem involves more than a simple cost/benefit analysis of the proposed technological development *vis-à-vis* other government programs. It also becomes a question of political power and feasibility. The acceptance of any program, and the ability of the government to increase or withdraw support, will be affected by the power position of the groups advocating or opposing it. If government's resources are expanding, then it may have a disposable surplus to allocate to new programs. If the resource base is stagnating, then competition for funds will tend to become zero-sum in nature (see Chapter VI) and vested interests supporting established programs will strenuously resist any proposal to further subdivide the fiscal pie, whatever its abstract merits.

4.   *Implementing the Fix*: After the politics of definition, assessment, and allocation comes the politics of implementation. No matter how well-conceived and supported, a technological fix may fail because of resistance to its implementation. As has already been noted, even if the governments of the world were willing to support the colonization of space it is hard to conceive how, given existing values and sensibilities, several billion people could be convinced or coerced to move there. Only limited success has been achieved in modest, earthbound colonization plans (as in the interior of the Amazon River basin and in Siberia). Similar problems of resistance affect less ambitiously conceived fixes, from population control to pollution abatement.

This experience with resistance does not mean that all technological fixes are necessarily going to encounter insurmountable obstacles, only that implementation is a political rather than a technical problem. The more a particular innovation goes counter to established values and habits, the more it disrupts the prevailing distribution of power, then the more opposition it will encounter.

The future of the technological fix, therefore, depends on political and social dynamics and questions of power, as much as on the intrinsic merit of any given innovation. In the international arena, moreover, there does not exist a recognized political authority even potentially capable of solving the problems of definition, assessment, allocation, and implementation; the lack further complicates the political problems of dealing with any global crisis. In fact, it seems reasonable to expect that if current attitudes continue, the politics of technological innovation will be subverted by the politics of greed. Perhaps the utilization of technology needs to be subordinated to a more basic shift in values, that is, to a cognitive fix and the politics of transcendence.

Future III: The Politics of Transcendence

In the vision of Future III, the material crises of modernity will be corrected not by the technological innovations of Future II, but through a massive restructuring of values and attitudes. This "inner revolution" would mean the abandonment of the materialism, hedonism, and value relativism of the modern world and their replacement by the transcendental, spiritual absolutes of an Ideational era. Such a shift in social values must necessarily affect the political process.

In a Sensate age like the twentieth century, political power is largely derived from the control of material power resources, such as economic wealth or coercive capability. These, in turn, can be used to generate increased immaterial resources, for example, status and legitimacy. So also, can certain kinds of information resources, which have also increased in value in modern societies; but these forms of knowledge and information are primarily valued for the contribution they make to the operations of complex technocratic organizations. Even the political credos of democracy and popular sovereignty, more honored in the breach than in the fact around the world, are related to the value relativism of a Sensate culture, in which each person's opinion is considered the equal of every other.

For Sorokin, the politics of greed are the inevitable accompaniment of a declining Sensate age:[15]

> Rude force and cynical fraud will become the only arbiters of all values and of all interindividual and intergroup relationships. Might will become right. As a consequence, wars, revolutions, revolts, disturbances, brutality will be rampant. *Bellum omnium contra omnes* —man against man, class, nation, creed and race

against class, nation, creed and race—will raise its head.

Freedom will become a mere myth for the majority and will be turned into an unbridled licentiousness by the dominant minority. Inalienable rights will be alienated, Declarations of Rights either abolished or used only as beautiful screens for an unadulterated coercion.

Governments will become more and more hoary, fraudulent, and tyrannical, giving bombs instead of bread; death instead of freedom; violence instead of law; destruction instead of creation. They will be increasingly shortlived, unstable and subject to overthrow.

If this deterioration does not culminate in ultimate destruction, then out of the ruins of Sensate politics, Sorokin believes, will emerge the new Ideational political order.[16] No longer will those who control material power resources be politically dominant. Rather, the primary political class will be composed of those who incarnate the absolute spiritual values of the Ideational culture. Since these values would most likely be grounded in some conception of the Deity, an Ideational political order would be theocratic in nature. The most valued resource, therefore, would be spiritual status, and a legitimate political system would necessarily reflect the spiritual absolutes. Law and public policy, which in the current era often simply disguise the private interests of powerful groups, would be derived from the requisites of this system of spiritual beliefs.

Ideational politics is, by definition, alien to that of the modern world. Precursors must be found in the politics of the early Middle Ages, in the era of the Judges in ancient Israel, or in the Tibetan theocracy. Just as the politics of twentieth-century Sensatism might lead to the pathologies predicted in Future I, the decay of an Ideational culture produces its own special perversions: dogmatism, intolerance, and the manipulation of a spiritual faith to preserve the power and privileges of a corrupt priestly caste. The decline of the Catholic church in the centuries prior to the Reformation illustrates what can occur when an Ideational political order begins to rot.

Future IV: The Politics of Evolution

Futures I and II foresee essentially linear development—the first a continuous material decline,the second an uninterrupted material advance. Future III, though, is basically cyclical in conception. The contradictions of one cultural era produce a compensatory alternative; presumably, the decline of an ideational order could result in a new Sensate age. In Future IV, the prevision is again one of linear advance, this time not so much in material or technological terms as in the evolution of human consciousness.

Teilhard de Chardin believes that this evolutionary advance is irreversible and inevitable. Certain moral principles (for one, love) encourage the development of "species consciousness," but Teilhard pays little attention to the specific political conditions that might accompany and support this evolution. Garcia, however, argues that the expansion of awareness cannot be taken for granted and must be deliberately pursued. He outlines the structure of an "ethical state"; that is, a structure designed to increase both individual and social awareness.[17]

The basic purpose of the ethical state, consequently, is the expansion of awareness—education. In contemporary societies, Garcia sees education as subordinated to other social operations. People are educated less for their own development than for service in the economic sector, for contributing to the national defense, or for operating government bureaucracies. He asserts this relationship should be reversed: The economic system should exist primarily to support the educational system, the military to defend it, and the government to administer it.

Nor does Garcia conceive of education as narrow, technical specialization, but rather as broadly generalist in nature. The basic program, *before* a person is allowed to specialize, would be equivalent to earning bachelor's degrees in mathematics, physics, chemistry, biology, earth sciences, engineering, psychology, anthropology, general behavioral science, humanities, and philosophy.[18] The state would support all those capable of completing such a program.

Other general policies also flow from the assumption that the fundamental purpose of the state should be to encourage the expansion of awareness. Garcia believes that leaders should be chosen on the basis of total awareness, that the less aware are not fit to govern. Accepting this basis means abandoning the conventional democratic selection process, insofar as only the most aware would be allowed to compete for office. Economic and political organizations are to be made competitive so as to insure that they receive continuous negative feedback (that is, information that they are not operating effectively, since Garcia believes that without competition, bureaucracies tend to screen out such information). Periodically, the least effective organizations should be disbanded to further encourage performance. Interestingly, Garcia thinks that men and women have somewhat different, but complementary talents, and, therefore, all major political offices should be filled by "candidate-pairs." In this way, organizations can benefit from the talents of both sexes.

Since Garcia is concerned with evolutionary advance, he believes that the ethical state should be given control over the propagation of the species (sometimes referred to as eugenics). This control implies that persons who are likely to produce defective offspring would be prevented from having children. He sees no danger in these policies, so long as the aim is to increase human awareness rather than to advance selfish, power-seeking goals.

In short, the politics of evolution can be viewed as a kind of humane "political Darwinism" in which competitiveness, negative feedback, and "creative tension" are maximized. In this way, the evolution of individual and general awareness would presumably be encouraged and the less aware, though not overtly eliminated, would eventually be winnowed out. In some ways—the emphasis on expanding consciousness, the selection of leaders on the basis of talent, the control of the propagation of the species—Garcia's political recommendations resemble those of Plato in *The Republic*. Plato also believed that the primary purpose of life is the pursuit of Truth (awareness), that philosophers should be kings, and that the state should practice eugenics to maintain and improve the quality of the species.

Garcia's opinions on the politics of evolution are clearly controversial. He admits that there is no agreed-upon standard for measuring the performance of bureaucracies whose output is not bought and sold in the market. A state-run eugenics program probably raises the most serious misgivings for, justly or unjustly, it suggests an unfortunate parallel with the Nazi pursuit of "racial purity." Even though Garcia repeatedly emphasizes that all he wishes to do is to keep the unfit from having children, there still remains the problem of determining what genetic characteristics are undesirable. The pursuit of a homogeneous hybrid may ultimately be much more destructive of human survival than the toleration of a diverse range of talents and capabilities, even those which may appear deviant. Not only does the toleration alternative retain the possibility for the creative recombination of genetic types, but furthermore an apparently deviant and worthless group may be preserving genetic material necessary for some future, unforeseen adaptation.

CONCLUSION

These speculations about the future could be extended indefinitely. The four introduced here serve only to suggest the range of possibilities confronting the human race. Some of these alternatives (III and IV) may seem rather remote, but one must remember that the world at the close of the twentieth century would seem equally remote to a person living at the beginning of the nineteenth. Other futures can also be imagined, such as the emergence of a near-perfect totalitarianism devoted to neither Ideational values nor to the evolution of consciousness.

Despite all the current efforts at prognostication, perhaps the only prediction that can be made with confidence is that the future will not be surprise-free. Whatever happens, as social arrangements differ further from what is currently commonplace, the politics, too, will become increasingly remote from contemporary practices. The primary challenge of political life, however, will remain the same: not only to manage unforeseen problems, but also to identify and protect the fundamental components of human dignity. Hopefully, the failures of the present will not be projected into the indefinite future.

Bibliography of Works Cited

Adler, Mortimer J. *The Idea of Freedom*. 2 vols. New York: Doubleday, 1958.

Afrifa, A. A. *Budget Statement for 1968-1969*. Accra: Ministry of Finance, 1968.

Afrifa, A. A. *The Ghana Coup: 24 February, 1966*. London: Cass, 1966.

Ahmad, Eqbal. "The Theory and Fallacies of Counterinsurgency." *The Nation*, August 2, 1971, pp. 70-85.

Almond, Gabriel A., and James S. Coleman, eds. *The Politics of the Developing Areas*, Princeton: Princeton University Press, 1960.

Almond, Gabriel A., and G. Bingham Powell, Jr. *Comparative Politics: A Developmental Approach*. Boston: Little, Brown, 1966.

Almond, Gabriel A., and Sidney Verba. *The Civic Culture; Political Attitudes and Democracy in Five Nations*. Boston: Little, Brown, 1965.

Anderson, Stanley V., ed. *Ombudsmen for American Government?* Englewood Cliffs, N.J.: Prentice-Hall, 1968.

Apter, David E. *Ghana in Transition*. New York: Atheneum, 1963.

Apter, David E. "Nkrumah, Charisma and the Coup." *Daedalus*, 97 (Summer 1968), pp. 757-792.

Apter, David E. *The Politics of Modernization*. Chicago: University of Chicago Press, 1965.

Aquinas, Thomas. *The Political Ideas of Thomas Aquinas*, Dino Bigongiari, ed. New York: Hafner, 1957.

Ardrey, Robert. *The Social Contract*. New York: Atheneum, 1970.

Arendt, Hannah. *On Revolution*. New York; Viking, 1965.

Aristotle, *Nicomachean Ethics*, trans. by Martin Ostwald. Indianapolis: Bobbs-Merrill, 1962.

Aristotle, *The Politics*, trans. by Ernest Barker. New York: Oxford University Press, 1962.

Bachrach, Peter, and Morton S. Baratz. "Two Faces of Power," in McCoy and Playford, eds., pp. 146-157.

319

Barkun, Michael. *Law without Sanctions: Order in Primitive Societies and the World Community*. New Haven: Yale University Press, 1968.

Bell, Daniel. "Twelve Models of Prediction" in Somit, ed.

Bellamy, Edward. *Looking Backward*. New York: Signet, 1963.

Berger, Peter, Brigitte Berger, and Hansfried Kellner. *The Homeless Mind: Modernization and Consciousness*. New York: Vintage, 1973.

Berlin, Isaiah. *Two Concepts of Liberty*. London: Clarendon, 1958.

Bienen, Henry, ed. *The Military and Modernization*. Chicago: Aldine-Atherton, 1971.

Bigongiari, Dino, ed. *The Political Ideas of St. Thomas Aquinas*. New York: Hafner, 1957.

Blondel, Jean. *Comparative Legislatures*. Englewood Cliffs, N.J.: Prentice-Hall, 1973.

Bluhm, William T. *Ideologies and Attitudes; Modern Political Culture*. Englewood Cliffs, N.J.: Prentice-Hall, 1974.

Boulding, Kenneth. *Conflict and Defense; A General Theory*. New York: Harper Torchbooks, 1963.

Boulding, Kenneth. "The Economics of the Coming Spaceship Earth," reprinted in Kenneth Boulding, *Collected Papers*, volume 2, *Economics*, ed. Fred R. Glahe. Boulder; Colorado: Associated University Press, 1971.

Brecht, Arnold. *Political Theory: The Foundations of Twentieth-Century Political Thought*. Princeton: Princeton University Press, 1967.

Bredvold, Louis I., and Ralph G. Ross, eds. *The Philosophy of Edmund Burke*. Ann Arbor: University of Michigan Press, 1960.

Bretton, Henry L. *The Rise and Fall of Kwame Nkrumah*. New York: Frederick A. Praeger, 1966.

Bronfenbrenner, Urie. "Response to Pressure from Peers versus Adults among Soviet and American School Children," in Sigel, ed., pp. 414-420.

Brooks, Harvey, and Raymond Bowers. "Technology: Processes of Assessment and Choice," in Teich, ed., pp. 214-232.

Brown, James Cooke. *The Troika Incident: The Coming of a Viable Human Society*. Garden City, N.Y.: Doubleday, 1970.

Brzezinski, Zbigniew, and Samuel P. Huntington. *Political Power: USA/USSR*. New York: Viking, 1964.

Burke, Edmund. *The Philosophy of Edmund Burke*, ed. Louis I. Bredvold and Ralph G. Ross. Ann Arbor: University of Michigan Press, 1960.

Campbell, Angus, *et al. The American Voter*. New York: Wiley, 1960.

"Can Nuclear Waste Be Stored?" *Newsweek*, Nov. 18, 1974, p. 56.

Casper, Jonathan D. *The Politics of Civil Liberties*. New York: Harper and Row, 1972.

Cirino, Robert. *Don't Blame the People*. Los Angeles: Diversity Press, 1971.

Clor, Harry M., ed. *Censorship and Freedom of Expression: Essays on Obscenity and the Law*. Chicago: Rand McNally, 1971.

Clotfelter, James. *The Military in American Politics*. New York: Harper and Row, 1973.

Cohen, Carl. ed., *Communism, Fascism and Democracy: The Theoretical Foundations*, 2nd ed. New York: Random House, 1972.

Cole, H. S. D., *et al.*, eds. *Models of Doom: A Critique of the Limits to Growth*. New York: Universe Books, 1973.

Commoner, Barry. *The Closing Circle: Nature, Man and Technology*. New York: Knopf, 1971.

Coser, Lewis. *The Functions of Social Conflict*. New York: Free Press, 1964.

Crick, Bernard. *Political Theory and Practice*. New York: Basic Books, 1973.

Cushman, Robert E., and Robert F. Cushman, eds. *Cases in Constitutional Law*, 3d ed. New York: Appleton-Century-Crofts, 1968.

Dahl, Robert A. *Democracy in the United States: Promise and Performance*. Chicago: Rand McNally, 1972.

Dahl, Robert A. "Power." In *International Encyclopedia of the Social Sciences*.

Dahl, Robert A. *Who Governs? Democracy and Power in an American City*. New Haven: Yale University Press, 1961.

Dahrendorf, Ralf. *Class and Class Conflict in Industrial Society*. Stanford: Stanford University Press, 1959.

Darlington, C. D. *The Evolution of Man and Society*. New York: Simon and Schuster, 1969.

Davies, James C. "The J-Curve of Rising and Declining Satisfactions as a Cause of Some Great Revolutions and a Contained Rebellion," in Graham and Gurr, eds., pp. 690-730.

Davies, James C. "Political Violence: The Dominance-Submission Nexus," in Hirsch and Perry, eds., pp. 52-71.

Dawson, Richard E. and Kenneth Prewitt. *Political Socialization*. Boston: Little, Brown, 1969.

The Declaration of Independence and the Constitution of the United States. House Document No. 189, 88th Congress, 2d Session. Washington: U.S. Government Printing Office, 1964.

Deutsch, Karl W. *Politics and Government; How People Decide Their Fate*, 2d ed. Boston: Houghton Mifflin, 1974.

Deutsch, Karl W. "Social Mobilization and Political Development," *American Political Science Review*, 55 (September 1961), pp. 493-514.

Deutscher, Isaac. "Pressure Groups," in Ploss, ed.

Diesing, Paul. *Patterns of Discovery in the Social Sciences*. New York/Chicago: Aldine-Atherton, 1971.

Domhoff, William G. *Who Rules America?* Englewood Cliffs, N.J.: Prentice-Hall, 1967.

Downs, Anthony. *Inside Bureaucracy*. Boston: Little, Brown, 1967.

Duverger, Maurice. *Party Politics and Pressure Groups: A Comparative Introduction*, trans. by David Wagoner. New York: Thomas Y. Crowell, 1972.

Dye, Thomas R. *Understanding Public Policy*. Englewood Cliffs, N.J.: Prentice-Hall, 1972.

Dye, Thomas R., and L. Harmon Zeigler. *The Irony of Democracy*, 3d ed. North Scituate, Mass.: Duxbury, 1975.

Easton, David. *The Political System: An Inquiry into the State of Political Science*. New York: Knopf, 1953.

Ebenstein, William. *Great Political Thinkers*. New York: Holt, 1960.

Eckstein, Harry, and Ted Robert Gurr, *Patterns of Authority: A Structural Basis for Political Inquiry*. New York: Wiley, 1975.

Edelman, Murray. *The Symbolic Uses of Politics*. Urbana: University of Illinois Press, 1967.

Ehrlich, Paul. "Eco-Catastrophe" in Toffler, ed.

Ellul, Jacques. *The Technological Society*, trans. by John Wilkinson. New York: Vintage, 1964.

Emerson, Rupert. *From Empire to Nation*. Boston: Beacon, 1962.

Enloe, Cynthia. *Ethnic Conflict and Political Development*. Boston: Little, Brown, 1973.

Epstein, Leon D. *Political Parties in Western Democracies*. New York: Praeger, 1967.

Etzioni, Amitai, and Edward Lehman, "Some Dangers in 'Valid' Social Measurement," in Gross, ed.

Fagen, Richard R. *Politics and Communications*. Boston: Little, Brown, 1966.

Fainsod, Merle. *How Russia Is Ruled*. Cambridge: Harvard University Press, 1963.

Field, G. Lowell, and John Higley. "Elites and Non-Elites: The Possibilities and Their Side-Effects." Andover, Mass.: Warner Modular Publications, Module 13 (1973). pp. 1-38.

Finer, Samuel E. *The Man on Horseback: The Role of the Military in Politics*. London: Pall-Mall, 1962.

Finkle, Jason L., and Richard W. Gable, eds. *Political Development and Social Change*, 2d ed. New York: Wiley, 1971.

Fischer, David Hacket. *Historians' Fallacies: Toward a Logic of Historical Thought*. New York: Harper and Row, 1970.

Fitzgerald, Francis. *Fire in the Lake: The Vietnamese and the Americans in Vietnam*. Boston: Little, Brown, 1972.

Flacks, Richard. "The Revolt of the Advantaged: An Exploration of the Roots of Student Protest," in Sigel, ed., pp. 182-191.

Foner, Philip S., ed. *The Black Panthers Speak*. New York: Lippincott, 1970.

Frank, Jerome. *Law and the Modern Mind*. New York: Doubleday Anchor, 1963.

Freud, Sigmund. *A General Introduction to Psycho-Analysis*, trans. by Joan Riviere. New York: Liveright, 1935.

Friedrich, Carl J., and Robert G. McCloskey, eds. *From the Declaration of Independence to the Constitution*. New York: Bobbs-Merrill, 1954.

Friedrich, Carl J. *Man and His Government: An Empirical Theory of Politics*. New York: McGraw-Hill, 1963.

Friedrich, Carl J., ed. *Nomos IV: Liberty*. New York: Atherton, 1962.

Friedrich, Carl J., and Zbigniew K. Brzezinski. *Totalitarian Dictatorship and Autocracy*. New York: Praeger, 1966.

Fromm, Erich. *Escape from Freedom*. New York: Holt, Rinehart & Winston, 1941.

Galbraith, John Kenneth. *American Capitalism*. Boston: Houghton Mifflin, 1952.

Galbraith, John Kenneth. *The New Industrial State*. Boston: Houghton Mifflin, 1967.

Garcia, John David. *The Moral Society: A Rational Alternative to Death*. New York: Julian Press, 1971.

Goffman, Erving. *Relations in Public: Micro Studies of the Public Order*. New York: Basic Books, 1971.

Gordon, Theodore J. "The Current Methods of Futures Research," in Toffler, ed., pp. 164-189.

Gordon, Theodore J., and Robert H. Ament. "Forecasts of Some Technological and Scientific Developments and Their Societal Consequences," in Teich, ed., pp. 5-20.

Graham, Hugh Davis, and Ted Robert Gurr, eds. *Violence in America: Historical and Comparative Perspectives*. New York: Bantam, 1969.

Green, Harold P. "The Adversary Process in Technology Assessment," in Teich, ed.

Greenstein, Fred I. "Personality and Political Socialization: The Theories of Authoritarian and Democratic Character," in Sigel, ed., pp. 260-276.

Gross, Bertram W., ed. *Social Intelligence for America's Future*. Boston: Allyn and Bacon, 1969.

Gurr, Ted Robert. *Why Men Rebel*. Princeton: Princeton University Press, 1971.

Gurr, Ted Robert, and Charles Ruttenberg, *The Conditions of Civil Violence: First Tests of a Model*. Princeton: Center for International Studies, 1967. Research Monograph No. 28.

Gurvitch, Georges. *The Social Frameworks of Knowledge*, trans. Margaret A. Thompson and Kenneth A. Thompson. New York: Harper Torchbooks, 1971.

Hagen, Everett E. "How Economic Growth Begins: A Theory of Social Change," in Finkle and Gable, eds., pp. 73-83.

Hardin, Garrett. *Exploring New Ethics for Survival: The Voyage of the Spaceship Beagle*. Baltimore: Penguin, 1973.

Hefner, Philip. *The Promise of Teilhard*. New York: Lippincott, 1970.

Heidenheimer, Arnold J., ed. *Political Corruption; Readings in Comparative Analysis*. New York: Holt, 1970.

Hess, Robert D. and David Easton. "The Child's Changing Image of the President." *Public Opinion Quarterly*, 24 (Winter 1960), pp. 632-644.

Hirsch, Herbert, and David C. Perry, eds. *Violence as Politics: A Series of Original Essays*. New York: Harper and Row, 1973.

Hobbes, Thomas. *Leviathan*. New York: Bobbs-Merrill, 1958.

Huntington, Samuel P., ed. *Changing Patterns of Military Politics*. New York: Free Press, 1962.

Huntington, Samuel P. "Political Development and Political Decay." *World Politics*, 17 (April 1965), 386-411.

Huntington, Samuel P. *Political Order in Changing Societies*. New Haven: Yale University Press, 1968.

Huntington, Samuel P. *The Soldier and the State: The Theory and Politics of Civil-Military Relations*. Cambridge: Harvard University Press, 1957.

Huntington, Samuel P., and Clement H. Moore, eds. *Authoritarian Politics in Modern Society: The Dynamics of Established One-Party Systems*. New York: Basic Books, 1970.

Ilchman, Warren F., and Norman Thomas Uphoff. *The Political Economy of Change*. Berkeley: University of California Press, 1969.

Janowitz, Morris. *The Military in the Political Development of New Nations*. Chicago: University of Chicago Press, 1964.

Janowitz, Morris. *The Professional Soldier: A Social and Political Portrait*. New York: Free Press, 1964.

Jaros, Dean. *Socialization to Politics*. New York: Praeger, 1973.

Jaros, Dean, Herbert Hirsch, and Frederick J. Fleron, Jr. "The Malevolent Leader: Political Socialization in an American Subculture." *American Political Science Review*, 62 (June 1968), pp. 564-575.

Johnson, Chalmers. *Revolutionary Change*. Boston: Little, Brown, 1966.

Johnson, John J., ed. *The Role of the Military in Underdeveloped Countries*. Princeton: Princeton University Press, 1962.

Kafka, Franz. *The Trial*, trans. by Willa and Edwin Muir. New York: Modern Library, 1956.

Kahn, Herman. *On Escalation: Metaphors and Scenarios*. New York: Praeger, 1965.

Kahn, Herman. *On Thermonuclear War*. Princeton: Princeton University Press, 1960.

Kaufman, Herbert. *Administrative Feedback*. Washington. D.C.: Brookings, 1973.

Key, V. O., Jr. *Politics, Parties and Pressure Groups*. New York: Thomas Y. Crowell, 1958.

Key, V. O. *The Responsible Electorate*. Cambridge: Belknap, 1966.

Kornhauser, William. *The Politics of Mass Society*. New York: Free Press, 1959.

Korpi, Walter. "Conflict, Power and Relative Deprivation." *American Political Science Review*, 68 (December 1974), pp. 1569-1578.

Kuhn, Thomas. *The Structure of Scientific Revolutions*. Chicago: University of Chicago Press, 1964.

LaPalombara, Joseph, ed. *Bureaucracy and Political Development*. Princeton: Princeton University Press, 1967.

LaPalombara, Joseph. *Politics within Nations*. Englewood Cliffs, N.J.: Prentice-Hall, 1974.

LaPalombara, Joseph, and Myron Weiner. "The Origin and Development of Political Parties," in La Palombara and Weiner, eds., pp. 3-42.

LaPalombara, Joseph, and Myron Weiner, eds. *Political Parties and Political Development*. Princeton: Princeton University Press, 1966.

Lasswell, Harold D. "The Garrison-State Hypothesis Today," in Samuel P. Huntington, ed., *Changing Patterns of Military Politics*.

Lasswell, Harold D. *Politics: Who Gets What, When, and How*. New York: P. Smith, 1936.

Lasswell, Harold D. *Psychopathology and Politics*. Chicago: University of Chicago Press, 1930.

Lasswell, Harold D., and Abraham Kaplan. *Power and Society; A Framework for Political Inquiry*. New Haven: Yale University Press, 1950.

Latham, Earl. *The Group Basis of Politics*. New York: Octagon, 1965.

Leggett, John C. *Taking State Power: The Sources and Consequences of Political Challenge*. New York: Harper and Row, 1973.

Leiden, Carl, and Karl M. Schmitt. *The Politics of Violence: Revolution in the Modern World*. Englewood Cliffs, N.J.: Prentice-Hall, 1968.

Leites, Nathan, and Charles Wolf, Jr. *Rebellion and Authority: An Analytical Essay on Insurgent Conflicts*. Chicago: Markham, 1970.

Lenin, V. I. *What Is to Be Done?* New York: International Publishers, 1943.

Levy, Marion J., Jr. *Modernization: Latecomers and Survivors*. New York: Basic Books, 1972.

Linden, Carl A. *Khrushchev and the Soviet Leadership, 1957-1964.* Baltimore: Johns Hopkins University Press, 1966.

Locke, John. *Two Treatises of Government.* New York: Hafner, 1947.

Lorenz, Konrad. *On Aggression,* trans. by M. K. Wilson. New York: Harcourt, 1966.

Lowi, Theodore J. *The End of Liberalism: Ideology, Policy, and the Crisis of Public Authority.* New York: Norton, 1969.

Luttwak, Edward. *Coup d'État; A Practical Handbook.* New York: Knopf, 1969.

McClelland, David C. "The Achievement Motive in Economic Growth," in Finkle and Gable, eds., pp. 83-100.

McConnell, Grant. *Private Power and American Democracy.* New York: Knopf, 1967.

McCoy, Charles A., and John Playford, eds. *Apolitical Politics: A Critique of Behavioralism.* New York: Thomas Y. Crowell, 1967.

MacIntyre, Alasdair. "Ideology, Social Science and Revolution." *Comparative Politics,* 5 (April 1973), pp. 321ff.

McLuhan, Marshal. *Understanding Media: The Extensions of Man.* New York: Signet, 1964.

Macridis, Roy C., ed. *Political Parties: Contemporary Trends and Ideas.* New York: Harper Torchbooks, 1967.

Malecki, Edward S. "Theories of Revolution and Industrial Societies." *Journal of Politics,* 35 (1973), pp. 948-985.

Marcuse, Herbert. "Repressive Tolerance," in Moore *et al.,* pp. 81-123.

Maslow, Abraham. "A Theory of Human Motivation." *Psychological Review,* 50 (1943), pp. 370-396.

Mason, Alpheus Thomas, and William M. Beany. *The Supreme Court in a Free Society.* New York: Norton, 1968.

Mayer, Lawrence C. *Comparative Political Inquiry: A Methodological Survey.* Homewood, Ill.: Dorsey, 1972.

Mazrui, Ali A. "Black Vigilantism and Cultural Transition: Violence and Viability in Tropical Africa," in Rosenbaum and Sederberg, eds., pp. 194-217.

Meadows, Donella, *et al. The Limits to Growth.* New York: Universe Books, 1972.

Meehan, Eugene J. *The Theory and Method of Political Analysis.* Homewood, Ill.: Dorsey, 1965.

Meyer, Alfred G. *The Soviet Political System: An Interpretation.* New York: Random House, 1965.

Michels, Robert. *Political Parties,* trans. by Eden and Cedar Paul. New York: Free Press, 1962.

Miller, Arthur R. *Assault on Privacy: Computers, Data-Banks, and Dossiers.* Ann Arbor: University of Michigan Press, 1971.

Mills, C. Wright. *The Marxists.* New York: Dell, 1962.

Mills, C. Wright. *The Power Elite.* New York: Oxford University Press, 1956.

Minte, Morton, and Jerry S. Cohen. *America Incorporated: Who Owns and Operates the United States.* New York: Dial Press, 1971.

Monoseritz, Martin, Gardner Lindzey, and Delbert D. Thiessen, eds. *Behavioral Genetics: Method and Research.* New York: Appleton-Century-Crofts, 1969.

Moore, Barrington, Jr. *Terror and Progress, U.S.S.R.: Some Sources of Change and Stability in the Soviet Dictatorship*. Cambridge: Harvard University Press, 1954.

Moore, Barrington, Robert Paul Wolff, and Herbert Marcuse. *A Critique of Pure Tolerance*. Boston: Beacon, 1970.

Moore, Clement H. "The Single Party as a Source of Legitimacy," in Huntington and Moore, eds., pp. 48-72.

More, Thomas. *Utopia*. In Ligeia Gallagher, ed., *More's* Utopia *and Its Critics*. Chicago: Scott, Foresman, 1964.

Morgenthau, Hans J. *Politics among Nations: The Struggle for Power and Peace*. New York: Knopf, 1967.

Muller, Herbert J. *Issues of Freedom: Paradoxes and Promises*. New York: Harper, 1960.

Myrdal, Gunnar. *Asian Drama: An Inquiry into the Poverty of Nations*. New York: Pantheon, 1968.

Natanson, Maurice, ed., *Philosophy of the Social Sciences*. New York: Random House, 1963.

Nieburg, H. L. *Culture Storm: Politics and the Ritual Order*. New York: St. Martin's, 1973.

Nisbet, Robert A. *Community and Power*. New York: Oxford University Press, 1953.

Nisbet, Robert. "The Year 2000 and All That," in Somit, ed., pp. 257-267.

Nogee, Joseph L., ed. *Man, State and Society in the Soviet Union*. New York: Praeger, 1972.

Nordlinger, Eric A. "Soldiers in Mufti: The Impact of Military Rule upon Economic and Social Change in Non-Western States." *American Political Science Review*, 64 (December 1970), pp. 1131-1148.

Nye, J. S. "Corruption and Political Development: A Cost-Benefit Analysis," *American Political Science Review*, 61 (June 1967), pp. 417-427.

O'Neill, Gerard K. "The Colonization of Space." *Physics Today* (September 1974), pp. 32-40.

Ono, Shin'ya. "The Limits of Bourgeois Pluralism," in McCoy and Playford, eds., pp. 99-123.

Orwell, George. *Nineteen Eighty-Four: Text, Sources, Criticism*, ed. Irving Howe. New York: Harcourt, 1963.

Palmer, Monte, *et al. The Interdisciplinary Study of Politics*. New York: Harper and Row, 1975.

Palmer, R. R. *The Age of Democratic Revolution: A Political History of Europe and America, 1760-1800*. 2 vols. Princeton: Princeton University Press, 1959, 1964.

Paret, Peter. *French Revolutionary Warfare from Indochina to Algeria*. New York: Praeger, 1964.

Parsons, Talcott. *The Social System*. New York: Free Press, 1964.

Peckham, Morse. *Art and Pornography: An Experiment in Explanation*. New York: Harper and Row, 1971.

Perloff, Harvey S., ed. *The Future of U.S. Government*. Englewood Cliffs. N.J.: Prentice-Hall, 1971.

Plato. *Euthyphro, Apology, Crito*, trans. by F. J. Church. New York: Bobbs-Merrill, 1956.

Plato. *The Republic*, trans. by Francis MacDonald Cornford. New York: Oxford University Press, 1963.

Ploss, Sidney I., ed. *The Soviet Political Process: Aims, Techniques and Examples of Analysis*. Waltham, Mass.: Ginn, 1971.

Prewitt, Kenneth, with Joseph Okello-Oculi. "Political Socialization and Political Education in the New Nations," in Sigel, ed., pp. 607-621.

Prewitt, Kenneth, and Alan Stone. *The Ruling Elites: Elite Theory, Power, and American Democracy*. New York: Harper and Row, 1973.

Price, Robert M. "Military Officers and Political Leadership: The Ghanaian Case." *Comparative Politics*, 3 (April 1971), pp. 361-379.

Polanyi, Michael. *Personal Knowledge: Towards a Post-Critical Philosophy*. Chicago: University of Chicago Press, 1958.

Proxmire, William. *Report from Wasteland*. New York: Praeger, 1970.

Pye, Lucian. "Armies in the Process of Political Modernization," in John J. Johnson, ed., pp. 69-89.

Pye, Lucian W., ed., *Communications and Political Development*. Princeton: Princeton University Press, 1963.

Pye, Lucian W. *Politics, Personality and Nation-Building: Burma's Search for Identity*. New Haven: Yale University Press, 1962.

Pye, Lucian W., and Sidney Verba, eds. *Political Culture and Political Development*. Princeton: Princeton University Press, 1964.

Ranney, Austin. *The Governing of Men*, 4th ed. Hinsdale, Ill.: Dryden, 1975.

Rawls, John. *A Theory of Justice*. Cambridge: Harvard University Press, 1971.

Rejai, Mostafa. ed. *Decline of Ideology?* Chicago: Aldine, Atherton, 1971.

Rejai, Mostafa. *The Strategy of Political Revolution*. Garden City, N.Y.: Doubleday, 1973.

Riesman, David. *The Lonely Crowd*. New Haven: Yale University Press, 1951.

Riggs, Fred W. *Administration in Developing Countries*. Boston: Houghton Mifflin, 1964.

Riggs, Fred W. "Bureaucrats and Political Development: A Paradoxical View," in LaPalombara, ed., *Bureaucracy and Political Development*.

Roeloffs, H. Mark. *The Language of Modern Politics*. Homewood, Ill.: Dorsey, 1967.

Rosenbaum, H. Jon, and Peter C. Sederberg. "The Occult and Political Development." *Comparative Politics*, 3 (July 1971), pp. 561-574.

Rosenbaum, H. Jon, and Peter C. Sederberg, eds. *Vigilante Politics*. Philadelphia: University of Pennsylvania Press, 1976.

Rosenbaum, H. Jon, and Peter C. Sederberg. "Vigilantism: An Analysis of Establishment Violence." *Comparative Politics*, 6 (July 1974), pp. 540-571.

Rostow, W. W. *The Stages of Economic Growth: A Non-Communist Manifesto*. Cambridge, England: University Press, 1960.

Roszak, Theodore. *Where the Wasteland Ends*. New York: Doubleday Anchor, 1973.

Royko, Mike. *Boss: Richard J. Daley of Chicago*. New York: Dutton, 1971.

Rousseau, Jean Jacques. *The Social Contract*, trans. by Charles Frankel. New York: Hafner, 1947.

Rustow, Dankwart A. *A World of Nations*. Washington, D.C.: Brookings, 1967.

Sabine, George H. *A History of Political Thought*, 3d ed. New York: Holt, 1961.

Sanford, Nevitt, and Craig Comstock, eds. *Sanctions for Evil*. San Francisco: Jossey-Bass, 1971.

Sargent, Lyman T. *Contemporary Political Ideologies*. Homewood, Ill.: Dorsey, 1969.

Sartori, Giovanni. *Democratic Theory*. New York: Praeger, 1965.

Sartori, Giovanni. "European Political Parties: The Case of Polarized Pluralism," in LaPalombara and Weiner, eds., pp. 137-176.

Schoeck, Helmut. *Envy: A Theory of Social Behavior*, trans. by Michael Glenny and Betty Ross. New York: Harcourt, 1969.

Schwartz, David C. *Political Alienation and Political Behavior*. Chicago: Aldine, 1973.

Scott, James C. *Comparative Political Corruption*. Englewood Cliffs, N.J.: Prentice-Hall, 1972.

Scott, James C. "Patron-Client Politics and Political Change in Southeast Asia." *American Political Science Review*, 66 (March 1972), pp. 91-113.

Sederberg, Peter C. "National Expenditure as an Indicator of Political Change in Ghana." *Journal of the Developing Areas*, 7 (October 1972), pp. 37-55.

Sederberg, Peter C. "Sheik Mujib and Charismatic Politics in Bangladesh." *Asian Forum*, 4 (June-September 1972), pp. 1-10.

Sederberg, Peter C. "Subjectivity and Typification: A Note on Method in the Social Sciences." *Philosophy of the Social Sciences*, 2 (1972), pp. 167-176.

Sharp, Gene. *The Politics of Nonviolent Action*. Boston: Porter Sargent, 1973.

Sibley, Mulford Q. *Political Ideas and Ideology: A History of Political Thought*. New York: Harper and Row, 1970.

Sigel, Roberta, ed. *Learning About Politics: A Reader in Political Socialization*. New York: Random House, 1970.

Skinner, B. F. *Beyond Freedom and Dignity*. New York: Bantam, 1972.

Skinner, B. F. *Walden Two*. New York: Macmillan, 1962.

Solow, Robert M. "How to Think Rationally about Exhaustible Resources." Address given at the University of South Carolina, April 18, 1974.

Somit, Albert, ed. *Political Science and the Study of the Future*. Hinsdale, Ill.: Dryden Press, 1974.

Sorauf, Frank J. *Party Politics in America*, 2d edition, Boston: Little, Brown, 1972.

Sorokin, Pitirim. *Social and Cultural Dynamics*. Boston: Porter Sargent, 1957.

Speer, Albert. *Inside the Third Reich*. New York: Macmillan, 1970.

Spiro, Herbert J. *Politics as the Master Science: From Plato to Mao*. New York: Harper and Row, 1970.

Statistical Yearbook, United Nations, 1973. New York: United Nations, Statistical Office, 1974.

Teich, Albert H., ed. *Technology and Man's Future*. New York: St. Martin's Press, 1972.

Teilhard de Chardin, Pierre. *The Future of Man*. New York: Harper and Row, 1964.

Teilhard de Chardin, Pierre. *The Phenomenon of Man*. New York: Harper and Row, 1965.

Thompson, William Irwin. *At the Edge of History*. New York: Harper Colophon, 1972.

Thorson, Thomas L. *Biopolitics*. New York: Holt, Rinehart and Winston, 1970.

Thucydides. *The Peloponnesian War*, trans. by Rex Warner. Baltimore: Penguin, 1954.

Tiger, Lionel. *Men in Groups*. New York: Random House, 1969.

Tocqueville, Alexis de. *Democracy in America*, trans. by Henry Reeves. New York: Schocken Books, 1961.

Toffler, Alvin. *Future Shock*. New York: Bantam, 1967.

Toffler, Alvin, ed. *The Futurists*. New York: Random House, 1972.

Toulmin, Stephen. *Foresight and Understanding*. Bloomington: Indiana University Press, 1961.

Truman, David. *The Governmental Process*. New York: Knopf, 1951.

Uphoff, Norman Thomas, and Warren F. Ilchman, eds. *The Political Economy of Development*. Berkeley: University of California Press, 1972.

Verba, Sidney. "Comparative Political Culture," in Pye and Verba, eds., pp. 512-560.

Vonnegut, Kurt. *Welcome to the Monkey House*. New York: Dell, 1970.

Waldman, Sidney R. *Foundations of Political Action: An Exchange Theory of Politics*. Boston: Little, Brown, 1972.

Waldo, Dwight. *Perspectives on Public Administration*. University, Ala.: University of Alabama Press, 1956.

Walker, Jack L. "A Critique of the Elitist Theory of Democracy," in McCoy and Playford, eds., pp. 199-219.

Walter, E. V. *Terror and Resistance: A Study of Political Violence*. New York: Oxford University Press, 1969.

Warner, H. Keith, and A. Eugene Havens. "Goal Displacement and the Intangibility of Organizational Goals." *Administrative Science Quarterly* 12 (March 1968), pp. 539-555.

Weber, Max. *The Theory of Social and Economic Organization*, trans. by A. M. Henderson and Talcott Parsons. New York: Free Press, 1964.

Weinberg, Alvin M. "Can Technology Replace Social Engineering." in Teich, ed., pp. 27-34.

Weiner, Myron. "Political Integration and Political Development." *The Annals of the American Academy of Political and Social Science*, 358 (March 1965), pp. 52-64.

Weiner, Myron, and Joseph LaPalombara. "The Impact of Parties on Political Development," in LaPalombara and Weiner, eds., pp. 399-435.

Welch, Claude E., Jr. "The Roots and Implications of Military Intervention," in Claude E. Welch, Jr., ed. *Soldier and State in Africa*. Evanston, Ill.: Northwestern University Press, 1970, pp. 1-59.

Weldon, T. D. *States and Morals; A Study in Political Conflicts*. New York: Whittlesey House, 1947.

Wertheim, W. F. *Evolution and Revolution: The Rising Waves of Emancipation*. Baltimore: Penguin, 1974.

Westin, Alan F. *Databanks in a Free Society*. New York: Quadrangle, 1972.

"What Is Taboo?" *Time*, May 15, 1972, pp. 55-57.

Wilner, Ann Ruth. *Charismatic Political Leadership: A Theory*. Princeton: Center for International Studies, 1968.

Wise, David. *The Politics of Lying: Government Deception, Secrecy and Power*, New York: Vintage, 1973.

Wolf, Eric R. *Peasant Wars of the Twentieth Century*. New York: Harper and Row, 1969.

Wolfenstein, E. Victor. *The Revolutionary Personality: Lenin, Trotsky, Gandhi*. Princeton: Princeton University Press, 1971.

Wolff, Robert Paul. *In Defense of Anarchism*. New York: Harper Torchbooks, 1970.

Notes

NOTES TO CHAPTER I (pages 2-23)

1. For an introduction to this controversy see Maurice Natanson, ed., *Philosophy of the Social Sciences*, 1963, especially Part III.

2. For a more extended version of this argument see Peter C. Sederberg, "Subjectivity and Typification: A Note on Method in the Social Sciences," *Philosophy of the Social Sciences*, 2 (1972), pp. 167-176.

3. Eugene J. Meehan, *The Theory and Method of Political Analysis*, p. 32.

4. Compare Thomas Kuhn, *The Structure of Scientific Revolutions*; Thomas L. Thorson, *Biopolitics*; and Stephen Toulmin, *Foresight and Understanding*.

5. Arnold Brecht, *Political Theory*, pp. 113ff.

6. Michael Polanyi, *Personal Knowledge: Towards a Post-Critical Philosophy*.

7. Brecht, pp. 117-118.

8. Based on Brecht, pp. 121-122.

9. Compare Meehan, p. 34.

10. Compare this discussion with that in Meehan, pp. 88-126, and Lawrence C. Mayer, *Comparative Political Inquiry*, pp. 3-66.

11. Meehan, pp. 116-125.

12. For an application of this approach to the social system see Talcott Parsons, *The Social System*; for a specifically political application see Gabriel A. Almond and G. Bingham Powell, Jr., *Comparative Politics: A Developmental Approach*.

13. Compare Brecht, pp. 28-29.

14. See, for example, Robert Ardrey, *The Social Contract: A Personal Inquiry into the Evolutionary Sources of Order and Disorder*; C. D. Darlington, *The Evolution of Man and Society*; and Lionel Tiger, *Men in Groups*.

15. Paul Diesing, *Patterns of Discovery in the Social Sciences*, 1971, pp. 321-323.

16. Based on Abraham Maslow, "A Theory of Human Motivation," *Psychological Review*, 50 (1943), pp. 370-396.

17.   Erving Goffman, *Relations in Public: Micro Studies of the Public Order*. Goffman explores the complexity of apparently trivial social behavior.

18.   See Alexis de Tocqueville, *Democracy in America*, any edition.

19.   Amitai Etzioni and Edward Lehman, "Some Dangers in 'Valid' Social Measurement," in Gross, ed. pp. 45-62.

20.   The phrase is from Etzioni and Lehman, p. 57.

21.   This section owes its inspiration to Dwight Waldo's essay "Reversing the Glass," in his *Perspectives on Public Administration*, pp. 1-25.

NOTES TO CHAPTER II (pages 24-32)

1.   For a discussion of this problem see Harry Eckstein and Ted Robert Gurr, *Patterns of Authority: A Structural Basis for Political Inquiry*, Chapter I.

2.   Monte Palmer, *et al.*, *The Interdisciplinary Study of Politics*.

3.   David Easton, *The Political System: An Inquiry into the State of Political Science*, pp. 130ff.

4.   See, for example, Walter Korpi, "Conflict, Power and Relative Deprivation," *American Political Science Review*, 68 (December 1974). pp. 1569-1578.

5.   See Gabriel A. Almond, "Introduction," on Almond and Coleman, eds., p. 7. Also see Max Weber, *The Theory of Social and Economic Organization*, p. 156.

6.   Thomas Hobbes, *Leviathan*, pp. 104-109.

7.   Hans J. Morgenthau, *Politics among Nations: The Struggle for Power and Peace*.

8.   V. O. Key, Jr., *Politics, Parties and Pressure Groups*, p. 5.

9.   See Charles A. McCoy and John Playford, eds., *Apolitical Politics: A Critique of Behavioralism*, especially Peter Bachrach and Morton S. Baratz, "The Two Faces of Power," pp. 146-157.

10.   The term is E. E. Schattschneider's, used at p. 150 in McCoy and Playford, eds.

NOTES TO CHAPTER III (pages 33-47)

1.   For an extensive development of this perspective see Warren F. Ilchman and Norman Thomas Uphoff, *The Political Economy of Change*; for a "classic" power approach, see Harold D. Lasswell, *Politics; Who Gets What, When and How*.

2.   For a collection of wide-ranging essays on corruption in the United States and elsewhere in the world see Arnold J. Heidenheimer, ed., *Political Corruption: Readings in Comparative Analysis*.

3.   For a brief and lucid introduction to Marxist analysis see C. Wright Mills, *The Marxists*, especially Chapter 4.

4.   Among numerous other works, see: Theodore J. Lowi, *The End of Liberalism*; also Morton Minte and Jerry S. Cohen, *American Incorporated: Who Owns and Operates the Unites States*.

5.   John Kenneth Galbraith, *American Capitalism*.

6.   John Kenneth Galbraith, *The New Industrial State*.

7.   Compare the discussion of authority in Carl J. Friedrich, *Man and His*

Government: An Empirical Theory of Politics, Chapter 12.

8. Max Weber, *The Theory of Social and Economic Organization*, pp. 358-363.

9. Ann Ruth Wilner, *Charismatic Political Leadership: A Theory*, p. 7.

10. Peter C. Sederberg, "Sheik Mujib and Charismatic Politics in Bangladesh," *Asian Forum*, IV (June-September 1972), pp. 1-10.

11. See Albert Speer, *Inside the Third Reich*, especially Chapter 5.

12. For analyses of the concentration of information resources see Arthur R. Miller, *Assault on Privacy: Computers, Data-Banks, and Dossiers*; or Alan F. Westin, *Databanks in a Free Society*.

13. For an extensive, though somewhat controversial, discussion of the idea of "totalitarianism," see Carl J. Friedrich and Zbigniew K. Brzezinski, *Totalitarian Dictatorship and Autocracy*.

14. Robert Cirino, *Don't Blame the People*.

15. For a discussion of various kinds of electoral "inducements," see James C. Scott, *Comparative Political Corruption*, pp. 109-112.

16. Ilchman and Uphoff, pp. 73-80.

17. For a discussion of the possibilities and limits of this process in one country, see David E. Apter, *Ghana in Transition*.

18. Norman Thomas Uphoff and Warren F. Ilchman, "Development in the Perspective of Political Economy," in Uphoff and Ilchman, eds. pp. 96-98.

19. This section is based on Samuel Huntington's analysis of the relative strength of institutions in Samuel P. Huntington, "Political Development and Political Decay," *World Politics*, 17 (April 1965), pp. 386-411.

20. Aristotle, *The Politics*, pp. 110-128.

21. Based on Robert A. Dahl, "Power," *International Encyclopedia of the Social Sciences*, volume 12, p. 408.

22. Dahl, at p. 414.

NOTES TO CHAPTER IV (pages 48-59)

1. Sociologist Erving Goffman has extensively examined the importance of apparently trivial behavior. See especially, *Relations in Public: Micro Studies of the Public Order*.

2. Max Weber, *The Theory of Social and Economic Organization*, pp. 341ff.

3. Plato, "Crito" in *Euthyphro, Apology, Crito*, pp. 51-65.

4. Plato, *The Republic*, pp. 175-220.

5. Elements of natural law theory are found in Greek and Roman thinkers, as well as Medieval theologians. Perhaps Thomas Aquinas (1225-1274) presents the most sophisticated exposition of the medieval conception of natural law. See *The Political Ideas of St. Thomas Aquinas*, Dino Bigongiari, ed., pp. 3-91.

6. Thomas Hobbes, *Leviathan*, Parts I and II, especially pp. 104-152.

7. Hobbes, pp. 243-44.

8. John Locke, *Two Treatises of Government*, especially pp. 121-247.

9. Thomas Jefferson, *A Declaration by the Representatives of the United States of America, In General Congress Assembled*, in *The Declaration of Independence*

and the Constitution of the United States, House Document No. 189, 88th Congress, 2d Session, p. 1.

10. Philip S. Foner, ed., *The Black Panthers Speak*, p. 4.

11. Jean Jacques Rousseau, *The Social Contract*.

12. No one philosopher can be associated with the idea of democratic legitimacy. The contemporary conception owes much to the thought of Locke, Rousseau, Jefferson, and Madison, as well as Alexis de Tocqueville, Jeremy Bentham, John Stuart Mill, T. H. Green, and Walter Lippmann. Giovanni Sartori, *Democratic Theory*, provides a useful synthesis of much of this material.

13. See especially Robert Paul Wolff, *In Defense of Anarchism*.

14. See William Ebenstein, *The Great Political Thinkers*, pp. 589-621.

15. I owe much of the substance of this argument to Professor Mulford Q. Sibley, though I take responsibility for the interpretation.

NOTES TO CHAPTER V (pages 60-80)

1. The title for this chapter is borrowed from Robert A. Dahl, *Who Governs? Democracy and Power in an American City*.

2. This argument is based on Warren F. Ilchman and Norman Thomas Uphoff, *The Political Economy of Change*, pp. 136-150.

3. Carl J. Friedrich, *Man and His Government: An Empirical Theory of Politics*, p. 302.

4. For an exposition of the pluralist thesis see David Truman, *The Governmental Process*, or Earl Latham, *The Group Basis of Politics*.

5. Gabriel A. Almond and G. Bingham Powell, Jr., *Comparative Politics; A Developmental Approach*, p. 75.

6. Almond and Powell, pp. 75-79.

7. See John Kenneth Galbraith, *American Capitalism*, pp. 108-134.

8. The idea of "veto" groups is developed by David Riesman in *The Lonely Crowd*, especially pp. 242-254.

9. For the positive consequences of pluralism see: William Kornhauser, *The Politics of Mass Society*; and Robert A. Nisbet, *Community and Power*, especially pp. 248-279.

10. See, for example, Alexis de Tocqueville, *Democracy in America*.

11. On the power-elite thesis see C. Wright Mills, *The Power Elite*. Other statements of the elite thesis appear in William G. Domhoff, *Who Rules America?*; John C. Leggett, *Taking State Power: The Sources and Consequences of Political Challenge*; and Kenneth Prewitt and Alan Stone, *The Ruling Elites: Elite Theory, Power, and American Democracy*.

12. David C. Schwartz, *Political Alienation and Political Behavior*, pp. 8-29.

13. Robert Michels, *Political Parties*, p. 365.

14. The term is that of Karl W. Deutsch in *Politics and Government: How People Decide Their Fate*, p. 258.

15. For a summary see Prewitt and Stone, pp. 53-77.

16. It runs throughout *The Power Elite*.

17. H. Mark Roeloffs, *The Language of Modern Politics*, especially Chapters 6, 7 and 8.

18.   See, for example, Thomas R. Dye and L. Harmon Zeigler, *The Irony of Democracy*, especially Chapter 5.

19.   The "countervailing elites" thesis is most commonly identified with the work of Robert Dahl. See *Who Governs?* and *Democracy in the United States: Promise and Performance*.

20.   Deutsch, p. 258.

21.   For a collection of critical essays on both the pluralist and the countervailing-elite theses see Charles A. McCoy and John Playford, eds., *Apolitical Politics: A Critique of Behavioralism*. The following points summarize the criticisms contained in this collection, especially the articles by Shin'ya Ono, "The Limits of Bourgeois Pluralism," pp. 99-123; Peter Bachrach and Morton S. Baratz, "Two Faces of Power," pp. 146-157; and Jack L. Walker, "A Critique of the Elitist Theory of Democracy," pp. 199-219.

22.   For a discussion of "strategic" elites see G. Lowell Field and John Higley, "Elites and Non-Elites: The Possibilities and Their Side Effects," Warner Module No. 13, 1973.

23.   Numerous books have been written on Soviet politics. The classic study is Merle Fainsod, *How Russia Is Ruled*. More recent collections of interpretations of the Soviet system are Joseph L. Nogee, ed., *Man, State and Society in the Soviet Union*, and Sidney I. Ploss, ed., *The Soviet Political Process: Aims, Techniques and Examples of Analysis*.

24.   Deutsch, pp. 271-72.

25.   Carl J. Friedrich and Zbigniew K. Brzezinski, *Totalitarian Dictatorship and Autocracy*, p. 22.

26.   Isaac Deutscher, "Pressure Groups," in Ploss, ed., pp. 267-269.

27.   Compare Field and Higley, p. 15.

NOTES TO CHAPTER VI (pages 81-101)

1.   Plato, *The Republic*, p. 18.

2.   For an extended discussion of the "coercion" and "integration" theories of society see Ralf Dahrendorf, *Class and Class Conflict in Industrial Society*, pp. 157-165.

3.   Dahrendorf, pp. 157-165.

4.   Plato, pp. 126-129.

5.   Dahrendorf, p. 176.

6.   For a similar view see Carl A. Linden, *Khrushchev and the Soviet Leadership, 1957-1964*, pp. 1-9.

7.   See, for example, Thomas R. Dye, *Understanding Public Policy*, pp. 39-67.

8.   For an extensive discussion of latent and manifest interests and conflict group formation see Dahrendorf, pp. 178-189.

9.   V. I. Lenin, *What Is to Be Done?*

10.   Ted Robert Gurr, *Why Men Rebel*, pp. 66-73.

11.   For a discussion of value hierarchies and conflict see James C. Davies, "Political Violence: The Dominance-Submission Nexus," in Hirsch and Perry, eds., pp. 52-71.

12.   Gurr, pp. 66-73.

13. Sigmund Freud, *A General Introduction to Psycho-Analysis*, pp. 288-296.

14. Ted Robert Gurr and Charles Ruttenberg, *The Conditions of Civil Violence: First Tests of a Model*.

15. See, for example, the extensive discussions in John C. Leggett, *Taking State Power: The Sources and Consequences of Political Challenge*.

16. Samuel P. Huntington, *Political Order in Changing Societies*, pp. 412-420.

17. The term is Myron Weiner's in "Political Integration and Political Development," *The Annals of the American Academy of Political and Social Science*, 258 (March 1965), pp. 52-64.

18. Weiner, pp. 52-64.

19. Dahrendorf, pp. 231-237.

20. Dahrendorf, pp. 231-237.

21. This discussion is based on, but is not identical with, that of Kenneth Boulding, *Conflict and Defense: A General Theory*, Chapter 15.

22. Compare Dahrendorf, pp. 225-226.

23. This section summarizes the major points developed by Lewis Coser in *The Functions of Social Conflict*.

NOTES TO CHAPTER VII (pages 102-125)

1. Based on H. Jon Rosenbaum and Peter C. Sederberg, "Vigilantism: An Analysis of Establishment Violence," *Comparative Politics*, 6 (July 1974), pp. 541-544.

2. For a discussion of various definitions of revolution see Mostafa Rejai, *The Strategy of Political Revolution*, Chapter 1; and Carl Leiden and Karl M. Schmitt, *The Politics of Violence: Revolution in the Modern World*, Chapters 1 and 2.

3. Compare Chalmers Johnson, *Revolutionary Change*, pp. 140-141.

4. This discussion of relative deprivation owes much to the analysis in Ted Robert Gurr, *Why Men Rebel*, Chapters 2 through 5.

5. James C. Davies, "The J-Curve of Rising and Declining Satisfactions as a Cause of Some Great Revolutions and a Contained Rebellion." In Graham and Gurr, eds., pp. 690-730.

6. Gurr, p. 70.

7. See the discussion of personal and systemic inefficacy in David C. Schwartz, *Political Alienation and Political Behavior*, pp. 12-14.

8. Schwartz, pp. 22-25.

9. Konrad Lorenz, *On Aggression*.

10. Compare Gurr, Chapters 6 and 7.

11. Nevitt Sanford and Craig Comstock, eds., *Sanctions for Evil*, *passim*.

12. Compare Gurr, Chapters 8 and 9.

13. Murray Edelman, *The Symbolic Uses of Politics*, especially Chapter 2.

14. Gabriel A. Almond and Sidney Verba, *The Civic Culture: Political Attitudes and Democracy in Five Nations*, especially Chapter 6.

15. Compare Warren F. Ilchman and Norman Thomas Uphoff, *The Political Economy of Change*, pp. 42-47.

16. For a good introduction to these wars see Eric R. Wolf, *Peasant Wars of the Twentieth Century*.

17. For a discussion of this problem see Francis Fitzgerald, *Fire in the Lake: The Vietnamese and the Americans in Vietnam*.

18. Eqbal Ahmad, "The Theory and Fallacies of Counterinsurgency," *The Nation*, August 2, 1971, pp. 70-85; also Peter Paret, *French Revolutionary Warfare from Indochina to Algeria*, especially Chapter 7.

19. See Nathan Leites and Charles Wolf, Jr., *Rebellion and Authority: An Analytical Essay on Insurgent Conflicts*, Chapter 6.

20. For an analysis of terror in Stalinist Russia see Barrington Moore, Jr., *Terror and Progress, U.S.S.R.: Some Sources of Change and Stability in the Soviet Dictatorship*. For a discussion of examples before the twentieth-century, see E. V. Walter, *Terror and Resistance: A Study of Political Violence*.

21. For an extensive development of this argument see Gene Sharp, *The Politics of Nonviolent Action*.

NOTES TO CHAPTER VIII (pages 129-153)

1. For a number of definitions see Frank J. Sorauf, *Party Politics in America*, pp. 7-12.

2. Leon D. Epstein, *Political Parties in Western Democracies*, p. 11.

3. Maurice Duverger, *Party Politics and Pressure Groups: A Comparative Introduction*, p. 1.

4. Cf. Joseph LaPalombara and Myron Weiner, "The Origin and Development of Political Parties," in LaPalombara and Weiner, eds., pp. 33-41.

5. For a summary of this debate see Lawrence C. Mayer, *Comparative Political Inquiry: A Methodological Survey*, pp. 216-226.

6. For an extensive discussion of the impact of "moderate" versus "extreme" pluralism in the party system see Giovanni Sartori, "European Political Parties: The Case of Polarized Pluralism," in LaPalombara and Weiner, eds., pp. 137-176.

7. Every political scientist seems to come up with a slightly different typology of political parties. In addition to the works cited above, the curious reader might consult the essays in Roy C. Macridis, ed., *Political Parties: Contemporary Trends and Ideas*.

8. For a discussion of patron/client parties see James C. Scott, "Patron-Client Politics and Political Change in Southeast Asia," *American Political Science Review*, 66 (March 1972), pp. 91-113.

9. Karl W. Deutsch, "Social Mobilization and Political Development," *American Political Science Review*, 55 (September 1961), pp. 493-514.

10. This discussion of the machine is indebted to James C. Scott, *Comparative Political Corruption*, pp. 92-157.

11. See Mike Royko, *Boss: Richard J. Daley of Chicago*, for a pungent analysis of Daley's machine.

12. Scott, *Comparative Political Corruption*, pp. 124-131.

13.   For studies of the appeals made to the American voter see Angus Campbell, *et al.*, *The American Voter*; also, V. O. Key, *The Responsible Electorate*.

14.   Cf. Sorauf, pp. 9-12.

15.   Myron Weiner and Joseph LaPalombara, "The Impact of Parties on Political Development," in LaPalombara and Weiner, eds., pp. 400-407.

16.   LaPalombara and Weiner, pp. 35-37.

17.   Some of these are discussed in a different format in Weiner and LaPalombara, pp. 407-435.

18.   Richard E. Dawson and Kenneth Prewitt, *Political Socialization*, p. 6.

19.   For a general introduction to the analysis of political communications see Richard R. Fagen, *Politics and Communications*; also, Lucian W. Pye, ed., *Communications and Political Development*.

20.   David E. Apter, *The Politics of Modernization*, pp. 236-237.

21.   Clement H. Moore, "The Single Party as a Source of Legitimacy," in Huntington and Moore, eds., pp. 48-72.

NOTES TO CHAPTER IX (pages 154-174)

1.   See Fred W. Riggs, "Bureaucrats and Political Development: A Paradoxical View," in Joseph LaPalombara, ed., *Bureaucracy and Political Development*, pp. 120-167.

2.   "From the Transcript: National Planning and the Office of the President," in Harvey S. Perloff, ed., *The Future of U.S. Government*, p. 298.

3.   Max Weber, *The Theory of Economic and Social Organizations*, pp. 329-341.

4.   Anthony Downs, *Inside Bureaucracy*, pp. 81-87.

5.   For a discussion of the concept of "infrastructure" see Warren F. Ilchman and Norman Thomas Uphoff, *The Political Economy of Change*, pp. 208-255.

6.   Carl J. Friedrich, *Man and His Government: An Empirical Theory of Politics*, pp. 54ff.

7.   Fred W. Riggs, *Administration in Developing Countries*, pp. 183ff.

8.   Compare J. S. Nye, "Corruption and Political Development: A Cost-Benefit Analysis," *American Political Science Review*, 61 (June 1967), p. 416.

9.   See James C. Scott, *Comparative Political Corruption*, pp. 90-91 for a discussion of the conditions under which corruption might aid economic development.

10.   Kenneth Prewitt and Alan Stone, *The Ruling Elites: Elite Theory, Power and American Democracy*, p. 97. See also Grant McConnell, *Private Power and American Democracy*.

11.   Alfred G. Meyer, *The Soviet Political System: An Interpretation*, pp. 131, 221.

12.   Compare Aristotle's definition of distributive justice in *Nicomachean Ethics*, pp. 111-145.

13.   Cynthia Enloe, *Ethnic Conflict and Political Development*, *passim*.

14.   Prewitt and Stone, pp. 184-223, summarize the arguments in this area.

15.   Herbert Kaufman, *Administrative Feedback*, pp. 77-78.

16.   Stanley V. Anderson, ed., *Ombudsmen for American Government?*

17.   See Sidney R. Waldman, *Foundations of Political Action: An Exchange Theory of Politics*, for an extensive application of this idea to political analysis.

18.   H. Keith Warner and A. Eugene Havens, "Goal Displacement and the Intangibility of Organizational Goals," *Administrative Science Quarterly*, 12 (March 1968), pp. 539-555.

19.   See Ilchman and Uphoff, *passim*, for an excellent discussion of how regimes might maximize scarce resources.

NOTES TO CHAPTER X (pages 175-202)

1.   Quoted in Dankwart A. Rustow, *A World of Nations*, p. 177.

2.   For more extensive discussions of the functions of military organizations see Henry Bienen, ed., *The Military and Modernization*, *passim*; Morris Janowitz, *The Military in the Political Development of New Nations*, pp. 75-83; Lucian Pye, "Armies in the Process of Political Modernization," in John J. Johnson, ed., *The Role of the Military in Underdeveloped Countries*, pp. 69-89. For a critique of the military's potential role see Eric A. Nordlinger, "Soldiers in Mufti: The Impact of Military Rule upon Economic and Social Change in Non-Western States," *American Political Science Review*, 64 (December 1970), pp. 1131-1148.

3.   Compare the discussion of bureaucratic pathology in Chapter IX.

4.   Morris Janowitz, *The Professional Soldier: A Social and Political Portrait*, pp. 22-31.

5.   James Clotfelter, *The Military in American Politics*, p. 229.

6.   Clotfelter, pp. 61-62.

7.   William Proxmire, *Report from Wasteland*, pp. 153-167.

8.   Harold D. Lasswell, "The Garrison-State Hypothesis Today," in Samuel P. Huntington, ed., *Changing Patterns of Military Politics*, pp. 51-70.

9.   See the discussion of types of intervention in Samuel E. Finer, *The Man on Horseback: The Role of the Military in Politics*.

10.   For a comparative analysis of these challenges to the civilian authorities in the Soviet Union and the United States see Zbigniew Brzezinski and Samuel P. Huntington, *Political Power: USA/USSR*, pp. 331-365.

11.   This discussion of the causes of military intervention draws on the analyses of numerous commentators. For further investigation consult Janowitz, *The Military in the Political Development of New Nations*, pp. 83-100; Edward Luttwak, *Coup d'Etat; A Practical Handbook*, *passim*; Claude E. Welch, Jr., "The Roots and Implications of Military Intervention," in Welch, Jr., ed., pp. 1-59.

12.   A. A. Afrifa, *The Ghana Coup: 24 February, 1966*; see also Henry L. Bretton, *The Rise and Fall of Kwame Nkrumah*.

13.   A. A. Afrifa, *Budget Statement for 1968-1969*, p. 11.

14.   For a survey of the weaknesses of the regime see Henry L. Bretton, *The Rise and Fall of Kwame Nkrumah*, and David E. Apter, "Nkrumah, Charisma and the Coup," *Daedalus*, 97 (Summer 1968), pp. 757-792.

15.   Rustow, pp. 187-188.

16. Janowitz, *The Military in the Political Development of New Nations*, pp. 65-66.

17. Robert M. Price, "Military Officers and Political Leadership: The Ghanaian Case," *Comparative Politics*, 3 (April 1971), pp. 361-379.

18. Samuel P. Huntington, *The Soldier and the State: The Theory and Politics of Civil-Military Relations*, pp. 464-465.

19. This summary of military values is based upon longer discussions in Clotfelter, pp. 29-52; Huntington, *The Soldier and The State*, pp. 59-79, and Janowitz, *The Professional Soldier*, pp. 215-279.

20. For a trenchant examination of the inpact of "national security" concerns on democratic politics see David Wise, *The Politics of Lying: Government Deception, Secrecy and Power*.

NOTES TO CHAPTER XI (pages 205-230)

1. The phrase is Alfred Schultz's. See the discussion in Peter Berger, Brigitte Berger, and Hansfried Kellner, *The Homeless Mind; Modernization and Consciousness*, pp. 4-5.

2. Sidney Verba, "Comparative Political Culture," in Pye and Verba, eds., *Political Culture and Political Development*, p. 513.

3. Gabriel A. Almond and Sidney Verba, *The Civic Culture: Political Attitudes and Democracy in Five Nations*, p. 14.

4. Gunnar Myrdal, *Asian Drama: An Inquiry into the Poverty of Nations*, volume I, pp. 54-69.

5. Georges Gurvitch, *The Social Frameworks of Knowledge*, especially pp. 162-173 and 199-206.

6. Almond and Verba, pp. 16-18.

7. Almond and Verba, pp. 20-21. They state that parochial cultures also could be said to demonstrate allegiance, alienation, or apathy, but this would be meaningless, if the parochial is defined as relatively ignorant of the wider political system. A person cannot be apathetic toward that of which he is unaware.

8. Almond and Verba, *passim*, especially p. 142.

9. For a collection of readings on the "end of ideology" debate see M. Rejai, ed., *Decline of Ideology?*

10. William T. Bluhm, *Ideologies and Attitudes: Modern Political Culture*, Chapter 1.

11. David E. Apter, *The Politics of Modernization*, pp. 267-270.

12. See, for example, Theodore J. Lowi, *The End of Liberalism: Ideology, Policy, and the Crisis of Public Authority*.

13. This discussion is indebted to T. D. Weldon, *States and Morals: A Study in Political Conflicts*.

14. Those wishing more detail can consult Carl Cohen, ed., *Communism, Fascism and Democracy: The Theoretical Foundations*, 2d ed., for a selection of original writings in the three ideologies. Lyman T. Sargent, *Contemporary Political Ideologies*, provides a summary of basic principles.

15. Compare Richard E. Dawson and Kenneth Prewitt, *Political Socialization*, pp. 25-36.

16. For discussions of various aspects of behavior genetics see Martin Monoseritz, Gardner Lindzey, and Delbert D. Thiessen, eds., *Behavioral Genetics: Method and Research*, especially sections 5 (intelligence), 8 (personality) and 9 (psychopathology).

17. See, for example, Lionel Tiger, *Men in Groups*.

18. See "What Is Taboo?" *Time*, May 15, 1972, pp. 53-54 for a discussion of this controversy surrounding William Shockley.

19. Dean Jaros, *Socialization to Politics*, p. 80.

20. Harold D. Lasswell, *Psychopathology and Politics*.

21. E. Victor Wolfenstein, *The Revolutionary Personality: Lenin, Trotsky, Gandhi*.

22. For extended discussions of the growth in complexity of political learning see Dawson and Prewitt, Chapter IV, and Jaros, Chapter 2.

23. Robert D. Hess and David Easton, "The Child's Changing Image of the President," *Public Opinion Quarterly*, 24 (Winter 1960), pp. 632-644. For a critique see Jaros, pp. 90-91.

24. Dean Jaros, Herbert Hirsch, and Frederic J. Fleron, Jr., "The Malevolent Leader: Political Socialization in an American Subculture," *American Political Science Review*, 62 (June 1968), pp. 564-575.

25. More extensive treatment of this subject can be found in Jaros, Chapter 3.

26. Dawson and Prewitt, pp. 83-86.

27. For general and comprehensive discussions of the agents briefly mentioned here consult, Dawson and Prewitt, Part III, and Jaros, Chapters 4, 5 and 6.

28. See, for example, Everett E. Hagen, "How Economic Growth Begins: A Theory of Social Change," and David C. McClelland, "The Achievement Motive in Economic Growth," respectively pp. 73-83 and 83-100 in Finkle and Gable, eds., see especially pp. 78-79 and 97-100.

29. Fred I. Greenstein, "Personality and Political Socialization: The Theories of Authoritarian and Democratic Character," in Sigel, ed., pp. 260-276.

30. Almond and Verba, pp. 284-287.

31. Richard Flacks, "The Revolt of the Advantaged: An Exploration of the Roots of Student Protest," in Sigel, ed., pp. 182-191.

32. Lucian W. Pye, *Politics, Personality and Nation Building: Burma's Search for Identity*, Chapter 13.

33. Flacks, pp. 189-190.

34. Almond and Verba, pp. 287-294.

35. Kenneth Prewitt, with Joseph Okello-Oculi, "Political Socialization and Political Education in the New Nations," in Sigel, ed., pp. 607-621.

36. Urie Bronfenbrenner, "Response to Pressure from Peers versus Adults among Soviet and American School Children," in Sigel, ed., pp. 414-420.

37. B. F. Skinner, *Beyond Freedom and Dignity*.

38. Karl W. Deutsch, *Politics and Government: How People Decide Their Fate*, 2d ed.

NOTES TO CHAPTER XII (pages 231-248)

1. Franz Kafka, *The Trial*, pp. 267-269.

2. *The Trial*, p. 269.

3. This is similar to, but not identical with Max Weber's definitions of "convention" and "law." See Max Weber, *The Theory of Social and Economic Organization*, p. 127.

4. Weber, p. 127.

5. For a critique of the "command theory" of the law see Michael Barkun, *Law without Sanctions: Order in Primitive Societies and the World Community*, especially pp. 60-65.

6. Compare the discussion of "counterpoint values" in W. F. Wertheim, *Evolution and Revolution: The Rising Waves of Emancipation*, pp. 105-110.

7. Barkun, p. 71. He considers this the essential definition of a "jural community."

8. Barkun, p. 154.

9. Compare the discussion of innovation in Morse Peckham, *Art and Pornography: An Experiment in Explanation*, pp. 285-286.

10. H. L. Nieburg, *Culture Storm: Politics and the Ritual Order*, p. 96.

11. This distinction is in part indebted to the ideas of William Kreml of the University of South Carolina, given in private discussions.

12. Harold D. Lasswell and Abraham Kaplan, *Power and Society: A Framework for Political Inquiry*, p. 230.

13. Lasswell and Kaplan, pp. 232-234.

14. This discussion is based on, but is not identical with the one in Joseph La-Palombara, *Politics within Nations*, pp. 135-136.

15. Karl W. Deutsch, *Politics and Government: How People Decide Their Fate*, 2d ed., pp. 199-200.

16. For a more extensive discussion of the reasons behind the decline of legislatures see J. Blondel, *Comparative Legislatures*, pp. 45-54; 136-140.

17. Lasswell and Kaplan, pp. 195-198.

18. Lasswell and Kaplan, p. 128.

19. Blondel, pp. 14-15.

20. Compare Nieburg, pp. 94-95.

21. This discussion is based upon that in LaPalombara, *Politics within Nations*, pp. 352-361.

22. Lasswell and Kaplan, p. 197.

23. For a discussion of this notion of the law see Austin Ranney, *The Governing of Men*, 4th ed., pp. 456-458.

24. Jerome Frank, *Law and the Modern Mind*, p. 134.

25. See *Gideon v. Wainwright*; *Escobedo v. Illinois*; *Miranda v. Arizona*; reprinted in Cushman and Cushman, eds., pp. 749-787.

26. For more extensive discussions of the problem of vigilantism see H. Jon Rosenbaum and Peter C. Sederberg, eds., *Vigilante Politics*, especially Chapter 1.

NOTES TO CHAPTER XIII (pages 249-264)

1.   This thesis has been advanced by Erich Fromm, *Escape from Freedom*.

2.   Norman T. Uphoff and Warren F. Ilchman, "The New Political Economy," in Uphoff and Ilchman, eds., pp. 12-14.

3.   For a discussion of the nature and effects of the Calvinist belief in predestination see George H. Sabine, *A History of Political Thought*, 3d ed., pp. 262-366.

4.   Individual determinism is a position derived from an interpretation of behaviorism. See B. F. Skinner, *Beyond Freedom and Dignity*, pp. 24-40. Historical determinism is generally associated with a simplified Marxist view of history. Marx, himself, may have been much less of a determinist than some of his followers. See Herbert J. Spiro, *Politics as the Master Science: From Plato to Mao*, pp. 115-125.

5.   David Hacket Fischer, *Historians' Fallacies: Toward a Logic of Historical Thought*, pp. 15-21.

6.   Carl J. Friedrich, *Man and His Government: An Empirical Theory of Politics*, pp. 15-17.

7.   This "negative" concept of freedom and the "positive" notion discussed in the next subsection are the subject of a more extended examination in Isaiah Berlin, *Two Concepts of Liberty*. For other extensive surveys of some of the problems discussed below see Mortimer J. Adler, *The Idea of Freedom*, and Carl J. Friedrich, ed., *Nomos IV: Liberty*.

8.   For a discussion of the vagaries of the concept of self-determination see Rupert Emerson, *From Empire to Nation*, Chapters XVI and XVII.

9.   John Rawls, *A Theory of Justice*, p. 203.

10.   Jonathan D. Casper, *The Politics of Civil Liberties*, p. 20.

11.   Alpheus Thomas Mason and William M. Beany, *The Supreme Court in a Free Society*, pp. 286-287.

12.   Herbert J. Muller, *Issues of Freedom: Paradoxes and Promises*, pp. 7-8.

13.   The term *freedom as self-perfection* is used by Mulford Q. Sibley, *Political Ideas and Ideologies: A History of Political Thought*, p. 583.

14.   Herbert Marcuse, "Repressive Tolerance" in Barrington Moore, *et al.*, *A Critique of Pure Tolerance*, pp. 81-123.

15.   For a number of essays examining the pornography problem see Harry M. Clor, ed., *Censorship and Freedom of Expression: Essays on Obscenity and the Law*.

16.   Bernard Crick, "Toleration and Tolerance in Theory and Practice," reprinted in Bernard Crick, *Political Theory and Practice*, pp. 63-96.

17.   Bernard Crick, "Freedom as Politics" in Crick, pp. 35-62.

18.   Crick, "Freedom as Politics," p. 51.

19.   As reported in Thucydides, *The Peloponnesian War*, pp. 118-119.

20.   Hannah Arendt, *On Revolution*, p. 124.

21.   Friedrich, *Man and His Government*, pp. 354-356.

22.   Friedrich, *Man and His Government*, pp. 367-384.

23.   This idea of order receives its fullest justification in Thomas Hobbes,

Leviathan (see numerous editions). Hobbes's social contract guaranteed no necessary freedom or equality, only that the sovereign would protect the members from bodily harm.

24.   The list of works that could be included here is extensive. The interested student might begin with Thomas More, *Utopia*; Edward Bellamy, *Looking Backward*; and, for a more "modern" view, B. F. Skinner, *Walden Two*. In a sense, Plato's *Republic* is based on a similar ideal.

25.   Friedrich, *Man and His Government*, p. 337.

26.   Dino Bigongiari, ed., *The Political Ideas of St. Thomas Aquinas*, pp. 42-64.

27.   See Arnold Brecht, *Political Theory: The Foundations of Twentieth-Century Political Thought*, pp. 182-185.

28.   The classic proponent of these views is Edmund Burke. See Louis I. Bredvold and Ralph G. Ross, eds., *The Philosophy of Edmund Burke*.

29.   Compare Chalmers Johnson, *Revolutionary Change*, p. 8.

30.   See Alvin Toffler, *Future Shock*, Chapters 15 and 16, for a summary of this research.

NOTES TO CHAPTER XIV (pages 265-281)

1.   R. R. Palmer, *The Age of Democratic Revolution: A Political History of Europe and America, 1760-1800*, volume 1, *The Challenge*, Chapter 8, pp. 213-235.

2.   Hannah Arendt, *On Revolution*, Chapter 2, pp. 53-110.

3.   Plato, *The Republic*, pp. 106-107.

4.   Aristotle, *The Politics*, pp. 11-14.

5.   St. Paul, in particular, advised submission to secular authority; see Romans 13:1-2.

6.   Peter Berger, *et al.*, *The Homeless Mind: Modernization and Consciousness*, pp. 89-90.

7.   See, for example, Helmut Schoeck, *Envy: A Theory of Social Behavior*.

8.   Kurt Vonnegut, "Harrison Bergeron," in *Welcome to the Monkey House*, pp. 7-13.

9.   Harold D. Lasswell, *Politics: Who Gets What, When, and How*.

10.   Aristotle, *Nicomachean Ethics*, p. 118.

11.   Aristotle, *Nichomachean Ethics*, p. 119.

12.   Plato, *Republic*, pp. 119-129.

13.   Plato, *Republic*, p. 108-109.

14.   See Herbert J. Spiro, *Politics as the Master Science: From Plato to Mao*, pp. 13-14.

15.   This discussion of utilitarian justice draws upon the summary provided in John Rawls, *A Theory of Justice*, pp. 22-27. In note 9 on pages 22-23, Rawls provides a brief bibliography of utilitarian writers.

16.   Plato, *Republic*, p. 60.

17.   Rawls, pp. 118-192.

18.   Rawls, p. 302.

19.   Rawls, pp. 72-75.

20.   Carl Friedrich, *Man and His Government: An Empirical Theory of Politics*, p. 251.

21. Friedrich, *Man and His Government*.

22. Based on Arnold Brecht, *Political Theory: The Foundations of Twentieth-Century Political Thought*, p. 396. See also Rawls, pp. 236-239.

23. This example was taken from Ali A. Mazrui, "Black Vigilantism in Cultural Transition: Violence and Viability in Tropical Africa," in Rosenbaum and Sederberg, eds., *Vigilante Politics*, pp. 194-217.

24. See H. Jon Rosenbaum and Peter C. Sederberg, "The Occult and Political Development," *Comparative Politics*, 3 (July 1971), pp. 561-574.

NOTES TO CHAPTER XV (pages 285-299)

1. Marion J. Levy, Jr., *Modernization: Latecomers and Survivors*, p. ix.

2. Garret Hardin, *Exploring New Ethics for Survival: The Voyage of the Spaceship Beagle*, p. 172.

3. Hardin, p. 170.

4. Some comparative figures for representative areas of production/consumption are:

	India	United States
1. Population (latest census)	547,949,809	203,235,298
2. Energy consumption per capita (in kilograms of coal equivalent)	186	11,611
3. Steel consumption per capita (in kilograms)	16	663
4. Rubber consumption per capita (in kilograms)	0.2	14.2
5. Motor vehicles in use	1,233,000	116,874,000

—*Statistical Yearbook, United Nations*, 1973.

5. William Irwin Thompson, *At the Edge of History*, p. 72.

6. Barry Commoner, *The Closing Circle: Nature, Man and Technology*, pp. 84-85.

7. This argument was provided by Dr. Michael McElroy, a Harvard scientist in testimony before the House Health and Environment Subcommittee. Reported in *The Columbia Record* (Columbia, S.C.), Monday, December 16, 1974, p. 6-B.

8. "Can Nuclear Waste Be Stored?" *Newsweek*, November 18, 1974, p. 56.

9. Quoted in Theodore Roszak, *Where the Wasteland Ends*, p. 211.

10. Hardin, p. 151.

11. For extensive discussions of this point see the works by Thompson and Roszak cited above; also Jacques Ellul, *The Technological Society*.

12. Peter Berger, Brigitte Berger, and Hansfried Kellner, *The Homeless Mind: Modernization and Consciousness*, p. 185.

13. Berger *et al.*, pp. 41-62.

14. See the discussion of Alasdair MacIntyre, "Ideology, Social Science and Revolution," *Comparative Politics*, 5 (April 1973), pp. 331-332.

15.   Robert Nisbet, "The Year 2000 and All That," in Somit, ed., pp. 257-267.

16.   This section is indebted to the discussion of methods by Theodore J. Gordon, "The Current Methods of Futures Research," in Toffler, ed., pp. 164-189.

17.   See George Orwell, *Nineteen Eighty-Four: Text, Sources, Criticism*, ed. Irving Howe.

18.   See, for example, Herman Kahn, *On Thermonuclear War*; also *On Escalation: Metaphors and Scenarios*.

19.   Paul Ehrlich, "Eco-Catastrophe," in Toffler, ed., pp. 13-26.

20.   James Cooke Brown, *The Troika Incident: The Coming of a Viable Human Society*.

21.   See, for example, Theodore J. Gordon and Robert H. Ament, "Forecasts of Some Technological and Scientific Developments and Their Societal Consequences," in Teich, ed., pp. 5-21.

22.   This list is partially drawn from Daniel Bell, "Twelve Modes of Prediction," in Somit, ed., pp. 40-67.

23.   Marshall McLuhan, *Understanding Media: The Extensions of Man*.

24.   For an analysis of Marx's prediction of revolution in advanced capitalist states see Edward S. Malecki, "Theories of Revolution and Industrial Societies," *Journal of Politics*, 35 (1973), pp. 948-985.

25.   W. W. Rostow, *The Stages of Economic Growth: A Non-Communist Manifesto*.

26.   Pitirim Sorokin, *Social and Cultural Dynamics*.

27.   Donella Meadows, *et al.*, *The Limits to Growth*.

28.   H. S. D. Cole, *et al.*, eds., *Models of Doom: A Critique of the Limits to Growth*.

NOTES TO CHAPTER XVI (pages 300-318)

1.   Alvin M. Weinberg, "Can Technology Replace Social Engineering?" in Teich, ed., pp. 27-35.

2.   This argument is indebted to an address by economist Robert M. Solow, "How to Think Rationally about Exhaustible Resources," given at the University of South Carolina, April 18, 1974.

3.   Gerard K. O'Neill, "The Colonization of Space," *Physics Today* (September 1974), pp. 32-40.

4.   Pitirim Sorokin, *Social and Cultural Dynamics*, pp. 487-489.

5.   Kenneth Boulding, "The Economics of the Coming Spaceship Earth," reprinted in Boulding, *Collected Papers*, volume 2, *Economics*, p. 491.

6.   For Teilhard de Chardin's futurist thought see *The Future of Man*; also *The Phenomenon of Man*. For a brief analysis of his thought see Philip Hefner, *The Promise of Teilhard*.

7.   Teilhard de Chardin, *The Phenomenon of Man*, p. 265.

8.   John David Garcia, *The Moral Society: A Rational Alternative to Death*.

9.   See Garrett Hardin, *Exploring New Ethics for Survival: The Voyage of the Spaceship Beagle*, pp. 113-118.

10.   Hardin, pp. 177-189.

11.   Hardin, pp. 129-130.

12.   Harvey Brooks and Raymond Bowers, "Technology: Processes of Assessment and Choice," in Teich, ed., pp. 223-224.

13.   Harold P. Green, "The Adversary Process in Technology Assessment," in Teich, ed., pp. 254-262.

14.   Brooks and Bowers, p. 224.

15.   Sorokin, p. 700.

16.   Sorokin, pp. 474-486.

17.   Garcia, especially pp. 213-266.

18.   Garcia, pp. 218-219.

Index